WALDEMAR ERDURTH

Waldemar Erfurth
General der Infanterie
Date of Birth: 4 August 1879
Place of Birth: Berlin
Died: 2 May 1971

Erfurth joined the Army immediately after leaving school and received his commission as second lieutenant on 27 January 1899. Promoted to Captain on 22 March 1922, on the same day he was appointed Director of Mapping and Surveying in Berlin. In World War I he served in various positions with the field forces and in the General Staff at the eastern and western fronts.

From 1919 to 1924 he served as Operations Officer and Chief of Staff of I Corps Area Headquarters in Königsberg, Eastern Prussia, later in the same position in a General Staff group in Berlin until 1929, when he was promoted Generalmajor. For the next two years he was Commander of Infantry, Schwerin, II Corps Area Headquarters, which assignment terminated with his promotion to Generalleutnant on 1 May 1931. Then Erfurth resigned and took up his studies in philosophy at the Freiburg University, remaining there from 1931 to 1934. Recalled to the Army in 1934, he became Chief of the Section of Practical Application of War Experience at Potsdam, and later, for two years, Chief, Military Science Branch, Berlin. After a term of four years, 1938-1941, as Fifth Senior General Staff Officer (O Qu V) handling military history, Erfurth was appointed German General Attached to the Finnish Armed Forces, which post he held until 1944. During this time he received his Ph.D. degree from Freiburg University.

During the last year of the war he was in the Officer Reserve Pool, OKH. General Erfurth was captured in his home at Marklaberg near Leipzig on 25 May 1945.

PREFACE

After the German surrender in 1945, the US Army began its Foreign Military Studies Program with the questioning of prominent German POWs. Encouraged by the results, the Army moved to written questionnaires, which was followed later by monographs from certain higher ranked officer.

The mission of the ETHINT (European Theater Historical Interrogations) program was to gather information about the German operations in the European Theater. It quickly grew to involve other theaters as well, eventually becoming a training aid in developing operational studies.

The authors were for the most part direct participants, at higher levels, in the events of which they write. While they were all POWs at the start of the program, their participation was voluntary. Later, after return to civilian life, many of them continued to write. They were supervised by a group of carefully selected higher ranking former German officers.

While there was some remuneration, these writings were mostly motivated by professional interest, as well as a desire for stronger ties and mutual defense. Many of the original writings were entirely from memory, perhaps with the aid of maps. Later, the authors were able to associate with former compatriots and to consult documentation.

These reports have languished in the National Archives on microfilm, for decades. Accessing these documents meant first finding them, ordering microfilm rolls then finding a way to read them. While newer technology has eased this process somewhat, it can still be tedious and time consuming.

These volumes present a selection of this material in a much more user-friendly format. This information is being presented as it was originally written, with only the lightest of editing for spelling, syntax problems in the translation, and consistency. The overall formatting will be slightly different from the original, but the material will not be changed. In this regard, there was no effort made to eliminate any repetitions, so that the reader could view exactly what the authors wrote.

The major beneficial change I have made to this is the inclusion of cleaner maps. The map sketches in the original reports were overlays that were later photographed. In the process, they lost all transparency and are now just good sketches. While still informative, the re-rendering of these maps, with keys and translations on the same sheet will give the reader a much better visual interpretation of the scene.

INTRODUCTION

This volume of the *In Their Own Words Series* combines two different US ARMY ETHINT reports written by General der Infanterie Waldemar Erfurth. The first is his history of Finland during what became known as "The Continuation War." The second is a report on his period as the liaison officer to the Finnish High Command. Some information will be repeated between the volumes, but it will not detract from the story. The official references for these two titles are:

1. MS C-073 The Last Finnish War (1941 – 1944)
2. MS P-041bb The German Liaison Officer With The Finnish Armed Forces

There was only light editing done, mostly to change syntax confusion in the translation. Two maps were added in order to assist the reader visually. Any reader that wishes a printable map can request it from Maps At War, by e-mailing tlhoulihan3@gmail.com

www.mapsatwar.com

TABLE OF CONTENTS

Book One
I   Pre-War History.. 5
II   The Outbreak of the War to the Entrance of the
Finnish Army.. 21
III   The Joint Finnish-German Offensive in 1941.................... 28
IV   The Soviet Russian Counter-Offensive in the
Beginning of 1942 and Trench-Warfare......................... 66
V   The Development of the Political Situation in Finland and
Diplomatic Negotiation..140
VI   The Red Army Offensive Against the Finns in the Summer
of 1944..165
VII   The End of the Brotherhood-in-Arms...........................188
VIII The German Retreat from Finland............................206

Book Two
I   Liaison Staff North
I. Mission..235
II. Composition...237
III. Echelons...238
IV. Helsinki Echelon..239
V. Mikkeli Echelon...242
VI. Characterization of Mannerhcim.................................242
II.   Participation of German General in Military and Political
Questions..245
I. The Finnish Army and the Fighting for Leningrad............245
II. Mannerheim's Plan for Operation Aiming at Soroka.........248
III. The German Plan for an Offensive Against Soroka
(Operation LACHSFANG)...252
IV. Operation Nordlicht...254
V. Deterioration of German-Finish Relations
(Spring 1943)..255
VI. Efforts by Paasikivi to Obtain Separate Peace
(Spring 1943)..258
VII. The German Embargo on Arms to Finland................261
VIII. The Soviet Offensive Against the Finnish Front..........264
IX. The Midsummer Pact Between Germany and Finland......268
X. Resignation of President Ryti...................................269
XI. Mannerheim Becomes President.............................275
XII Secession of Finland...279
XIII Conclusion..283

PART ONE

CHAPTER I: Pre-War History

Finns born at the turn of the century have lived through three heavy, bloody wars with Russia, known in Finland as the Three Wars of Independence. This indicates that the Finnish nation each time fought for its freedom. In the first War of Independence, which during its last years was officially call the "Civil War," the Bolshevist revolutionary flood, which threatened to swallow the whole country, had to be stemmed and repulsed. Actual fighting lasted for only a few months (from the end of January until the middle of May 1918), and the war ended with the preservation of Finnish Independence, which had been proclaimed by the freedom loving Finnish people on 6 December 1917 shortly after the October Revolution in Russia.

That the First War of Independence, which had been started by the Finns quite without preparation, with about 1000 rifles and no trained troops or cadres, could be brought to a victorious end seemed a miracle. The giant eastern empire, weakened by World War I and by two revolutions, recognized the independence of the Finnish people in the Peace of Dorpat (14 October 1920).

For scarcely two decades could the Finnish people enjoy peace. In September 1939 World War II broke out between the Great Powers of Central and Western Europe, and storm clouds of a new war with Soviet Russia also appeared at the Finnish frontiers. When the Finns refused to consider the cession of territory demanded by the Soviet Union (a base at Hangö, the Karelian Isthmus with Viipuri and islands in the Gulf of Finland), the Second Finnish War of Independence, frequently called the Winter War,[1] began on 30 November 1939 with a surprise attack of Soviet Russian land, naval and air forces against Finnish territory. This campaign waged during a particularly hard winter, brought the heroic defense of a small nation against the Soviet Russian millions before the eyes of the world. Posterity has not always handed laurels to him who has emerged victoriously from combat. A war waged against the principles of eternal right will bring neither real honor nor posthumous fame to the victor. No great poet will praise violence and unchecked thirst for conquest on the

---

[1] The Soviet Russian version of the outbreak of the Winter War may be derived from the publication "The Western Powers and Hitler" in the "Tägliche Wundschau" of 18 February 1948, according to which the cause of the War was the refusal to accept the friendly proposals of the Soviet Government. The causes of this outbreak of hostilities, as seen by the Russians, were hostile Finnish actions and provocations at the Soviet-Finnish border.

part of the strong toward the weak. But he who is defeated, who fights for a lost cause with all the greatness inherent in a human being will win the esteem and sympathy of present and future generations, because his resistance against violence, his fight for the right appears more estimable than the success of an enemy superior in force. The brave attitude of a nation which is ready for any sacrifice will be rewarded in the judgment of history. The sentence of Lucan: '*Victrix causa diis placuit, sed victa Catoni*[2]' applied also in the Winter War to Mannerheim and his Finns. Their accomplishments have attracted the attention of the whole world and won admiration and sympathy. Nevertheless, after three and a half months of war, Finland was still facing a powerful enemy alone, whose strength kept on increasing in spite of tremendous losses. The League of Nations had proved incapable of ending the war. Owing to the conditions prevailing in Europe, the Great Powers who were perhaps interested in the fate of the Finnish people lacked the opportunity to intervene on behalf of Finland and the chances of the Finns to continue the war became less and less. On 13 March 1940, therefore, they gave up the unequal struggle and accepted severe peace conditions, which delivered to the Soviet Union almost all the battlefields on which the Finnish soldiers had shed their blood and accomplished wonderful feats. The Finnish soldier knew, however, that he had been honorably defeated. Nor had the war on the Finnish home front, where innumerable air attacks had spread death and terror amongst women and children, been a failure.[3] With unheard of tenacity the Finnish soldier had held on to every inch of his native soil and had even boldly and successfully attacked enemy units superior in strength. The short Winter War had been fought with the greatest severity and recklessness on both sides, for the Red Army also had its traditional, incredible perseverance and toughness in attacks and in beating off Finnish counterattacks. The heroic spirit which animated the Finnish people in this war has been accurately characterized by the proud words of Mannerheim at its conclusion:

> "Soldiers! I have fought on many battlefields, but I have never seen warriors like you. I am as proud of you as of my own children, equally proud of the man from the northern tundra as of the sons of the Ostrobothian plains, the forests of Karelia, the gay countryside of Savo,

---

[2] The conquering cause pleased the gods, but the conquered one pleased Cato.

[3] Expressly confirmed by Field Marshal Mannerheim, Commander in Chief of the Winter War, in his order of the day, dated 14 March 1940.

the rich farms of Haeme and Satakunta, the birch groves of Uusimaa, and the heart of Finland."

Not like a defeated field marshal, but like a valiant hero of bygone times returning from chivalrous combats covered with glory and honor, the Finnish commander in chief addressed his soldiers and his people with these encouraging words, raising their self-respect:

"We shall do everything in our power to provide a home with what is left us to those who have become homeless, to create better living conditions for all, and we shall continue to readily defend our smaller native land with the same vigor and determination with which we have defended our undivided country. "

In the last words of his order of the day of 14 March 1940, Mannerheim with the magnificent bearing and the strong self-confidence of a descendant of an old family addressed his aroused people with a side glance at the reluctant Great Powers, who left little Finland in the lurch in its desperate struggle:

"Proudly conscious of our historical mission, we shall continue in the future to defend western civilization as has been our inheritance for centuries. But at the same time we are aware that we have paid our debt to the Occident to the last cent."

In the Moscow Peace Treaty (1940) Finland lost considerable territory on the Karelian Isthmus and north of Lake Ladoga, as well as the districts of Salla and Hangö, Finnish soil which the Finnish people had cultivated for centuries. The ceded territory was of particular value to Finland, since it was here in particular that new industry was fast developing. The loss of Viipuri, the flourishing capital of Karelia, situated at an incomparably beautiful site on a bay of the Gulf of Finland, was felt especially severely.

As a serious consequence of the Winter War the Finns were placed in a position of uncertainty because of the sudden outbreak of war and by the lack of assistance from other powers. The Finns felt deserted and believed that their mighty eastern neighbor had further evil designs against their country with the ultimate object of destroying its independence, in the same way as the Baltic States had lost their freedom to Soviet Russia in the autumn of 1939. The fate of the ethnically related Estonians on the other side of the Gulf of Finland considerably worried the Finnish people. The months following the conclusion of the Peace of Moscow were, therefore, not used for peaceful reconstruction but were passed in anguish and sorrow. Conscious of their insecure position, the Finns were dominated by the feeling of becoming involved momentarily in another defensive war. Information from the other side of the eastern frontier had a disquieting effect. There were many indications that Soviet Russia was preparing a new attack in order to occupy Finland entirely. It was a matter of course that the Finnish politicians observed the world situation with the greatest attention and did not remain inactive. In particular they watched the relations between Soviet Russia and Germany. The German policy at the beginning of World War II had heavily handicapped German-Finnish relations, specifically Ribbentrop's first trip to Moscow on 23 August 1939 which led to the conclusion of a non-aggression pact between German and Russia and, after the defeat of Poland, his second trip on 27 September 1939 when the two powers came to an agreement on their zones of interest, which surrendered Finland to the eastern influence. The German policy of disinterestedness in Finland during the Winter War did not originate from German-Russian amity but from concern about Swedish ore. If Sweden were involved in a Russian-Finnish war, it was feared that no Swedish ore would be shipped to Germany. When, therefore, in winter 1939/40 the Finnish war situation worsened, the German government was obliged to demand strict neutrality of Sweden, which particularly strongly condemned the Russian attitude. The cool reserve of the German press towards the fate of the Finnish people during the Winter War had been unfavorably received in Finland. The Finns had enough reason for complaint against the German politics. Nevertheless, Finland, after its sad experiences with the League of Nations and the Great Powers during the Winter War, had to find a way of not again facing alone any further demands of the giant eastern empire. The ability and energy of the Finnish statesmen found that way. It had not escaped their notice that relations between Germany and the Soviet Union, which still appeared unclouded in the summer of 1939, had cooled down shortly thereafter and seemed to develop with growing tension. It was, therefore, obvious that the Finnish politicians would look for rapprochement with Germany, which, after the quick and great successes of World War II, alone seemed able to come to the aid of the threatened Finnish freedom.

Contact between a representative of the German Army and the Finnish officials was established through a short visit at the end of June 1940 by Generaloberst Halder, who met Finnish statesmen and generals but not Field Marshal Mannerheim, who was sick at the time. This trip was merely a formal call to return a visit of General Österman to Germany. The trips of Österman and Halder did not serve any political purpose but revived the Finnish-German brotherhood-in-arms created in

World War I (The Finnish Volunteer Light Infantry Battalion in Germany and the German auxiliary forces in Finland during the Civil War in 1918). On 22 September 1940 a Finnish-German agreement was concluded with regard to the passage of German troops through northern Finland, which considerably facilitated the supply of the German forces in northern Norway. This agreement was of a purely military and not of a political character. No objections against this Finnish-German agreement could be raised by the Soviet Union, since it had previously demanded the right of transit for the troops of the Red Army through southern Finland in order to supply the newly leased territory of Hangö which Finland had had to grant. Trains provided under the terms of the agreement ran daily at a time along the Leningrad-Hangö line carrying Russian army supplies; since 22 September 1940 Finnish trains ran on the lines from the Bothnian ports to Lapland carrying German troops and army supplies bound for northern Norway. These transports went by rail to Rovaniemi and thence in overland march on the Arctic Highway through the Petsamo area to Kirkenes.

In the middle of November 1940, Russian Foreign Minister Molotov paid a visit to Berlin. During the discussions between Hitler and Molotov on 12 and 13 November, the difference between the German and Russian standpoints with regard to Finland became evident. The Soviet Union demanded a free hand against Finland and German non-intervention there. The Russian foreign minister made no secret of the Russian intention of winning back the border countries on the western Russian frontier, which had been lost after the October Revolution. Hitler declared himself unwilling to accept this policy of the Soviet Union and held his hand protectively over Finland. He did not want the war to spread to the Baltic. Since no common ground could be reached, Molotov departed without having achieved his objective. Molotov's conference with Hitler was a great diplomatic failure for the Russian foreign minister and strongly prejudiced future German-Russian relations. This conference became the hour of destiny for Germany and Europe and represents a decisive moment in history.

Several versions of the conference among Molotov, Hitler and Ribbentrop at Berlin have since been published. In his proclamation to the soldiers at the Eastern Front of 22 June 1941 Hitler refers to it more or less in the following words:

> "The Soviet Foreign Minister demanded the clarification of and the consent of Germany to the following four questions: Question #1 referred to Rumania, question #2 to Finland, question #3 to Bulgaria, question #4 to the Dardanelles. Question #2

ran as follows: Russian felt again threatened by Finland. Would Germany be prepared to render Finland no assistance at all and, above all, to withdraw immediately the German forces marching through to Kirkenes? Our answer was that now, as before, Germany was politically disinterested in Finland. But another war waged by Russia on the tiny Finnish nation was considered intolerable to the German Government, so much more since we did not believe Finland to be any threat to Russia. Besides, we did not at all desire that a theater of war be again created in the Baltic."

The Finnish problem, which had disturbed relations between German and the Soviet Union, was again discussed on the occasion of the visit of the Japanese Foreign Minister Matsuoka to Berlin in March 1941. In a stenographic report presented to the International Court in Tokyo and published for the first time on 25 November 1947 (by German New Agency – International News Service) it is stated that the Soviet Union had almost joined the Axis. But its demands had been too high, so that Hitler had not acceded to them. According to notes taken at a conference, which took place on 27 March in Berlin between the German Foreign Minister von Ribbentrop and the Japanese Foreign Minister Yosuke Matsuoka, Ribbentrop had declared that Russia would have joined the Three Power Pact had her demands been fulfilled. According to the report, Ribbentrop defined the demands as follows:

1.	Germany must give up her interests in Finland
2.	Russian must get bases along the Dardanelles
3.	Russia insists on a dominating position in the Balkans, particularly in Bulgaria

The demands raised by Russia and declined by Germany with regard to Finland in

November 1940 became known in Finland much too late and in too vague a form to explain the development of public opinion in favor of a rapprochement with Germany, which undoubtedly took place in the winter of 1940/41.

Neither the German-Russian negotiations at Berlin in November 1940 nor the understandable ill feeling and bitterness caused by the hard Moscow Peace were the decisive reasons underlying this sudden change in Finnish feeling. Much more it was various additional demands of the Soviet Union, not based on the Moscow Peace Treaty, which caused a deterioration of Finnish sentiment, as for instance subsequent alterations of the new frontier; surrender of large quantities of railroad material; demand for permission to initiate transit traffic with Russian trains through southern Finland to the new Russian naval port at Hangö; claims of participation in the administration and production of the Petsamo nickel plants; Russian objections to the tone of Finnish descriptions of the Winter War; the Russian veto against the idea of a joint defense of Finland and Sweden with had arisen right after the termination of the Winter War (prior to 9 April 1940 including Norway); Soviet speeches on the occasion of the incorporation of the former Finnish province Viipuri into the territory of the Karelian Soviet Republic, held at Petrozavodsk alluding emotionally but unmistakably to the future union of all Finnish races, that is to say the annexation of entire Finland as a part of the Soviet Union. A very bad impression was created in Finland, when after the death of President Kallio and a short time prior to the election of a new president, Russia informed the Finnish ambassador at Moscow that the election of several leading statesmen enumerated by name would be considered by the Soviet Union as an expression of lack of sincerity to act upon the terms of the Moscow Peace Treaty.

This intervention and the repeated veto raised against Finland signing a defense pact with Sweden probably created a much stronger distrust in the intentions of Russia than the uncertain rumors, known to a small circle of persons only, of the Russian demands at Berlin. The repeated bad experiences of Finland increased her feeling of distrust toward the Soviet Union to fever pitch and brought about an agreement with Germany. In the general belief of the Finnish people, German protection appeared the only means possible to avoid the impending destruction of Finland's political independence. Although the Finnish people had developed this way of thinking as early as the autumn of 1940 and it waxed stronger in the course of the winter, it still must be admitted that no official steps were taken to foster a rapprochement with Germany. The various attempts at contact between German and Finnish official agencies during the first half of 1941 were without exception due to German initiative. In order to avoid erroneous impressions of the importance of these approaches, the individual events must be dissected in some detail. These overtures included a visit of General Heinrichs, the Chief of the Finnish General Staff, (end of January 1941 at Berlin and Zossen) and a visit of Colonel Buschenhagen (February-March in Finland), later there were discussions between German and Finnish officers at Salzburg and Berlin on 25 and 26 May, and finally a second visit of Colonel Buschenhagen to Helsinki in the beginning of June. The development marked by these visits was exclusively determined by the Germans.

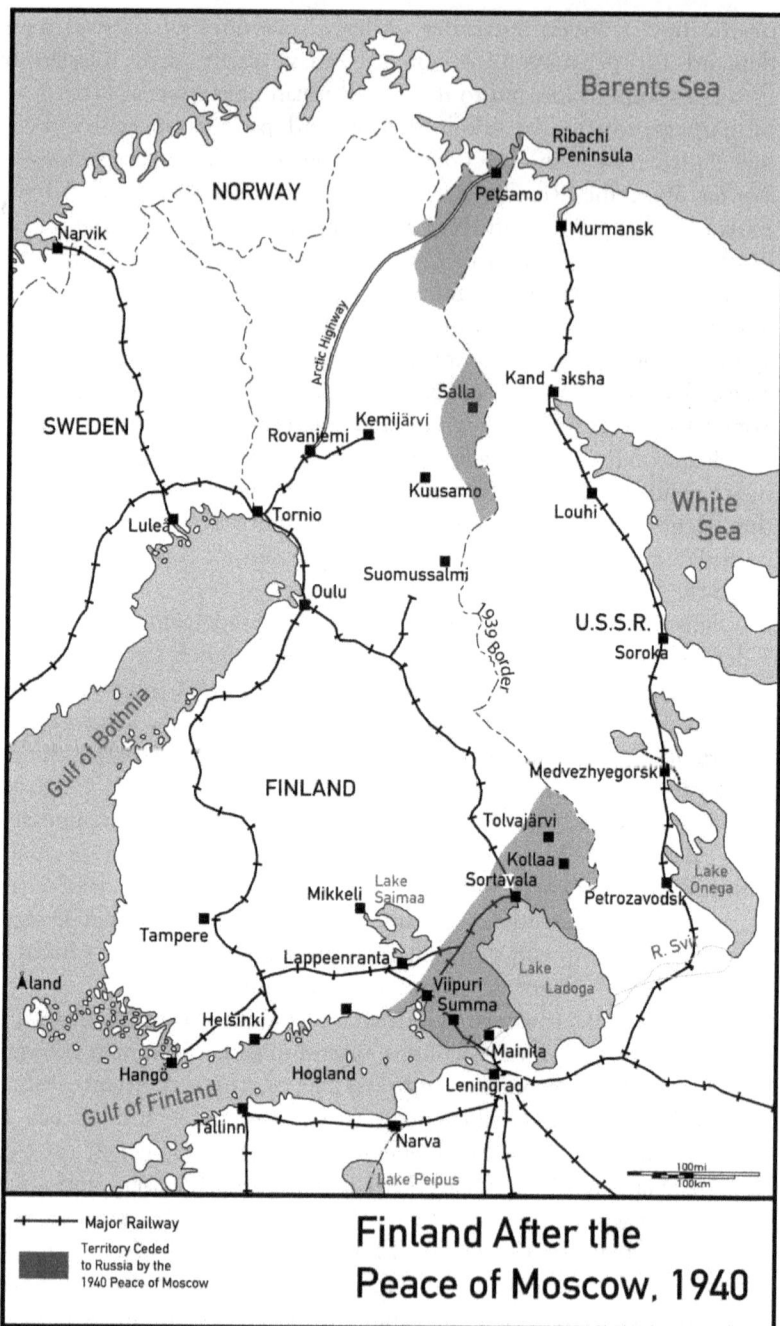

Barents Sea

NORWAY

Ribachi Peninsula

Petsamo

Narvik

Murmansk

Arctic Highway

SWEDEN

Salla

Kand aksha

Kemijärvi

Rovaniemi

Kuusamo

White Sea

Luleå

Tornio

Louhi

Oulu

Suomussalmi

1939 Border

U.S.S.R.

Soroka

Gulf of Bothnia

FINLAND

Medvezhyegorsk

Tolvajärvi

Kollaa

Lake Onega

Mikkeli

Lake Saimaa

Sortavala

Petrozavodsk

Tampere

R. Svi

Åland

Lappeenranta

Lake Ladoga

Viipuri

Summa

Helsinki

Hango

Hogland

Mainila

Leningrad

Gulf of Finland

Tallinn

Narva

100mi
100km

Lake Peipus

Major Railway

Territory Ceded to Russia by the 1940 Peace of Moscow

Finland After the Peace of Moscow, 1940

Map 1

Upon an invitation of the German Army High Command to the Finnish High Command to send an officer to Germany to give a lecture on the Finnish Winter War to the senior officers of the Army High Command, General Heinrichs came to Germany at the end of January 1941. Since the steamer was greatly delayed by the freezing over of the Baltic, the lecture had to be postponed for several days. Neither Generalfeldmarschall von Brauchitsch, Commander in Chief of the German Army, nor Generaloberst Halder, Chief of the German General Staff, was able to attend the lecture of the Finnish guest owing to the pressure of work. The visit to Generaloberst Halder required by military protocol, which General Heinrichs had to pay after his arrival in Germany was very short. No negotiations took place. The idea of German-Finnish cooperation was neither mentioned by the Germans nor by the Finnish General during the report at Zossen or the dinner at the Finnish legation in Berlin, which took place in the usual way in accordance with the rules of protocol. Heinrichs returned to Finland in the first days of February. Nothing came to his knowledge during his visit to Germany of German plans regarding a war against the Soviet Union (Operation BARBAROSSA).

The first visit of Colonel Buschenhagen to Helsinki in February 1941, according to his own statements, served the purpose of getting in touch with the Finnish General Staff in order to discuss joint operations in case of a German-Soviet war. The Finns, however, deny that the motive of the visit was so explained to them. On the contrary, the reason for the visit given the Finnish General Staff consisted of the question of transit traffic for German forces through northern Finland, in which Colonel Buschenhagen in his capacity as Chief of Staff of the Army Headquarters in Norway was particularly interested. Buschenhagen, who during his visit hinted at certain apprehensions with regard to Russian designs on Finland, is said to have mentioned on this occasion that it was his personal conviction that Germany would not remain an inactive onlooker to a possible new Russian aggression against Finland. He had pointed out that the forces of the Army High Command in Norway were geographically in the best position to come to the aid of the Finns under such circumstances. He was, therefore, in his capacity of Chief of the General Staff of the German Army in Norway exceedingly interested in the terrain conditions of northern Finland. Following a visit at Rovaniemi, where Buschenhagen was making arrangements in regard to transit traffic affairs, he was given the opportunity by the Finnish High Command, as a result of his statements, to inspect the eastern boundary regions of Lapland accompanied by a Finnish officer. It is true that this survey of the north Finnish region could only be hasty, as little time was available and the season was particularly unfavorable for terrain reconnaissance. This superficial reconnaissance resulted perhaps in the erroneous impression of the difficult conditions in this theater of war, which had an unfavorable effect on later operations of the AOK NORWEGEN (Army High Command Norway). No negotiations or discussions concerning a possible future cooperation between the Germans and the Finns took place during Buschenhagen's visit to Helsinki or anywhere else. The Finnish authorities in question categorically deny that any negotiations about a German or German-Finnish offensive against Murmansk or the White Sea took place during Buschenhagen's visit to Finland from the end of February to the beginning of March 1941. A contrary statement by Buschenhagen is perhaps due to confusion on his part with discussions which took place on a later visit to Helsinki (beginning of June). The Finnish version is supported by a report of the OKW on the situation dated 1 June 1941, according to which "preparatory negotiations" to possible German-Finnish cooperation were first held at Salzburg on 25 May.

Before describing the Salzburg negotiations, we must recapitulate the situation which had developed between Germany and the Soviet Union in the early part of 1941. Tension between the two countries increased during these months. Although the exchange of goods continued smoothly and without delay in conformity with the treaty, mutual distrust of each other's intentions increased on both sides. As a result of the breakdown and division of Poland, Germany and the Soviet Union had a common boundary. Increasingly stronger military forces assembled on either side of the frontier. It became known in Germany that further age classes were being drafted in the Soviet Union. New German divisions were continuously transferred from France to western Poland. The purpose of the concentrations on both sides remained unclear.

The sinister tension of the political situation in Europe could not remain unnoticed in Finland, where everyone lived under the pressure of the Russian menace and was aware that the chance for security offered by a pact with Sweden was lost due to the Russian veto. Any possibility of preserving neutrality in the tremendous clash, which appeared more and more threatening in the spring of 1941, seemed to vanish. No lasting attitude of neutrality towards the two Great Powers would possibly be maintained, in case of a German-Russian war, by the comparatively small Finnish forces. The Finns had not yet forgotten that in the beginning of the Winter War the Red Army had crossed the Finnish frontier and started the war without a formal declaration of war.

Amid this atmosphere of high tension, the German government suggested an exchange of opinions with Finnish experts on the military and political situation. Ambassador Schnurre, who had been sent to Helsinki by Adolf Hitler in May, was the bearer of an invitation from the latter to Finnish President Ryti, to send representatives of the Finnish General Staff to German Headquarters in order to receive information and to discuss questions of common interest for the headquarters of both countries. President Ryti gave his consent. Field Marshal Mannerheim's first intention to send a branch chief of the General Staff to Germany did not seem to meet with Ambassador Schnurre's approval and it was decided to send the Chief of the Finnish General Staff to the German Headquarters, accompanied by his most important assistants. General Heinrichs was, therefore, accompanied to Germany by Colonels Tapola, Maekinen and Rooa, as well as Commodore Sundmann. The Finnish guests arrived at Salzburg on 25 May. The discussion took place on the same day in a hotel opposite the railroad station, defining German-Russian relations and concluding with the possibility of a military clash of the two countries. He expressed his conviction that Finland could under no circumstances remain neutral in such a war but would willingly or unwillingly be drawn into it sooner or later. Jodl did not discuss any operational details but hinted in broad outlines at a possible advance of the German left wing through the Baltic countries, without, however, demanding or discussing Finnish cooperation against Leningrad. He explained that in case of a German-Russian war, the German Army in Norway would advance against the Murmansk railroad through Finnish territory. "All that we expect of Finland," said Jodl, "is that it will by its own action hold down at least those Russian forces at its frontier, which will be there at the outbreak of hostilities."

When Jodl had finished, Heinrichs immediately answered. He declared explicitly that Finland would certainly wage no war unless it was attacked. Even in case a new Russian aggression would draw Finland into a war, the Finnish officers had no authority to make any, even hypothetical arrangements. Jodl accepted this declaration without any objection. He simply pointed out that after all one could discuss conditions and possibilities, which was then done without any obligations. When the Finnish delegation left, Jodl held out the prospect of a visit of a senior German staff officer to Helsinki at a somewhat later date in order to hear the opinion of the competent Finnish political and military authorities with regard to Jodl's statement and to continue the discussions if necessary. From the above and from the statement of the OKW dated 1 June 1945 in the time table for Operation BARBAROSSA that preparatory negotiations were initiated on 25 May, it follows clearly that no agreement was reached at Salzburg. There would have been no possibility in view of the short time available. Nothing was done at Salzburg beyond giving information on the general situation and discussing the particular situation of Finland in a German-Russian conflict, followed by a short exchange of questions and answers. Nor were the Germans intent on reaching any agreements on this occasion. The Finnish officers had no authority to enter into any engagements, not even hypothetical ones. According to the statements of General Jodl, it seemed entirely uncertain whether or not there would be a war between Germany and the Soviet Union.

In a discussion with Generaloberst Halder at Berlin on the following day (26 May 1941), the German wishes with regard to the attitude of the Finns in case of a German-Russian war were defined more precisely. The Chief of the German General Staff stated the desirability of German-Finnish cooperation against Leningrad, whereupon General Heinrichs immediately remarked that, although he had no authority, he believed that he was in a position to assure the Germans that this particular operational plan would never be approved by the political and military authorities in Finland. The Finnish officers present had the impression that after the declaration of the Finnish Chief of Staff, Halder waived the idea of a Finnish advance across the Karelian Isthmus.[4] He continued calmly speaking about a possible direction of attack of the Finnish army through the territory north of Lake Ladoga, paying particular attention to the Finnish supply facilities for such an operation. During the Berlin discussions, General Heinrichs again emphasized that Finland would only join the war if attacked, but no agreements were arrived at in Berlin with regard to such a hypothetical case. All questions regarding possible military cooperation remained open. In Berlin too it was mentioned that senior officers would be sent to Finland to continue the discussions and to gain acquaintance with official Finnish opinion.

It struck the Finns that, while at Salzburg Jodl spoke only of a desirable "binding activity" on the part of the Finns, Halder in Berlin hinted at major operations. General Heinrichs drew the attention of Kapitän zur See Bürckner, Chief of the Foreign Group, to this matter and inquired how the different attitude of the German agencies should be interpreted. Bürckner declared that Jodl's statements of were to be considered authoritative. Besides, he added, those questions would be later discussed at Helsinki.[5]

The visit of a senior officer of the German General Staff to Helsinki, as promised by Jodl and Halder, did not take place, but in the beginning of June, Colonel Buschenhagen accompanied by Colonel Kinzel, Branch Chief in the Army General Staff, returned to Finland to discuss unsettled matters. This visit resulted in repeated conferences with the Chief of the Finnish General Staff. The over-all operations of the German eastern armies in case of war were not discussed on this occasion. The discussion

---

[4] This operational idea was repeatedly suggested to the Finnish Headquarters by Wehrmacht Operations Staff but was always declined by Field Marshal Mannerheim.

[5] Already on this occasion the lack of coordination between the ideas and plans of the Wehrmacht High Command and the Army High Command became apparent, which during the whole war proved an obstacle to operations on the Finnish theater of war.

dealt with the local cooperation of the Finnish V Corps (which soon after was renamed III Corps) and the forces of the Army Headquarters Norway, stationed in or to be sent to Lapland, as well as with practical measures resulting therefrom. The Finns always hedged those discussions with the reservation that their results should be valid only in case Finland be drawn into the war by a Russian attack. Regarding the abovementioned questions of possible cooperation of German and Finnish forces in northern Finland, a general agreement was reached. Its conditions as well as the arrangements to be made by the Finnish High Command the agreement became effective were communicated to President Ryti, who raised no objections.

Apparently Colonel Buschenhagen during his last visit at Helsinki before the outbreak of the war had still another, far more important mission. He tried repeatedly and with the utmost energy, obviously by order of the OKW, to attain a pledge from the political leaders in Finland of cooperation in the threatening German-Russian war. But neither the Finnish president, nor the government, nor the military leaders gave such a guarantee.

After the war, Buschenhagen was known to have said that he had been received together with Colonel Kinzel at the end of his last stay in Helsinki by Field Marshal Mannerheim in the latter's home and that the Marshal had on that occasion expressed his satisfaction with the agreement reached by the two general staffs. The Finns give a different version from that of Buschenhagen. According to them, the Marshal had received the two Germans at the urgent request of Buschenhagen, but the questions which Buschenhagen had raised when speaking with General Heinrichs were not touched upon nor had Buschenhagen and Kinzel mentioned them. Anyone knowing Mannerheim's great gift of guiding a conversation in the direction he wanted it to go, avoiding ticklish questions, will have no doubt that the Finnish version is correct.

When trying by means of the sources available to reconstruct pre-war history and the overtures between the Germans and the Finns prior to the outbreak of the war, and when evaluating the results in accordance with their importance, the conclusion must be reached that the Germans always took the initiative in entering into negotiations, while the Finns showed reticence in meeting the German desires and did not commit themselves by any binding declarations. The political and military leaders of Finland, by the attitude of the German participants in the conferences and particularly by the statements of General Jodl at Salzburg at the end of May 1941, became aware of the great probability of a German-Russian war and the intention of the Germans in such a case to advance through north Finnish territory against the area of the Murmansk railroad. Should Finland prevent that and was it able to do so? It is easy to understand that the Finnish people at that time had no sympathy for the Soviet Union. There was a firm, general belief in a German victory in case of a campaign in the East. It is no wonder that German observers gained the impression that in case of war a pro-German attitude was to be expected in Finland. This impression, the correctness of which was corroborated by later events, was probably strong enough to allow the German Wehrmacht to renounce the idea of a political or even of only a military agreement with Finland, since the conviction prevailed that in the long run events would automatically take the course desired by Germany. Finland could, as Jodl had openly said at Salzburg, not remain aloof from a German-Russian war, once the dice had been cast.

Russian bombing of Finnish towns in the first days of the German-Russian war hastened the expected development. When Soviet air warfare against Finland commenced, the veil of uncertainty was torn down which had hidden the true situation from the eyes of the Finnish statesmen and military authorities. Fate took its course.

There is no doubt that the position of the responsible men in Finland in the last days before the outbreak of the war was a particularly difficult one. Political tension in the world was increasing daily, but complete uncertainty reigned with regard to the paramount question of whether or not there would be war with the Soviet Union. Under these circumstances it was very difficult for the Finnish government to take the necessary measures for the security of the country. It could not expose the Finnish people to the risk of being involved in a sudden war without any defense preparations. On the other hand the danger existed of rousing the suspicion of the Soviet Union by military preparations, even if the political crisis did not lead to war. The decision to call in the reserves was, therefore, repeatedly postponed. On 17 June, however, a further postponement of mobilization was no longer considered advisable. On this day, President Ryti, dictated by anxiety for the security of the Finnish people, took the fateful decision to order immediate mobilization. On the same day, German S-Boats and mine layers under Kapitän zur See Bütow arrived in southern Finnish ports in order to secure the Gulf of Finland against the Russian Baltic Fleet stationed in Kronstadt. The Finnish mobilization proceeded in the next days according to plan. It was not announced by public proclamation but by induction orders sent to those liable for military service. The brave, soldierly Finnish nation followed its government's call to arms with admirable calmness. Everybody witnessing these days at Helsinki was deeply impressed by the attitude of the population. All good qualities inherent in the Finns became apparent during these days. All men capable of bearing arms promptly came from the immense forests and from remote, desolate places to the assembly points in their parishes. The Finnish railroad system, which had not too great a capacity, mastered all difficulties. Trains were only a few hours late. The mobilization days were governed by a sense of duty and reliability. Everyone took his place in the quiet and serious Finnish way.

General Jodl had promised at Salzburg that a German general would come to Finland as a liaison officer of the Wehrmacht and the Germany Army and would be attached to the Finnish High Command. In this capacity, General der Infanterie Erfurth landed on 13 June 1941 at Malmi Airport near Helsinki and on the same day assumed his duties at the Finnish Headquarters as "Commander of Liaison Staff North." Through the suggestions of the OKW transmitted after the outbreak of hostilities by General Erfurth and voluntarily accepted by Field Marshal Mannerheim, the Finnish operational plans with regard to the concentration of the army were to a certain extent influenced by Germany. It was, however, in keeping with the very independent way of Mannerheim who knew so well how to guard his position as Finnish Commander in Chief against any German or Finnish attempts to influence him, and who steadfastly clung to what he deemed the right thing to do, that the Finnish Commander in Chief was influenced in his decisions by advisors only in so far as was justified in the interest of the country. The welfare of his own people was his supreme law. The Finnish offensive in summer 1941 was not carried out to help the Germans nor in order to fulfill any obligations towards brothers in arms, but to keep the devastations of war away from Finnish territory. There were, therefore, no agreements with the Germans tying the hands of the Finnish Marshal in the beginning of the war.

As applied to the local sector in northern Finland, in which Generaloberst von Falkenhorst, arriving on 15 June at Rovaniemi, took over the command of the German and Finnish forces with part of the Army Headquarters Norway,[6] certain guiding principles had been discussed orally with regard to the hypothetical case of Finland being drawn in to the war by an act of Russian aggression. In this connection General Siilasvuo, the Commanding General of the Finnish III Corps, was placed under the command of Generaloberst von Falkenhorst. If necessary, this assignment could be cancelled in the same way, as was actually done later in the course of the war.

Germany tried repeatedly during the war to bind Finland to the Reich by the conclusion of a formal alliance. The Finnish government always evaded these requests. The Finnish people and its government did not want to get involved in the war of the Great Powers. The Finns regarded their Third War of Independence as a continuation of the Winter War, as

---

[6] The former V Corps (3rd and 6th Divisions), assembled there, was renamed Finnish III Corps on that day.

a defensive war, as an affair concerning only the Finns and the Soviets. For their relationship toward the German soldier, the Finns chose the name "brothers-in-arms." The official Finnish agencies carefully avoided calling the German brothers in arms "allies." This differentiation did not prove harmful to mutual good understanding.

German-Finnish friendship during World War II won the fullest and unanimous support of the German people. The strong sympathy felt in Germany for this honest and clever people was increased by the reports of the German soldiers fighting in Lapland, who after having become accustomed to the strange conditions prevailing in the northern regions took a great liking to Finland and to their Finnish comrades. Of all peoples who fought during the last war alongside Germans, the Finns were those with whom the German soldiers had the best relationship.

War between Germany and the Soviet Union began early in the
morning of 22 June 1941. Mountain Corps Norway, arriving from
Kirkenes, marched into the Petsamo region on this day. Finnish and
German naval forces jointly began to seal off the eastern part of the Gulf
of Finland by laying mine fields. The Soviet Russian naval base of Hangö
was bombarded by German air forces approaching it from the south from
the area of Army Group North. Russian bombers attacked Finnish
battleships and fortifications on the skerries of Turku, as well as Finnish
coastal vessels southwest of Porvoo. On the morning of 22 June, the
Russian artillery fire opened from the leased Territories of Hangö into
Finnish territory, and in the evening Russian infantry fired the Finnish
border east of Imatra. Similar frontier violations also occurred on the
following days.

On 23 June the impression was gained by the AOK NORWEGEN at
Rovaniemi that the hilly area of Salla, which after the Winter War had
been ceded to the Soviet Union, was very little or not at all occupied by
the Russians. Generaloberst von Falkenhorst decided to get this
important mountain range into his possession by a surprise attack, since it
would be difficult to take it if strongly defended. Since Field Marshal
Mannerheim considered such an attack based from Finnish territory
inopportune for political reasons at a time when war had not yet been
declared between Finland and the Soviet Union, Falkenhorst had to desist
from his plan.

The Finnish Army at that time had occupied defense positions along
the border and concentrated behind the security zone along the long
eastern frontier in the assembly areas of the divisions. The fortifications
along the new frontier had been constructed during the short time of
peace after the Winter War, but, despite strenuous labor, were ineffective
because of the vast area that had to be covered. The Finnish High
Command was therefore particularly concerned about the important
industrial district of Imatra situated only a few kilometers behind the
border, which could be but weakly protected. Imatra's loss would have
had incalculable consequences.

New bombing attacks followed on 25 June on Helsinki, Turku,
Jönsuu, Heinola and many other places in the interior of Finland. War had
come again to Finland.

On this day the Finnish High Command occupied its war
headquarters at Mikkeli, where Field Marshal Mannerheim had had his
headquarters during the last months of the First War of Independence
and during the Winter War. The quarters of the Finnish High Command

were not moved to any other location during the entire duration of the war. In the school building of Mikkeli, not far from the large town church, the Marshal of Finland spent many work-filled days and nights, more and more anxious as the war continued. The town of Mikkeli, as the site of the Finnish Headquarters in three major wars, claims a special place among the towns in the history of Finland. In gratitude and in acknowledgement of its hospitality, Mannerheim bestowed upon the town two crossed batons for its coat of arms. The German Liaison Staff North, which remained in close contact with the Finnish Headquarters during the entire war, occupied billets for the next two months at Heimari, about two miles south of Mikkeli, a little way from the road to Lappeenranta. Since the quarters were only suitable for summer, the German staff moved to Mikkeli on 1 November.

On account of Russian air attacks against Finnish towns President Ryti broadcast an address to the Finnish people on 26 June, declaring that a state of war had thereby been created between Finland and the Soviet Union. From this day on Finland fought shoulder to shoulder with its German brothers-in-arms against its powerful eastern neighbor. The future of Finland now depended on the issue of the war.

While the main body of the Finnish forces assembled in the area between the Gulf of Finland and Jönsuu, conferences were held at the Headquarters of Field Marshal Mannerheim on how to launch the Finnish offensive. As the situation in the sector of the German Army Group North developed, the bulk was to advance either west or east of Lake Ladoga in the direction of Leningrad or against the Svir River. The successes of the German forces in western Russia were considerable and began to exercise their effect on the Finnish Front. The Red Army reserves which had assembled immediately east of the Finnish frontier (particularly on the Karelian Isthmus) and which probably had the mission to carry out an attack against the Finnish front, now seemed to have been withdrawn to the German front. It is possible that the Russian Army Command, affected by the difficult situation at the German front, gave up its initial idea of launching a major counterattack across the Finnish border. Since the Russian fleet did not dare to leave the Bight of Kronstadt, Russian offensive operations were limited to air attacks on Finnish towns. The Finnish air force was too weak to prevent the Russian raids. The southern towns especially suffered from these raids. It was here that the bulk of the Finnish population and athe main industries were located.

The fact that the enemy bombers approached southern Finland as a rule from the south across the Gulf of Finland was very unfavorable for the Finnish air warning service and air defense. The vulnerability to air attacks of the southern Finnish towns had already been severely felt in the

Winter War. Now the disadvantages, well known from experience in the last war, reoccurred, especially since the airfields in Estonia were available to the Red Air Force. The air raids came generally as a surprise so that no air alert was sounded until the first bombs were dropped. The population of the towns because very uneasy, particularly the inhabitants of the capital where the political and economic life of the country was concentrated. Many new Russian airfields had been built and old ones had been repaired in the territory on the Karelian Isthmus and east of Lake Ladoga lost to Moscow as a result of the dictated peace treaty of the previous year. The Soviet Union had made good use of the short time following the Winter War to transform Karelia into a base for attack against Finland and had also constructed roads and railroads, the capacity of which by far exceeded the needs of the thinly-populated region.

Consideration of how to capture the Russian airdromes, therefore, played a major role in the plans of the Finnish High Command. It was hoped that through the advance of Army Group North the threat from the air from Estonia would soon be removed by the German troops. But in Karelia the air situation could only be corrected by a Finnish offensive.

Most Finns wished with all their heart to win back lost West Karelia and to expel the Russians from soil which had been part of Finland for centuries. Over and above this desire, which seemed a matter of course to the Finns, many Finns also had the ardent with to liberate East Karelia[7] too from Soviet rule. Field Marshal Mannerheim, therefore, addressed his soldiers in the order of the day of 28 June 1941 as follows:

> "I call upon you to take part in a holy war against the enemy of our people. Our dead heroes are rising from their fresh, green graves at this moment in order to rejoin us as brothers-in-arms of a mighty Germany in a crusade against our enemy to secure the future of Finland.
>
> Brothers in arms: Follow me for the last time, now that Karelia is rising and Aurora will light a new day for the Finns."

---

[7] It is often called Far Karelia by the Finns. The area colonized by the Karelians is not confined to strict boundaries. The Karelian Isthmus between the Gulf of Finland and Lake Ladoga and Ladoga-Karelia (the country east and north of Lake Ladoga) are closely connected with the FInnish People and have for a long time been politically within the eastern Finnish boundary. East Karelia, on the other hand, the country between the Svir River and the White Sea, has been under Russian rule for quite a long time and since early times under the sway of the Orthodox Church.

As the Finns saw it, based on the experiences of all former wars against Russian, the main theater of war had to be the Karelian Isthmus. The Russian breakthrough in the Lähde sector (east of Summa) on the Karelian Isthmus in the middle of February 1940 had caused the disastrous changes of the situation in the Winter War. The shortest way for a Russian invasion of southern Finland and Helsinki led through the Isthmus. Furthermore, enticing objectives for a Finnish offensive (rich Viipuri and the developing industrial area along the Vuoksi River) were located on the Karelian Isthmus, which was the most densely populated of all Karelian areas, highly cultivated, and provided with a good road net. It was, therefore, quite natural that the thoughts of the Finnish Commander in Chief were occupied chiefly with the Karelian Isthmus as the main theater of war of the planned Finnish offensive. The deployment of Finnish forces was carried out mainly in accordance with this idea.

The German brothers-in-arms had other plans, however. The greater the success of the German offensive in western Russian, the more pressing became the demands of the German High Command that Field Marshal Mannerheim should not direct the main thrust of this army by way of the Karelian Isthmus toward Leningrad, but east of Lake Ladoga toward Ladeynoye Pole on the Svir. The German Army High Command desired that the strongest possible Finnish forces advance to the Svir and there unite for a decisive operations with Army Group North which was proceeding across the Volkhov River. In order to emphasize the importance attached by the German Command to the Finnish offensive east of Lake Ladoga, the OKW expressed on 27 June the wish that the German 163rd Division arriving by rail from Norway should be brought forward to the Finnish point of main effort east of Lake Ladoga. This division had originally been earmarked by the OKW for an attack on the Russian naval base at Hangö, the land entrance to which had been sealed off by the Finnish 17th Division since the beginning of the war. On account of the length of time needed for transportation by water around the North Cape to Petsamo and the threat by British submarines on that route, the German government had requested transportation of the 163rd Division by rail on German rolling stock by way of Sweden to Finland. The Swedish government agreed reluctantly. After the great German successes, the Swedish government acknowledged with a certain justification the possibility for a quick German victory over the Soviet Union. According to the previous German plans, the 163rd Division was to have attacked Hangö jointly with the Finnish 17th Division and to have occupied this Russian naval base in order to make possible uninterrupted sea traffic to Helsinki and Kotka. Now, however, the German High Command declared its readiness to postpone the attack on Hangö for the present, in order to strengthen the Finnish offensive toward East Karelia.

On 28 June Field Marshal Mannerheim made his decision. He decided that the Finnish offensive was to head in a southeasterly direction along both sides of Lake Jänia. The forces participating in this operation, whose further mission was to advance east of Lake Ladoga to the Svir, were organized as the "Karelian Army" under the supreme command of General Heinrichs, the Chief of the Finnish General Staff. As a general rule, the Finnish Corps were under the immediate command of Finnish Headquarters, without the interposition of an army headquarters. The signal communications from Mikkeli to the corps on the Karelian Isthmus were equal to all demands of the high level command. On the other hand it seemed doubtful whether an offensive into Karelia undertaken by several corps could be directed from Mikkeli. Since, for several reasons, it did not seem feasible to transfer the headquarters from Mikkeli to the rear of the Finnish main attack wing, it was decided to organize the Karelian Army. At the General Headquarters, General Tuompo, Chief of the Command Section, acted for a short time as deputy of the Chief of the General Staff; later on General Hanell, Chief of Fortifications, acted as deputy. Colonel Tapola was assigned as Chief of Staff of the Karelian Army to General Heinrichs. His former place as Chief of the Operations Branch at General Headquarters was assumed by Colonel Mäkinen, then by Colonel Karikoski and later Colonel Viljanen.

At the beginning of the offensive in June 1941, the Finnish front between the Gulf of Finland and Liekaa was organized as follows (from the right to the left wing):

1. IV Corps (Major General Ösch) with its right wing on the Gulf of Finland, opposite Viipuri, with the left wing on the Vuoksi River.

8th Division	12th Division
10th Division	4th Division

2. II Corps (Brigadier General Lastikainen) between the Vuoksi and the northwestern Corner of Lake Ladoga to Lake Pyhae.

2nd Division	15th Division
18th Division	

3 Karelian Army (Major General Heinrichs) from Lake Pyhae to Korpiselkä

    a. VII Corps (Brigadier General Hägglund) from Lake Pyhae to the outskirts of Värtsilä

19th Division	7th Division

    b. VI Corps (Brigadier General Talvela) from Värtsilä to Korpiselkä

11th Division	I Light Infantry Brigade
5th Division	

    c. Oinonen Task Force (in and north of the Ilomantsi area)

II Light Infantry Brigade Cavalry Brigade

d. 1st Division Army reserve behind the Karelian Army.

4. 14th Division (Colonel Raspana) in the Lieksa area.

5. The German 163rd Division was to follow behind the Karelian Army as Mannerheim's reserve. It was to assemble in and east of the Jönsuu area on 30 June.

6. 17th Division. Temporarily before Hangö

The area adjoining to the north as far as the Arctic coast was occupied by German and Finnish forces formed into an army under the command of AOK NORWEGEN. The Commander in Chief was Generaloberst von Falkenhorst; Chief of the General Staff, Colonel Buschenhagen.

On the right wing of this army was the Finnish III Corps (Brigadier General Siilasvuo), in the Suomussalmi and Kuusamo areas:

Finnish 3rd Division   Finnish 6th Division

Adjoining to the north was the German XXXVI Corps Headquarters (General der Kavallerie Feige) in the Lake Kämi area:

German 169th Division   Assigned Finnish forces
German SS Brigade Nord

Located in the Petsamo area was German Mountain Corps Norway (General der Gebirgstruppe Dietl):

2nd Mountain Division   3rd Mountain Division

The organizational command at Finnish Headquarters[8] was as follows:

Commander in Chief: Field Marshal Mannerheim, as of 4 June 1942, Marshal of Finland

Chief of the General Staff: Major General Heinrichs, until beginning of 1942 detached to command the Karelian Army and represented by Major General Hanell

Chief of Army Supply and Administration: Brigadier General Airo

Chief of the Operations Branch: Colonel Käkinen, succeeded by Karikoski, Viljanen and finally Colonel Nihtilä

Chief of the Command Staff: Brigadier General Toumpo

Chief of the Reconnaissance Branch: Colonel Melander, succeeded by Colonel Paasonen

Chief of the Supply System: Colonel Roos

Commander in Chief of the Navy: Major General Valve

Commander in Chief of the Air Forces: Major General Lundquist

---

[8] The Headquarters were organized along French lines. The Chief of Army Supplies and Administration was in charge of operations.

Artillery Inspector: Major General Henonen
Engineer Inspector: Major General Sarlin
Signal Inspector: Colonel Ekberg

CHAPTER III: The Joint Finnish-German Offensive in 1941

As previously agreed upon, the attack of the Finnish-German front did not begin simultaneously in all sectors, but started from the left wing. The attack by AOK NORWEGEN began on 29 June with the Mountain Corps Norway advancing from the Petsamo area toward Murmansk. After that, on 1 July, the German-Finnish troops of the XXXVI Corps the border formed by the dictated Peace of Moscow, in the direction of the hilly Salla region.

On the same day, forces of the German Army occupied Riga. The Dvina River was reached between Dvinsk and Riga on a wide front. On the following days, the Finnish III Corps advanced from the Suomussalmi and Kuusamo area and crossed the Russian border in the direction of Uhtua and Kiestinki.

The objective of AOK NORWEGEN'S eastern offensive was the Murmansk railroad. The Front sectors in the Arctic region were designated the objectives assigned to the three corps groups of the Falkenhorst Army. They were the Louhi, Kandalaksha, and Murmansk sectors. The final objective of the offensive was to reach the Murmansk railroad in order to cut the Soviet supply line from overseas. The region into which this offensive led was a pathless, uninhabited, boulder-strewn wilderness in which even the Finns were strangers. Perhaps there is no other area in Europe as lonesome and remote as this vast desert between the long eastern Finnish border and the Murmansk railroad. The southern and central sectors are covered by immense virgin forests and moors, often intersected by large and small lakes and streams running into the White Sea. The northern sector belongs to the treeless tundra, which merges into the boulder-strewn coast of the Arctic Sea. Most of the time the region is buried under snow and ice. Winter in the Arctic is very hard for Central Europeans (all bodies of water are covered with ice; deep snow, very low temperatures, long nights). A mud period forms the transition between winter and summer, during which the few roads become impassable or are difficult to use. Summer in the north is short but extreme in consequence of the long period of sunshine. By the middle of summer, the sun does not set in Lapland. In Karelia the sun disappears below the horizon for only two hours. No sooner does dusk set than the new day dawns in the east. Here one can at midnight sit in a room reading a book without putting on a light. Whereas the temperature in winter sinks to forty centigrade below zero, the thermometer rises in summer to thirty-five centigrade above zero. Gnats in the forest wilderness are a plague in summer. The German-Finnish offensive in the arctic region took place during the time of endless daylight.

The peculiarities of the theater of war became immediately apparent in all sectors and affected the conduct of war. In particular, those German soldiers who had grown up in towns were faced with almost insurmountable problems by the closed terrain, the general impassability of the wilderness. All movements depended on the few bad roads, on which traffic was only possible by means of light carts or sleighs.

The boundary near the Arctic Sea was crossed in the last days of June. Within a short time the Mountain Corps Norway gained thirty to forty kilometers until the German front came to a standstill in the Litsa sector half-way to its objective owing to lack of forces and could not be set in motion again. Heavy fighting ensued putting the Mountain Corps to a severe test. When Russian troops landed in the rear of the German front and General Dietl had no reserves for clearing the country behind the Mountain Corps of enemy forces, Generaloberst von Falkenhorst approached Field Marshal Mannerheim with a request for help. On 8 July 1941 Mannerheim sent the Finnish 14th Infantry Regiment to the aid of the German brothers-in-arms. That regiment had at first occupied the Aland Islands and then, being superfluous there, had been brought forward to the Riihimaki area as GHQ reserve. Soon after its arrival in the Petsamo area, the gravity of the situation eased. On 7 September the Mountain Corps Norway again began an attack on Murmansk, which likewise proved unsuccessful. In the Litsa sector the German forces went into position, with their left wing on Motovski Bay and remained until the end of the war in that same position. Repeated Russian attempts to break the defense line of the German Mountain Corps at the Murmansk front remained unsuccessful until the capitulation of Finland. Thus, stubborn attacks of the Soviet troops between 21 and 26 December 1941 amidst heavy frost and snowstorms were frustrated. A Soviet Russian offensive in May 1942 suffered the same fate. After that, calm reined in the Arctic. It is true that the OKW, which at first had accepted the fact that the German offensive along the arctic coast had come to a standstill, later demanded a resumption of the offensive against Murmansk and the occupation of the Rybachy Peninsula late in Winter 1941/42, but this did not take place since the forces necessary for an offensive could not be made available and the supply of major forces did not seem possible. The mission of Mountain Corps Norway was, therefore, after the discontinuation of the offensive restricted to the protection of the nickel mines of Kolosjoki, the security of the Arctic Highway and the protection of the arctic coast.

The XXXVI Corps Headquarters, which had been given the mission of occupying the Salla hills and then to proceed to Kandalaksha also became engaged in heavy fighting, immediately bringing home to the German troops the characteristics of this theater of war. The German-

Finnish advance in this area was carried out on a wide front; far to the south the Finns began their advance from Hautajärvi to Tuntijärvi and Vuorijärvi. While the German artillery fired upon the Russian positions in the Salla hills, the SS Brigade 'Nord" attacked along the road from Keiloselkä on 1 July. This attack, which ran up against a fortified Russian position not previously recognized,[9] came to a standstill under heavy SS losses.

SS-Kampfgruppe Nord had been formed by units of the Waffen-SS stationed in Norway and had been transferred to Finland. It consisted of the 6th and 7th Motorized SS Infantry Regiments equipped with Czech arms, supplemented by two artillery battalions activated in the Zone of the Interior, one SS signal battalion, one SS reconnaissance battalion, one SS medical company, and a 20-mm antiaircraft battery. The Kampfgruppe consisted of elderly men without combat experience and was an improvised unit, over which hovered an unlucky star. During transport 105 casualties had occurred as a result of a fire aboard ship. Losses on 1 July owing to the unsuccessful attack included one regimental commander, one battalion commander and 600 men. As in all improvisations there was a lack of training, leadership, and combat experience.

Northwest of the hilly country, a German combat unit advanced toward Salla by way of Saja. Still further to the north, a regiment of the 169th Division marched on corduroy roads many kilometers long, across the border and after being delayed by large-scale forest fires, reached the Salla-Korja road. At the outer northern wing, raider units penetrated to the east on both sides of the Tennio River. The first attempt to capture the strongly fortified mountain area governing the approach road to Kandalaksha was a failure. There, too, reserves were lacking to add new vigor to the attack which had come to a standstill. Strong Russian counterattacks with tank support took place on 2 July but were beaten off. The enveloping units in the north and south made good progress. On 3 July the front was attacked seven times by the Russians, with their point of main effort north of Salla. The German attack on either side of the Savukoski-Salla road reached a small height in front of Salla. The employment of dive bombers brought some relief to the German forces. The northern tank force wheeled to the south and advanced as far as the Kuola River. The Finns reached Jahrhämäjärvi in the south and on Vuojärvi 4 July. Whereas the two northern task forces took up contact with one another at the Keinuvara ridge, the German attack on the height

---

[9] Ed. Note: In point of fact, Finnish Military Intelligence was aware of this line of fortifications. German intelligence officers scorned this report, however, and didn't even bother to translate it into German.

immediately north of Salla made no progress. Forces were lacking to give a new impetus to the frontal attack. Generaloberst von Falkenhorst, looking about for assistance, pinned his hopes on the 163rd Division on its way from Sweden, whose rear regiment had not yet passed Tornio. Falkenhorst asked for and received permission to reroute the last third of the 163rd Division from Tornio to Rovaniemi and to bring it forward to the Salla sector. Though this help did not prove necessary after all (Salla was captured on 7 July at a time when the regiment of the 163rd Division had not yet arrived before the town) the fact remained during this campaign that the 163rd Division was torn into two parts, naturally influencing the efficiency of the division which joined the Karelian Army with only two regiments.

On 5 July the XXXVI Corps was reorganized for a concentric attack on Salla. On 6 July the last assault was carried out on the Russian fortifications south of the Kuola River, supported by German dive bombers. The northern combat unit reached the fork in the Salla-Kairala road. Again Russian counterattacks followed. The combat unit advancing on the extreme northern wing crossed the Kuola and captured a Russian barracks east of Salla in the evening of 6 July. A northern auxiliary column reached the fork at the eastern fringe of Salla. The fact that fifty Russian tanks were destroyed by 6 July served to indicate the severity of the fighting.

The Finns had by this time reached Lake Kapa and consequently were on the flank of the Russian forces. Russian resistance abated on 7 July. In the evening Salla was captured.

On 8 July the Russians withdrew from action, fighting as usual on such occasions with great ability and bravery. The Finnish southern group encountered prepared Russian rear positions south of Mikkeli. The enemy retired from the German center forces and the SS Brigade Nord. The northern forces advanced toward the railroad. Advance detachments with tanks and cyclists advanced on the road to Kandalaksha in the direction of Kairala. In the evening of 8 July all of the Salla Hills were in German-Finnish hands.

After the capture of the Salla Range, the XXXVI Corps headquarters continued the offensive in the direction of Kandalaksha. The Russians had retired in the south behind a line Lake Vuori and Lake Aapa, and in the north to the Maaseljän Hills, on which they occupied new bunkers which had been blasted into the rock. The line of advance of the XXXVI Corps led through the Kairala Narrows. Russian defenses, skillfully placed, necessitated long enveloping movements through impassable country which caused much trouble. The 169th Division advanced in the north, the Finnish 6th Division in the south. The Russians offered stubborn resistance and stormed for four weeks against the German northern wing on the Jungoiva. Slowly the ring closed around the Russians. In the battle of encirclement at Kairala, which now began, Germans and Finns endeavored to surround the bravely resisting enemy, resulting in heavy fights with alternating success. On 19 August 1941 the Finns and Germans advanced against the Nurmi Height to the south of the Lehtokangas Height and there reached the road to Lake Vuori. A German enveloping detachment advanced northeast of the Nenäpalo Height, the northern combat unit advanced lunging in a wide sweep further to the east. On 20 August the Finns reached the Kairala-Alakurtti road east of Nurmi Height. Units of the SS Brigade Nord blocked the lake front of Lakes Kuola and Aapa, while the northern envelopment detachment sealed off the Nurmi River crossings. On 21 August the Kairala-Alakurtti road was blocked by the Finns east of the spot where the railroad crossed the road, whereupon they thrust a spearhead in the direction of Uulantoin Hill. A Russian pocket of resistance northeast of Lehtokangas was destroyed. The right Finnish wing now advanced to the Lake Vuori-Alakurtti road and blocked the bridge across the Sulahaavan River, while the northern enveloping detachment penetrated to the south as far as north of Kynailorthamoselkä. A northern group held Aukkisrova.

On 22 August the Russians tried to open the Kairala-Alakurtti road and withdrew in the south to Lake Vuori. The northern enveloping detachment reached the bridge across the Nurmi River.

On 23 August the Russians made numerous attempts to break through to the south. The Finns advanced further in the area south of Uulantoin Hill to the northeast and northwest. A German task force reached Lehtokangas. Fighting on the Nenäpalo Height continued.

On 24 August the Russians evacuated the Maaseljän Hills and continued their withdrawal. The German encircling column on the north advanced in the depth of the retreating enemy's flanks to the south. The Russians once more offered bitter resistance on the Nurmi Height. After their front in the Lake Vuori sector had collapsed, the Russians tried on 25 August to break through the Finnish switch position at Nauttoselki. In the northern sector, the pursuit of the retreating Russians led to the opening of the Kairala Narrows. On the Jukku Height the Russians offered strong resistance to the northern encircling detachment. The German attack on the railroad crossing was continued from Uulantoin Hill.

On 26 August the bridge across the Kairala Narrows was finished. The Mikkola Narrows were also opened. The Russians retired from the Nensepalo Height and in the south too they withdrew to Alakurtti.

A focal point of the encircling battle was on the Jukkulampi Height, where the Russians made repeated attempts to break through the northern German encircling columns.

On 27 August the Russians withdrew in the north too heading eastward, thus bringing to an end the nine days' battle of encirclement of Kairala, in which the Russian XXXVI Corps was decisively beaten. All German-Finnish combat units had now reached the road to Alakurtti. The SS Brigade Nord penetrated to the east north of the railroad line, the Finns advanced along the road and south thereof.

At the end of August, the Tuntsa River was crossed north of the road and a bridgehead formed across the river. German infantry penetrated into Alakurtti from the north, Waffen-SS from the west. In the south, the Finns reached the Nuotta Hills and continued their advance. The Russians retreated to the former Finnish-Russian boundary.

The hilly ranges of the Lyssaja (425 meters) and Wojta (411 meters) rise from the valley of the Wojta River, commanding the road and the railroad to Kandalaksha. The advance of the 169th Division came to a halt in front of the bunkers on these ranges. Some of the units of the division succeeded in crossing the Wojta River sough of the hills and in forming a bridgehead. At the southern wing of the German XXXVI Corps was the Finnish 6th Division at the northwestern point of Lake Tolwand. The elongated lake protected the Russian flank. The Russian positions could, therefore, only be enveloped from the north, which accordingly began during the first days of September. The envelopment was planned on a large scale and brought complete success, as both the Lyssaja and Wojta Ranges were captured.

When reaching Lake Verman, the striking power of the German troops was exhausted, so that combat activity in this sector declined and passed over into trench warfare.

The northern group of the Finnish III Corps had advanced from the Kuusamo area in spite of bad roads across the Sohjana Plateau and captured Kiestinki on 8 August. In the end of August, beginning of September 1941 the Russians in the Kiestinki sector made counterattacks which were temporarily successful, pressing back the Finnish front to rear positions. A Russian partisan unit cut the Finnish withdrawal route so that the situation became critical, but it was finally gotten under control by the brave defenders (Finnish and German troops under the command of General Palojärvi). Severe fighting was still taking place in this sector in November with alternating success, in the course of which the Finns suffered heavy losses but finally pressed the Russians further to the east. But then the front also became stabilized here east of the narrows between Toposero and Pjawosero.

The southern group of the Finnish III Corps, after heavy fighting, reached the Uhtua area where both sides dug in.

The 14th Division (Colonel Raapana), which did not belong to the AOK NORWEGEN but formed a detached group of Mannerheim's

Finnish front, had begun to attack from the Lieksa area in the beginning of July. The Finnish Commander in Chief did not order the division south to join the Karelian Army, but ordered it to march toward the east in the direction of the Murmansk railroad. The division formed the link between the northern German-Finnish front advancing to the east and the Karelian Army directing its offensive operations toward the southeast in the direction of the Svir. The 14th Division, marching toward Kom, was separated from both the Finnish III Corps and the Karelian Army by large patches of virgin Karelian forest and was, therefore, entirely dependent on its own resources. It had, nevertheless, obtained considerable successes with comparatively small losses. On 6 July the division occupied Repola and thereupon encircled strong enemy forces to the northeast of this town. When this "motti"[10] had been eliminated on 23 July, the Finns advanced further against continued enemy resistance. Owing to the skill of the Finns when fighting in the wilderness and the unexcelled command of Colonel Raapana, the Finns were able to press the Russians further and further eastward.

On 11 September the division conquered Rukajärvi on the road to Kotshkoma. After this success combat activity declined in this sector too and passed over to trench warfare.

The advance of the Karelian Army from the area Lake Pyhae-Korpiselkä-Ilomantsi across the border into Aunus Karelia[11] began on 10 July. A few points on the other side of the border had previously been occupied by the Finns. The general plan of the Karelian Arm was to defeat the enemy occupying the frontier and then to advance on a wide front to the east and southeast. The point of main effort was in the Lake Jänis-Korpiselkä sector by the VI Corps under Brigadier General Talvela. In order to cover the flanks of this main attack group, a Kampgruppe South was to attack between Lakes Pyhä and Jänis to advance to a line Lake Pyhä-Sortavala, and then to penetrate through the isthmus between Lakes Ladoga and Jänis, while Kampgruppe Nord was to attack from the area north of Korpiselkä as far as Ilomantsi and on the road Korpiselkä-Tolvajärvi.

Russian resistance quickly collapsed under the weight of the Finnish attack, particularly in the Värtsilä-Korpiselkä sector. Although individual pockets offered stubborn resistance, it became apparent that the main thrust of the Finns had hit a soft spot in the Russian front. Through the gap created in this way, the courageous Finnish riflemen immediately

---

[10] Motti is a Finnish expression created in the Winter War, indicating the encirclement and starving out of particularly stubbornly defensed Russian bases.

[11] Aunus (Russian Olonez) is the main town in the southern part of Far Karelia.

penetrated deep into the territory occupied by the enemy in the direction of Tolvajärvi. The Russians had fortified every stream and every village in the Korpiselkä-Tolvajärvi directions. After hard fighting, Kokkari was taken by storm on 12 July and on the same day the village of Tolvajärvi.

Light forces of the 1st Light Infantry Brigade[12] under the command of bold and enterprising Colonel Lagus advanced from Kokkari southward in the direction of Uksuu-Mauanto. In the meantime, the Finnish forces which had come from Havavaara and Värtailä, were engaged in fighting with the enemy who was putting up a stubborn defense in the rolling country of Soaplahti. The 1st Light Infantry Brigade, which had reached a line Unkau-Muaanto on 14 July, detached some of its forces to the rear of this enemy. While units of the VI Corps at Tolvajärvi made the position secure to the east, the main body advanced southward in a forced march across the line Uukau-Muuanto. General Talvela saw his opportunity and went boldly ahead. He immediately committed all mobile troops for the capture of Loimola in order there to intercept the railroad to Petrozavodsk and to cut the enemy in front of the Karelian Army off from his railroad connection to the east. Heavy corps weapons were brought forward from Uuksu to the battle for Soanlahti.

The blow against Loisola was successful. The Finnish armored infantry battalion pushed into the town on 15 July and dispersed its Russian garrison. At that point an even greater operational objective offered itself to General Talvela. It seemed possible by a quick thrust to the coast of Lake Ladoga as far as Koirinoja and Pitkäranta in order to cut off the enemy units still resisting on both sides of Lake Jänis from their road connection to the east. This bold decision was immediately carried out. While the bulk of the Finnish mobile troop was committed in the direction of Koirinoja, flank securing forces advanced in the direction of Lappäsyrjä and Kitalä, as well as in the direction of Käsnäselkä. Koirinoja fell into Finnish hands by 16 July. On the same day the security battalion succeeded in taking Käsnäselkä. On 16 July enemy resistance was also broken in the area north of Soanlahti. The enemy speedily retired by way of Suistamo to the isthmus between Lakes Ladoga and Jänis.

On 17 July the Finnish forces pursuing from the north had reached the Jänis River line with their front to the west. The troops of the VI Corps had with a tremendous élan, dispersed the enemy and by quick action prevented him from carrying out a scorched-earth policy.

It was now the mission of the Karelian Army High Command to secure the successes thus far obtained and to reorganize and build up to the Finnish offensive.

---

[12] The 1st and 2nd Light Infantry Brigades had been equipped with bicycles in summer and were therefore very mobile.

The 1st Division, which so far had been a reserve of the Karelian Army, had been advanced on 15 July to Loimola in order to relieve the weak security forces of the VI Corps. This measure served to prevent a possible threat to the left wing by enemy reinforcements brought forward from the Petrozavodsk area. On 16 July, Field Marshal Mannerheim placed the 163rd Division, which had advanced on the road Jönsuu-Sortavala as far as Tohmajärvi, under the Karelian Army High Command with the mission of occupying the Suojärvi and Nikkola area, an important railroad and road junction. Finally the Finnish Commander in Chief ordered the 17th Division, which had been relieved at Hangö by other Finnish forces, transported by rail to join the Karelian Army. The division (Colonel Snellman) assembled west of Värtailä.

In the meantime the VI Corps had been assigned the task of occupying a line Salmi-Lake Tulea. The units of the corps which had advanced southward of Lake Jänis as far as the Jänis River (11th Division) were removed from corps control, since a special mission had been assigned to them in the impending fight for Sortavala. In their stead another division was assigned General Talvela to continue the offensive to the east by way of Käsmäselkä-Lake Tuleme. The VI Corps had indefatigably pushed forward, spearheaded by the valiant infantry under the excellent command of Colonel Lages.

Russian resistance on the road leading along the coast of Lake Ladoga, on which the Finns had continued their advance by way of Pitkäranta, was broken in the night of 18 July, and the Salmi area was reached on 19 July, where the Finnish riflemen were engaged in heavy fighting. The Russians had received reinforcements and, favored by the terrain, offered stubborn resistance.

Salmi was not occupied until 21 July after heavy fighting and the offensive continued in the direction of the old historic boundary. On 22 July they reached the old boundary-stone which had been erected by Sweden's heroic King Gustaf Adolf II at Rajakontu. General Talvela could on this day proudly announce to his commander in chief: "After the capture of Mamesila today at 1130 hours, the Russians have been chased out of Finland in the operational area of the VI Corps. The area, whose rear boundary is formed by a line Korpiselkä-Jänis River, has been freed from our hereditary foe.

In the evening of 17 July Finnish forces had also left Käsnäselkä for the east. On 18 July this attack column crossed the old boundary in the direction of Lake Tulema and captured the northernmost village on the lake on the same day. On the following day the Finns occupied the widely scattered settlements on the shores of Lake Tulema and on 20 July Palalahti on its southern shore. The offensive proceeded without interruption to the east and reached Vieljärvi on 20 July. The Russians had put up a strong resistance at Rajakonu which could not be overcome until 23 July. The advance of a Finnish column from Palalahti in the direction of Vitele favorably influenced the course of the combat at Rajakontu, since after having broken the enemy resistance at Suurmäki under heavy fighting it threatened the Russian line of retreat along the shore. When on 24 July this column reached Vitele simultaneously with the forces advancing from Rajakontu, the town was taken after light skirmishes. The Finnish front on the northern shore of Lake Ladoga now shifted to the Tuulos River.

The Finnish forces which had advanced from Lake Tulema by way of Vielärvi reached the lake area of Tsokkila by 22 July where they secured toward the southeast, east and north.

The important Lake Sä area was still in Russian hands. An attempt on 16 July from Loimola to occupy Suojärvi by employing light forces had failed. The enemy consequently continuously threatened the flank and the rear of the VI Corps from this direction. For his own protection and in order to support a renewed attempt with stronger forces to conquer the Lake Sä area, General Talvela sent forces ahead from Lake Tulema in the direction of Sotjärvi and Hyrsylä. These Finnish units reached the Suojärvi-Petrozavodsk railroad at Pyraylä by 26 July and thereby cut the railroad connection of the Russians in the Lake Suo area.

The Finnish operations in Ladoga-Karelia, crowned by such great successes, were favored by splendid summer weather. Summer 1941 in Finland was dry and uniform; the roads were solid and usable. By day it was very hot. Owing to the long drought the forests easily caught fire when shelled by artillery. The smoke of smoldering forest fires covered the countryside and mingled with the dust raised by the marching troops. But neither heat nor smoke nor dust could dampen the Finnish fighting spirit.

The German 163rd Division did not fare as well as the Finnish VI Corps. On 20 July it had been engaged in fighting for the first time at Lake Tolva and met with exceedingly difficult conditions for an offense. The road of advance of the division from Kokkari by way of Lake Tolva to the Lake Suo area led through one of the finest scenic areas of Karelia, but the highway winding through this lake-filled forest area actually forms a single, narrow defile stretching over many kilometers, and makes an ideal terrain for defense. For the attacker this area, rich in intersections and natural obstacles, is almost insurmountable. Heavy fighting had taken place in this region between Finns and Russians during the Winter War.

The 163rd Division lost much sweat and blood here and made slow progress. Repeatedly the German troops, confronted by entirely unfamiliar conditions, with little combat experience in the wilderness but with much too heavy trains, believed that they were faced with a hopeless task. On 29 July the Division's attack had come to a deadlock before Äglajärvi. Behind the town it was established that increasingly numerous fortified Russian positions had been formed on the Vegarus and Aitto Rivers along the road to Lake Suo. It became evident that the German division, now seriously feeling the absence of its regiment detached to the Salla sector, was too weak to conquer the Lake Suo area. Stronger forces had to be brought forward, which, the situation being as it was, could only be taken from Finnish units of the Karelian Army. A new attack to be carried out from two directions (south and west) needed systematic preparation. Several weeks went by before its execution. The first relief for the 163rd Division came from the group on the left wing of the Karelian Army the cavalry brigade (Colonel Oinonen) and the 2nd Light Infantry Brigade (Colonel Sundman) assembled in the Ilomantsi area. After the Karelian Army had started its offensive on 10 July, the Finnish cavalry pressed the Russians back across the old Finnish border east of Ilomantsi and gained ground step by step in the direction of the upper Aitto River in cooperation with the 2nd Light Infantry Brigade. During the first half of August, when the operation against the Lake Suo area was to be set in motion again, these Finnish forces were merged with the 163rd Division into Kampfgruppe Engelbrecht under the command of the German division commander.

While the VI Corps rushed forward through Ladoga-Karelia, the right wing of the Karelian Army (VII Corps), which had on 10 July begun its offensive from the Lake Pyhä area and the northern tip of Lake Jänis southward pressed the Russians slowly but surely back in the direction of Sortavala, reaching at the end of July an approximate line of Ruskeala-Harlu. Under the threat of encirclement by the Finns who had advanced east of Lake Jänis, the Russians between Lakes Jänis and Ladoga River had withdrawn in the direction of Sortavala, so that the entire Jänis River on which the Finns advancing from the west and east had met was in Finnish hands by the end of July. The rest of the Finnish front between the Gulf of Finland and Lake Pyhä had been comparatively quiet. The Finnish soldiers who had been elated by the news of the great victories of the Karelian Army impatiently waited for the order to begin the offensive. At Finnish Headquarters the question as to whether to widen the attack area by engaging the Finnish troops to the right of the Karelian Army increasingly assumed more importance in discussions toward the end of the month. As long as the Finns on the wide front between the Gulf of Finland and Ruskeala kept quiet, the Russians could quite calmly shift their forces and bring forward reinforcements to the battlefield east of Lake Ladoga by weakening their positions on the Karelian Isthmus. Field Marshal Mannerheim was not a man to make precipitate decisions. He had gained experience in five great wars and had learned to bide his time.

He did not like to throw his sword onto the scale until the time was ripe and had by his mastery of the art of leadership often saved the lives of his soldiers.

On 31 July the Finnish Commander in Chief ordered II Corps (General Lastikainen) to begin the attack. Thus started the second and more important phase of the Finnish offensive. The Corps attacked southward from the area between Imatra and Uukunjami. A strong artillery preparation had preceded the attack. In the beginning the point of main effort of the Finnish offensive was at Hiitola. In order to support this attack from the depth, Field Marshal Mannerheim ordered the 10th Division (up to that time employed in the area of the IV Corps) to be withdrawn from the front and concentrated behind the II Corps west of Simpela. On 8 August the road from Elisonvaara to Käkisalmi, which ran along the shore of Lake Ladoga, was reached near Hiitola, thereby cutting the two Russian groups which had remained on the northwestern shore of Lake Ladoga (a larger one near the Kurki River and a smaller one in the Sortavala area) off from their land communication. Lahdenpohja and Elisanvaara were occupied by the Finns on 9 August.

Furthermore, units of the Finnish II Corps had been committed form the Ilmee-Hiitola area against the narrowest part of the Vuoksi River at Paakkola-Poelläkkmallä. Other Finnish forces advanced a little further to the east toward Kivinjemei and Eaipale. The Finns in these operations had the great advantage of being thoroughly acquainted with the terrain of the Karelian Isthmus. Thus for example on 18 August Finnish troops crossed the Vuoksi River northwest of Paakola at the same spot where the river had been crossed during the great Finnish maneuvers in the summer of 1939. Shortly after 20 August, the whole region on the Karelian Isthmus between the Vuoksi and Lake Ladoga was in Finnish hands. Käkisalmi was occupied by the Finns on 21 August.

While the Finns fought successfully for the line of the Vuoksi, the fate of the Russian forces cut off on the northwestern shore of Lake Ladoga was also sealed. In the Kurki River area, two Russian divisions put up fierce resistance in spite of their desperate position. Hard pressed by the Finns, they withdrew to the large island of Kilpola, connected with the mainland by a causeway. The Russians tried to escape across Lake Ladoga under great losses of men, ships and barges.

Upon request of the Finnish Headquarters, a Ju 88 wing of the German Luftflotte 1 carried out armed reconnaissance after 5 August over the northern part of Lake Ladoga, harassing the Russian lake transports from the northwestern shore to Valmo Island.

On 24 August the fighting at Kilpola concluded with a complete Finnish victory.

During the early part of August the left wing of the Finnish II Corps began to attack from the west in a general direction toward Sortavala. The Russian division fighting in this sector was pressed against the short of Lake Ladoga between Lahdenpohja and Sortavala and surrounded at Rautalahti. Also in this area the Russians tried to escape on ships, first to Valamo and then further on to Leningrad. On 20 August these Russian forces were eliminated.

The battle for Sortavala had already come to an end sometime before. The Russians could not hold out for long against simultaneous Finnish attacks from the west, north and east. On 16 August the Finnish liberators entered this town, cherished by all Finns because of its history and incomparably beautiful site.

So the Finnish front on the Karelian Isthmus now ran from Virolahti on the Gulf of Finland to Enso and from there along the Vuoksi and Suvanto Rivers to Taipale on the shore of Lake Ladoga. The whole northwestern and northern shores of the lake were also in Finnish hands.

South of the Gulf of Finland, Army Group North (Feldmarschall Ritter von Leeb) had made good progress toward achieving its mission of breaking through the Stalin Line running along the Latvian-Russian boundary and simultaneously of defeating the Red Forces in Estonia.

The Sixteenth Army (Generaloberst Busch) and the armored forces of Generaloberst Höppner fighting in the same sector had succeeded in a bold attack in breaking through the strongly built and stubbornly defended positions south of Lake Peipus. Ostrov and Pskov were taken after a short and hard battle. Thus the groundwork was laid for Army Group North to wheel to the north and to initiate the attack on Leningrad. In spite of difficult road conditions, bitter resistance and utmost strain on the troops occasioned by marches and fighting, the left wing of the German forces advancing between Lake Peipus and Lake Ilmen was able to penetrate almost as far as Narva in order to block the isthmus between Lake Peipus and the Gulf of Finland.

The German Eighteenth Army (Generaloberst von Küchler) operating in Estonia took the strongly defended towns of Tartu, Viljandi and Pärnu, defeated the Russian divisions in numerous violent battles and threw them back to the north beyond Tapa. On 8 August the German troops fighting in Estonia captured Rakvere and penetrated to the shore of the Gulf of Finland.

In the sector of the Karelian Army, operations had temporarily ceased during the first half of August with the exception of the Lake Suo area. The pause was utilized for rehabilitating the army for new tasks.

The 17th Division, formerly at Hangö and now detrucked west of Värtsilä, was assigned on 2 August to the High Command of the Karelian Army.

The VII Corps Headquarters (General Hägglund) which had become available in the Sortavala area was inserted between the VI Corps and Kampfgruppe Engelbrecht.

On 19 August a new attack began from two fronts against the Lake Suo area. The VII Corps advanced from a southwesterly direction. Kampfgruppe Engelbrecht attacked from a northwesterly direction enveloping the Russian positions with its mobile units. This thoroughly prepared and well organized attack was a complete success. Closely following the retreating enemy, the German and Finns mopped up the strongly contested area as far as the frontier and advanced across the frontier to Sjamosero. The 163rd Division, whose burden had been particularly heavy during the preceding days, was withdrawn from the Finnish front and stationed at the rear of the Karelian Army as Mannerheim's reserve.

The deeper the German Army penetrated into western Russia, the more important the question of operational cooperation at or east of Leningrad became for the German and Finnish High Command.

On 2 August word was received by the Finnish Headquarters from the OKH that the German advance which had been temporarily suspended, would be resumed and that the German attack on Leningrad was scheduled to being on 6 August. The Finnish Commander in Chief was asked to support the German attack on Leningrad by an advance of the Finnish main forces toward Lodeynoye Pole on the Svir. This request came at an inopportune moment, since the offensive of the Karelian Army had come to a standstill after reaching the old boundary at the end of July, and Field Marshal Mannerheim did not think it possible to resume the offensive of VI Corps towards the Svir until the enemy had been dislodged from the Lake Suo area, from where the Russians could threaten the flank and the rear of the VI Corps.

The course which the operations of the AOK NORWEGEN had taken in the month of July did not come up to the expectations of the OKW. In none of the three sectors had a decisive victory been obtained. A continuation of the attempts to reach the Murmansk railroad at one place of another offered little hope.

A Führer Decree[13] was, therefore, issued on 2 August to AOK NORWEGEN ordering the discontinuation of the attacks on Kandalaksha.

---

[13] Operations of the German Army in Russia were conducted by the OKH. Discussions about cooperation of Army Group North and the Finnish front on the occasion of the attack on Leningrad or the "rendezvous on the Svir" were therefore held between the OKH and the Finnish Headquarters. Lapland, on the other hand, was considered a OKW theater of war. Corps Headquarters Norway was assigned immediately to the OKW. The Finnish Commander in Chief was only responsible to his government. Wishes of the German Wehrmacht or OKH directed to Field Marshal

The point of main effort of the operations in the theater of war between the Gulf of Finland and the arctic coast was to be in the sector of the Karelian Army east of Lake Ladoga. But in order to give a new impetus to the attack of the Mountain Corps Norway against Murmansk, which had come to a standstill at Litsa Bay, the Führer Decree promised the transfer of the 6th Mountain Division from another theater of war as reinforcement.

The attack of Army Group North on Leningrad scheduled to take place on 6 August was delayed by a few days. When on 10 August the German attack started, the OKH suggested that the Finns join the attack on Leningrad from the direction of the Karelian Isthmus. The request was repeated on 20 August. The early occupation of Hangö was also considered desirable by the Germans.

On 21 August, that is to say at a time when the II Corps had reached the Vuoksi River and the northwestern shore of Lake Ladoga, a new chapter in the Finnish summer offensive began. The IV Corps now began its attack between Virolahti and Enso, being the last sector of the Finnish front to participate in the offensive. Simultaneously the Finnish forces on the Vuoksi pivoted partly to the west in the direction of Viipuri, partly proceeded to the south toward Rajajoki. Through these operations the Viipuri area was encircled from the north, northeast and east. Since Finnish units crossed from the western shore of the Bay of Viipuri to the opposite shore at the same time and cut off the road along the shore as well as the connection with Koivisto Island, a Finnish ring closed around the capital of Karelia. Owing to the hopelessness of the situation the Russians gave up their resistance and evacuated the city which was occupied by the Finns on 30 August. The Russian garrison of Viipuri found no retreat route available. About ten kilometers south of the town, at Porlampi, the Russians were encircled. They defended themselves bravely as is the custom of Russian soldiers. On 1 September this motti was eliminated. A rich booty fell into Finnish hands.

Finnish forces had in the meantime advanced without encountering any resistance across the Karelian Isthmus in the direction of Rajajoki and Koivisto. The old frontier was reached on 31 August near Mainila,[14] well known from the history of the Winter War; Koivisto was occupied on 2 September. A little later, the Russians in the eastern part of the Karelian Isthmus were also dislodged from the Valkjärvi and Metsäpirtti areas and

---

Mannerheim were couched in the form of a request or suggestion through the German General at Finnish Headquarters.

[14] According to the Soviet Russian version, the Winter War was caused by artillery firing from the Mainila area on Russian territory. The Finns always repudiated the Russian version.

fled across the border. Thus the entire Karelian Isthmus was liberated from the enemy. The last islands in Lake Ladoga (Valam and Konevitsa) were occupied at the beginning of September, so that the whole former Finnish territory in this reign was returned to its rightful owners.

The Finns in this situation were confronted by the question whether the Finnish offensive should stop at the old border or whether the advance should continue beyond it. On 1 September Field Marshal Mannerheim decided to push forward across the frontier as far as necessary to obtain tactically favorable positions for the encirclement of Leningrad, which would also have the advantage of saving forces. By taking this decision the Finnish Commander in Chief also went along with the German point of view. The question of crossing the frontier was not only a military but also a political question, which had to be handled with great care in view of the inner political opposition. In his order of the day for 3 September, Mannerheim hit the nail on the head by saying:

The frontier has been reached. The fight goes on."

Further great successes had also been obtained on the southern shore of the Gulf of Finland by Army Group North. A strongly fortified and defended Russian position between Lake Ilmen and Lake Peipus, after a bitter struggle lasting for several days, had been pierced on 21 August. The towns of Novgorod, Kingisepp, and Narva were taken by the German forces. The Eighteenth Army made steady progress at the front before Leningrad and Estonia. The German troops advanced on Tallinn through Estonia in a concentric circle. On 29 August, units of the Eighteenth Army in cooperation with the Kriegsmarine and Luftwaffe occupied the strongly fortified naval port of Tallinn. On the same day units of Army Group North advanced to the naval base, Port Baltic, and occupied it. The transport fleet which the Russian employed for evacuating troops and equipment from Tallinn stumbled into the German minefield and suffered heavy losses. Several Soviet transport vessels were sunk in the Gulf of Finland by German planes.

On 4 September General Jodl, Chief of the Wehrmacht Operations Staff, paid a visit to Finnish Headquarters. In the forenoon he landed at Mikkeli airport and had a long conversation with Field Marshal Mannerheim about the situation on the German front and the continuation of operations. By order of the Führer, Jodl presented Mannerheim with all three classes of the Iron Cross in order to honor the victorious Finnish Army in the person of its Commander in Chief. Furthermore Jodl brought the promise that Germany would furnish

15,000 tons of rye to Finland in order to bridge over the time before the new harvest.[15]

The Finnish Commander in Chief informed his German guest that the Karelian Army had begun a new offensive against the Svir Line that very day, which meant the fulfillment of a request repeatedly brought up by the German brothers-in-arms. Both partners were highly satisfied with the result of the conversation. The quiet and authoritative attitude of Jodl and his reliable and congenial personality made a very good impression on Field Marshal Mannerheim.

Early on 4 September, the Karelian Army again began its offensive from the area Tuloksa-Sjamozero. It made splendid progress. On 7 September the Finnish riflemen reached the Svir at Ladeynoye Pole.[16] On the following day[17] the Murmansk railroad was intercepted at the Svir station. The left wing of the army (VII Corps reinforced by the 4th Division from the Karelian Isthmus) under the command of General Hägglund occupied at the same time the important road crossing at Pryazha, forty kilometers west of Petrozavodsk. It was thereby possible to advance on Petrozavodsk from various directions. The concentric Finnish attack on the town began on 18 September. The brave 1st Rifle Brigade under Colonel Lagus, advancing along the Murmansk railroad, approached the town from the south. Other forces attacked Petrozavodsk from the west along the road from Pryasha and across the great forest area south of the road.[18] Besides, other forces (the II Corps under General Laatikainen which had been transferred from the Karelian Isthmus to the East Karelian theater of war) advanced toward Petrozavodsk from the northwest. These attack operations made simultaneously from different directions, which are reported in the annals of the war as a glorious feat of the Finnish command and its brave divisions, led to the capture of Petrozavodsk, the capital of Eastern Karelia[19] on 1 October. Petrozavodsk was beautifully situated on the sloping western shore of Lake Onega, and, with the exception of part of the town near the harbor, did not suffer greatly from Finnish artillery fire.

Thus the great successes of the Finnish army in East Karelia had led to the formation of two fronts. One front ran on the Isthmus of Aunus along the Svir, where the Finnish front line of defense above Ladeynoye

---

[15] Finland had asked for 25,000 tons.

[16] Called Lotinapelto by the Finns.

[17] On this day Shlisselburg was taken by Army Group North.

[18] The 1st Division carried out the amazing feat of crossing the trackless forest wilderness south of the road fro Pryasha to Petrozavodsk with considerable speed.

[19] The town during the Finnish occupation was officially called Äänislinna.

crossed the river in some places in order to obtain more favorable positions. Below Ladeynoye Pole, the German 163rd Division, which was again assigned by Field Marshal Mannerheim to the Karelian Army, was placed in the front line. Combat activity on the Svir now declined, and the Finns took up permanent positions in this sector, too.

The second front in East Karelia stretched from Petrozavodsk in the direction of Syamozero and from there toward the north. In this area, the Finns continued their attacks in the north and east although a severe and early winter had set in. The Finnish divisions advancing from Petrozavodsk and Porozero (called Porajärvi in Finnish) cooperated excellently and pressed the Russians in this particularly difficult river and lake district slowly together by clever maneuvering into the area of Medvezhyegorsk (Karhumäki in Finnish) – Lake Seg. On 19 October, II Corps advancing to the north had reached the Suna sector and the area west of Lake Seg. On 3 November Kondoboga was captured. Soon afterwards on 5 November, Finnish troops coming from the north and from the south united at Lizhma. Strong Russian forces, unable to prevent the juncture at Lizhma of the Finns advancing from different fronts, withdrew to Medvezhyegorsk. The offensive of the Karelian Army became more and more difficult and slowed down as winter set in and the continuous strain on the Finnish troops through months of mobile warfare began to show. The General Headquarters reflected on how to reinforce the Karelian Army. The more severe winter became, the more acute became the transportation problem of the Finnish railroads, which made it impossible to carry out the transfer of one division and several heavy batteries from the Karelian Isthmus to the Karelian Army for the attack on Medvezhyegorsk. Around 16 November the strength of the Finns seemed to have come to an end. Their offensive came to a stop before Medvezhyegorsk. The terrain which has a subalpine character and had become almost impassable by deep snow seemed to form a firm obstacle to further Finnish advance. Under these circumstances it was the strong will of General Laatikainen which inspired the brave corps to make another supreme effort. Through snow up to their knees and in bitter cold the Finnish II Corps in a lighting attack on 5 December penetrated into Medvezhyegorsk, the next day captured Povenets (Finnish Pventsa) on the Stalin Canal and two days later destroyed the large Russian motti formed south of Medvezhyegorsk. In order to obtain better defense positions toward the north, the Finnish positions were advanced to the heights dominating the Isthmus between Lake Onega and Lake Seg.[20] After that, the front in this sector also stabilized.

Combat activity along the long Finnish eastern boundary continued during the winter. In the southern and northern sectors of the Army Headquarters Norway, the initiative passed from time to time to the Russians, which created rather critical situations because of the lack of operational reserves and transverse connection between the sectors. It became apparent that the Russian command was placed in an advantageous position through the existence of the Murmansk railroad which made a quick transfer of forces from one sector to the other possible, whereas it took a great many days for the Germans to withdraw forces from one sector to march them to the Arctic Road, to transfer them by motor transportation and to march them again to the threatened sector which needed reinforcements. The German command was bound to fall behind in respect to its operations. This situation could have only been improved by the construction of a railroad from Rovaniemi to Petsamo. The OKW made such a proposal at the end of September 1941. The Finnish government agreed on condition that the railroad be built with German labor and material. The construction of such a railroad met, however, with so many difficulties that it was not carried out.

Around 7 September, the situation in the sector of the Finnish III Corps became critical. The Russians attacked in the Kiestinki sector with strongly superior forces. AOK NORWEGEN which had no forces available for reinforcing the threatened sector turned to Finnish Headquarters for help. Since the Finns could not help either, The Finnish III Corps had to withdraw to a rear position more favorable for defense, which settled the crisis in the Kiestinki sector.

Difficult situations in the sector of the AOK NORWEGEN repeatedly impelled Generaloberst von Falkenhorst to ask the Finnish Headquarters for help. On 25 August 1941 Falkenhorst requested the transfer of the 163rd Division to give new impetus to the stalled attack on Kandalaksha. It was impossible to grant this request, since the Finnish Commander in Chief had just decided to launch an attack of the Karelian Army toward the Svir. This Finnish offensive could not be accomplished without the 163rd Division, all the more so since the German Army High Command again and again requested the Finnish Commander in Chief to appear as soon as possible, and with the strongest possible forces on the Svir and to form a bridgehead below Ladeynoye Pole from which to cooperate with the forces of Army Group North advancing across the lower Volkhov.

---

[20] This isthmus formed the watershed between the Gulf of Finland and the White Sea. The Finns called this front the "Maaselkä (isthmus) Front." On the Russian maps it is called Maselskaya, after a village and station of the Murmansk railroad.

The success of a joint Finnish-German offensive was not aided by the fact that the German operations were not based on a uniform plan. South of Leningrad, as mentioned above, Feldmarschall von Brauchitsch, Commander in Chief of the German Army was in charge of operations. He aimed at a rendezvous with the Finns on the Svir or further south in the area between it and the Volkhov, whereas in northern Finland the German Commander in Chief, who was assigned to the OKW, had directed his attention to the Murmansk railroad and desired the participation of more and more Finnish forces in his eastward offensive as difficulties increased in the course of the time. The OKW was to take a clear operational decision about the point of main effort, but even the highest German command agency did not master this problem. The damaging dual mission remained, an offensive against the Leningrad area and an offensive against the Murmansk railroad. On 23 September Adolf Hitler addressed a letter to Mannerheim informing his that the 163rd Division should first form a bridgehead on the Svir and should then "in due time" be transferred to AOK NORWEGEN. At that time (end of September) it was already obvious that the 163rd Division after having once crossed the Svir could never arrive in time to take part in the campaign for the Murmansk railroad, for the situation at the German front south of Leningrad had by that time become very tense. The Red Army, in spite of its numerous defeats and retreats, had preserved an astonishing power of resistance, again and again making counterattacks which could be repulsed only with difficulty by the decimated German divisions which had been fighting without interruption since June 1941 and were exhausted.

Even during the war German critics, who, however, had to act very cautiously in expressing their opinion, considered the strategic objectives too great in the 1941 offensive against Russia and gave this as reason for the failure of the campaign against Leningrad. The OKW intended to conquer Leningrad, Moscow and Kiev simultaneously, for which forces were lacking as was subsequently found out. The difficult situation in the Leningrad area in December 1941 was created because forces urgently required for continuing the offensive against Leningrad were withdrawn too early from Army Group North for the offensive against Moscow. The German High Command's communiqué of 21 October reviewing the preceding operations came to the conclusion that considerable units of Army Group Leeb and of Luftwaffe Group Keller had been withdrawn a long time ago and been employed in other operations at other sectors of the eastern front. The release of these German forces was the result of a great illusion of the OKW with regard to the ratio of forces of attacker and defender in the east. It was not sufficiently taken into consideration that the political development in the Balkans in Spring 1941 had caused a considerable alteration in the German plans for marshaling forces against Russia and that the German eastern army had lost considerable fighting power as a result of an extensive and lengthy offensive far into Russia. The forces grew more and more overexerted from week to week. Wise economy in the setting of objectives and a timely cessation of the offensive before severe cold had set in would probably have prevented the serious crisis which threatened the German eastern flank in Winter 1941/42.

There is no doubt that for a commander in chief it is difficult to arrive at the decision to stop a victoriously advancing army and to let it take up winter positions. The German High Command did not do this at any rate and believed that by continuing the offensive in winter the war could be definitely decided. There was no lack of warning voices alluding to experiences in former wars against Russia, but no attention was paid them. The overwhelming successes of the Wehrmacht lured it deeper and deeper into Russia. Although by the middle of September continuous rain announcing the approach of winter had transformed the roads in White Russia and Ukraine into a terrible state, the German armies penetrated deeper and deeper into the vast Russian area, crossed the Dnieper, continued their advance toward the industrial area in the Donets basin, and victoriously fought the great encirclement battle 200 kilometers east of Kiev. Kiev and Poltava were successively taken. The German spearheads reached the area north of the Sea of Azov early in October. By the middle of October, the center of the eastern front against Army Group Timoshenko led by the middle of October to the great encirclement battles of Vyazma and Bryansk. The German forces steadily approached the outer defense lines of Moscow.

In order to eliminate Russian influence in the Baltic Sea, an operation had been started in the latter part of September against the Baltic Islands off the Gulf of Riga. Verms, Muhu, Riimaa and Saaremaa were taken by the German troops in quick succession, with the able help of the Finnish naval forces. The OKW had been deceived by the great German victories in the East and allowed itself to be persuaded that the war with Russian was finished. But when reviewing the results of the German offensive in 1941, one arrives at the conclusion that, notwithstanding extraordinary successes, the actual operational results remained far behind expectations and what had been achieved had taken much more time than calculated beforehand. When looking at things soberly, a final conclusion of the war with Russia was out of the question.

On 3 October Generaloberst von Falkenhorst again expressed a desire to Mannerheim. He asked for the Finnish 1st Light Infantry Brigade for commitment in the direction of Louhi or Kandalaksha. This brigade, which owing to its great successes during the offensive of the Karelian

Army had attracted the attention and admiration of the German authorities, was stationed after the occupation of Petrozavodsk at the East Karelian capital, thus securing the shore of Lake Onega. The Finnish High Command declined the transfer of the brigade rather coolly.

Marshal Mannerheim's standpoint was that in the discussions preceding the outbreak of war only two Finnish divisions were to have been provided in northern Finland and that after the occupation of Salla at least one Finnish division ought to have been given back by Generaloberst von Falkenhorst. Furthermore, Mannerheim was of the opinion that the Luftwaffe had promised to help the Finns but had not done it when at the end of August the Commander in Chief of the Luftwaffe had been asked to prevent the flight of the Russians across Lake Ladoga. The Marshal was angry that the Germans made more and more requests, whereas they did not fully live up to their own promises. Mannerheim's discontent still increased when by the middle of November 1941 the Finnish 3rd Division suffered heavy losses during an offensive in the Kiestinki sector, ordered by Generaloberst von Falkenhorst, in which it lost one third of its officers (83) within a week. Mannerheim rather enraged told the General Erfurth at Mikkeli that he could not afford and that he had no way to replace such heavy losses.

Besides, the frequent change in German plans decreased the readiness initially existing of the Finns to agree to German requests. The Finn keeps his word and sticks unflinchingly to what has been agreed upon. General Lundquist, the Commander in Chief of the Finnish Air Force, who was of very independent nature and who already in the winter 1941/1942 viewed the development of the war situation with great skepticism, made the following remark to the Luftwaffe liaison officer attached to his staff:

"The Finns begin to be fed up with being led by the nose by the Germans. Considering the large ground organization needed by the Lufwaffe, we Finns cannot adapt ourselves every four weeks to another plan. That costs too much personnel and materiel. For the time being we shall do nothing and wait how the situation develops. Our economy is being bled white and needs new substance. Besides, General Hanell with all labor and building material available is busy constructing new fortifications on the Karelian Isthmus in order to give the Finns a sense of security in that area, since they have grown suspicious of the further development of the situation in the sector of the Army Group North. If the Germans should not be able to achieve the encirclement of Leningrad, we Finns expect a Russian push to the north, for which we want to be prepared in time."

It is quite natural that there were differences of opinion between the Germans and the Finns with regard to the war against Russia and that those differences increase in the course of the years. Differences of opinion exist in all coalition wars. From the Finnish standpoint, the Karelian war was by far the most important segment of entire World War II. For the German High Command, on the other hand, there were more important theaters of war than the Karelian Wilderness. From the German point of view, the region between the Gulf of Finland and the Arctic Sea was a secondary theater or war. One was happy when the situation in the arctic region remained static and satisfied with the fact that the Finns were reliable brothers-in-arms who splendidly accomplished their missions. That was all the more important since transportation from German to Finland (particularly to Lapland) was exceedingly difficult, which excluded quick help in case of critical situations. If the German High Command at Rovaniemi was in difficulty and needed help, the easiest solution was to apply to Mikkeli. Help from Germany could not be reckoned upon. That explains why Generaloberst von Falkenhorst and later Generaloberst Dietl always turned to Marshal Mannerheim whenever they were in difficulties.

On 14 October, a new Führer Directive, reorganizing conditions in the northern areas according to the wishes of Falkenhorst and Mannerheim, addressed to AOK NORWEGEN, came to the knowledge of the Finnish Headquarters. The Directive ordered that AOK NORWEGEN'S offensive against the Murmansk railroad should be temporarily suspended. German and Finnish units had been very much intermixed in the sectors of Army Headquarters Norway owing to mutual rendering of help during the preceding combat. The Führer Directive, therefore, requested that by interchange of units a purely Finnish southern front under Mannerheim and a purely German northern front under Mannerheim and a purely German northern front under Falkenhorst should be created. This clarification was much welcomed be the Finnish Headquarters, as the supplying of the Finnish units interspersed in the German front had caused a great deal of trouble. The German High Command, on the other hand, was reluctant in releasing the Finnish units, since the Finnish soldier was highly esteemed by the German forces as a very capable man, experienced in forest warfare. The Finnish combat elements also liked to fight within German units, as the German mess contained many items which could not be supplied by the Finns and also since the leaders of Finnish units felt more independent under German command than was possible in the rigid organization of the Finnish Army. The relationship between German and Finnish soldiers of all ranks was excellent. In spite of a difference in language they understood one another very well and appreciated each other's military efficiency and national character. The difference in nationality of Finnish and German soldiers fighting and living side by side never caused any trouble during the whole war up to the capitulation of Finland, since they respected and helped each other wherever possible.

The Führer Directive of 14 October also stipulated that the construction of the Rovaniemi-Petsamo railroad be postponed, but it promised to build a road from northern Norway by way of Karasyok to Ivalo-Inari, which was actually built later on and proved of great importance during the last phase of the war.

The situation on the German front south of Leningrad in the autumn of 1941 had not developed as expected by the Wehrmacht and German Army High Command, although mobile divisions of Army Group North had on 8 September reached the Neva east of Leningrad on a wide front and had taken Shlisselburg by storm. The German-Finnish ring around Leningrad was thus closed and the town cut off from all land communication. Furthermore, Army Group North had succeeded on 14 September in penetrating into the outer fortifications south of Leningrad. But after that, the German attack met with ever-growing resistance and made no progress. There was no doubt but that Leningrad would be defended to the utmost by the Russians. This defense was active and accompanied by praiseworthy bravery. The Russians may properly look back with pride on this episode. Repeated breakout attempts took place on the part of the defenders. For instance, on 6 October Soviet forces tried to land west of Leningrad, supported by the fire of the Kronstadt forts, naval and coast artillery, and renewed attempts were again made on 11 October. On 1, 2 and 5 November the Russians tried with great audacity to cross the Neva in numerous boats. Another major breakout attempt was made on 12 November by forces concentrated at the southern front of Leningrad, but it was beaten off by the Germans, the Russians suffering heavy losses. On 30 November the defenders of Leningrad continued their attempts to break through with strong forces on the Neva front. In the attacks across the ice of the Neva the Russians had large and bloody losses, including prisoners and tanks. Renewed attempts on 4, 6 and 7 December to break out were frustrated. Russian history will always count the defense of Leningrad as a special page of glory for the brave defenders and the large population which courageously bore all the sufferings of prolonged siege.

The German attack south of Lake Ladoga to the east also met with more and more stubborn resistance. On 1 September the OKW had informed the Finnish Commander in Chief that Army Group North should first carry out a narrow encirclement south of Leningrad before the planned German-Finnish joint effort southeast of Lake Ladoga would begin. The Finns, who had been stationed on the Svir since 7 September, believed they had honestly fulfilled their obligations toward the Germans by concentrating strong Finnish forces on the Svir, which was to be carried out during the next few days, and, moreover, by advancing their positions above Ladeynoye Pole to the southern bank of the Svir. Conscious of having done their duty in the joint offensive, they took up permanent positions on the Svir and waited for the German attack south of Lake Ladoga to be continued across the Volkhov in the direction of Tikhvin and the lower Svir. However, nothing came of this for the time being. Heavy fighting began south of Lake Ladoga, which brought the XXXIX Corps into a rather critical situation so that on 26 September the German Army Headquarters thought it expedient to ask the Finnish Headquarters for relief of the hard-fighting German corps by demonstrative activity on the Svir front. The Finns, however, we note capable of doing so since they had at that time concentrated all available forces for an attack on Petrozavodsk. As long as the Russians were in a position to hold out at Petrozavodsk with strong forces, the Finnish Commander in Chief believed the rear of his Svir front seriously threatened. Immediately upon reaching the Svir, Field Marshal Mannerheim, therefore, had decided to consider the capture of Petrozavodsk as a new task of prime importance, and he emphatically defended the decision to drive the Russians from Petrozavodsk.

Until this point, all phases of the Finnish offensive from 10 July until late in autumn had been carried out with entire success, but it was clear to the sober thinking Finnish Commander in Chief that, when the over-all situation of the Finnish Army was considered, the poor communications between the individual theaters of war formed a weak point. Shifting of forces from the Karelian Isthmus to Eastern Karelia cost a great deal of time. The Finnish railway system could only with difficulty do justice to all its tasks, constantly increasing as they were. Traffic near the front was only partly possible owing to destruction of the railway tracks.[21] It had cost time and trouble in the beginning of October 1941 to transport the 8th Division from the Karelian Isthmus to the Karelian Army. During the following weeks it became quite obvious that the situation of the Finnish front on the Svir could be no means be considered secure. On 15 October a Russian attack began against the 7th Division (left wing of the Svir front), which continued during the following days and also involved the 5th Division, adjacent to the 7th Division. In addition the Germans requested the Finns to support the planned advance of the German 163rd Division to cover the Svir and, after it had reached the opposite bank, to

---

[21] For instance the important Elisenvaara-Sortavaala-Matkaselkä Line, which was of special importance for transports from one front to the other, could not operate until 4 December 1941.

cover the left flank. In order to comply with the German request, two thirds of the Finnish 11th Division were brought forward from the operational area north of Petrozavodsk to the Svir front and assembled in the rear of the 163rd Division.

On 6 November the Svir began to freeze over. Until the ice was thick enough, it was impossible to cross the river below Ladeynoye Pole. Finnish Headquarters, therefore, considered letting the 163rd Division effect the crossing east of Ladeynoye Pole where the Finnish front was already south of the Svir.

The advance of Army Group North south of the Volkhov River in the direction of Tikhvin slowed down more and more. Initially the OKH had demanded the rapid concentration of the 163rd Division within a few hours for the attack toward the south in order to take part in the battle of Army Group North, but the deadline had to be extended in order not to expose the troops unnecessarily to the hard winter weather. Eventually the news arrived, so anxiously expected by the Finns, that German troops had entered Tikhvin in the night of 8 November. On 10 November Mannerheim expressed to General Erfurth his appreciation of the German successes at Tikhvin and in the valley of the Volkhov in the direction of Vikhovstroy. From his words could be gathered how much the Finns would welcome the actual and definite closing of the ring around Leningrad and the final solution of the Leningrad problem by the Germans. The Marshal said that forces would then be released. At present he had not enough troops, as had also been true during the whole campaign.

The idea of an operational cooperation between German and Finnish troops south of the Svir, on which the Finnish offensive in eastern Karelia was based, seemed to near realization by the occupation of Tikhvin, but it soon became apparent that the crisis had by no means been overcome. The Russians were far from giving up the fight east of Tikhvin, but instead began a counteroffensive against Army Group North with new forces, which had partly been withdrawn from the front before the Karelian Army. The German OKH, therefore, requested Finnish Headquarters bind Russian forces by increased combat activity of the Karelian Army. Furthermore, the wish was expressed that the Finnish 5th Division should join the 163rd Division in its assault against the southern bank of the Svir. The German-Finnish forces coming from the north should work their way at least as far as the Oyat River towards the German troops advancing from Tikhvin. The annual autumn bad weather, which is a prelude to winter, had also caused many difficulties during October for the German troops advancing in Russia. Nevertheless, the German High Command's communiqué of 23 October could report that the outer defense line of Moscow had been pierced from the southwest and west during the last days. At some places German spearheads had worked their way to within sixty kilometers of the Soviet capital. Kharkov and Byelgorod had been in German hands since 24 October. The German troops reached the upper course of the Donets River on 30 October on a wide front.

It appeared that not even the mud period and the Russian winter were going to stop the victorious advance of the eastern German Army and that in the days of the motor the vastness of Russia which had destroyed Napoleon I was no longer an obstacle to a German invasion.

It was not until the end of November that luck began to turn against the Germans. A change in the dramatic struggle set in by the end of November and beginning of December, when the troops of Generaloberst von Kleist had to evacuate Rostov on the Don, which had been taken on 22 November, on account of a large-scale Russian counteroffensive. In the north, Tikhvin was the point where the offensive of the German eastern front came to a standstill and then went into reverse. At the Moscow front, attacks of the German infantry and tank forces met with more and more tenacious Russian resistance in the beginning of December. The Russians made any further approach to the Soviet capital impossibly by increasingly powerful counterthrusts.

By the first week in December 1941, the offensive of the German eastern army in Russian had come to a halt at every point, not as a result of the wise decision of the command but owing to the Russian winter and the powerful counterattacks of the Red Army, which through its tenacity and incredible power of resistance surprised the whole world. In the hard December fighting, in which the German troops were entirely confined to the defensive and ran into more and more difficulties, the "Russian National War" was born, which soon became the common cause of the Russian people. For the first time in World War II the German Army was facing a serious crisis, as in spite of all propagandist camouflage measures may be clearly derived from Hitler's proclamation on 19 December 1941 upon assuming command of the German Army. It ran as follows:

> "The armies in the east, after their unforgettable victories, unparalleled in history, over the most dangerous enemy of all times, must now pass over from mobile into trench warfare owing to the sudden arrival of winter. It will be their task to hold as fanatically and to defend as tenaciously until spring what they have won up to now with immense heroism and under the heaviest sacrifice."

It had now become obvious to everybody that Soviet Russia was not a house of cards which would collapse at the first push but rather that the gigantic eastern empire possessed tremendous inherent strength which was to determine the issue of World War II. From now on the struggle in the East was not only to determine the fate of the Soviet Union but also the existence of the Third Reich. A great run of destiny had happened as occurs but seldom in the annals of mankind.

The Finnish Commander in Chief experienced anxious hours during these weeks. He was asked for help from all sections of Finland, and felt unable to comply with all requests. Notwithstanding the great successes of the Finnish Army on the Karelian Isthmus and in Eastern Karelia, Field Marshal Mannerheim, the Finnish Government and the Finnish people were on the whole disappointed with the result of the Finnish-German offensive of 1941 between the Gulf of Finland and the Arctic Sea. Nowhere along the extensive Finnish boundary had a definite decision been arrived at nor had the threat from Russia been definitely removed. The great success hoped for in the battle for Leningrad did not appear; the junction of Germans and Finns on the Svir became more and more doubtful; the advance toward the Murmansk railroad had come to a standstill in all sectors without having reached its goal. When the war against the Soviet Union began in June 1941, the Finns under the impression of the lightning German offensives in Poland, France and the Balkans had relied upon a short duration of the war against Russia and deluded themselves with hopes that the Russian empire would quickly collapse and the main work be finished by autumn 1941. The dream of a short war had induced them to exert all forces to the utmost at mobilization and also to call the older age classes to arms. Men under arms, including the women and girls of the Lotta[22] service, are said in summer 1941 to have numbered sixteen percent of the Finnish population. An admirable performance but a tremendous burden too, under which the population suffered more and more from week to week after just having surmounted the Winter War with all its sacrifices. The consequences of this overexertion were felt everywhere.

The Finnish economy threatened to come to a standstill owing to lack of labor, transportation became more and more paralyzed. The urban population, particularly at Helsinki, suffered from lack of food and heating material. Large parts of the population urgently demanded the return of at least the oldest age classes to their families and work. The many problems of the Finnish people reached Marshal Mannerheim in many ways, who was held in the highest esteem and the greatest confidence by all classes of the Finnish people. His headquarters at Mikkeli during the entire war was a place of pilgrimage for all Finns in

---

[22] Women and girls served voluntarily in Finland in the Lotta Svärd Organization, the name of which goes back to Huneberg's ballad of that name featuring a Finnish ideal that has become immortal.

authoritative positions of public life. The President, the Prime Minister, the cabinet members, the Finnish ambassadors abroad, the leaders of the political parties, the leading men in the Finnish economic set-up, all came to the Finnish Headquarters if they were in trouble and did not know a way out, in order to discuss their troubles with the Field Marshal and to ask the opinion of the man who towered over all Finns in wisdom and experience. Mannerheim took an active interest in all questions of public life and was excellently informed on all events of local and world interest in consequence of his astonishing intellectual freshness and his unusually large capacity for work in spite of his age. There has probably seldom been a general who has had such a deep insight into his country's conditions as Mannerheim. He knew exactly the needs of the common soldier and demanded that his co-workers at Headquarters informed him in detail of minor occurrences at the front. Nothing that happened beneath the surface in Finland escaped his watchful eye.

It was, therefore, natural that he enjoyed the confidence of all Finns and that his opinion was of immense importance. It goes without saying that his chief care was the maintenance of the Finnish Army's striking power, for which purpose a plan had been worked out in November 1941 at the Finnish Headquarters aiming at reorganizing the Finnish Army. The Finnish divisions were to be reorganized in the course of the winter, as far as the situation at the front permitted, into brigades of four battalions. The Headquarters hoped this plan to have the following advantages:

1. The possibility of dismissing the older age classes.
2. The procurement of labor for industry and agriculture.
3. The increase of mobility of the Finnish Army.

Brigades were believed to be more suitable for mobile operations in the Karelian wilderness than the divisions with much stronger infantry. In order to make up for the older age classes withdrawn from the Finnish front, order was given on 27 November that one and a half age classes of newly trained young men be brought forward to the front from the training centers. On 23 November, age class 1923 was ordered to report for active duty at the training centers at the beginning of 1942.

To improve the supply of the Finnish troops, Field Marshal Mannerheim had on 24 October requested the OKW help their Finnish brother-in-arms by supplying uniforms and underwear. On 1 November the Germans promised to provide the clothing, a promise which surely was not easy for the German agencies. Many headaches were caused the Government and the High Command by the transportation crisis of the Finnish railroads which increased from week to week. Since the area to the supplied by the Finnish railroads had considerably widened as a result of the occupation of the Karelian Isthmus and large regions in Eastern

Karelia, and since both the requirements of the Finnish front and the rather high ones of the Army Headquarters Norway had to be taken care of, little transportation space remained for the Finnish civil population. Owing to the early arrival of a very severe winter, the North Finnish ports in the Gulf of Bothnia froze over early so that transportation for the army in Lapland had to be switched over to the southern Finnish ports, thus taxing the Finnish railway system even more.

On 24 October, the Chief of the Supply Service at Finnish Headquarters, Colonel Roos, an expert of note, received dictatorial power to cope with the Finnish transportation situation which had in the meantime become critical. On 12 November, Field Marshal Mannerheim explained in a lengthy letter to the OKW the rapidly increasing difficulties of the Finnish railroads and asked the Germans to help with trucks, locomotives, and railroad cars. Since the Finnish railroads use the Russian gauge and it was impossible to consider the special Finnish wishes in the German manufacturing program during the war, German help was restricted to the placing of captured Russian railroad material at the disposal of the Finns, which however, could only be delivered in limited quantities and partly in a damaged state.

The Finnish Commander in Chief had the earnest desire of extending the intended reorganization of the army as soon as possible to the divisions fighting under the command of AOK NORWEGEN. These units included a large percentage of older age classes, the withdrawal of which was not possible as long as the battalions were committed in the front line and engaged in heavy fighting. It had not been possible to carry out the OKW order of 14 October to stop the offensive against the Murmansk railroad and to exchange the intermixed units. Fighting had continued particularly in the Kiestinki sector and led to heavy losses, especially of Finnish forces. Moreover, the OKW had on 9 November issued regulations for an extensive relief of German divisions in the sector of AOK NORWEGEN, which was contrary to the desire of Mannerheim to withdraw the Finnish divisions for reorganization. For obvious reasons, Generaloberst von Falkenhorst primarily obeyed the order of the German High Command, which, however, was in contradiction to the request of the Finnish Commander in Chief. Upon Mannerheim's increasingly urgent requests, the OKW in an order to Generaloberst von Falkenhorst, dated 11 November, demanded that the activity of the Finnish III Corps in the Kiestinki sector should pass over to the defensive. This directive, however, was not to the liking of Generaloberst von Falkenhorst who believed a great success just within reach of III Corps, since Russian resistance in the Kiestinki sector appeared to be lessening. He hesitated to carry out the OKW's order. The difference of opinion in the proposals reaching the OKW from Mikkeli and from Rovaniemi was felt more and more. The complete accord between the Finns and the Germans with regard to a joint conduct of operations which had existed during the summer offensive no longer was in evidence.

On 15 November 1941, General Warlimont, Deputy Chief of the Wehrmacht Operations Staff, came to Helsinki to attempt to clarify the situation. He discussed matters on 15 and 16 November with General Erfurth whose duty it was to present the frame of mind of the Finnish Headquarters and with General Buschenhagen who defended the attitude of AOK NORWEGEN. The following points were discussed by the three German generals:

1. Relief of the German troops in the area of AOK NORWEGEN.
2. Withdrawal and reorganization of the Finnish troops under the command of Generaloberst von Falkenhorst.
3. Chances of a continuation or resumption of the offensive against the Murmansk railroad.
4. Reorganization of the AOK NORWEGEN.

The latter point referred to the intention of the OKW to replace General von Falkenhorst with General Dietl, former Commanding General of Mountain Corps Norway. General von Falkenhorst was to return to Norway and his authority to be restricted to the command of the Norwegian area. The character of Dietl, who stood in high favor with Hitler, offered the guaranty of smooth cooperation with Mannerheim, for whom a stronger influence on the joint conduct of war in the extreme north had been intended by the Germans. On the occasion of these confidential discussions the idea was mentioned for the first time, which in later phases of the war was often taken into consideration and which might have removed many difficulties, to offer the Finnish Field Marshal the supreme command over the entire Finnish-German front between the Gulf of Finland and the Arctic Sea. In early spring 1941, Mannerheim would perhaps have accepted this proposal if a generous gesture had at the time been made by the Germans. This, however, did not occur.

As a result of the Helsinki discussions, the OKW insisted on the execution of its directive to AOK NORWEGEN to let the Finnish III Corps immediately assume the defensive. The request of Marshal Mannerheim to withdraw and reunite the Finnish divisions which were in the area of the German Army should be complied with as soon as possible. The Uhtua sector was to be separated from the front of the German Army and included into that of the Finns.

AOK NORWEGEN received a Führer Directive on 21 November to prepare an attack on Kandalaksha in March 1942 in order to resume the offensive against the Murmansk railroad.

The plan of the offensive in the Kandalaksha sector was communicated to the Finnish Commander in Chief on 24 November by a letter of Field Marshal Keitel. Mannerheim was asked to make two Finnish ski brigades available for this offensive if possible and a Finnish general for the command of the southern attack group.

Mannerheim replied on 5 December; he did not decline the German plan, but made a stronger Finnish participation in the intended campaign against the Murmansk railroad dependent on a previous juncture of the German and Finnish forces on the Svir in order to relieve the Finnish southern front. The Finnish Commander in Chief thereby clearly indicated the correlation between the battle for Leningrad and an offensive against the Murmansk railroad. The Finnish defense front on the Karelian Isthmus and on the Svir required so many forces that Finish participation in the campaign against the Murmansk railroad was out of the question unless the southern Finnish front had actually been relieved. Mannerheim considered the Finnish position on the Svir an Achilles' heel. In case of an enemy penetration at this point, the whole Finnish position on Lake Onega would become untenable. East Karelia would remain safely in Finnish possession only as long as all went well in the south, where, however, the situation seemed rather doubtful.

The spearhead of Army Group North, which had advanced as far as Tikhvin, had run into more and more difficulties as a result of the Russian counterattacks and the hardships of the severe Russian winter. The question arose whether the position at Tikhvin could be held. From the daily communiqués from the German eastern front it could be derived that the German eastern Army had been taken by surprise by the enemy counteroffensive and by the Russian winter. The tone of Radio Moscow had become very confident of victory. The news arriving at Mikkeli from the German eastern front led to the conclusion that the German Army was not sufficiently prepared for winter warfare in Russian and that its strength had been spent to a great extent by the preceding long offensive. The Russian soldier was much less affected by the Russian winter than the German soldier. He was more suitably dressed and knew better how to deal with the demands of winter warfare. In former wars too, the Russian Army preferably started its offensives in winter.

Political power in Russia had proved considerably more strong and stable than expected by the highest German authorities. It became obvious that the war in Russia had developed into a national struggle, in which all segments of the Russian people participated eagerly and with all their energy.

The exchange of thoughts between the Finnish Headquarters and AOK NORWEGEN regarding the relief and exchange of forces in the area of command of the German High Command, which had been initiated by the Helsinki discussions on 15 and 16 November and the subsequent directives of the OKW, was immediately continued but led to no result. In order to thrash the matter out, Mannerheim went to Rovaniemi on 13 December 1941. He was accompanied by General Airo, the Chief of Army Supply and Administration, Colonel Isakson, the Chief of the Organization Branch, and the German General at Finnish Headquarters. On the request of Mannerheim, General Siilasvuo, the Commanding General of the Finnish III Corps, and Colonel Viiklas, the Commander of the Finnish 6th Division committed with its bulk in the Kandalaksha sector, were also called to Rovaniemi. The discussion took place on 14 December at General Falkenhorst's headquarters. Falkenhorst declared himself in no position to withdraw the Finnish divisions from the front line in order to make them available to the Finnish Commander in Chief behind the front. Mannerheim stipulated that the taking over of the Uhtua sector was dependent upon the transfer to this sector of the same number and strength of forces as had been stationed there before. This, however, Falkenhorst could not grant, since he had received an order from the OKW to evacuate the SS Group Nord from the Uhtua sector to Germany, where it was to be rehabilitated and reorganized into a division. Forces to replace it, however, were not available to the Commander in Chief of AOK NORWEGEN. Under these circumstances Mannerheim declined to take over the Uhtua sector.

Also no agreement between the Finnish and German Commander in Chief could be reached with regard to the resumption of the offensive against the Murmansk railroad. Falkenhorst wished to resume the attack as soon as possible with Finnish reinforcements in the Kandalaksha area. Mannerheim referred to Finnish experience in winter warfare in the arctic region and recommended the first half of March as the deadline for the offensive. Besides the Kandalaksha sector did not seem to him suitable for a winter offensive, and he also declined the Kiestinki sector. He proposed Soroka as objective (on Russian maps called Byelomorsk), the point where the railroad leading south of the White Sea to Oboserskaya (on the Archangelsk-Velogda line) branches off from the Murmansk railroad. This branch line had been constructed by the Russians as late as 1938/41. Soroka, no doubt, was a point of particular importance, since the branch line south of the White Sea represented for the Russians a substitute for the sector of the Murmansk railroad between the Svir and Medvezhyegorsk lost as a result of Finnish occupation. In case the line would be cut at Soroka, communications between the important harbor of Murmansk and the interior of Russia would cease.

Mannerheim's proposal was communicated by the General Erfurth to the OKW, where it evoked great interest. The Germans were glad that the Finns now proposed to resume the offensive against the Murmansk railroad, since it was immediately recognized that they would have to bear the brunt of the fighting at Soroka, while the task of the German troops would only be of secondary nature. On 20 December the OKW dispatched a directive to AOK NORWEGEN cancelling the offensive against Kandalaksha.

The German 7th Mountain Division, whose transfer to Army Headquarters had been planned, was placed at the disposal of the Finnish Headquarters for the Karelian Army's attack against Soroka. Field Marshal Mannerheim accepted the offer. Coordination of the German and Finnish plans of operation appeared to have been reached. But immediately upon the return of Marshal Mannerheim from Rovaniemi to Mikkeli a change took place. Highly disquieting news arrived from the German eastern front. The Finns, naturally, were particularly interested in the situation in the sector of Army Group North, where the narrow German spearhead at Tikhvin had no longer been able to ward off the Russian counterattacks and had under great losses retreated behind the lower Volkhov. The Russians pressed strongly in pursuit. The situation of the German troops south of Lake Ladoga became critical. On 26 December a call for help from the OKW arrived at Finnish Headquarters, requesting the following assistance:

1. Enemy forces should be tied down by lively combat activity at the Finnish front on the Karelian Isthmus.
2. The Russians should be led to believe by means of misleading reports that a Finnish attack from the north against Leningrad was impending.

The news of the German retreat from Tikhvin had exceedingly depressed all Finnish circles and may have sounded like a shrill alarm signal to the cabinet members and congressmen. Naturally Field Marshal Mannerheim was also alarmed. He wondered how it was possible that the German eastern army had fallen into such a difficult situation. The recall of Field Marshal von Brauchitsch, Commander in Chief of the German Army, which took place on 19 December, underlined the importance of the failure.

The fact that Adolf Hitler decided to take over the command of the German Army himself failed to make a great impression on the sober Finns. It is possible that Christmas 1941 brought the farsighted and experienced Mannerheim the first doubt whether Germany would be able to win the war.

The strong optimism characteristic of the German communiqués had considerably toned down in December 1941. The German communiqué admitted on 8 December that continuation of the operations and methods of combat in the East would in future by determined by the Russian winter. More and more frequently, enemy attacks against the German eastern front were mentioned, which were beaten off under heavy fighting. From the Wehrmacht communiqué of 17 December could be gathered that the German eastern army had in several sectors not been able to hold its positions against the Russian attacks and was involuntarily retreating. This passage read as follows: "Improvements and shortening of various sectors of the eastern front have at present become necessary owing to the transition from offensive operations to winter trench warfare." Hitler's order of the day addressed to the Wehrmacht on 31December 1941 stated with utter frankness: "The year 1941 now lies behind us. It was a year of most difficult decisions and extremely bloody fighting." This admission opened the eyes of the German public to the truth of the course the Russian campaign had taken, so far hidden from it.

From many reports arriving at the Finnish Headquarters at Mikkeli in December, it became obvious that the German eastern army had passed through a grave crisis. The common fate with their ally made the Finns too view the situation in Russia with great anxiety. Thus at the end of 1941 dark clouds had appeared on the Finnish horizon.

In our description of the events during the first year of war, some particulars might have been omitted with regard to the events along the Finnish coast and in Finnish waters.

Soon after the outbreak of the war, strong British naval forces appeared off Murmansk. At the end of July 1941, enemy air attacks were made on Liinahamari and Kirkenes from aircraft carriers belonging to this fleet. After that, the situation in the Arctic Sea became quiet, but Finnish export trade was entirely blocked.

In the Gulf of Finland, the Finnish Navy, reinforced by German naval units, defended the Finnish coast. Extensive minefields in the Gulf of Finland confined the Russian Baltic Fleet at Kronstadt to inactivity. The German-Finnish minefields proved fatal to the Russian naval forces and transports when Tallinn was evacuated by the Russians at the end of August. Before the Gulf of Finland froze over, German and Finnish naval units penetrated deep into the gulf and reinforced the minefields toward Kronstadt Bay. The Luftwaffe sank a cruiser and a destroyer on 23 September in the Kronstadt area and bombarded the Russian battleships in Kronstadt Bay on the following days.

On 14 September, the German-Finnish naval forces simultaneously suffered heavy losses. For unknown reasons, three German mine sweepers exploded in the harbor of Helsinki. The Finnish armored ship ILAARINEN apparently struck a mine and sank at the same time southwest of Hangö, being a total loss.

When the eastern part of the Gulf of Finland began to freeze over, the Russians probably considered defense of the islands off Koivisto useless and evacuated them. The Finns occupied them during the first days of November.

At the beginning all was quiet at Hangö. The Finns confined themselves to encircling the leased territory from both land and sea. The Russians kept quiet and remained within the leased territory. The situation changed, when the Gulf of Finland began to freeze over. A Russian naval formation put to sea from Kronstadt Bay on 3 November, heading for Hangö, and arrived unharmed by the minefields.

Slowly it dawned on the Finns that Hangö was going to be evacuated and given up by the Russians. On 4 December the Finns reoccupied the leased territory from the land side without meeting any resistance. Numerous Russian boats leaving Hangö and heading for Kronstadt struck Finnish-German mines and suffered losses. The 12,000-ton troop transport STALIN was heavily damaged by several mines and was brought in by German patrol boats. German naval assault detachments occupied Osmussaar Islands. At the time the Germans planned for the first time to occupy Suursaari Island, the possession of which was very important for securing sea traffic in the Gulf of Finland. Since ice conditions did not admit the transport of strong forces to the island however, and no German forces were available for the operation, the plan was postponed to a more opportune time.

Finland's air defense had in the time between the Winter War and The Third Finnish War of Liberation been energetically increased. Lundquist, the able General of the Finnish Air Force had been remarkably successful in its organization, the results of which now showed. The Finnish fighter planes could successfully stand their own against a highly superior enemy. In numerous air fights, for instance over Lahdenpohja on 9 July and Rautjärvi on 1 August, the Finnish fighter pilots showed their great aerial ability and splendid fighting spirit. Finnish bombers and reconnaissance planes repeatedly took part in ground operations. The reinforced Finnish antiaircraft artillery succeeded much more efficiently than in the Winter War to protect the Finnish towns, but the Finnish Air Force and the Finnish air defense, which was small in relation to the vast Finnish territory, were not able to prevent bombing attacks on the towns altogether. Thus an air attack was made on Helsinki on 3 November which caused considerable damage.

The Luftwaffe's mission was to cooperate in the fight for Leningrad and to conduct air warfare in the arctic region. During the last months of 1941 German bombers repeatedly attacked installations of the Murmansk railroad, transport trains and the port of Murmansk, as well as cantonments on Ribachi Peninsula.

In December, the road across the ice on the southern part of Lake Ladoga, which was an important supply route for the besieged city of Leningrad, was repeatedly bombed by German planes.

It was to be expected that in the common German-Finnish conduct of war both nations used their utmost energy, and that, in relation to the greater potential of the Reich, Germany was in many cases the giver and small Finland the taker, but yet it did not develop into a partnership in which the stronger took advantage of his superiority. The German brother-in-arms was always ready to help and magnanimously shared its resources with the Finns without Finnish policy thereby becoming dependent on German demands. The representatives of both governments negotiated on the same level. Nor did the responsible German agencies in Finland attempt to introduce the ideology of the autocratic regime into democratic Finland. Both partners respected each other's individuality, and in consequence the Finnish and German agencies treated with great impartiality and in full confidence all questions which arose. The economic requirements of both were settled and made mutually dependent on one another by negotiations of government representatives sitting in conference from time to time. In these negotiations, which took place partly in Berlin and partly at Helsinki, Germany was regularly represented by Ambassador Schnurre, who was advised by the German Embassy at Helsinki. The leadership of the Finnish delegation changed several times. The results of the negotiations were formed into bilateral commercial treaties. In addition there must be added the large, entirely one-sided German armament assistance to Finland, since the Finnish war economy was not sufficiently developed to satisfy the requirements of her Armed Forces in wartime. The Finnish requests with regard to armament assistance were advanced by the Finnish Commander in Chief through the German General at Finnish Headquarters to the OKW and generally quickly settled. Technical particulars of the Finnish armament program were dealt with by General Grandell, Chief of the Finnish Economic Staff, and Kapitän zur See Koch, the German economic officer attached to the staff of General Erfurth at Finnish Headquarters and only came to Finnish Headquarters at Mikkeli if required.

Since Finnish requests found quicker fulfillment through military channels by way of the German General at Finnish Headquarters than through the diplomatic channels of the German Embassy at Helsinki, Field Marshal Mannerheim occasionally also made use of the former in case of a state of emergency in the Finnish economy (for instance if rye or coal were required), or in case of requests of the Finnish government. In the first year of war the German General supported the following Finnish requests before the OKW:

9 July 1941	Request for the supply of captured Russian ammunition
1 September 1941	Request for the supply of 25,000 tons of rye (15,000 tons were granted at once. The balance was taken over by the German-Finnish commercial treaty).
24 October 1941	Request for the supply of uniforms, underwear and linen.
12 November 1941	Request for the supply of trucks, locomotives and railroad cars.
14 November 1941	Large requests for the supply of war materiel, fuel, provisions.

But Finland too was ready to help her German brother-in-arms if an opportunity for doing so arose. When the OKH asked on 24 September 1941 whether the Finnish Commander in Chief was ready and in a position to place Finnish instruction groups for winter warfare at the disposal of the German eastern armies, Field Marshal Mannerheim answered in the affirmative. The Finnish High Command responded generously to the German request, making available not only the body of instructors, but also all necessary equipment for successfully carrying out the courses. The first course on winter warfare took place after Christmas in the Kankaanpää camp. German officers and noncommissioned officers had been brought to Finland as pupils. The second course in February 1942 had to be held in Germany, as the German participants could not be brought to Finland by boat owing to the frozen state of the Baltic Sea. It took place at the Grossborn training camp. These courses, which not only transmitted to the German Army Finnish experiences in forest and winter warfare, but also served to strengthen the mutual comradeship between them, were welcomed by all participants and gave the Finnish officers acting as instructors an opportunity to make the German participants acquainted with Finnish hospitality so characteristic of the Finnish people. The courses were continued at regular intervals later on and with the exception of the second one all took place in Finland. During the summer, instructions on forest combat were given. The German participants were attached to the German General at Finnish Headquarters, who prepared the program of instruction with the Finnish instruction group.

CHAPTER IV: The Soviet Russian Counter-Offensive in the
Beginning of 1942 and Trench Warfare

German-Finnish Plans for a Resumption of the Offensive
1. January – June 1942

In the beginning of December, the Russians began a large-scale offensive against the German front in Russia. The Russian attacks continued with undiminished force and in severe cold in January 1942. Particularly heavy fighting raged in the central sector of the German eastern front (battle of Moscow). In the northern sector of the eastern front, the Valdai Hills were a scene of heavy fighting. Bitter fighting also went on at Feodosiya in the Crimea where the Russians had landed and where German and Rumanian troops successfully counterattacked.

On New Year's Day a Russian offensive began against the Finnish front between Povenets and Lake Seg, where bitter fighting raged between 1 and 11 January. The Russians made their customary attacks across the frozen lakes and streams against the Finnish positions. The hardest struggle took place for the tongue of land at Povenets. Since, however, the Russians could be beaten back and could also be repulsed at other sectors of the Finnish front, this offensive ended without any Russian success worth mentioning.

In the first days of January it was temporarily considered at Finnish Headquarters not to bring the 7th Mountain Division, whose transport had been announced, forward to eastern Karelia (it was to be transferred to reinforce the Finnish forces which were to attack Soroka), but to commit it on the Karelian Isthmus in order to release Finnish units for the Karelian Army. It was believed that the German supply service for this German division would work easier if the latter was employed near the coast of the Gulf of Finland instead of south of Medvezhyegorsk.

On about 5 January the impression was gained at Finnish Headquarters that the Russians had received reinforcements north of Medvezhyegorsk, so that the Finnish front protruding far into eastern Karelia seemed threatened. The Commander in Chief was also alarmed by the news from the German eastern front. In order to get a clear overall picture of the situation and to arrive at definite decisions, Mannerheim decided to send General Heinrichs, the Commander in Chief of the Karelian Army, to visit the OKW. Heinrichs left by plane for German on 6 January. His mission consisted of procuring definite answers to Mannerheim's questions as to whether the retreat of major parts of the German front in Russia would come to a halt and whether the operations against Leningrad would be resumed and brought to a conclusion. Heinrichs, who was received in the Führer's Headquarters by Field Marshal Keitel and General Jodl and also paid a visit to General Halder at the Army Headquarters, received reassuring promises. Finally Heinrichs proposed as ordered by Mannerheim the replacement of the Finnish III Corps by German forces in order to be able to employ this Finnish corps at Medvezhyegorsk, where Mannerheim considered the situation tense. The German generals at the Führer's Headquarters, who apparently wished to keep the Finnish Marshal in good humor, agreed to Heinrich's proposal.

On 8 January the OKW sent a directive to AOK NORWEGEN to withdraw the Finnish 6th Division which Mannerheim had vainly tried to obtain at the conference in Rovaniemi on 14 December, from the front of the German Army and bring it forward to the Karelian Army.

The 7th Mountain Division was then no longer destined for the Finnish front. This division together with the 5th Mountain Division, which followed behind it, was gradually to take over the sector of the Finnish III Corps (Kiestinki and Uhtua) under the German XVIII Corps Headquarters which was heading for Finland. The released Finnish forces were to be made available to the Finnish Commander in Chief as soon as possible. The execution of these OKW orders was made difficult and delayed by the situation at the front. By the middle of January, the Russians opposite Kiestinki received reinforcements, and the withdrawal of the last units of the Finnish 6th Division was delayed. Whatever forces the division could send back were assembled in the Kayasni area to carry out the reorganization. Opposite Medvezhyegorsk the Russians also displayed some activity although the attacks had been beaten off. The Karelian Army was, therefore, reinforced by the III Brigade (originating from the reorganized 12th Division) withdrawn from the Karelian Isthmus.

In the second half of January another lull occurred on the Karelian Army's front. Several changes in the Finnish and German organization took place during this period. The AOK NORWEGEN (command post at Rovaniemi) was renamed AOK LAPLAND. General Dietl took over the command of the German Army in northern Finland in place of General von Falkenhorst, who returned to Oslo. The first transports of the 7th Mountain Division began to arrive in Finland on 14 January.

The German Luftflotte 5 set up an extensive program for the enlargement of its ground organization which considerably taxed Finnish economy with regard to building material, particularly wood. In contrast to the self-sufficient Finnish soldiers, the German demands, especially those of the Luftwaffe, appeared very extensive to the Finnish agencies. There is no doubt that the Finnish forces acted with greater economy than the Wehrmacht. The almost extravagant expenditure which formerly was unknown to the Wehrmacht and had been introduced by the National Socialists was particularly favored by the new branches of the Wehrmacht

(Luftwaffe, Waffen SS) and this attitude was little appreciated by the Finns. They themselves practiced a strict economy, which was recognized as imperative by all agencies and carefully watched over by the Finnish congress.

On 17 January, Generaloberst Stumpf, Chief of the Luftflotte 5, came to Mikkeli in order to discuss the plan for the offensive against Soroka with General Hanell, Deputy Chief of the General Staff, General Lundquist, Commander of the Finnish Air Force, and the German General at Finnish Headquarters. The Finnish generals remained very reserved during the discussion so that the German generals gained the impression that Field Marshal Mannerheim had not yet made a final decision on the offensive.

The Finnish Commander in Chief decided at this time to reorganize his forces into the following three fronts:

> a. Karelian Isthmus
> b. Svir
> c. Maaselkä

The following commanders were appointed to the respective fronts:

> a. Major General Ösch
> b. Major General Öhquist
> c. Brigadier General Laatikainen

When the plan was later carried out, Generals Ösch and Öhquis exchanged places.

Mannerheim's intention remained to dissolve the High Command of the Karelian Army and to place the commanders of the three fronts under his own command. General Heinrichs, the Commander in Chief of the Karelian Army, was to return to his old post as Chief of the General Staff at Headquarters. His former representative, General Hanell, was to take charge again of the fortification system. The OKW's agreement to exchange General Öhquist, Finnish General at the German Headquarters, for General Talvela was solicited and granted on 19 January.

After Mannerheim had decided to dissolve the High Command of the Karelian Army, Finnish Headquarters considered exchanging the site at Mikkeli, which was too far from the front, for other quarters nearer to it. Several departments at Mikkeli occupied themselves after 18 January with reconnoitering and preparing new quarters at Sortavala.

During the engagements in the first half of January, the Russians had succeeded somewhat in pushing back in the Finnish positions near the Murmansk railroad. Finnish counterattacks against this salient were carefully prepared without undue hurry and successfully carried out, resulting in the destruction of the Russian division in the protruding salient. This success was due to sufficient supply of ammunition, through which German help was available to the Finns to a much larger extent than in the Winter War.

Around 19 January a strong ski unit of the Finnish 14th Division made a long range reconnaissance operation against the Murmansk railroad. The Finns, led by Colonel Hannula, succeeded in penetrating to the railroad and in raiding the Russian supply base at Segeshea (south of Kochkoma), interrupting for some time the traffic on the Murmansk railroad. After this outstanding performance the Finnish unit returned without any major losses.

The situation on the German eastern front, particularly south of Lake Ilmen, at this time became more and more critical. The great Russian winter offensive made more and more progress to the west. The German eastern army suffered heavily from the severe Russian winter. Forces were lacking to seal off enemy penetrations or to counterattack enemy units which had broken through. Wider and wider sectors of the German front had to be given up.

Transportation by water from German to Finland ceased on 27 January because the Baltic Sea froze over; the consequences for the Finnish-German front were most inconvenient. Not only did the current supply service to the German troops in Finland and the furlough traffic cease, but also the armament transports for the Finnish Armed Forces and grain transports for the Finnish population were ice-bound in the Baltic for an indefinite period. Transportation of the 7th Mountain Division, which had just started, came to a complete standstill. For a time, contact between Germany and Finland was as good as cut off, since communications by air were also hampered by the severe cold.

On 28 January Field Marshal Keitel wrote a letter to the Finnish Commander in Chief broaching again the question of the Finnish-German offensive against Soroka, which Mannerheim on 14 December had promised would take place in the beginning of March.

The overall situation had however, taken a turn for the worse during the last six weeks and important prerequisites upon with Mannerheim had been able to count on 14 December had in the meantime been lost. That was made clear when General Dietl, the new Commander in Chief of AOK LAPLAND, paid his courtesy call on the Finnish Commander in Chief at Mikkeli on 2 February. Since the arrival of the 7th Mountain Division was delayed for an uncertain period, the Finnish III Corps in the Kiestinki sector could not be relieved for the time being. For the arrival of the 5th Mountain Division, which was to be transferred to Finland after the 7th Mountain Division, a time schedule could not be laid down at all. The German Commander in Chief at Rovaniemi lacked, therefore, the necessary forces to participate in the Finnish advance on Soroka by attacking in one of his own sectors. Dietl was of the opinion that sufficient forces for offensive operations would not be available to him until the beginning of summer. Mannerheim also believed that in view of the changed over-all situation an offensive against Soroka was no longer possible. Keitel, therefore, received a negative answer from Mannerheim on 8 February. The southern Finnish front had not been relieved by the unfavorable development of the situation in the center of Army Group North, and it was precisely this demand which the Finnish Commander in Chief had considered the most important prerequisite for a Finnish offensive. The operation against the Murmansk railroad was, therefore, indefinitely postponed. When Ambassador Schnurre came to Mikkeli on 15 February to extend the Finnish German commercial treaty and visited the Commander in Chief, Mannerheim, commenting on the offensive against Soroka, said, "I shall not attack anymore." It was not clear to the ambassador whether Mannerheim's refusal referred only to the present situation or had a broader sense and referred to Finnish foreign policy in general.

While violent seesaw fighting continued uninterrupted in severe cold along the eastern front, combat activity at the Finnish-German front abated. The lull was utilized for reorganizing the divisions. The older age classes were withdrawn, particularly from the infantry, and partly given home leave, partly assembled behind the front in special battalions (so-called "senile battalions"). Those to be dismissed numbered 111,500. The first reorganized units were the following:

a. The 1st Light Infantry Brigade, which had been relieved at Povenets by the 1st Division and transferred to the western shore of Lake Seg after reorganization.

b. The 12th Brigade reorganized from units of the 6th Division, which was brought forward from Kajaani to the 14th Division in the Rukajärvi sector.

In the Maaselkä sector, the following forces remained:
1st Division
II Brigade
4th Division
8th Division (in reserve)

The reason given by the Finnish Headquarters for the regroupings in the sectors of Maaselkä and Rukajärvi was a possible offensive with limited objectives in the direction of the Murmansk railroad.

Soviet attacks continued in February along the eastern front in spite of bitter cold and large snow drifts. In the first week of February the Russians renewed their attempts at breaking out of Leningrad with strong forces, which, however, could be repelled by the besieging forces. The artillery of Army Group North continued firing at objectives of military importance in Leningrad and Kronstadt.

By the middle of February the cold in Russia was abating, but fighting continued in the east with undiminished violence. Particularly bitter fighting took place at the Donets front, where German, Rumanian and Croatian troops counterattacked in the middle of the month throwing the Russians back in spite of tenacious resistance.

In the central sector of the eastern front, enemy forces had succeeded in breaking through the German lines south of Vyazma. After hard fighting the Russians were encircled in counterattacks and destroyed. General Model's army in the central sector of the front was remarkably successful at the end of February. In a four-week long battle under most difficult terrain conditions, it encircled and destroyed the bulk of a Soviet Russian army. Strong units of another army were also eliminated. Uninterrupted bitter relief attacks on the part of the Russians were repulsed. Heavy seesaw fighting continued throughout February in the central and northern sectors. Bloody fighting also went on in the Crimea, particularly before Sevastopol and on the Kerch Peninsula.

In the beginning of March the Wehrmacht communiqué announced that heavy defensive operations continued in the Crimea, at the Donets front and southeast of Lake Ilmen. The cold had become more severe again in March, but, in spite of this, the battle continued to rage at many places along the eastern front.

On 4 March the regrouping and renaming of the Finnish fronts came into force. The High Command of the Karelian Army had been eliminated as intermediary between the headquarters and the fronts.

The supply service of the Finnish III Corps was also finally reorganized on 9 March. The OKW performed a great favor in supplying this corps from German stocks even after its separation from AOK LAPLAND. No change too place although the channels of requisition and supply were switched over from AOK LAPLAND to the German General at Finnish Headquarters.

Around 8 March the plan to occupy the islands in the Gulf of Finland made a new appearance. It was suggested by Army Group North, and also the Finnish Headquarters showed strong interest. Taking the planned operations of the Finnish naval and air forces in summer into account, Marshal Mannerheim deemed it necessary to occupy Suusaari Island before the end of winter.

On 14 March, however, participation of Army Group North in the operation became doubtful, since the situation at its front did not permit the withdrawal of forces.

On 17 March Mannerheim decided to act independently of the German brother-in-arms, whose cooperation became more and more doubtful, and to carry out the attack on Suursaari singlehanded, since further delay was not possible owing to the fact that ice conditions in the Gulf of Finland were expected to change soon. Sufficient forces, belonging for the most part to the 18th Division, were, therefore, assembled near Kotka and thorough preparations made by the Division Commander General Pajari. On 24 March, German participation in the attack on the island was definitely countermanded. All that Mannerheim demanded was the cooperation of the Luftwaffe. In the night of 26 March the Finnish forces began the attack on Suursaari Island. The island was taken on 27 March, and on 1 April Tytärsaari Island was also occupied. The Finnish garrison on the latter island was replaced on 4 April by a German garrison. During the relief action a Soviet attack on the island was made but repulsed by the joint German and Finnish forces. In the time to follow Tytärsaari remained occupied by German troops, whereas Suursaari retained its Finnish garrison. These extremely difficult operations were carried out under very unfavorable weather conditions within an unbelievably short time and with small losses. A longer delay in carrying out the operation could not have been allowed, since a few days after the capture of the islands the ice in the Gulf of Finland had already lost adequate carrying capacity.

The Finnish Air Force achieved great successes in these days over the Gulf of Finland. On 26 March in bitter air battles brought about by the surprise attack on the islands, Finnish fighter planes succeeded in downing twenty-seven Soviet planes. During the whole war, the Finnish fighter planes were far superior to the Russian planes, and even isolated Finnish planes used to attack at once regardless of the number of enemy planes. The demands made on the modest Finnish Air Force during these days in spring were very great, since the Germans also made considerable demands. On 5 April Luftflotte 1, which was heavily engaged in the sector of Army Group North, requested larger Finnish participation in fighter protection over the Gulf of Finland. On the same day Luftflotte 5 requested the Finnish Air Force to put itself at the disposal of AOK LAPLAND. Naturally it was not possible to fulfill these demands, and the Finns were justified in concluding from the calls for help that the Luftwaffe was overtaxed by the great Russian winter offensive.

The German request made on 6 April to be allowed to station two bombardment groups of Luftflotte 1 on the Malmi airdrome near Helsinki in order to be able to approach Leningrad from the north was declined by Field Marshal Mannerheim for political reasons. He made it a principle to avoid creating difficulties for the Finnish capital. In place of Malmi, Utti Airport was placed at the disposal of Luftflotte 1, which served the purpose just as well. Utti was re-evacuated by the Luftwaffe on 27 October 1942.

Some of the Finnish grain ships coming from Germany, which had been ice-bound off the Swedish coast, arrived on 6 April in southern Finnish ports. A Russian counterattack on Tytärsaari was repulsed on 8 April by the German garrison of the island.

A proposal made on 8 April by AOK LAPLAND regarding a joint German-Finnish long distance operation against the Murmansk railroad under participation of the Finnish II Corps and the Finnish 14th Division was declined by Finnish Headquarters, since at that time a Finnish offensive was felt undesirable for political reasons. From the beginning of March the Finns were subjected to diplomatic pressure by the United States aiming at bringing about reconciliation with the Soviet Union or at least of averting a Finnish offensive against the Murmansk railroad.

At the end of March the Arctic Sea also became a scene of heavy fighting. An enemy convoy heading for Murmansk, which had on 29 March been the target of German air attacks, was attacked on 30 March by German destroyers. A 10,000-ton transport on its way from New York with a cargo of tanks and ammunition, was sunk by artillery fire and torpedo hits. At dawn a naval engagement with superior allied escort forces, consisting of cruisers and destroyers took place. A torpedo hit a British cruiser of the "city" class, but owing to the snowstorm the result could not be ascertained. A German destroyer was lost in this engagement. On the next day, the convoy was again attacked in the Murmansk area by German submarines. Two heavily loaded freighters of a total tonnage of 11,000 tons were sunk at the entrance of Kola Bay. A third transport was hit by a torpedo. Another large freighter was damaged by air attacks.

German bombers raided an escorted Allied convoy in the Arctic again on 12 April. Two freighters were set afire, another damaged.

When the snow began to melt, the Russians made an attack on the Svir from Lake Onega as far as Ladeynoye Pole with strong forces and large expenditure of ammunition. The brave Finnish defenders were able to beat off all attacks of the Russians and inflicted heavy losses on the enemy in front of the Finnish positions. Only in the center, in an extensive, closed forest area where no continuous front existed, did the Russians succeed in penetrating about ten kilometers deep into the Finnish lines. Here, however, the Russians were sealed off and almost annihilated by the Finns, who employed all heavy weapons available. This annihilation battle lasted for ten days. On 21 April the situation stabilized again at the Svir front. The ice on the Svir and the Gulf of Finland began to break up. In southern Finland the mud period started.

When toward the end of the month the ice began to melt in the Kiestinki sector, the Russians took the offensive in that area too. Since in the Murmansk sector a large-scale Russian attack had begun by the middle of April, which led to interminable seesaw battles, AOK LAPLAND, to whom no reserves were available, ran into difficulties and on 1 May asked Finnish Headquarters for help. Dietl requested that the Finnish XII Brigade, which was not too far from the Kiestinki sector, be placed at his disposal for commitment together with the Finnish III Corps. The Finnish Headquarters made a counterproposal. It now saw a chance to make some headway with the exchange of Finnish and German units, which had come to nothing up to this point.

The Finnish High Command offered to replace the 163rd Division, committed on the Svir, by Finnish forces from the Maaselkä sector, and then to bring the 163rd Division forward to Army Headquarters Lapland, under the condition that it would get in exchange the Finnish 14th Infantry Regiment from the Kiestinki sector, whose return Field Marshal Mannerheim was particularly concerned about.[23] Marshal Mannerheim also declared himself ready to take over the Uhtua sector with all forces committed there (also the German forces!). Enemy attacks in the Kiestinki sector increased and facilitated Dietl's decision with regard to the Finnish proposal. Under pressure of events an agreement was quickly reached. The entraining of the 163rd Division was speeded up as much as possible, but nevertheless some time elapsed until the help brought by the division was felt. The Russian attempt to destroy the Finnish-German front at Kiestinki was finally frustrated, but a short time after 1 May the enemy succeeded in penetrating into the area northwest and west of Kiestinki by means of an outflanking movement through dense virgin forest. Here, however, the Russians were surrounded and destroyed, as in April on the Svir front. The remainder of the enemy was thrown back to their jumping-off position after difficult forest fighting lasting for about one month. On 15 May began the Finnish-German counterattack at Kiestinki, which reached the former positions on 23 May. On 31 May Army Headquarters Lapland was able to report that the counterattack at Kiestinki conducted by German and Finnish forces had been successfully terminated.

In the Murmansk sector, too, the situation had become very serious at the end of April. The enemy not only attacked the front of the Mountain Corps Norway on the Litsa River, but also landed forces in Motovski Bay at the German rear. Fighting in the vicinity of the Arctic Sea took place under very severe weather conditions. Snowstorms raged with unbelievable force across the tundra and the German troops suffered great hardships from the inclemency of this spring weather. The counterattack against the enemy who had penetrated into the German

---

[23] The 14th Infantry Regiment had been assigned to AOK NORWEGEN since 8 July 1941 and had at first been employed in the Murmansk sector.

lines required superhuman efforts. On 11 May the counterattack came to a halt at the Litsa River. The troops seemed completely exhausted. These violent fights on the coast of the Arctic in which the German mountain infantrymen gloriously stood their test, ended on 15 May with a clear German defensive victory. The Luftwaffe also achieved great successes in the spring battles in the Arctic. It repeatedly hurled its forces against the far superior enemy and won many air victories. On 11 May, for instance, German fighters shot down twenty-seven Soviet planes, while losing only one plane themselves. Dive bombers and bomber formations damaged one large freighter in Litsa Bay and successfully bombed the harbor of Murmansk as well as installations of the Murmansk railroad.

How many efforts had to be made, what perseverance and tenacity was needed to frustrate all Russian attacks along the Finnish-German front in spring 1942! Finnish-German brotherhood-in-arms triumphed in this heavy fighting and can with clear conscience face future critics. Better soldiers than Finns and Germans do not exist. This proud conviction was brought to the mind of the fighters at the Svir front and at Kiestinki and all participants in the bloody spring fighting on the Arctic coast in 1942. Brave feats in bygone days too have been carried out along the extended Finnish eastern border, but the heroism of the Finns and Germans during the last war will shine brightly through all times and will never be forgotten.

At this time the Finnish Commander in Chief made an important organizational decision. The plan formed in autumn of the preceding year to reorganize the Finnish Army was re-examined and altered. The transformation of divisions into brigades had been carried out very slowly, and the advantages hoped for had not been realized. On 16 May Field Marshal Mannerheim ordered the discontinuation of the reorganization. Only the already reorganized 6th and 12th Divisions (now XII and III Brigades) and the newly organized I Light Infantry Brigade were to remain brigades. With regard to the relief of the Finnish III Corps, AOK LAPLAND had worked out a fixed plan after navigation in the Baltic had reopened and the transfer of the 7th and 5th Mountain Divisions was possible again. The plan was adopted by Marshal Mannerheim on 9 June.

At the end of May it was learnt at Finnish Headquarters that the Russian had begun to evacuate the population of Leningrad. Finnish-German circles considered how to prevent Russian traffic in both directions across the southern part of Lake Ladoga. Traffic across the ice in a direct line between the two coast points Sumskaya and More had been very lively during the winter. After the ice had melted lively shipping traffic between those two points was to be expected. Both the Finns and Germans were interested in preventing this.

Lieutenant Colonel Siebel, the inventor of a flat bottom landing craft, paid a visit to Finnish Headquarters on 5 June in order to gather information on the employment of his boats on Lake Ladoga. A discussion took place at Headquarters on 14 June about the commitment of the forces promised by the Kriegsmarine (German S-boats and Italian Mas-boats) and the Seibel boats brought by the Luftwaffe to Finland. The operation received the code name KLABAUTERMANN. Since the Finnish headquarters gave the German agencies complete freedom of action, but the latter could not coordinate their operations, the paradoxical situation was created that the Kriegsmarine was to begin its operation on 1 July and the Luftwaffe on 1 August.

In the last days of May, an air and naval battle, which proved successful for the Germans, had taken place in the Far North against an American-British convoy (the sixteenth) which coming from the United States and heading under strong escort for Murmansk had been discovered by the German reconnaissance in the brightness of the polar summer night and had been attacked jointly by the Kriegsmarine and Luftwaffe ever since 25 May. During the long winter the convoys had proceeded through the Arctic without being discovered and had brought much war materiel to the Soviet Union. The convoy was attacked for days at the end of May during storms, high seas and ice. A British 10,000 ton cruiser was sunk by a torpedo hit. A German destroyer flotilla took up the fight against the superior flotilla escort and damaged several enemy destroyers. A German destroyer suffered major damage. Two ships with a total of 12,000 tons belonging to the convoy were torpedoed by destroyers. Submarines sank a 6500-ton ammunition transport and torpedoed another ship. Bombers on 27 May sank eleven ships totaling 72,000 tons and damaged numerous other vessels. The balance of the convoy withdrew to the most northern waters that were still free from ice but were persistently pursued by the German air and naval forces in spite of bad weather. For the first time in human history the Arctic Sea had become the scene of major battles.

Heated fighting also took place during the second half of May in the southernmost part of Russia. The battle on the Isthmus of Kerch ended with the destruction of the Russian forces which had been surrounded there. The pursuit of the beaten enemy went on without respite. The town and harbor of Kerch fell into German hands on 16 May. The balance of the Soviet forces northeast of the town were narrowly pressed together on the eastern tip of the peninsula and were annihilated during the following days. Russian forces fleeing across the Kerch Strait suffered large losses through air attacks. A spirited struggle for the fortress of Sevastopol went on for many weeks. The attack of the German and Rumanian forces against this strong point made gradual progress in spite of bitter resistance and great terrain difficulties. Tenaciously defended heights and fortifications were taken in stiff fighting. On 19 July the attacking forces stormed in bitter hand to hand fighting the main works in the northern part of the strong fortification system and approached the entrance of the harbor to within efficient range of the guns. That brought the decision. The annihilation of the still resisting remnants of the enemy made daily progress. On 1 July the Wehrmacht communiqué could announce that Sevastopol had fallen. After a twenty-five day struggle the resistance of the strong land and naval fortress had been overcome. On 5 July 1942 the battle for the Crimea ended.

A large battle of encirclement had developed in the Kharkov area in the second half of May. A Soviet attack with strong forces on 12 May had broken down under heavy enemy losses. The German counter-attack began on 17 May resulting in the encirclement of three Soviet armies. All attempts of the Russians at breaking out south of Kharkov were frustrated and heavy losses were suffered. On 30 May the Wehrmacht communiqué announced that the great battle for Kharkov had ended. Rumanian, Italian, Hungarian, Croatian and Slovak units had fought side by side with the German troops and shared in the victory.

In the swampy Volkhov area too, forces of Army Group North brought a battle to a victorious conclusion at the end of June, which was followed by the Finns with particular interest. Strong Soviet forces, pushing north of Lake Ilmen across the frozen Volkhov River, had succeeded in February 1942 in making a deep penetration into the German defense front. After bitter fighting for months under difficult weather and terrain conditions, these Russian forces were first of all cut off from their rear communications, then slowly pressed together and finally annihilated on 26 June. A large-scale breakthrough offensive of the Red Army across the Volkhov with the object of relieving Leningrad had thereby been frustrated and developed into a great Russian defeat.

News of a victory also came from North Africa. On 2 June, German and Italian forces under the command of General Rommel took the fortress of Turku, which was defended by British forces. The Axis troops pursued the beaten British in the direction of the Libyan-Egyptian frontier and capture on 30 June the fortified town of Mersa Matruh.

Thus the situation at the end of June 1942 had taken a turn for the better on all fronts. With admirable energy the winter crisis had been overcome, and the Germans and Finns looked forward with great hope to the impending offensive of the German eastern front in the summer of 1942. It seemed possible that the German forces might be sufficient to enforce a definite decision against Russia. Confidence in the power of German and the hope of bringing the war to a victorious conclusion had been strengthened again in Finland too when the second great offensive in the east began.

AOK LAPLAND was renamed Twentieth Mountain Army (AOK 20.) on 22 June by order of the OKW. A positive necessity for this change probably did not exist. It may be that the new name was given in honor of Dietl who particularly enjoyed Hitler's favor. The latter, when visiting Finland on 4 June, had promoted him General der Gebirgsjäger.

In the first half of 1942 the economic and armament assistance given the Finns by the Germans had steadily increased. The Finnish requests were dealt with, as before, through diplomatic channels (German Embassy) or through military channels (German General at Finnish Headquarters). Finnish-German commercial treaty negotiations, in reality, went on without interruption, and their results were from time to time checked by government committees. The Helsinki press proved to be very much satisfied with the results of the economic negotiations in the beginning of February. Ramsay, the leader of the Finnish delegation, expressed the same opinion when arriving at Mikkeli on 15 February together with Ambassador Schnurre in order to report to the Commander in Chief on the state of affairs. The fact that further German supplies were granted the Finnish III Corps after its replacement by German troops had been ordered was also to be considered a generous move on the part of the OKW.

The harbor installations at Oulu were not sufficient to serve as a supply base for the German troops in Lapland. The OKH, therefore, planned to extend them, and the Finnish Government agreed on 30 March. The rather high cost was assumed by the German Reich.

New negotiations took place on 5 May at Helsinki concerning Finnish wishes for the supply of war materiel. The Finns were again represented by General Grandell, the Germans by General Becker, Chief of the Wehrmacht Economic and Armaments Office, who had come to Helsinki with Colonel Radtke, his Chief of Staff. The German General at Finnish Headquarters was as usual represented by Kapitän zur See Koch.

On 20 May renewed Finnish-German economic negotiations took place on the subject of the good-sized Finnish requests for motor vehicles, fuel and leather. Naturally, as the duration of the war increased, the German partner had more and more difficulties in fulfilling all the wishes of the Finnish brother-in-arms, particularly in regard to certain scarce items, where even German requirements could only be met to a limited extent. That applied to trucks, which were again and again included in the Finnish list of wishes. Probably all countries participating in World War II experienced equally the fact that the requirements of the war machine were growing faster than production could satisfy them. Although the latter was increased by all available means, it lagged behind the steadily growing war consumption. At any rate, the Finnish newspapers expressed their satisfaction again around 12 June with regard to the result of the Finnish-German economic negotiations.

On 23 May an old wish of the Finnish Ministry of Defense found its fulfillment by the conclusion of a German-Finnish agreement regulating the reimbursement for use of the Finnish signal communication system and hospital installations by the Germans, and fixing a lump sum to be paid the railroad for German transports according to the Finnish requests. The agreement on the use of Finnish communications was supplemented by a request of the Finns on 15 October 1942 by which the German liability was made retroactive.

In order to improve the rear communications in the Kiestinki sector, the construction of a field railroad from Hyrynsalmi by way of Kianta to Taivalkoski was ordered. The construction was carried out by German labor forces and with German material. In the course of construction, the technical difficulties of the project were discovered to have been considerably underestimated by the engineers with a consequent great delay in finishing the project.

The beginning of the summer brought some change in the chain of command and organization of the Finnish-German front.

On 2 July, General Engelbrecht, former commander of the 163rd Division, left Finland on another assignment. For the time being, the division remained under the command of Colonel Wachsmith, the senior regimental commander.

On 3 July the German XVIII Mountain Corps (General Boehme), which had arrived in the meantime, took over responsibility on the Kiestinki front sector from the Finnish III Corps. Simultaneously the new border between the Finnish Army and the Twentieth Mountain Army north of Uhtua came into being.

The front sectors of the German Lapland Army were occupied as of July 1942 as follows:

Louhi sector:	XVIII Mountain Corps Headquarters with the 7th Mountain Division and SS Division Nord in the area between Lake Top and Lake Kovi. Corps Headquarters at Kanainen.
Kandalaksha sector:	XXXVI Corps Headquarters with the 163rd and 169th Divisions. Corps Headquarters at Alakurtti.
Murmansk sector:	XIX Mountain Corps Headquarters

with the 2nd and 6th Mountain
Divisions. Corps Headquarters at
Parkhina.

GHQ troops assigned to Army Headquarters:
 388th Infantry Regiment
 93rd Infantry Regiment
 4th Machine Gun Battalion
 13th Machine Gun Battalion
 67th Bicycle Battalion
 12 Army coastal batteries and a few coastal naval units.
 5 Finnish frontier guard light infantry battalions (of which only
  the independent Petsamo Battalion remained with the
  German Army in Spring 1943)
Corps troops:
 Signal battalion
 Engineer battalion
 2 construction battalions

Added to the above forces between autumn 1942 and spring 1943
were the following units:
 210th Infantry Division (consisting of five fortress infantry
  battalions)
 503rd Luftwaffe Field Regiment
 Staff of Division Group Petsamo
 139th Mountain Infantry Regiment (left behind by the 3rd
  Mountain Division).
 Naval Commander Kirkenes with about eight naval coastal
  batteries

The two mountain divisions were stationed on the inland front (2nd to
the right, 6th to the left) and on the coast the two coastal divisions
(Division Group Petsamo to the right, 210th Division to the left). The
latter adjoined the 230th Division of Army Group Norway.

The XIX Mountain Corps had the following missions: Protection of
Kolosyoki (nickel mines), securing the Arctic Highway, protection of the
Arctic coast. The XIX Mountain Corps was supplied only by way of
Kirkenes.

The German Lapland Army's front extended on land over 650
kilometers, along the coast of the Arctic (as far as Gamvik which lay on
28° longitude) about 600 kilometers.

Between the XXXVI and XIX Corps was a gap in the front about
300 kilometers long.

The strength and composition of the Luftwaffe changed a great deal. The command post of Luftflotte 5 was at Oulu and Kemi. From 1943 on there was a Commanding General of the Luftwaffe in Finland.

Four airfields were in the area of the XIX Mountain Corps (Kirkenes, Luostari, Salmijärvi, Hautsi).

The heart of the whole defense positions in the Murmansk sector was the Litsa Front. The positions in this sector consisted of a chain of individual bases with all-round defense. The meshes of the strong point system along the security front were much wider. To the south it extended in a thin line (scattered outposts). In the southernmost sector, the Finnish Petsamo Battalion held a front about 110 kilometers wide. The rocky tundra in the north consists of open country, something intermediate between low mountains and hills. In the south the country is covered by virgin forest.

The lifeline of the Finnish Petsamo Battalion passed through the small town of Ivalo, from where the Finns build a 120 kilometer long road along the Lutto brook to the security front.

The coastal front along the Arctic Sea extended from Kutovaya Bay on the eastern shore of Ribachi Peninsula to Gamvik (that is almost to the North Cape).

The purpose of the front was to secure the German convoy traffic to Kirkenes and Liinahamari and to protect the Luftwaffe base from which Anglo-American convoys were attacked. Furthermore, it aimed at protecting the rear of the inland front against enemy landings. The main points of defense were the ports of Kirkenes and Liinahamari.

The nickel plants at Kilosyoki consisted of pits and smelting plants around Kolosyoki, of a dam and hydro-electric plant at Jäniskoski, the up-stream dam at Niskakoski and the eighty kilometer long power line.

The total supplies of the Murmansk sector include the current requirements for about 100,000 men (XIX Mountain Corps, including Luftwaffe, Kriegsmarine and Organization Todt) and, by order of Hitler, also reserve supplies for twelve months. Giant depots and cold storage plants were, therefore, erected in the Arctic Region. Cold storage boats were also stationed at Kirkenes. Finland supplied only water and firewood.

2. July – December 1942

A conference at Rovaniemi on 9 July between Generals Dietl and Erfurth on the situation at the front gave the impulse for new operational planning. The conference was occasioned by the fact that it seemed paradoxical for the Finnish and German forces between Leningrad and the Arctic coast, amounting to 500,000 men in all, to remain inactive, while the German Eastern Army fought in the interior of Russia for a second time for a final decision in the campaign. The German summer offensive of 1942 had begun in the last days of June. The point of main effort of the Germans and considerable forces of their allies was in southern Russia. No particular mission had been assigned the Finnish-German forces in the plans of the OKW.

In autumn 1942 or later, Twentieth Mountain Army had, according to the directives of the OKW, to prepare an attack against the Ribachi Peninsula. This mission did not appear worthwhile to Dietl. He also did not believe in resuming the attack against Murmansk, since he considered a stronger force necessary for an attack on the Arctic coast than could possibly be supplied there. Opinions of the OKH were divided as to whether an offensive against the Murmansk railroad offered better prospects in the Kandalaksha or in the Kiestinki sector. Dietl was in favor of attacking in the Kandalaksha sector as recommended by the Commanding General of the XXXVI Corps, whereas his Chief of Staff believed conditions in the Kiestinki sector better.

Prerequisite for a German attack, however, as Dietl saw it, was a simultaneous Finnish attack on Soroka. Mannerheim's agreement to a participation of the Finns was expected to be dependent on a previous clarification of the situation in the Leningrad area. Not until that had been done would he be able to raise the necessary forces for an attack against the Murmansk railroad. From whatever side one looked at the problem, one was caught in the vicious circle of a situation in which a free hand in the east could only be obtained after first getting a free hand in the south. Leningrad remained the key to all planning at the Finnish-German front. The forces necessary to cope with the problem of Leningrad could only be supplied by the OKW.

It was a favorable coincidence that immediately after 9 July General Jodl paid a short visit to Dietl at Rovaniemi. Dietl oriented him on the discussion with Erfurth, and Jodl was won over to the opinion of the two German generals. The result soon became apparent. On 22 July, AOK 20 received a new Führer Directive for the operation against the Murmansk railroad to be prepared under the code name LACHSFANG. The attack on Ribachi Peninsula was to be postponed for the present. The OKW agreed to Dietl's plan for an offensive in the Kandalaksha sector. It was hoped that they had a clear conception of the importance of Leningrad for any Finnish decision and that it would also consider the necessary consequences. News arriving in Finland that the Germany heavy artillery was on its way from Sevastopol to Leningrad could be interpreted in this sense. In Finland the impression reigned around 1 August that the great German summer offensive in southern Russia was advancing from success to success. According to the Wehrmacht communiqué of 31 July, the lower course of the Don River had been crossed by the Axis troops on a 250 kilometer wide front. The spearheads of the German armies stood 180 kilometers south of the Don, and the Krasnodar-Stalingrad railroad had been crossed on a wide front. Still fighting had developed in the large Don bend, since the Red Army made strong counterattacks in this area.

As foreseen, the attitude of Mannerheim toward the attack against the Murmansk railroad, which was presented to the OKW on 2 August, was strongly bound to certain prerequisites. He left no doubt that Finnish participation depended on the prior capture of Leningrad. Under this condition would the Finnish Commander in Chief make the following forces available for the operation against Soroka:

Two divisions from the Karelian Isthmus, as well as the III and XII Brigades in the Medvezhyegorsk area.

The armored division west of Lake Seg (Finnish Headquarters had begun on about 23 July to activate an armored division.

Further two divisions from the Karelian Isthmus and the 14th Division in the Rukajärvi area.

The two divisions which were present at the Maaselkä front (1st and 4th Divisions) were to follow as second waves and support the attack.

It may be assumed that if Mannerheim's operation plan had been carried out, it would have been a complete success. The operation was well planned and was to be launched with strong forces from two fronts. If the Russians at the same time were strongly attacked in the Kandalaksha sector, which would prevent them from reinforcing their defense forces at Soroka, the Finnish thrust might have reached the important railroad junction of Soroka and the shore of the White Sea. But the employment of forces planned by Mannerheim makes it quite clear that he expected to relieve four divisions, that is to say, almost the entire forces on the Karelian Isthmus, by the elimination of the enemy in the Leningrad sector. Such a situation could naturally only arise if Leningrad were actually in German hands so that occupation of the Karelian Isthmus by the Finns would have become superfluous.

On 15 August, General Talvela, Finnish General at German Headquarters, reported the German viewpoint with regard to Operation LACHSFANG to Mannerheim at Mikkeli. The answer ran as follows:

1. The occupation of Leningrad requested by the Finnish Marshal will be carried out and prepared by the OKH

2. Participate of the Luftwaffe in the Finnish attack on Soroka, as desired by Mannerheim, is granted by the OKW.

3. The Finnish demands for fuel (which were considerable) for Operation LACHSFANG are likewise granted.

4. If Mannerheim insists upon an advance of Army Group North south of Lake Ladoga eastwards to a point south of Lake Onega prior to the offensive on the Murmansk railroad, the entire Operation LACHSFANG will have to be cancelled. In this case the promised 5th Mountain Division will not be brought forward to the Twentieth Mountain Army but will be committed before Leningrad in the sector of Army Group North.

Like a skilled fencer, Mannerheim, obliged to make a clear decision by paragraph four of the German reply, evaded a precise written answer and ordered his Chief of Staff to discuss the matter verbally. General Heinrichs went by plane on 24 August together with General Talvela to the German OKH and by his explanations, removed the difficulties which had arisen in the German-Finnish discussions.

When Heinrichs returned to Finland, LACHSFANG seemed to be getting on well. But fate had decided otherwise. The situation in the sector of Army Group North became more unfavorable. On 30 August, the OKW was forced to inform Finnish Headquarters that Operation LACHSFANG would have to be postponed. Moreover, the German High Command requested immediate cooperation of the Finnish Army in the attack on Leningrad (code name NORDLICHT). A witness of the Finnish-German negotiations in the summer of 1941 concerning a joint attack on Leningrad was surprised that a new attempt was made to obtain Mannerheim's assent. A change in the standpoint of Mannerheim and the Finnish government was out of the question. It was, therefore, to be expected that negotiations with the Finnish brother-in-arms would make no headway.

Nevertheless Mannerheim did not flatly decline Finnish participation in Operation NORDLICHT in his answer of 4 September 1942, which was as usual couched in polite terms. He pointed out, however, that the capacity of the Finnish Army was only a limited one. Finnish forces would not be released until Operation NORDLICHT had been successfully carried out – which brought matters back to where they started from. The capture of Leningrad (through German forces) remained the Alpha and Omega of all Finnish planning. The course of events in Russia did not favor the Finnish wishes. At the end of August it became clear that in spite of great initial successes the German offensive in southern Russia in the summer of 1942 was not going to bring about the decision and that the Red Army had retained its maneuverability to strike a counterblow. It is true that the German attack in southern Russia had made astonishing progress and that the German occupation had attained its broadest expansion of the war. The main objective of the entire offensive had not been achieved, however, the destruction of the Red Army, the vital strength of the Soviet Union. In contrast to its behavior in the summer of

1941, the Russian Army avoided all encirclements, thus saving most of its personnel at least.

Finnish Headquarters followed with close attention the dramatic course of events on the eastern front in the summer of 1942.

On 4 August the German eastern army reached the Kuban River east of the Sea of Azov. German and Rumanian troops advanced further to the east between the Sal and Don Rivers. Continual attacks of the Red Army in the large Don bend were repulsed. The Luftwaffe uninterruptedly attacked the enemy who withdrew to the Caucasus Mountains and bombed Russian railroad transport installation with disastrous effect. In the Rzhev area, on the other hand, the Russians extended their attacks, carried out with strong forces, to other sectors of the front and engaged the German Army in heavy defense operations which involved larger and larger areas.

On 9 August the German, Rumanian, and Slovak troops reached the northern slopes of the Caucasus on a 400 kilometer wide front. Krasnodar, capital of the Kuban region, and Maykop, center of the oil district on the northern fringe of the Caucasus, were taken by storm. The Wehrmacht communiqué reported on 12 August that a Soviet army had been surrounded and destroyed by forces of General Paulus in the great Don bend west of Kalach.

Between the Volga and Don the German attack made further headway, and fighting became more severe in the Voronezh area. The heavy defensive battle at Rzhev continued with alternating success. While in southern Russia the German troops penetrated further into the Caucasus and advanced toward the Volga, fighting in the central sector of the German eastern front had developed into heavy defensive actions in the second half of August. It was quite obvious that the initiative was in Russian hands in this region. The Red Army proved in the battles of Voronezh, east of Vyazma, and at Rzhev an opponent to be taken seriously. Also southeast of Lake Ilmen and at the Volkhov front the Russians uninterruptedly and vehemently attacked the German front.

By the end of August the situation in Russia more or less found the Germans and their allies in the Caucasus area making slow progress in bitter fighting in the mountains.

Northwest and south of Leningrad, the attack of the German divisions, which had crossed the Don, gained further ground in spite of desperate Soviet defense. Russian resistance and counterattacks continually increased in force. Strong Russian counterattacks at Kaluga and Medyn failed, while seesaw fighting still went on at Rzhev. Local fighting southeast of Lake Ilmen flared up again. Repeated breakout attempts of the Russians from Leningrad were frustrated.

At the end of August a large-scale offensive of the Red Army began south of Lake Ladoga, which was followed with close attention in Finland. From now on the situation in the sector of Army Group North worsened from week to week, and the events south of Leningrad made all former discussions about NORDLICHT and LACHSFANG appear nebulous. To Finnish ears it sounded suspicious when the OKW announced on 17 September that four German divisions, which had been earmarked for Operation NORDLICHT, could not be brought forward to the assembly area southwest of Leningrad but had been wheeled to the so-called bottleneck. The bottleneck was that part of the front of Army Group North, which like a narrow wedge extended southeast of Shlisselburg to Lake Ladoga and cut off the Leningrad area southeast of the town on the land side. This wedge, which was threatened by the Russians from both east and west, had become critically narrow. The Russians attacked it on 27 August 1942 and the following days in the area between Lake Ladoga and the Mga-Leningrad railroad from the east, and as of 8 September 1942 from the direction of the Neva. If it were intended to maintain the encirclement of Leningrad, this vulnerable bottleneck had to be held against all attacks and widened if possible. That, however, was not achieved since the Russian endeavors aimed at nibbling away at the positions and preparing the bottleneck for storming. In the September and October battles south of Lake Ladoga the Germans did not succeed in improving the positions encircling Leningrad in the southeast.

In a counteroffensive lasting from 29 September until 15 October the Germans regained their old positions, but later on bad weather upset the operational plans. The short northern summer drew near its end, and an offensive at the Finnish-German front in 1942 became more and more unlikely. After the experience of the previous year, the OKW was reluctant to undertake an offensive in the northern regions which would extend into the bad weather season. By order of the OKW on 7 October, the Twentieth Mountain Army was to pass over entirely to the defensive and the plan to capture Ribachi Peninsula was also dropped. The preparations for Operation NORDLICHT, however, were continued on a modest scale. The laying of a new cable line between Helsinki and the Eleventh Army Headquarters was approved by the OKW for instance. The Eleventh Army Headquarters coming from the Crimea had arrived before Leningrad and had been committed on the left wing of Army Group North, attached directly to the OKH. The top level command intended to place Field Marshal von Manstein in command of Operation NORDLICHT. Manstein had a wide reputation after his victorious campaign in the Crimea.

The German General at Finnish Headquarters contacted him in order to gain clarification on the state of affairs. On 12 October the disappointing answer came from Manstein to Mikkeli that the attack on Leningrad would be definitely postponed. He was, however, considering a more narrow encirclement of Leningrad for which limited Finnish participation was desirable. General Heinrichs, however, who was taken into the confidence of the German General at Finnish Headquarters, was disinclined to accept this plan. He drew attention to the "solemn promise," which the Finnish government at the hour of birth of the Finnish state had given the capitals of Europe and the United States to the effect that no inconvenience should ever be cause the Russian capital by the proximity of the frontier of the newly created Finnish state. Participation of the Finnish Army in Operation NORDLICHT, even in the modest form proposed by Manstein, could not be expected. In addition to the political scruples of the Finns came the deterioration of the situation at the German eastern front. The fact that the offensive of the Red Army in Russia, which had been in full swing since the middle of September, was making good progress and that the German Army had so far nowhere been able to launch an effective counterattack, all this did not remain hidden from the Finnish Government and the Finnish Headquarters, who received reports from their agencies abroad and in addition to broadcasts from foreign countries were amply supplied with news from Sweden. That naturally had a paralyzing influence on the Finnish Government's and Finnish Headquarters' intentions.

Combat activity in the central and northern sectors of the eastern front abated in consequence of the deterioration of the weather by the middle of October. The battle for Stalingrad, on the other hand, went on with undiminished force. Step by step the Germans penetrated into the town, which the Russians defended with utmost tenacity. Every inch of ground was bitterly contested in hand to hand fighting for individual blocks of houses and barricades.

The world had never before seen more obstinate fighting than at Stalingrad. The arrival of winter did not moderate the intensity of the struggle. Over and over again the Russians made counterattacks in the Stalingrad area which led to bitter battles, costly in manpower. In the last days of October, the German forces and their allies faced the attacking Russians on the entire eastern front in a long, thin line. The troops were exhausted, the materiel worn out. The dreaded Russian winter was in sight and with it the threat of a large-scale winter offensive of the Red Army. Every endeavor was made to strengthen those sectors of the front which were considered threatened, but the attempts remained unsuccessful owing to a general lack of forces and insufficient transport facilities. Since Hitler declined any withdrawal on principle and particularly for reasons of political prestige, he could not make up his mind to give up the Caucasus front in time.

In North Africa too, the situation of the Axis Powers deteriorated in autumn 1942. In the last week of October, the British began a large-scale counteroffensive at the western Egyptian border, which led to heavy fighting for the El Alamein position. The German and Italian forces were not able to hold the latter. After the positions of Army Group Africa had been broken through, the army had to retreat westwards, and this retreat to prepared positions had to be admitted in the Wehrmacht communiqué of 6 November. The British troops continued their attacks and the Axis forces were obliged to withdraw further and further westward under heavy losses. A large tank battle developed on the Libyan-Egyptian border, the result of which was a further withdrawal of the German-Italian forces. On 14 November, the fortress of Tobruk, which changed hands several times in the war, was relinquished to the British.

On 8 November, the Americans began to land on the North African coast. The report caused great alarm in Finland and apprehension in all official circles. The Allied action came as a surprise to the OKW at a critical moment and caused a decisive turn for the worse in the Axis position. The fact that the Germans would have great difficulty in taking countermeasures because of lack of operational reserves and as a result of too many improvisations was immediately felt at Finnish Headquarters.

On 30 October it was learned at Mikkeli that the OKW had sent the following message to the Twentieth Mountain Army: "The prospects for Operation LACHSFANG are getting worse. It is still intended to bring a division forward in the beginning of May 1943 which is to be employed either for Operation LACHSFANG or for strengthening the northern area, as the situation may require." The plans for a German-Finnish offensive in the Arctic region had become quite uncertain. The OKW had lost the initiative.

Finnish Headquarters in August and September 1942 had on several occasions consulted the Finnish President with regard to the offensives planned by the OKW against Soroka (LACHSFANG) and Leningrad (NORDLICHT), which however came to nothing afterwards, thus undermining Finnish faith in the Germans.

When the above-mentioned report of the OKW of 30 October arrived at Mikkeli and was discussed by General Erfurth with the Finnish Chief of Staff, General Heinrichs remarked that he would be pleased if the Finns were not put into action too early. In any case some positive result would have to develop from the negotiations, for the state of affairs in Finland required the Marshal to act in agreement with the President, and the latter would insure his own position by drawing the Prime Minister and the President of Congress into his confidence. If, however, nothing came of the whole matter, as had been the case in autumn 1942 with Operation LACHSFANG and NORDLICHT, the affair would become awkward for Finnish Headquarters.

Little indeed was left in the beginning of winter of the hopeful plans which had been discussed between the Germans and Finns ever since July 1942. South of Voronezh and on the Don southwest of Stalingrad the Soviet Russian counteroffensive developed into a serious threat to the German eastern front. It was of more than symbolic importance that the Eleventh Army Headquarters left its quarters on the southern shore of the Gulf of Finland. The new mission of Field Marshal von Manstein was not known in Finland.

By the middle of November, the situation at the front in southern Russia became critical. Like an evil omen a large-scale Russian offensive began to shake the German eastern front northwest and south of Stalingrad on 19 November. The offensive started with an attack by strongly superior forces against the Rumanian and German front in the area south of Stalingrad and on the lower Don, overrunning and routing the Rumanian Third Army. As water quickly spreads when a dike bursts and in swift succession tears down those parts of the dike which at first remained standing, so disaster quickly took hold of the neighboring fronts on the Don and Volga and tore Italian, Hungarian and also German divisions into a whirlpool of defeat. A battle of tremendous size developed in the last third of November between the Volga and Don, at Stalingrad and in the large Don bend.

The situation at the German eastern front became extremely critical since the Russians began their expected large-scale attack on 25 November on a wide front in the central sector south of Kalinin, and in the area southwest and west of Torpets. The fact that the Red Army was still capable of such great effort naturally caused anxiety to its opponent and surprised the world.

The hope that the Russian winter would bring about a decrease in combat activity did not materialize. The offensive of the Red Army went on at the same sectors of the front uninterruptedly throughout December. Fighting in the Volga-Don area increased in the second half of December to utmost intensity. Another Soviet large-scale offensive began on 12 December south of Rzhev, where the Russians tried to break through the German front by employing unusually strong infantry and armored forces.

On 21 December, the Russians succeeded in making a deep penetration into the German defense front on the Central Don, whereby the former positions were lost necessitating a withdrawal to rear positions. The battle went on with undiminished intensity. In these seesaw battles the German eastern front became more and more disrupted and lost the straightness of its frontline. The German islands of resistance, which had been bypassed by the waves of the enemy offensive, and which continued their isolated struggle, were surrounded by the Red Army and had to be supplied by the Luftwaffe. Thus Velikiye Luki became an advanced strong point whose brave garrison held its own firmly against the all-around attacks of the Russians.

In North Africa things were also going badly for the Axis Powers. Benghazi had to be evacuated on 20 November. The German-Italian forces in Cyrenaica withdrew further to the west. The Americans, who had landed in French Africa and penetrated to the east, reached the Algerian-Tunisian frontier region. Since German-Italian resistance in Tunisia was only improvised and their forces much inferior to those of the attacker, events quickly took a turn for the worse.

At this juncture, Finnish Headquarters for the first time indicated to the German General at Mikkeli its dissatisfaction with the scarcity of information given by the Germans on the events in other theaters of war. The daily communiqués of the German Attaché Branch, which were regularly forwarded to Finnish Headquarters, had become meager and meaningless and did not disclose the actual state of affairs. Place-names were hardly mentioned in the German reports so that it was practically impossible to follow the actual situation on the map. General Talvela pointed out to the German General at Finnish Headquarters in a confidential conversation on 25 November that Marshal Mannerheim would believe that the concealment of obvious failures was a sign of a lack of confidence that would hurt him. He added that General Paulus' Sixth Army at Stalingrad was as good as encircled. This had, however, been concealed in the reports of the German Attaché Branch, a procedure with was out of place when dealing with the Commander in Chief of an allied power. Full confidence ought to have been placed in him. If Mannerheim received personal orientation, one could rely upon it that he would treat it in strict confidence. This complaint of General Talvela was repeated by General Heinrichs in a later conversation with General Erfurth. The Finnish Chief of Staff said as follows:

"For the first time in this war we are obliged to pin our flags onto he maps according to the announcements of the Russian radio. Today the Minister of Communications was here who said that at Helsinki everybody listens in to Stockholm in order to hear the Russian news broadcast. Place yourself into the difficult position of the Marshal. He is to cheer up and encourage the members of the government and must admit at the same time that he has no definite information."

In early December the OKW sent word that it expected a landing of Allied forces in Norway between Trondheim and Narvik simultaneously with a Russian offensive in the Finnish northern region, that it had, therefore, ordered a strengthening of the defense forces in the area of the Twentieth Mountain Army (reactivation of a Luftwaffe field division, transfer of a police regiment, perhaps later on of the 28th Light Infantry Division). It appeared unlikely that the Anglo-Americans had enough shipping space available to attempt another major landing in the north of Europe soon after the landing in North Africa. Perhaps the repeated news of intended landings in Scandinavia had been spread in 1942 with the purpose of misleading Germany and of concealing the actual landing intentions on the African coast.

The OKW announcement was followed by negotiations with Finnish Headquarters with regard to the port of debarkation of the German reinforcements to be sent from Tallinn to Finland. The German transportation authorities desired debarkation at Helsinki in order to use the shortest sea route, but Marshal Mannerheim declined in agreement with the Finnish Government that Helsinki be used for the transshipment of German forces. The reasons offered for the Finnish attitude were the increased air danger through the passage of German troops and men on leave through Helsinki, for which none of the Finnish authorities wanted to be responsible. The last air attacks on Helsinki had taken place on 23 November, and Finnish precaution, therefore, seemed justified. An agreement was finally reached to drop Helsinki and Tallinn as transshipment ports and to transfer the transportation of troops and men on leave from Tallinn to Ventspils, Liepaja and Danzig, with Hangö as destination for troops and Turku port of shipment for men on leave. The Finns wished to keep Helsinki entirely free of German soldiers on leave. Extensive barracks were erected at Hangö as temporary quarters for the arriving Wehrmacht personnel who could not be transferred at once. When the port of Turku froze over in January 1943, the entire furlough traffic of the Twentieth Army was also directed by way of Hangö.

Summer at the Finnish-German front between the Gulf of Finland and the Arctic Sea had passed quietly, in contrast to the German eastern front which was a scene of uninterrupted, heavy fighting from the end of June onward. Only at isolated places had fighting occurred, which, however, in comparison to the giant battles in the Russian area was of no importance at all.

This also referred to the employment of the forces of the German Navy and Luftwaffe on Lake Ladoga. Though its success was limited, Operation KLABOUTERMANN deserves to be remembered in history. It will remain a unique, memorable event in Finnish history that German and Italian barges and boats conducted wartime operations on the wide surface of Lake Ladoga in summer 1942. As had become obvious during the discussion of the operation at Finnish Headquarters on 14 June, two operations of the Kriegsmarine and Luftwaffe went parallel to one another without being correlated as to time, nor was it possible during the whole operation to procure a uniform control. Finnish Headquarters did not feel responsible for KLABOUTERMANN and remained reserved with regard to the tactical employment of the boats. It had not been consulted by the agencies concerned when the plan was made and restricted its activity now to placing all necessary Finnish installations generously at the disposal of the foreigners. By order of Finnish Headquarters, Colonel Järvinen, Commander of the Coast Protection Brigade Ladoga, took over the role of host at Sortanlahti. The boats and landing craft had been brought to Lake Ladoga under great difficulties but with the energetic support of the Finnish authorities. Their base was first at Sortanlahti, later at Lahdenpohja. The over-all purpose of the operation was to interrupt the Russian supply service across the southern part of Lake Ladoga, but opinions on how to accomplish this were at variance. Both the Kriegsmarine and Luftwaffe claimed command of all boats and landing craft participating in the operations. Since no agreement could be reached it was inevitable that they worked parallel to each other, which proved harmful. When the Siebel landing craft were ready for employment on 1 August, the German E-Boats and Italian Mas boats had roamed about on Lake Ladoga for four weeks, drawing the attention of the Russians toward Lahdenpohja, which had been made the base of the landing craft. Before even the first Siebel landing craft had been launched, the town, therefore, was made the target of frequent Russian air attacks.

Besides, it soon turned out that the lake was at many places too shallow and not very suitable for the boats, having many rocks directly underneath its surface. The Germans also complained that Finnish air protection was insufficient. The Finnish Air Forces, however, with their limited means were not in a position to give better fighter protection. All this contributed to a situation in which the German and Italian boats did not feel at ease in the strange, northern waters, and out of fear that they would have to pass the winter there, they began to urge their own early withdrawal. As early as 31 July an inquiry from the OKW arrived at Finnish Headquarters with regard to the withdrawal of the German and Italian boats. The Marshal of Finland, however, who had just begun to take a lively interest in the proposed Operations LACHSFANG and NORDLICHT did not agree. He considered it absurd that at the very moment when the long announced but always postponed attack on Leningrad was about to materialize one should let an opportunity slip by to exert additional pressure on the city. In a decisive battle for Leningrad, the interruption of the Russian supply lines from Nova Ladoga to

Leningrad would have been especially important. Mannerheim's answer resulted in the silencing of the crews' desire to return home. At the end of September the wish of the landing craft to return as soon as possible was again introduced by the Commander in Chief of the Luftwaffe. Simultaneously it was learnt at Finnish Headquarters that the crews were busy making preparations for their departure.

The Marshal, who at that time did not cherish any particular hopes as to the outcome of Operation NORDLICHT, agreed on 29 September to the withdrawal of the foreign boats on Lake Ladoga but proposed at the same time to purchase some of the Siebel landing craft and naval boats for the Finnish Armed Forces. That made negotiations necessary delaying the withdrawal of the boats for a few weeks.

On 22 October, Finnish Headquarters were surprised by the news of a major engagement on Lake Ladoga. Before leaving, the German boats had decided to strike a last blow at the Russian supply lines across the southern tip of the lake. At dawn they had made a surprise attack across Lake Ladoga in spite of unfavorable weather conditions. The objective was the Sucho lighthouse (Sumskaya in Russian) northwest of Nova Ladoga. In spite of considerable losses the attacking boats succeeded in landing forces and in blowing up the lighthouse. On their way back the boats were attacked by the Red Air Force causing further losses. Damage at Sucho appears to have been small and to have been soon repaired by the Russians. The losses were not quite in proportion to the successes obtained, but the daring spirit of the German crews did not fail to impress the Finns. The Marshal who as an old cavalryman appreciated knightly heroism and boldness sent a congratulatory telegram and paid a visit to the German units at their base.

After the injuries and damages suffered in the attack on Sucho had been cared for and repaired, and after the sale negotiations had been concluded, the boats returning to Germany were withdrawn from Lake Ladoga on 6 November. The reports on the experiences of the boats were written in a reserved tone. A renewal of the operation in summer 1943 was not recommended by any German agency, nor did the Finns file any such request.

A new kind of warfare characteristic of our age was the guerrilla warfare aimed against the occupation forces in the rear operational areas by partisan bands frequently of considerable size. This kind of warfare was hardly found in World War I. At that time there was no possibility of dropping forces behind the enemy front and of supplying them from the air. Besides, no radio system had yet been established to give instructions to the partisan bands and to incite the population in the occupied territory to resist the enemy. The possibility of conducting warfare in the rear of the enemy field army was only created by modern technology. The result in World War II was partisan warfare which developed in all countries of Europe and particularly in the rear of the German Eastern Army. There is no doubt that it exercised a pernicious influence on the conduct of war and sharpened attack and defense methods.

In Finland in the first year of war, there was as yet no partisan warfare in the rear area. There was no underground movement on the part of the population which could have served as a source of strength for partisan warfare. The border population on this side of the Finnish frontier supported the Finnish forces in every respect in this fight against guerrillas. On the other side of the border, in the Karelian Isthmus and in East Karelia, the Russians had evacuated most of the civil population in their withdrawal in the summer of 1941. Only in more densely populated areas, as for instance Petrozavodsk and the villages around Lake Tulama, did the population slowly reappear after the tidal wave of war had rolled over them. In the summer of 1941 now and then individual groups of dispersed Russians were discovered in the lonesome forest areas of Karelia, who had lost contact with their units during the retreat of the Red Army and had hidden in the woods. Forced by hunger they gradually reappeared and were easily arrested and disarmed. These remnants of the battered Russian front, who were called "forest Russians" by the Finns, were rather harmless and required no special defensive measures.

The situation changed, however, in summer 1942, when real partisans to an increasing extent harassed the rear of the Twentieth Army, particularly in the Salla area, that is to say bands who were sent over by the Russian to the Finns with a certain combat mission, and who not only suddenly fell upon the Finnish-German outposts but also harassed the Finnish border population. Since the flanks in the Kandalaksha sector had no contact with adjacent units, the Russian partisans were able to bypass the flanks of the XXXVI Corps and penetrate into the border area, occasionally even as far as the Arctic coast. The population was kept in a state of unrest by the guerrilla nuisance, and traffic behind the front was made difficult, so that defense measures had to be taken. The XXXVI Corps tried as far as possible to prevent enemy raiding parties from penetrating around its wings into the rear territory. Special mobile companies or battalions were advanced for that purpose beyond the wings of the front into the trackless wilderness on the border, where they carried on mobile guerrilla warfare and tried to cut off the return route of the partisans. That was difficult in summer but easier in winter after the first snow had fallen.

The Finnish border police and "Sissi" (raider) battalions were particularly suited for this kind of border warfare and very much appreciated by their German brothers-in-arms. They consisted of settlers, lumbermen, hunters, trappers and reindeer breeders living on lonely farms along the Finnish eastern border and were far superior to the German soldiers in this kind of warfare. Nothing escaped their ears. With unswerving instinct they noticed every noise, every movement, every footprint in the forests and swamps and as successfully detected the partisans as hunting dogs smell out game. The German commanders were aware of the excellent assistance the Finnish Sissi battalions gave to them and tried to retain them in their command area. General Dietl, who himself was an expert hunter, an experienced mountaineer and a passionate skier, was particularly fond of this excellent force and wrestled tenaciously for months with Field Marshal Mannerheim for the four battalions which after the relief of the Finnish III Corps had been left behind in the Twentieth Mountain Army sector.

The growing pressure on the Finnish people found its expression in the directives issued by the government and headquarters in the second half of 1942 with regard to questions of organization and economy. The underlying idea was to create a situation in which the country could carry on to the end even in case of a protracted war. The dream of a short war, which a large proportion of the Finnish people had had in the summer of 1941, had vanished. In the second year of the war, most Finns willingly carried the heavy burden of war with true Finnish realism and a strong sense of duty.

The Finnish economy suffered as it always had from lack of a labor force. The older age classes, which had been dismissed in the preceding winter, did not bring the relief hoped for. Many of them had not returned to their old places of employment but had migrated to the north to find employment through the agencies of the Wehrmacht. Though care had been taken that the German agencies did not pay higher wages than the Finns, many a released veteran was lured by the Wehrmacht food and agreeable working conditions. Owing to this fact, a conference took place at Rovaniemi on 10 July 1942 between the German General at Finnish Headquarters and Hillilä, the Governor of Lapland, in order to discuss the request of the Finnish Government to reduce to 3,500 the estimated 10,000 Finnish laborers in German service.

An agreement was reached to call together a labor conference consisting of interested Finnish and German parties at Rovaniemi from time to time to examine labor questions with due regard to the requirements of the Finnish economy. General Erfurth promised that the German agencies would act in accordance with the decisions of the labor conference. This he was able to do because the necessary power had been given him through a directive of the OKW of the previous winter authorizing him to protect the Finnish economy against the demands of the Wehrmacht.

A steady cause of concern for the government and congress of Finland during the war was to find the most economic expenditure of public funds. In order not to let the Finnish finances get into disorder in spite of the long duration of the war, the ministries endeavored to get back from the German brother-in-arms any expenses made on their account. Thus the Ministry of Defense filed on 5 August 1942 extensive demands with the German General with regard to wages and other expenses made in the interest of the Wehrmacht (maintenance of roads, fortification works, rental of real estate).

On 6 August a Finnish law was issued in agreement with the German authorities dealing with the sale of goods to German soldiers. Though the purchasing power of the German soldiers in Finland had on request of the Finnish Government been restricted by the fact that only a fraction of their pay was in Finnish currency, the danger nevertheless existed that the interest of the population would be injured by purchases on the part of the Wehrmacht. In order to avoid a complete clearance of the goods still left in Finnish stores, most articles were rationed by the law of 6 August. The German soldier needed a purchase permit issued by the Liaison Branch of the Finnish Ministry of Defense. Only a few articles, of which there was an abundant stock, could be freely sold (for instance writing paper, wood carvings and so forth).

During the economic negotiations in October 1942 in Berlin the Finns announced their intention of withdrawing from the Bushenhagen-Kredit (named after *Oberst* Buschenhagen, the German negotiator in 1941). This credit of 300,000,000 Finnmarks monthly had been granted by the Finnish Government to the Reich in the beginning of the war for the pay and wages of the occupation forces to be charged in account against the demands of the Reich resulting from the Finnish-German commercial treaty.

After expiration of the Buschenhagen-Kredit, the Wehrmacht Economic Representative had to apply to the German Minister of Economics for the Finnmarks required to pay the German troops in Finland, who made the amount available from funds of the Finnish – German commercial treaty.

In the Berlin economic negotiations of October 1942 an important concession had been made to the Finnish delegation, that the Finnish population would in future get the same bread ration as the German. The slogan that the German people would share its last crust of bread with the Finnish people was coined at that time.

On 12 November, new Finnish economic demands were set forth. Mannerheim addressed a letter directly to Adolf Hitler on account of coal shipments from Germany, which had been delayed owing to air attacks on the mining districts and lack of transportation. Hitler decided in favor of the Finnish demands and against the German Center for Coal Distribution, which created the impression in German circles that the Finns could obtain everything from Hitler. Thus the atmosphere of the Finnish-German economic negotiations was influenced in favor of the Finns. The Finnish brothers-in-arms were highly respected everywhere in Germany and their performance for the common cause honestly appreciated.

In the last ten days of November 1942 Helsinki was repeatedly attacked from the air. The Finnish air defenses again proved inadequate. The Finnish antiaircraft artillery was unable to reach high flying enemy planes, and range finding was insufficient in view of the increasing speed of the Russian planes. Mannerheim, therefore, ordered the Finnish General at German Headquarters to use his influence in inducing the Commander in Chief of the Luftwaffe to make the most modern German antiaircraft equipment available for better protection of the capital and the Malmi airdrome, that is to say Messerschmitt planes, radar, and 105mm antiaircraft artillery. The granting of this request was expected to meet with great difficulties, since Germany was at that time already exposed to heavy air attacks and urgently needed the whole German production for the protection of its own population.

A proof of the fact that hopes for a favorable outcome of the war had been shaken in Finland was the Marshal's commission on 5 December to General Isakson, who had returned to Finnish Headquarters as general on special assignment, to examine the military administration in East Karelia and see that investments in the occupied territory would serve only present and not postwar purposes.

After the spring offensive on the Svir, at Kiestinki and the Arctic coast had been repulsed, the Finnish-German front remained very quiet. Days passed without a shot being fired. Fortifications and positions were everywhere improved. The great skill of the Finns in handling axe and saw aided the erection of livable quarters. Wooden houses, some of which were very attractive, saunas and other installations were built, making life at the front bearable and even comfortable. For example the Finnish "Korssu style" even satisfied artistic demands and was employed for the following construction: quarters of the Staff of the 18th Division on the Karelian Isthmus near the Gulf of Finland, the VI Corps Headquarters at Nurmoila, Headquarters of the 17th Division on the Svir front, the camp of GeneralÖsch at Kolatselkä, quarters of the staff of 14th Division at Rukajärvi, and of the III Corps Headquarters at Suomussalmi. This enumeration could be extended by many other examples, and these sites recall to all war participants the true Finnish soldierly spirit, comradeship, orderliness and cleanliness.

Morale at the Finnish front considerably improved after the winter of 1941/42. The older age classes were withdrawn from the front, dismissed or given home leave. Leave was arranged by a general settlement in such a way that all soldiers could return to their families for a few days every three months. This also had a favorable effect on Finnish economic life since the businessmen among the soldiers could look after their affairs during leave. How much worse off was the German soldier, whose mail communication with Germany required very much time or did not function at all as shipping discontinued in winter, and whose turn to go on leave came only after seventeen to eighteen months.

Though the whole front was very quiet after the Russian spring offensive, the regularly occurring casualties, whether dead, wounded or sick, were excessively high[24]. Mannerheim, who had the fate of his soldiers at heart and received a daily report on the casualties, particularly after major engagements, was very much concerned about the steady decline of the Finnish Army's fighting power and pondered a way how to reduce the high losses at the front. As former president of the Finnish Red Cross, he was particularly interested in hospitals and often visited the wounded himself or received the reports of Generals Wetzer, Wilkama and Admiral Bonsdorff on their impressions in the hospitals and the morale of the wounded, to whom they brought by order of Marshal Mannerheim the medal to the Finnish Cross of Liberty.

On 5 September half of the 1924 age class was called to arms for 15 October. The deadline was later postponed to 27 October. The Marshal altered his decision with regard to the transformation of Finnish divisions into brigades. It was doubtful whether brigades were indeed superior to divisions and the reorganization came to a halt. Headquarters decided on 21 September to remerge the 12th Infantry Regiment returning from the Kiestinki sector with the 12th Brigade in order to revive the former 6th Division, but the execution of this plan was delayed. The 12th Regiment remained for a few months at Kajaani and was not transferred to the area south of Medvezhyegorsk until 24 January, where it was again merged with the 12th Brigade into the 6th Division. The Finnish officers' corps had a considerable increase at the end of 1942, since more than 700 new officers were graduated from the officer candidate schools at Santahamina and Niinisalo and sent to the front. These young officers represented the elite of the Finnish armed forces and did their part in raising the morale of the Finnish Army.

Important changes took place in the Wehrmacht in the period dealt with above. The resignation of *Generaloberst* Halder became known in

---

[24] The Finnish losses in the Third War of Liberation as of 30 September 1942: 32,303 dead, 82,282 wounded, 3,390 missing.

Finland on 24 September. His place as Chief of Staff was taken by General Zeitzler, who was a complete stranger to the Finns. The resignation of Halder came as a surprise to the Finns and caused general regret at Finnish Headquarters. After the sudden resignation of Field Marshal von Brauchitsch in December 1941 and repeated changes in the high level command at the German eastern front in the course of summer 1942, the removal of Halder, which had a direct connection with the outcome of the German offensive in the summer of 1942, was much discussed by the Finns.

The German Liaison Staff North attached to Finnish Headquarters was changed on 4 November into a Wehrmacht agency called German General at the Finnish Armed Forces High Command. The second echelon of the Liaison Staff North at Helsinki was dissolved in consequence of this reorganization. The Wehrmacht Signal Office became an independent agency but remained in service matters assigned to the German General.

The German General was given by the Wehrmacht High Command the mission of a Wehrkreis Commander in South Finland, and all German agencies in Finland outside the area of the Twentieth Mountain Army were assigned to him.

A Wehrmacht Post Headquarters was erected at Helsinki which established Wehrmacht billets near the Helsinki main railroad station for improving the care for and transit facilities of the Wehrmacht personnel coming to Helsinki.

The courses of instruction in winter warfare for German officers continued in the winter of 1942/43. The third course began on 23 November at Kankaanpä. A number of Hungarian officers also took part.

The contractual settlement of expenses made by the Finns in the interest of the Wehrmacht (maintenance of roads, fortification works, real estate rentals) had been delayed. The Finnish Minister of Defense approached the German General on 20 December and asked him to use his influence with the OKW to get an early refund of the sums advanced by the Ministry of Defense. Cooperation between the Finnish Ministry of Defense and the German General continued smoothly and agreeably.

On 1 January 1943, Colonel Roos was appointed Director General of the Finnish Railroads, while he retained his position as Chief of Transportation at Finnish Headquarters. Although the transport situation of the Finnish railroads was not as tight as in the winter of 1941/42, the demands made on the railroads could only be met with difficulty. The consolidation of the highest offices in the hands of an experienced expert like Colonel Roos guaranteed that everything possible would be done by the Finnish transportation system administration.

At the end of the year, the Arctic Sea was the scene of a naval engagement. On 31 December near Bear Island German naval forces attacked a British squadron escorting a convoy. In a battle lasting several hours, both sides suffered losses. Bad weather made observation of the result difficult.

3. January – June 1943

Finnish Headquarters received on 2 January an estimate of the situation by the Chief of the Wehrmacht Operations Staff. The report began with the unwelcome statement that a German attack on Leningrad was not possible for the time being. The OKW expected, on the contrary, an early Russian attack against the German front encircling the town in the east. Furthermore, the OKW believed it possible that toward the end of winter a decisive Russian attack would take place against the front of the Twentieth Mountain Army, probably in the sector of XIX Mountain Corps (formerly Mountain Army Norway), perhaps coupled with an Allied landing on the Arctic coast. The letter of General Jodl concluded with the remark that one SS regiment, one Luftwaffe field regiment and later on perhaps further reinforcements would be brought forward to the Twentieth Mountain Army. In spring, the Wehrmacht Operations Staff expected a Russian large-scale attack in the northern theater of war. The construction of field fortifications along the Norwegian coast was to be begun as a preventive measure. If necessary an additional division would be transferred to AOK NORWEGEN.

The expected attack against the forces encircling Leningrad actually began on 16 January. Heavy fighting developed south of Lake Ladoga. On 19 January the great misfortune happened. The Russians broke through the German positions at Shlisselburg and pierced the bottleneck. Overland communication from Leningrad to the east had thereby been reopened. An attempt of Army Group North to restore the situation south of Lake Ladoga failed since sufficient forces were not available. This bad news fell like a bombshell in Finland. The first report of this catastrophe which shattered many Finnish hopes was given out over Radio Moscow. Since the Wehrmacht report came only after a great delay, the Finnish public as at first dependent on the Russian news service which announced the Russian victory with great exaggeration. Finnish morale sank as the alarming news piled up in the first weeks of 1943, including that from other sectors of the German eastern front. The Helsinki press used to publish in the first place the original wording of the Anglo-American and Russian communiqués on the foreign theaters of war, whereby the precarious situation of the Italian-German forces in North Africa and Russia was made clear to the Finnish people. Headquarters, government and members of congress followed the development of the military situation in southern Russia with the greatest concern. Large-scale fighting had been going on there for weeks. After the unlucky outcome of the decisive battles, the armies of Germany and its allies were retreating from the Volga and Don to the Dnieper, while dark clouds hung over the fate of the German Sixth Army encircled at Stalingrad.

At the end of January the tragedy of Stalingrad entered its last phase, as strong German forces tried under hopeless conditions to avert the threatening calamity. This inevitable catastrophe of the strong German Sixth Army filled the Finns with amazement. Between the lines of the Wehrmacht communiqué one could read that the Luftwaffe was unable to supply the encircled army. The possibility of relief grew smaller and smaller and finally vanished altogether. The distress and dire need which had become the fate of the German brother-in-arms became quite obvious now to Finnish eyes and could not be belittled by German attempts at hushing up and propagandist exaggerations. A serious political crisis arose in February 1943 at Helsinki as a result of the precarious German situation at the eastern front and in North Africa. This crisis and its consequences will be dealt with in Chapter Five.

News of an impending large-scale Russian attack against the Finnish-German front had been repeatedly reported in Finland. The Commander in Chief of the 20.Geb.Armee believed these reports to be true and ordered complete preparedness of his army and close attention to be paid to possible Russian attack preparations. The blow against the Arctic front was expected in the beginning of February.

The nervous atmosphere in Helsinki was reflected in the pessimistic impression caused by a report on the situation delivered by Colonel Paasonen, Chief of the Finnish Reconnaissance Section, before members of the Finnish Congress on 9 February.

In the first half of February new reports arrived about the enemy which made the situation look still more complicated. On 8 February, the impression was gained by the 20.Geb.Armee that the Russians were withdrawing forces before the front of the German army. How could that be explained? Had the enemy given up his offensive plans?

In the meantime, the battle along the shores of Lake Ladoga continued. On 10 February the Russians resumed with fresh forces their attack against the Eighteenth Army, which was fighting in the northern sector of Army Group North, and attempted to penetrate into the German front south of Kolpino. Heavy fighting ensued at the front between Volkhov and Lake Ladoga, and before Leningrad, which continued during the next days and again and again revived during the following weeks. Marshal Mannerheim was worried lest the Russian successes south of Leningrad would increase further and threaten the security of the Finnish positions on the Karelian Isthmus. He decided on

12 February to replace the Finnish cavalry brigade which had so far protected the shore of Lake Ladoga by the rehabilitated 6th Division, and to transfer the cavalry brigade to the Karelian Isthmus east of Viipuri, to be held there at his disposal.

The insecurity about the enemy plans was increased on 19 February by rumors arriving at Finnish Headquarters about an impending Allied landing at Petsamo, which seemed to originate from American sources. Russian attack intentions, which were also reported through other channels, were, however, not confirmed by reconnaissance at the front. On the contrary, the impression gained was that the enemy had made no attack preparations whatever.

News of a Soviet war council, which was said to have taken place in January at Moscow, came to Mikkeli on 26 February. According to this report, the plan of a winter offensive in the Arctic region had been abandoned, and it had been decided to leave only indispensable forces opposite the Finnish-German front. But the report went on to speak again of an offensive of the Red Army in May with a simultaneous Anglo-American landing in Norway.

As was found out later, all reports of a landing and an offensive were wrong and disseminated by the enemy only for misleading purposes. They were repeated several times again in the course of the spring but made less impression since it became obvious that the Russians were withdrawing forces from the Arctic front.

We shall now try to answer the question of the morale of the Finnish officers in the beginning of January 1943.

In the eyes of the Finnish officers, Germany had lost tremendous prestige with the massive defeat at Stalingrad. The front officers mostly adhered with complete conviction to the German brotherhood-in-arms and in many cases felt sincere friendship for the German soldiers. Their confidence in Germany was not shaken by the unfavorable news from the eastern front, and they hoped that the German Army would survive the setbacks suffered and march on to new victories. Their judgment was more or less influenced by sentiment and they lacked insight in the actual facts. But the opinions of many officers in leading positions at Finnish Headquarters differed from that of officers at the front in view of the bitter struggle in the vastness of Russia and the unlucky course the fighting in Africa was taking. They saw with sober observation that the chances of Germany had worsened from month to month since the autumn of 1942. They admitted that the strongest forces of the time, the Anglo-American armaments potential and the manpower of the Soviet Union, had joined together and influenced the scale holding the German fate. Such were the reasons for the divergence in Finnish public opinion which became noticeable in the beginning of 1943 and not only found its expression in the pessimism of Headquarters and the optimism of the front, but also led to an increase of the opposition in congress and was reflected in the Helsinki press.

Marshal Mannerheim remained outwardly calm in this storm, but anxiety about the further development of the war and the future of Finland weighed heavily on his mind. After the die was cast at Stalingrad, he probably harbored no illusions and was prepared for an unsuccessful end of the war with his usual foresight and true Finnish realism. His remark on 4 March to General Erfurth, "I do not attack any more, I have lost too many men already," led to the conclusion that he had lost faith in another Finnish-German offensive. Obviously he did not believe that a change of the situation could be caused by Germany's reseizure of the lost initiative. He attached small importance to the noisy German propaganda which predicted new huge efforts on the part of the Reich and said to the German General at his Headquarters on 19 March 1943, "You may be sure that for each million men scraped from the bottom of the barrel in Germany there will be as many in Russia too."

Remarks from the ranks of the senior officers at Headquarters doubting the final victory increased in the spring of 1943. The development of the situation in Africa rightfully caused the Finnish officers great anxiety. The realistically thinking Finns realized early that the German-Italian forces in Tunisia fought a losing battle. Now and then remarks were made at Mikkeli that Germany would do well in employing old and experienced diplomats once again in order to find a way out of the imbroglio by diplomatic means. Confidence in Ribbentrop was not great. The antipathy felt against him at the Finnish Ministry of Foreign Affairs began to be shared by Finnish Headquarters.

The fears of the Finns were confirmed by the announcement from the Führer's Headquarters on 13 May 1943 that the heroic struggle of the German and Italian forces had come to an end, that the last groups resisting in the vicinity of Tunisia have been forced to cease fighting after having used up their entire ammunition.

Here too, lack of judgment prevented the OKW from giving up in proper time the North African theater of war, which could not be defended.

At the end of the winter of 1942/43, Mannerheim was in rather poor health. In March he contracted a serious case of pneumonia, and the small circle of persons who knew of his illness was plunged into great anxiety for the life of the irreplaceable soldier. Thanks to his tough constitution and the skill of Dr. Kalaja, his excellent doctor, Marshal Mannerheim recovered from his illness after a long confinement in bed. Seconded by President Ryti, the doctor urgently demanded a vacation in a mild climate in order that he regain his health completely. Since the beginning of the mud periods made any major Russian operation at the Finnish front seem unlikely, Mannerheim with a small escort went to Lugano, Switzerland, on 17 April 1943. During his leave, he was represented in his capacity as Commander in Chief by General Heinrichs, his Chief of Staff.

The Marshal returned to Finland in May. He had made a good recovery, and immediately on his arrival at Mikkeli he plunged again as usual into his work which filled his time from early morning till far in the night.

Calm at the Finnish-German front continued after the thaw set in. But the partisan activity in the rear of the Twentieth Mountain Army increased to an unpleasant extent. Even traffic on the Arctic Highway was at times intercepted by partisans. For instance the mail bus was attacked near Ivalo on which occasion the Bishop of Oulu lost his life. The lives of Finns or Germans travelling alone in northern Finland were no longer safe, nor were Finnish women spared who fell into partisan hands. Finnish Headquarters and the 20.Geb.Armee reflected on a way to improve matters. General Dietl proposed reinforcement of the Finnish frontier guards or evacuation of the civilian population living in the border areas to the road Kuusamo-Salla-Ivalo. Marshal Mannerheim neither approved of evacuating the border population nor of reinforcing the frontier guards, which could have been done only at the expense of the Finnish Field Army. Finnish Headquarters arrived at the decision to activate a motorized unit for the protection of the Arctic Highway. This unit was placed under the command of Colonel Villamo, the Finnish liaison officer at Rovaniemi, who was familiar with conditions in Lapland and particularly suited for this task as a long-time member of the frontier guard. In addition, arms were handed out to the Finnish border population.

Negotiations between Mikkeli and Rovaniemi concerning the withdrawal of the Finnish battalions, which after the relief of the Finnish III Corps had remained in the area of the Twentieth Mountain Army, stretched over several weeks. Both sides attached great importance to this question. The more insecurity increased in the border region, the less Dietl believed himself able to do without the Finnish battalions. Mannerheim, on the other hand, once he had set his mind to something, did not desist from it. The struggle for these battalions continued with great tenacity. Negotiations began on 11 January 1943 when General Heinrichs requested for the first time the return of the four Finnish battalions still employed at the front of the Twentieth Mountain Army. Since no headway was made and the OKW, to which the 20.Geb.Armee had turned, did not wish to annoy the Marshal of Finland in view of the steadily deteriorating situation at the front, General Erfurth at Finnish Headquarters was instructed by the OKW on 6 February to mediate between Germans and Finns with regard to the four battalions demanded back by Mannerheim.

Thereupon Mannerheim immediately increased the Finnish demands and on 7 February asked in addition for the return of the Ivalo Battalion which was employed for the protection of Petsamo. After protracted discussions about the rate and sequence of withdrawal, an agreement was reached. The Marshal agreed to the plan of the 20.Geb.Armee and made the concession that the Ivalo Battalion should for the time being remain in the German area. Mannerheim was entirely satisfied with the result of the negotiations, whereas Dietl was somewhat discontented since he looked at the matter merely from a military standpoint and felt somewhat uncomfortable at having made a bad bargain with regard to the five battalions.

A thorny question causing a wide divergence of opinion between Finns and Germans was the treatment of young Estonians who beginning in spring 1943, arrived in increasing numbers illegally in Finland. The reason why the Estonians fled from their country to Finland was to escape the military service introduced in Estonia by the German authorities. From the German point of view, these Estonians were deserters who violated German laws. The German frontier police closed the border and made illegal flight a punishable crime. The property of the deserters was confiscated. It proved impossible, however, to prevent the escape of young Estonians across the Gulf of Finland and they came to Finland in an increasing number. Soon they began to inconvenience the Finnish authorities since they refused to enter the labor service and became a burden to the Finns who had to supply them with food. General Heinrichs acquainted General Erufth with these facts on 22 April in a confidential manner.

It went without saying that the Finnish Government could not deny the fugitives the right of asylum so that a forced evacuation was out of the question. The Finns considered the Estonians blood-relations and took a lively interest in their fate. The measure and methods of the German administration in Estonia were not approved of by many Finns. Out of sympathy with the fate of the Estonian people private organizations were established in Finland whose mission it was to assist the young Estonians in escaping to Finland. The Finnish authorities kept entirely aloof but treated the whole problem with caution and reserve. General Heinrichs intimated the intention of Finnish Headquarters to send the young Estonians from Helsinki to the front. The German General did not raise any objections but pointed out that he was not competent for these matters. If there would have to be any discussion, it ought to take place between the Finnish Ministry of Foreign Affairs and the German Embassy. But apparently there seemed to be no inclination for treating the matter officially. No change took place in the actual state of affairs. The illegal entry of Estonians in Finland continued during the following months. They were not allowed to stay at Helsinki but sent to the front and organized there into an Estonian infantry regiment.

Perhaps in connection with these affairs, Finnish Headquarters expressed the wish on 17 June to establish a Finnish military agency at Tallinn. Since the Finns obviously placed great value on having this request granted and the German authorities at Tallinn raise no objections, the agency was organized under the command of a Finnish general staff officer and remained until Finland withdrew from the war.

At the suggestion of Finnish Headquarters, conditions at the boundary between the Finnish and the German forces were made the subject of discussions. The Finns proposed in order to escape other obligations that the boundary be shifted northwards (occasioned by the return of the Finnish Waffen-SS battalion, to be dealt with in Chapter Five). Twentieth Mountain Army agreed to the Finnish proposal. The new boundary chosen, through which the southern part of the German sector at Kiestinki became part of the Finnish front, was determined by the terrain. The area south of Toposero was situated outside of the Kiestinki sector, and the German XVIII Mountain Corps had difficulty in reaching it. By attaching this region to the Finnish front at Uhtua, the left wing of the Finnish Army became well anchored on the Toposero. The 7th Frontier Guards Battalion, whose reputation had made it well known to the Germans, took over on 12 July the sector from which the XVIII Mountain Corps withdrew. Negotiations about minor questions went on for a few weeks between Finnish Headquarters and the 20.Geb.Armee. Finally the boundary question was settled by direct negotiations on the spot in a way which satisfied both partners.

History will bear witness that the Finns did not slacken their efforts during the war. In the dark month of February 1943, when the fateful outcome of the battle of Stalingrad echoed in the hearts of all Finns, and when news from the North African theater of war became more and more hopeless, the responsible Finnish leaders decided to call further young Finnish men to arms. An announcement was made on 27 February that the second half of age class 1924 would be inducted by 8 March. The first half of age class 1925 was to be inducted by 12 March.

The efforts of Finnish Headquarters to improve and modernize the air protection of Helsinki with German help were crowned with success. When General Lundquist, the Commander in Chief of the Finnish Air Forces, visited German on 17 January 1943, the Commander in Chief of the Luftwaffe gave him the assurance that General Talvela's request for radar and Messerschmitt planes would be fulfilled. Moreover, he offered the Finns a number of Ju88 planes.

For Germany it became more and more difficult to satisfy Finnish demands for fuel for motor vehicles. Though the conversion of the latter to wood-gas had been speeded up, gasoline could not be dispensed with for certain categories of motor cars (for instance personnel carriers in the field). A rather large fuel demand of the Finnish Armed Forces, therefore, remained to be reckoned with in spite of utmost economy and elimination of cars with powerful motors. The OKW requested that General Erfurth in future to make proposals concerning the amount of fuel to be allotted to the Finns monthly. Allotments by the OKW were then based on these proposals. This procedure became the rule as the time went on and stood its test. The lack of trucks, on the other hand, a situation which had existed from the beginning of the war, became increasingly inconvenient. The war created tremendous wear and tear on motor vehicles and at the same time there was a very large demand for equipment for Germany's many newly activated units; Germany could scarcely meet its own requirements. The nation was, therefore, not able to fulfill the Finnish demands, which were repeatedly put forward. Actually the predicament was no so much in evidence because of the long period of trench warfare. If a major offensive had occurred at the front considerable trouble would have arisen as a result of the insufficient motor vehicles in the hands of the Finnish Armed Forces.

When the snow in North Finland had to be cleared in March 1943, for instance, the lack of heavy vehicles was seriously felt and Finnish Headquarters were not able to comply with the request made by 20.Geb.Armee on 2 March for assistance from Finnish trucks.

After Finnish Headquarters had decided to activate an armored division, Marshal Mannerheim eagerly desired to obtain modern tanks from Germany for this division and sent a request to the OKW on 1 June to let him have up to fifty Russian T-34 tanks. On 6 June he received the reply that no captured tanks were available. But in order to satisfy their brothers-in-arms as much as possible, Finland was promised thirty assault guns. Since the design of the new Sturmgeschutz (StuG) was unknown in Finland, the Finns were at first rather disappointed. Later on, however, they expressed their satisfaction at the excellent quality of the StuG, which had already been of valuable service in stemming the Soviet offensive in June and July of 1944.

The reorganization decreed on 8 June 1943 of the 6th Light Infantry Battalion for use by the Finnish Cavalry Brigade, and the activation of a special battalion for long-range reconnaissance decreed on 15 July 1943 (fourth independent battalion) assigned to the Reconnaissance Battalion at Headquarters and billeted near Mikkeli, was part of the overall reorganization which aimed at improving the quality of the Finnish Army. Finally, the return from Germany to Finland of the Finnish Volunteer

Battalion, which had belonged to the Waffen-SS, and its reincorporation in the Finnish Army took place during this period. These volunteers had won great fame when serving in the German Army and all of them were suited for employment as noncommissioned officers in the Finnish Army. The political background of this event, which in July was much discussed in Finland, will be treated in Chapter Five.

The third training course of German officers in winter warfare began before Christmas at Kankaanpä and continued in 1943 in a somewhat changed form. Simultaneously and at the same location, the first instruction course for regimental commanders and the first long distance run training course for German officers and soldiers began on 11 January 1943. They took place chiefly at Tuusola and at times on the Karelian Isthmus on account of more favorable snow conditions. Both training courses, which had been a success, were repeated after 15 March with the same training schedule The beautiful site of Tuusola and the comfortable billets in the modern defense corps training school will always remain a pleasant memory to all German participants.

In consequence of the deterioration of the situation in the most important German theaters of war (Russia and Sicily where the Allies had landed on 11 July), the Swedish Government became more reserved towards the Reich and began to reduce the concessions it had previously made. On 18 July 1943 it fixed the end of July as deadline for the entrance of German motor vehicles to Sweden for maintenance purposes and announced on 29 July its withdrawal from the transit agreement for German personnel on leave. Although both measures were of no great importance and a way out could be found, the German conduct of war in the Arctic was made more difficult by Sweden's attitude. For the 20.Geb.Armee it was inconvenient to be forced to send damaged motor vehicles to Germany, which up to that time could easily be repaired in Sweden.[25] In any case, the attitude of the Swedish Government proved that the chances of a German victory were not believed by the Swedes to be very great.

After Stalingrad and the secession of Italy, Sweden began to influence Finland to withdraw from the war.

4. July – December 1943

The situation at the Finnish-German front remained quiet. Feeble trench warfare went on between the Gulf of Finland and the Arctic Sea. Neither side made any efforts to stir up a combat activity which had completely died out. Both friend and enemy contented themselves with

---

[25] Spare parts for the repair of cars of German make were as a rule lacking in Finland.

holding their positions and improving their trenches, shelters, and routes of communications. This complete lull offered a striking contrast to the dramatic events at the German eastern front, where bitter fighting took place. In the Byelgorod area, for instance, and south of Orel a large battle developed in July 1943, when the Germans tried to cut off the protruding salient of the Russian positions around Orel (Operation ZITADELLE). After initial successes, luck went against the Germans. A strong Russian counteroffensive from the Kursk area frustrated the German attack and forced the German front to retreat from the sector in question. The battle spread to the southern front and increased in intensity. The whole German eastern front between the Sea of Azov and Byelgorod became involved, and forces were lacking to throw back enemy penetrations by making counterattacks. In consequence new and repeated withdrawals had to be made without being able to fall back on covering positions (Hitler did not allow the construction of covering positions in Russia.) so that even the gigantic rivers in Russian did not bring the Russian offensive to a standstill.

The news arriving in Finland from the Russian front revealed that the German eastern army had been bled white and that trained reinforcements were lacking to replenish the units whose combat strength had considerably diminished.

Conditions in the Russian theater of war were naturally well known to Finnish Headquarters. The Marshal of Finland received regular reports from his General at German Headquarters and the Finnish military attaches at Stockholm, Budapest, Bukarest and Ankara. General Talvela the Finnish Liaison officer to German Headquarters, was an officer of great acumen and experience in war, who often came to Mikkeli from Germany in order to report to the Marshal on his impressions at the German eastern front. The OKW granted General Talvela all facilities for inspecting the German front.

The chief of the Finnish Reconnaissance Section was Colonel Paasonen, a very intelligent officer who was exceedingly active and utilized every opportunity to obtain an intelligent and accurate picture of the situation at the German-Russian front. The Wehrmacht High Command granted General Talvela all facilities for inspecting the German front, on which he made a personal report every night to the Marshal. There can be, therefore, no doubt that the Marshal and his Headquarters had an accurate resumé of conditions at the front. Finnish judgment was perhaps too favorable and relied too much on the ability of the Third Reich to bring new forces to bear on the hope that new kinds of weapons would soon be employed. But Mannerheim watched the retrograde movement of the German eastern front with increasing anxiety, particularly the events in the sector of Army Group North. Repeated

Soviet attacks south of Lake Ladoga had been repulsed by the German defenders in July and August. Army Group North (the Eighteenth Army) had passed over to a counterattack in August and in heavy fighting frustrated the breakthrough intentions of the Russians.

On the strength of reports from Finnish sources, Finnish Headquarters believed in the beginning of September 1943 that the Germans had begun to evacuate Riga. On 10 September, General Heinrichs asked General Erfurth how things stood with regard to Riga. On 14 September, Erfurth handed the OKW's reply to the Marshal explaining that the events which had obviously had come to Mannerheim's knowledge did not imply an evacuation of Riga but simply the liquidation of superfluous offices. The OKW assured the Finns that it would get into contact with the Finnish High Command prior to taking any measures liable to influence the Finnish front.

General Talvela also reported on 16 September that the German Army High Command had informed him of its intention to hold its positions in the northern sector of the German eastern front under all circumstances, even if other sectors in southern Russian might be forced to continue the retreat. For these reasons and out of consideration for the Finns, particularly strong forces had been assigned to Army Group North.

General Talvela further reported that assurance had been given him that no forces would be withdrawn from the sector of the Twentieth Mountain Army, which was welcome news to Mannerheim. These promises, however, were not enough to completely dismiss the anxiety that had taken roots in the heart of the Marshal. On 29 September he informed the German General that he felt concerned about alleged German preparations to retire the front south of Leningrad. The OKW replied on 3 October that all reports about an intended retirement of the German front before Leningrad were incorrect but that rear preparations for use in case of an emergency were being prepared in the Narva sector. The Finns could have no objections to this explanation, since General Hanell had been busy for weeks constructing a second fortifications line behind the entire Finnish front. This work was given special priority on the Karelian Isthmus, but switch positions were also being constructed in the rear of the fortifications on the Svir front. Most progress had been made at Medvezhyegorsk where the terrain favored the construction of a second fortification line. All available forces and building material were employed for this work under the experienced and active command of General Hannel and occasionally inspected by Marshal Mannerheim. In view of the complete lull at the Finnish front it was obvious that the second Finnish fortifications line was intended for an emergency case only, as a natural precaution of any far-seeing army command. The corresponding German preparations ought not, therefore, to have made

Finnish Headquarters nervous, unless the confidence of the Finns in the stability of the German eastern front had been shaken by the German retreats which repeatedly occurred after the autumn of 1942.

A particularly far-seeing Finn, governor of the province of Lapland, confidentially asked an officer on General Erfurth's staff at Mikkeli on 26 September 1943, to pass the information on to Erfurth that he no longer believed in a Russian breakdown. Any such reasoning was merely wishful thinking without any foundation. As he saw it, Germany should try to come to an understanding with Russia. It might already be too late but it should be tried.

In retrospect, a critic cannot overlook the fact that a striking disparity of forces existed in the autumn of 1943 on the entire eastern front from the Black Sea to the Arctic. In Russia proper, between the Black Sea and the Gulf of Finland, a permanent crisis had been created by the fact that the superiority in number of the Red Army in all sectors could not be counterbalanced by any measures of the German command or the employment of fresh forces. On the Finnish-German front conditions were in direct contrast. The withdrawal of forces by the Russians, which had begun in the spring of 1943 and had been continued throughout the summer, had led to a considerable weakening of the Russian forces on the northern front as compared to the situation in the summer of 1942. An estimate of the situation by Finnish Headquarters on 15 September 1943 assessed the total strength of the Russians on the Finnish-German front to be only 270,000 men, 180,000 of which were in front of the Finnish sector. Since the Finnish Army was at that time about 350,000 strong and the German troops in the sector of the Twentieth Mountain Army numbered about 200,000 men, the Finnish-German Army was twice as strong as the Russians in the autumn of 1943 (550,000 Finns and Germans as compared to 270,000 Russians). During the entire war with Russia a ratio more favorable to the Germans probably never existed. This superiority was not only in numbers but also in quality. Finns and Germans between the Arctic and Gulf of Finland were well-rested and in good form. No major engagements had taken place since the spring of 1943. Both the physical and mental condition of the troops was excellent. In the reports arriving at Finnish Headquarters the morale of the Finnish forces was always considered good. The agitation aroused by the opposition party in congress (we shall refer to the campaign of the "thirty-three" in Chapter Five) was universally disapproved by the men on the Finnish frontlines. Without exaggeration the Twentieth Mountain Army was in the autumn of 1943 the strongest and best German army available. The gaps in the army in Lapland had been completely filled by reinforcements, the troops were familiar with the special conditions of their theater or war, and there was no lack of arms and equipment. It is a simple matter of arithmetic that a joint Finnish-German offensive would have had at that time the best chances for a quick and decisive success. The 550,000 Finns and Germans would surely have finished off the 270,000 Russians thoroughly and quickly.

Not only would the problem of the Murmansk railroad have been successfully solved, but the bulk of the Finnish-German Army would have been able, after breaking through the Russian front between Lake Onega and the Murmansk coast, to turn to the south in order to relieve Army Group North. Why did not the Finnish and Wehrmacht High Commands make the seemingly obvious decision in the autumn of 1943? This question was repeatedly asked by Finnish generals who became conscious of the paradoxical situation on the Finnish-German front and were depressed when they saw that the Germans were being weakened in heavy fighting while the Finnish front led a comfortable life. Was the Finnish attitude of reserve justifiable? Could not the German soldier expect more of his Finnish brother-in-arms? Many a brave soldier at the front at that time passed harsh judgment on Finnish Headquarters and the political leaders of the Finnish Republic. To his way of thinking, President Ryti lived in a world which did not exist, Mannerheim was too old to make energetic decisions, the generals surrounding Mannerheim were under the influence of the politicians and so forth.

These judgments came from the hearts of the soldiers but were based on the military viewpoint and did not take political problems into consideration. In a war or coalition political motives will always rank before military ones, and that was the case in Finland in the autumn of 1943. The men responsible for the government and the armed forces saw clearly that a new Finnish offensive would immediately be followed by a declaration of war by the United States against Finland. The political majority in Finland did not intend to allow that to happen. The Finns maintained that the present Russo-Finnish hostilities were a continuation of the Winter War, that is to say an affair which concerned only Finland and the Soviet Union. No Finn wanted war with the United States. Finnish Headquarters exercised great care to take no steps for which congress might hold them responsible if the United States entered the war. A Finnish offensive was therefore out of the question. Both Germany and the Soviet Union were probably fully aware of such internal Finnish scruples. The political events at Helsinki, which will be dealt with in Chapter Five, were clear and could easily be interpreted abroad from the frank comments of the Finnish press. For that reason the OKW probably did not even attempt to persuade the Marshal to launch an offensive, and the Soviet Union did not run any great risk by withdrawing more and more forces from the Finnish-German front in the summer of

1943. All players in this card game knew who had the trumps. Military decisions in Finland depended in increasing measure on politics.

The Finnish-German command avoided major problems and occupied itself with minor decisions of local importance, as for instance, the storming of a ridge in the Kiestinki sector by the German 7th Mountain Division in the second half of August, or a German request on 10 September 1943 for stronger commitment of the Finnish Air Forces over the Gulf of Finland in order to relieve the German naval units at the Suursaari-Tytärsaari barrier. For some time the Russians had shown more activity at the eastern end of the Gulf of Finland, launching increasing aerial attacks on the German warships on blockade duty. They also began to clear the mines laid by the Germans and Finns and to damage the net obstacle. On 18 September 1943, Admiral Böhmer, commander of the German obstacle construction units, went with Admiral von Bonin, the German Military Attaché at Helsinki, to Mikkeli Headquarters to discuss blocking and security measures and defense against Russian nuisance raids. Both officers were received by Marshal Mannerheim who availed himself of the opportunity to praise the cooperation of German and Finnish naval forces, which remained excellent until the very end of the war.

The situation at the German fronts deteriorated considerably in September. On 9 September, strong Allied forces landed in the Bay of Salerno and soon afterwards the Fascist regime was overthrown in Italy. The Axis position in the Mediterranean was badly shaken. The concern which Marshal Mannerheim obviously felt in the autumn of 1943 about the outcome of the war may be gathered from a request which General Heinrichs passed to the German General by order of the Marshal. Mannerheim expressed the desire to have Finnish officers reconnoiter positions in the rear area of the Twentieth Mountain Army, which might gain importance in case of a withdrawal of German forces from Lapland. Finnish Headquarters evidently intended to let General Hanell carry out the construction of fortifications in the rear of the German front even at this early juncture. Since Headquarters stressed this point and wished to continue the discussions on the following day, the German General reported the Finnish requests on 7 October to the OKW.

This report induced General Jodl to visit Finland on 14 and 15 October. His mission, by order of Adolf Hitler, was to orient Marshal Mannerheim on the overall war situation and the German plans and to discuss pending questions. Jodl carried a personal letter from Adolf Hitler to President Ryti which was delivered to the President by the German ambassador. Jodl was treated by the Marshal and Headquarters with great consideration. Since the landing of large planes on Mikkeli airport always involved a certain risk, the plane coming from German Headquarters landed at Malmi on 14 October. The German guest was received at the airport by the Chief of Staff, General Heinrichs, and brought by the Marshal's special train from Helsinki to Mikkeli.

In the afternoon a rather lengthy meeting took place between the Marshal and Jodl, whose factual report and straightforward manner made a strong impression on the former. The Marshal was so satisfied by the explanations of the German guest that he requested the extension of Jodl's trip in order to give General Walden, the Minister of Defense, an opportunity to receive and hear Hitler's special envoy. Late in the evening of 14 October, Jodl traveled in the Marshal's special train, accompanied by the German General, from Mikkeli to Helsinki. The German generals were welcomed at the station by General Grandell and accompanied to Walden's residence at Brunsparken, where the Minister of Defense gave a luncheon in honor of his German guests. After lunch a confidential discussion took place between Walden and Jodl.

As on the previous day at Mikkeli, Jodl's statements also made a strong impression on the Minister of Defense. These discussions included Mannerheim's wish for Finnish offers to reconnoiter the terrain behind the German front in Lapland. Jodl had given assurance that Germany did not intend to withdraw her troops from Finland. Mannerheim, nevertheless, insisted on his request, asking the OKW to consent to the intentions of Finnish Headquarters, which obviously were dictated not only by military but also by political reasons.

An indication of Marshal Mannerheim's farsightedness is the fact that in the autumn of 1943, when the withdrawal of the Germans from Finland did not seem to be within the bounds of possibility, he began to worry about a situation which became reality in September of 1944. On 26 October the OKW agreed to the intended Finnish reconnaissance.

On 4 November, General Thomaschki, a senior artillery commander at Eighteenth Army Headquarters, came to Mikkeli and gave a lecture to the Finnish officers at headquarters on artillery problems. His statements made it clear that the Eighteenth Army Headquarters expected an early Russian large-scale attack from the Volkhov bridgehead and the Oranienbaum area. The great danger of such a pincer attack was obvious since it threatened the entire positions of the Eighteenth Army. Thomaschki gave assurance that the Eighteenth Army intended to hold its positions under any circumstances and would not withdraw to the Narva positions. When Thomaschki made this statement, the Marshal said calmly, "I gladly believe you have such an intention and I hope that you have the power to carry it out." The Marshal probably had the large withdrawal movement in mind which during the last months had been carried out by the German eastern armies as far as behind the Dnieper, and the evacuation of the Zaporozhye bridgehead. An experienced general like the Finnish Commander in Chief was of course fully aware that such a vast territory would only be abandoned in war in case of need and for lack of forces.

Thomaschki was informed by the German General of the views at Finnish Headquarters and was asked to draw the attention of Eighteenth Army Headquarters to the importance for the Finnish-German brotherhood-in-arms of holding out on the Volkhov and south of Leningrad under any circumstances. The German General left no room for doubt that a withdrawal of the Eighteenth Army to the Narva position would exercise a disastrous influence on Finnish politics.

The situation in the sector of Army Group North deteriorated in the course of November as a result of a deep penetration made by the Russians southwest of Velikiye Luki at Nevel on 5 November, which tore up the front of the Sixteenth Army to great depth. An increasing number of Estonians fled to Finland in the wake of the retreat of the German front in North Russia.

Even more than by the success of the Red Army at Nevel, Mannerheim was worried by the obvious German inability to stem the enemy advance west of Nevel and to eliminate the thrust or at least to make it smaller. On the contrary, the penetration area was widened by the Russians in the course of November. The collapse of the newly organized Sixth Army also astounded Mannerheim and caused him grave concern. He asked the German General at Finnish Headquarters on 4 November 1943: "How is it possible that the enemy is advancing on an average of thirty-five kilometers daily in South Russia between the Sea of Azov and the Dnieper? Where are the Germans? They cannot have been taken prisoner since Radio Moscow says nothing about it."

Information from Germany gave no clear picture of the situation, and it was not possible to follow the march of events by means of the Wehrmacht communiqués. Contradiction between the news from Radio Moscow and the Wehrmacht communiqués increased daily. Both reports were prepared for propaganda purposes and colored so that it was not easy to discover the truth.

The Winter War had taught the Finns that when the enemy broke through, to attack him from all sides, to encircle him, press him together, and finally to destroy him. That was the gist and the purpose of the "motti tactics" they developed. On the German eastern front, however, Russian penetrations constantly gained in depth, like the bursting of a dike that cannot be stopped. The German forces employed in counterattacks were as a rule insufficient.

To an attentive observer the thought suggested itself that the German Army was not able to recover from the terrible catastrophe suffered at Stalingrad and was no longer a match for the unceasing attacks of the Red

Army. President Ryti incidentally told the German Ambassador, and Mannerheim told the German General they were astonished that important sectors of the German eastern front were abandoned although they had been assured a little while ago by high level German sources that those sectors would be held at all costs. Such remarks revealed not only the anxiety with which the Finnish statesmen followed events at the German eastern front, but also the doubts of the Finns in the power of resistance of the Wehrmacht.

In the second half of 1943 Finnish Headquarters made new efforts to maintain and to increase the striking power of the Finnish Army. On 21 August, the second half of age class 1925 had been conscripted for 12 October. A little later, on 25 October, members of older age classes, so called D-personnel, were inducted.

On 28 October Finnish Headquarters announced its new plan for the activation of three new mixed brigades. In the previous weeks repeated requests had been made for the supply of artillery equipment from Germany. The Marshal had been excellently advised in this matter by General Henonen, Inspector of Artillery, who was a real expert in that field, and Mannerheim intended to simplify and modernize the Finnish artillery. The OKW had promised on 18 September to grant Mannerheim's request and equip the armored division with assault guns. When General Jodl paid his visit on 14 October, the Marshal handed him a long list of requests including equipment for the activation of eight new artillery battalions (light field howitzers) for the three new brigades. The Headquarters attached great importance to an early delivery of the artillery in order to have the new brigades ready for employment as soon as possible. Most of the Finnish demands for artillery were granted by the OKW, but the required early delivery could not be met with the result that the brigades, which were ready at about the end of the year, initially lacked the artillery expected from Germany.

Upon a Finnish request, a German training team arrived in Finland on 14 December in order to assist the Finnish armored division in handling the assault guns which had come from Germany.

After the good experience enjoyed in the preceding two winters with the training courses in winter warfare, the OKH approached Finnish Headquarters in the summer of 1943 with the request that such courses for German officers be held also during the summer in Finland. These courses were to deal only with forest warfare according to season, since the Finns were masters of this art of fighting. Mannerheim readily complied with the German request. The training courses took place at Parola, a Finnish summer camp, the site of which was well suited for the purpose. The close proximity of Hämeenlinna allowed the noncommissioned officer school there to participate in the courses too.

The first training course began on 11 July, the second on 14 August. The Finnish instructor was Lieutenant Colonel Suvantola, an experienced general staff officer, who was particularly suited to such an assignment owing to his expert knowledge and his excellent character.

A conference of the Labor Commission was convoked by Governor Hillilä on 22 September at Rovaniemi in order to discuss measures for reducing the quota of Finnish laborers, which moreover had been exceeded by the German authorities. In addition a minimum age limit for female workers at German administration centers was fixed by request of the Finns. It was decided that underage workers would be replaced by older women. Germany's economic assistance was as usually negotiated by government committees. As a great favor, coal, which in wartime is a precious raw material, was placed by Germany at the disposal of Finnish industry in accordance with its requirements. The German delegate gave assurance that Finland would get an annual supply of 1,200,000 tons of coal. This promise was kept in spite of the bad effect of the air attacks on production and transportation. The Finnish gasoline quota, however, had to be curtailed. In the economic negotiations of December 1943 at Berlin, most of the Finnish demands were complied with. The German-Finnish commercial treaty was prolonged until 1944.

In the course of the autumn of 1943 several changes took place with regard to the German generals assigned in Finland. General Schörner, the former commanding general of the XIX Mountain Corps left Finland on 25 October. His name will remain connected in the history of the war with the victorious defense against the Russian offensive in the Murmansk sector in May 1942, when Schörner proved himself a particularly energetic and unflinching officer. He was called away from the quiet Arctic front and entrusted with greater tasks. His successor was General Ritter von Hengl, the former commander of the 2nd Mountain Division.

On 2 November, Generaloberst Stumpf, commander of the Fifth Air Fleet was recalled to Germany and a new mission assigned to him. These changes caused at the same time an alteration of the organization. The operational area of the Fifth Air Force was extended to Denmark, its command post being transferred from Kemi to Oslo. The Luftgau (the administrative area of an Air Fleet) Staff Finland, which so far had had only administrative functions, was changed to an agency of the commanding general of the Luftwaffe in Finland. This agency took over the command of all Luftwaffe units employed in Finland.

5. January – 8 June 1944 (until the beginning of the Soviet Russian offensive in June against the Finnish front on the Karelian Isthmus)

1943 drew to a close with heavy fighting all along the German eastern front. The German eastern army, bleeding from many wounds, withdrew from one position to another. Nikopol, Krivoy Rog, Kremenchug, Kiev, Gomel, Smolensk, and Reval were the focal points of bitter fighting. Also south of Lake Ladoga Russian attacks flared up now and again. The end of 1943 brought with it great anxiety for the Finnish Government and Army headquarters. The Finns, who were not at all influenced by propaganda, looked at the situation with sober eyes and harbored no hopes that the outcome of the war would be favorable to the Finns and Germans. All friends of the Finnish-German brotherhood-in-arms could not conceal the fact that the constant deterioration of the situation at the German eastern front caused great uneasiness to Finnish public opinion. Finnish internal politics were very unstable in the beginning of the new year, and many things contributed to lower morale. The Russian radio station waged a war of nerves against Finland and broadcast malicious propaganda on the outrages of the Finnish military administration in Karelia. The Russian propaganda was very inconvenient to the Finnish authorities who feared that it might unfavorably influence the relationship between Finland and the United States. In view of the outcome of the war, which appeared gloomier from day to day, all political circles attached great importance to the maintenance of good relations with the United States, which were, however, deteriorating daily. The uneasiness of the urban population was increased by frequent Russian air raids and particularly by reports of the devastating effect of the air attacks on Germany.

Feeling at Finnish Headquarters was rather pessimistic in the first weeks of the new year under the pressure of responsibility and the strong influence of the unfavorable situation at the German eastern front. The Marshal pondered how to improve air protection of Helsinki. For fear that Mikkeli would again become the target of systemic air attacks in this war as had been the case in the Winter War, the Marshal on 12 January ordered the dispersion of individual branches of Headquarters to different sites in the surroundings of the town. The transfer was to be prepared immediately and to be carried out with utmost speed. It throws some light on the pessimistic attitude of individual officers at Headquarters, naturally expressed in various degrees of severity, that for the first time the possibility of a separate peace was openly discussed. It was a matter of concern whether the Finns in case of a German catastrophe should feel pledged to remain brothers-in-arms of their allies, or whether it were permissible or possible to separate from Germany before the latter crashed into the abyss, and thus not to be drawn into the whirlpool of the dying Third Reich. The air at Helsinki and Mikkeli was close and oppressive as before a thunderstorm. One had the feeling of impending disaster.

News that a strong Russian offensive against Army Group North had begun on 17 January north of Novgorod, south of Leningrad and at Oranienbaum struck the nervous tension of the Finns like a thunderbolt. While Radio Moscow was broadcasting reports of a great victory, the Wehrmacht communiqué only announced that the Russians had attacked with increasing violence north of Lake Ilmen, in the area south of Leningrad and south of Oranienbaum, but that their attempts at breaking through had been frustrated in bitter fighting. It soon became apparent, however, that the enemy offensive was actually a great success and had quickly penetrated deep into the German positions. The German front on the Gulf of Finland between Uritsk and Peterhof had to be retired since the German positions further to the west in the Oranienbaum area had been overrun. Because of this and also the Russian successes north of Novgorod, the Eighteenth Army ran into great danger. If the center of the army remained in its positions, and envelopment of the wings was threatened, which would cut the army off from its rear communications to the west.

The Wehrmacht communiqué of 21 January 1944 admitted that heavy defensive fighting south of Leningrad and south of Oranienbaum continued and that the town of Novgorod had to be evacuated in order to straighten out the local front. Actually, it was not a question of a local correction of the front; the entire Eighteenth Army was in full retreat. The Wehrmacht High Command's order that Army Group North was to hold the Luga position had also been communicated to Finnish Headquarters, where it was received with great skepticism sine the latter had reason to doubt the existence of a Luga position and no pertinent information could be obtained from Army Group North. As Mikkeli saw the situation, the Germans would have to be glad if they succeeded in saving the remnants of the Eighteenth Army by reaching the Narva position.

There could be no doubt that the pincer attack of the Red Army would penetrate to the south and west and try to cut off the withdrawal route of the bulk of the Eighteenth Army. Heavy fighting went on in the large swamps west of Novgorod, along the Pskov-Leningrad railroad and in the Kingisepp area. Kingisepp had been evacuated on 22 January after bitter fighting. Whether it would be possible to build up a new and firm defense line depended to a large extent on the strength and condition of those segments of the Eighteenth Army which succeeded in falling back behind the Narva sector. Finnish Headquarters had no clear conception of this at the end of January. The Finnish Minister of Foreign Affairs, who maintained close relations with Headquarters, made a remark on 1 February which gave rise to much discussion: "In case Narva cannot be held, a new situation for Finland will be created." The Wehrmacht communiqué of 9 February proved that without stopping at intermediate positions, but the bulk of the artillery including the unwieldy group "heavy flat fire" could be safely brought back into new positions, which could be held against strong attacks. This retreat under almost hopeless conditions was a performance of command and troops beyond all praise. Estonian volunteers fighting within Army Group North distinguished themselves too. Thanks to the combined efforts of the Germans and Estonians most of the Narva sector was held. The loss of the German positions south of Leningrad, however, was a great success for the Red Army and led to a further deterioration of the situation at the eastern front. The Finnish positions on the Karelian Isthmus and on the Svir had now lost any connection with the German eastern front and the possibility of cooperation had been lost. Now that the important traffic center of Leningrad and its surroundings was again dominated entirely by the Russians, the Russian could, if he wanted, easily assemble large forces opposite the Finnish southern front. The possibility of operating in the Leningrad area had considerably changed in favor of the Russians since the retreat of the Eighteenth Army, a fact which was quickly recognized by both Finnish Headquarters and the Wehrmacht High Command. In consideration thereof, the OKW proposed of its own accord to Marshal Mannerheim on 31 January that he submit his wishes for strengthening the Finnish defense front to the OKW, which would then try to comply with them as much as possible.

In order to reassure the Marshal, who was correctly believed by the OKW to be in low spirits, the message of 31 January contained the assurance that the forces of the Twentieth Mountain Army would remain in the Far North in full strength in spite of the obvious withdrawal of enemy forces. Prior to the receipt of this letter, Mannerheim had already requested the expedition of the delivery of artillery for the three newly activated brigades. Upon the request of the OKW to set forth their demands, Finnish Headquarters made a long list of new arms to be supplied which was sent to the OKW on 3 February. These far-reaching wishes of Mannerheim included among other things a request for 4,000 machine guns of the 1942 model, 300 captured Russian 152mm guns and sixty 122mm guns. Moreover, the Marshal expressed the surprising desire to have the Finnish 3rd Division in the Uhtua sector relieved by forces of the Twentieth Mountain Army. General Dietl protested immediately but the OKW rejected Dietl's protest on 6 February, obviously trying to soothe the Marshal, and agreed to the relief of the Finnish 3rd Division. An early delivery of the brigade artillery had already been promised previously (on 6 February).

A senior officer at Headquarters who had a particularly good judgment of the internal and external political situation said on 22 January

1944 to the German General at Mikkeli that there was nobody at Finnish Headquarters who still believed in a German victory if the coalition between the Soviet Union, the United States and England lasted until the end of the war. The only way out according to the Finns was the possibility of German diplomacy succeeding in removing either the Russians or the British from the fighting.

In spite of German endeavors to comply with all Finnish wishes[26] to increase the Finnish defense power by German assistance, uneasiness on the part of both government and population mounted abetted by the war of nerves against the Finnish people. A strong air raid on Helsinki took place on 6 February which did much damage to the inner city. Many window panes were broken, a very inconvenient situation for the inhabitants in view of the prevailing cold. On 9 February the United States initiated a political offensive which was to have a great influence on the development of the internal political situation in Finland. Further particulars will be given in Chapter Five.

Finnish Headquarters always kept a sharp eye on public opinion in the capital. Mikkeli had an exact knowledge of what was discussed there in government circles, among the members of congress, journalists, the political parties or the working population. Every day Mannerheim held long telephone conversations with General Walden, the Minister of Defense. General Heinrichs and Foreign Minister Ramsay were also in frequent telephone communication with one another. Particularly in these tense days of February 1944 the restless atmosphere of the capital influenced Mikkeli Headquarters by many channels. The Marshal, therefore, set his heart on improving the air defense of Helsinki for which he needed the material help of his German brother-in-arms. As a result of Mannerheim's efforts, German night fighters arrived on 15 February at Tallinn and Helsinki to support the Finns. This was very valuable assistance, made available only by reducing the defense of the German towns which were suffering enormously from the relentless air warfare.

Immediately after the news of the outcome of the battle south of Leningrad arrived, Finnish Government and Headquarters on 13 January called the first half of the 1926 age class to arms for 21 February. On 21 January, General Dietl paid a short call on the Marshal at Mikkeli. At that time a clear conception of the extent of the disaster that had befallen the Eighteenth Army was not yet formed. Dietl told the Marshal that he intended to build a covering position in the Uhtua sector behind the Finnish 3rd Division adjacent to the Sofjanka sector, for the construction

---

[26] Keitel had replied to Mannerheim's list of wishes on 6 February that everything would be examined with greatest care. Only the demand for thirty captured T-34 tanks could not be fulfilled.

of which he needed Finnish help. Dietl's intentions coincided with Mannerheim's wishes. No agreement was reached, however, about Finnish participation in this matter, since the Finnish construction units were at the time fully occupied with other missions. Negotiations about the construction of the Sofjanka position went on between the 20.Geb.Armee and Finnish Headquarters during the next weeks after the establishment of a new boundary line between the Finnish and German fronts had become necessary because of Mannerheim's demand for the relief of the Finnish 3rd Division.

Another consequence of the tension built up in Finland at the front and in the zone of the interior was the Marshal's decision to recall General Talvela, his representative to the OKW, and to replace him with General Österman. This switch afforded a certain insight into the reasoning of the Commander in Chief. General Talvela was in high favor with Mannerheim and was preferably employed by him in important missions which required particular acumen and sound judgment. It was a sign of Mannerheim's confidence that he sent General Talvela to Berlin in January 1942 as his representative, when he became aware that a long war was to be expected before a decision between Russian and German could be reached. This far-seeing general was at that time more important for the Marshal in Germany than at the Finnish front, which was obviously passing over to quiet trench warfare. When Mannerheim decided on 10 February 1944 by way of General Erfurth, to ask for the agreement of the OKW to the replacement of Talvela by Österman, he seemed to be taking into account the possibility of decisive engagements along the Finnish front in the near future. For this he would need Talvela, who had highly distinguished himself as commanding general during the offensive in Karelia in the summer of 1941. At the present Talvela was more important to him as commander of a front sector in Karelia than as Finnish observer of the events in the Reich in Berlin.

To Finnish eyes, the Karelian Isthmus was always the most important front, for the security of which everything possible was done. On 13 February the Marshal ordered that the Finnish armored division, which so far had been occupied with training and in securing the shore of Lake Onega in the Petrozavodsk area, be transferred to the Viipuri area where the division was to continue training and to construct the "Third Position."

Negotiations for establishing a new boundary line between the Finnish and German fronts were initiated on 14 February between General Heinrichs and the German General. The natural consequence of the relief of the Finnish 3rd Division in the Uhtua sector by German forces was that this sector was included in the area of the Twentieth Mountain Army. The boundary between the two fronts was to be shifted to the south by the width of one division. It will always be difficult and require careful study to establish tactical boundaries if all possibilities are taken into consideration. In the present case it was no simple matter to arrive at a decision satisfactory to both parties. The question was, therefore, discussed several times again during the following weeks.

By the middle of February, feeling at Helsinki had risen to fever point. The situation report of Army Group North indicated on 14 February that the Red Army had crossed the Narva River south of that town. It became doubtful whether the Russian advance in the Narva sector could be brought to a halt. On that day the Helsinki press published an account to the effect that Passikivi, Councilor of State, had left by plane for Stockholm in order to get acquainted with the Russian conditions for a separate peace with Finland. The name of Passikivi signified a definite program to all Finns that is to say, agreement between Finland and the Soviet Union. Though politically a Conservative (party composed of men possessing various political views), Paasikivi had always advocated agreement with Russia. He was the proper person for the job of renewing the broken ties between Finland and the Soviet Union. Chapter Five, which deals with internal political development, will go into detail on the trip of Paasikivi.

The seriousness of the situation was stressed by a remark of Foreign Minister Ramsay to German Ambassador von Blücher on 16 February that a new situation would be created for Finland if the Germans would have to withdraw to the lower Dvina. The alarming reports in the Finnish and Swedish press concerning Paasikivi and his trip to Stockholm roused great attention in German official circles, (the German press published no news of these events.), and the OKW sent an inquiry to the 20.Geb.Armee and General Erfurth asking whether the situation was considered so tense that the shifting of forces to replace the Finnish 3rd Division, which had begun, should be stopped. Both German agencies replied in the negative to the question. The German General, who in these days of strain had frequent discussions with General Heinrichs, and who was on friendly terms with many Finnish officers owing to his long stay at Finnish Headquarters, was still convinced that nothing decisive had happened and that the Finnish Government was keeping all doors open. He warned, therefore, against taking hasty decisions which might prejudice the brotherhood-in-arms. General Erfurth's judgment was in full agreement with that of the German Ambassador at Helsinki. The difficult position of these two representatives of the Reich in Finland during the critical year of 1944 had led to an animated exchange of opinions between the Ambassador and the German General which resulted in showing their complete harmony on all important questions. Not often perhaps have there been equally harmonious and frictionless relations between military and diplomatic representatives abroad during the war.

On 21 February, General Österman reported at the Führer's Headquarters as General Talvela's successor. At his reception by Adolf Hitler and Field Marshal Keitel he emphasized that he would not have come to Germany if there was any possibility of Finland concluding a separate peace. Since Österman was considered in Germany a sincere friend of the Reich and a champion of the Finnish-German brotherhood-in-arms, his words were given the proper prominence.

The political crisis initiated by the trip of Paasikivi to Stockholm dragged on for more than two months. Its length proved that all questions arising from the crisis were examined in detail. The Finns have a cool temper and do not like hasty decisions. They prefer to think matters over carefully. Since it was a matter of life or death to the Finnish people, events strictly followed the rules of democracy. All constitutional authorities (president, cabinet, congress) participated in mastering the situation, and the press discussed matter with the openness guaranteed by the constitution. The mere spectator was strongly impressed by the cool objectivity with which Finnish fate was discussed and differences of opinion settled. The sterling qualities of the Finns, their sense of responsibility, self-discipline and patriotism came to the fore. A survey of all phases of the political crisis will be given in Chapter Five. While politicians at Helsinki struggled for weeks to arrive at a decision on war or peace, the daily routine went on as usual at Finnish Headquarters.

The serious news on the effect of enemy air raids on German towns caused the Marshal on 21 February to order all military agencies at Helsinki transferred to the country. The German General, thereupon, ordered the few German agencies which were at Helsinki to follow this exodus from the capital in the interest of better cooperation with the Finnish authorities. The evacuation caused, as expected, considerable difficulties in the prompt dealing with service matters.

In the meantime General Talvela reported to Mikkeli Headquarters. On 24 February Mannerheim ordered a reorganization of the Finnish front. The Karelian Isthmus was divided into two corps sectors under the command of General Laatikainen (western half) and General Siilasvuo (eastern half). General Talvela was appointed Commander in Chief of the Maaselkä group. Generals Blick and Svenson continued to be in command along the Svir River, under General Ösch as Commander in Chief (Headquarters at Kolatselkä).

Another air raid on Helsinki took place on 27 February which caused considerable destruction. The German Embassy, which was in the vicinity, suffered major damage from bombs. Another attack was carried out in the night of 6 March on the port of Kotka, an important base for the Finnish and German naval forces during the summer months.

On 2 March Mannerheim received the German General for a lengthy discussion of the situation. The Marshal openly expressed his doubts whether Germany had sufficient soldiers in the east to ward off the attacks of the Red Army at all sectors of the front. "One hopes for many things in war but not everything comes true," Mannerheim said with resignation. Alluding briefly to the Finnish negotiations with the Soviet Union, Mannerheim then declared that the Russian peace conditions transmitted by Paasikivi were unacceptable. He saw his main task as commander in chief in strengthening the Finnish Army as much as possible. He had already had the first half of the 1926 age class inducted on 21 February and had besides given the order to prepare for the induction of the second half of that age class. He emphasized with great seriousness that maintenance of the Narva sector by the Germans was a decisive prerequisite for the Finns whether to continue in the war or not.

The Red Army offensive had meanwhile come to a standstill at the Narva front. Although the German defenders had not succeeded in throwing the Russians back across the river, the situation became more and more stabilized at this part of the front. Russian attempts further to the south to advance across the ice of Lake Peipus and thus to open the isthmus between that lake and the Gulf of Finland were also repulsed by the Eighteenth Army. The German authorities could not have the slightest doubt about the importance of the Narva position for Finnish-German relations, since it had been again and again impressed upon them by the German Ambassador and the German General. The reports on the situation in the sector of Army Group North in the first half of March had a confident ring and did not fail to make an impression on Finnish Headquarters. The stabilization of the German front at Narva had no doubt also a favorable effect on the issue of the internal political crisis in Finland.

The 20.Geb.Armee and Finnish Headquarters gained the impression around 13 March that the Russians were withdrawing forces from the Maaselkä front and so reinforced the Kiestinki and Kandalaksha sectors. On 13 March, Finnish Headquarters received a request from Dietl not to withdraw the Finnish 3rd Division, which had been disengaged from the Uhtua sector and placed at the disposal of the Finnish Commander in Chief, but to leave it at the boundary between the Finnish and German fronts. The German Commander in Chief further asked that two Finnish battalions be left in the Uhtua sector for four weeks. General Dietl wanted to be prepared for all emergencies until the mud period set in. Mannerheim readily agreed to leave the two battalions behind and declared his readiness to leave the reinforced 11th Regiment of the Finnish

3rd Division in the Suomussalmi-Kuusamo area but insisted on the evacuation of the bulk of that division to the Karelian Isthmus as intended.

Further Russian forces were obviously withdrawn in March from the Finnish front in Karelia. It appeared that the Russians while negotiating with the Finns intended to strike a strong blow against the German front. That was the reason for a renewed appeal from Dietl to Mannerheim on 22 March to transfer a Finnish division to Central Finland.

Everything in these days appeared to indicate that a major Russian offensive against the Twentieth Mountain Army was imminent. The OKW shared this opinion. All measures were taken to strengthen the defense in the threatened areas.

General Dietl's great energy acted like a powerful motor to put the German Army in the Arctic region into a state of utmost preparedness, ready to repulse any Russian advance. Dietl issued a stirring order of the day on 23 March to his army, ending with the words, "There is no road back."

In these days which were under the shadow of the pending Finnish-Russian peace negotiations, Mannerheim was particularly friendly and ready to help his German brothers-in-arms. He agreed to Dietl's request and decided on 25 March to transfer the Finnish 3rd reinforced Brigade to the Lake Kemi-Lake Joutsi area. If the expected Russian attack had taken place, the German army in Lapland would undoubtedly have put up a gallant fight as in the spring of 1942, and the goddess of victory would perhaps have once again bestowed laurels on the Commander in Chief of the Twentieth Mountain Army, the victor of Narvik. But fate had decided otherwise. The expected Russian attack did not occur. Why the offensive was not carried out has remained a mystery. The Russians perhaps never intended to attack and the measures which had been observed were only part of a large-scale and successful camouflage operation intended to divert the Wehrmacht High Command's attention from other focal points.

Since Finnish attempts to approach Moscow had not yet been concluded, the OKW abandoned the attitude of reserve it had held up until then. On 2 April, a teletype message from the Chief of the OKW to the Finnish Commander in Chief arrived at Mikkeli thanking the Marshal for the transfer of the Finnish 3rd Brigade as requested by the Germans. This readiness of the Finns, Keitel felt, indicated their intention of continuing the war. He hinted at the possibility that the fighting spirit of the Finnish Army might suffer from the peace policy of the Government, and, counting on the Finns' strong interest in the Narva front, he suggested at the same time that the Finnish Commander in Chief assure himself of the stabilized situation in the sector of Army Group Narva[27] by sending officers of his headquarters there. In southern Russian, too, he continued, the Russian advance would be halted. Keitel's teletype letter contained an invitation for the officers to be sent by Mannerheim.

The Marshal accepted the invitation on 3 April. He thanked Keitel for the invitation and announced that the delegation would be led by Colonel Nihtilä, Chief of the Operations Branch at Finnish Headquarters. With his usual dexterity of expression Mannerheim rejected in respectful form but without injuring anyone the idea that the fighting spirit of the Finnish Army might have suffered. He did not see that the negotiations with Moscow poised any danger for the morale of the Finnish Armed Forces, who would continue to do their duty.

The trip of the Finnish officers was eagerly prepared by both sides. It took place in the second week of April, was well-planned by the German authorities and impressed the Finnish visitors favorably. It was made possible for Colonel Nihtilä, a particularly experienced and far-seeing general staff officer, to proceed to the foremost German position near the town of Narva and to convince himself of the good state of the German forces. The personality of General Friesner, the commander of the Army Group and his assurance that the Army Group would either hold the Narva front or perish, made a strong impression on Nihtilä.

General Österman, the Finnish General at German Headquarters, who had been ordered to report to the Marshal at Mikkeli, was received prior to his departure on 4 April by Field Marshal Keitel. The Chief of the OKW pointed out in this conversation that the attitude of the Finnish press toward the Hungarian question had caused resentment (this referred to German Military measures against Hungary). He added that the negotiations with Moscow were liable to react strongly on the Finnish people, the Finnish Army, and even on the German Army of General Dietl. Österman was requested to use his time in Finland to obtain a clear answer from Marshal Mannerheim as to his future attitude. By the time when Passikivi's second approach to Moscow became known, the OKW had already discussed whether a further delivery of German arms to Finland was advisable. That was a clear warning to the Finnish Commander in Chief and his government.

---

[27] The elements of the Eighteenth Army which had retired to the isthmus between the Gulf of Finland and Lake Peipus had been transferred from that army and assigned as Army Group Narva directly to Army Group North. The front sector of Army Group Narva at first extended from Narva to Lake Peipus and was later on increased to include the western shore of Lake Peipus southward as far as Fustres on the northwestern shore of the lake.

The Commander in Chief of the Twentieth Mountain Army expressed the desire in the beginning of April to discuss the situation at his own front with the Finnish Commander in Chief again. Mannerheim was always ready to receive Dietl at Mikkeli as he was fond of the honest, natural manner of the German Commander in Chief. Dietl, on the other hand, knew how to treat the Marshal with due respect in view of his great popularity with the Finnish people and his advanced age. Prior to his departure from Rovaniemi to Mikkeli, Dietl addressed his army as follows:

> "The reasons for the surprising reserve of the Russians in front of the Mountain Army may perhaps lie in events in the political arena. They may be preparing an advance on the Mountain Army on the chance that the Finns will withdraw from the war. The Finnish attitude has meanwhile stiffened. The enemy's intention must be discovered by increased employment of reconnaissance."

Early on 6 April Dietl arrived by night train at Mikkeli and left in the evening again by way of Helsinki. He explained to the Marshal the situation in the sector of his army and the extensive Russian attack preparations at Kandalaksha. Enveloping the northern wing of the German positions, the enemy had advanced his trenches more and more westward and threatened in the direction of Alakurtti and the main supply route of the XXVI Corps to Salla. The situation had become very tense through the Russian activity. Mannerheim himself admitted that the German positions were threatened by the enveloping movement of the Russians. Dietl's plan to anticipate the Russians by attacking them and piercing their line of encirclement greatly appealed to the Marshal. He endeavored to encourage Dietl's attack intentions and offered to relieve the German security forces at the Kolosjoki nickel plant by the Finnish 3rd Brigade. Obviously he was much interested in inducing Dietl to attack in the Kandalaksha sector without committing any Finnish forces. Dietl, however, postponed his decision with regard to the Marshal's proposal, declaring that the German security forces at Kolosjoki were unsuited for an attack. He departed without having reached a definite decision. Dietl also avoided mentioning various German complaints. If Mannerheim had offered that the Finnish 3rd Brigade join the attack, Dietl's plan might yet have taken shape. The OKW also became interested in a German-Finnish attack in the Kandalaksha sector and instructed the German General at Finnish Headquarters on 11 April to induce Mannerheim to allow the participation of Finnish troops if Dietl's army would launch an attack with limited objectives in the Kandalaksha sector. As expected, however, the

Marshal did not like this plan. The endeavors of the German General, therefore, came to nothing.

By the middle of April the offensive preparations of the Russians waned again and the mud period was impending, so that major operations against the Mountain Army were not likely. The Luftwaffe, therefore, transferred forces to the south again. Only a fighter group and a bomber group remained in Finland.

In the meantime, the Finnish-Russian peace parleys came to an end. On 18 April, the Finnish answer declining the Russian conditions was delivered at Stockholm. The internal political tension in Finland thus came to a close, but calm was not to last for long. There is no doubt that Mannerheim approved of the Finnish Government's policy to obtain an interpretation of the Russian conditions at Moscow. Mannerheim said on 26 April to the German General at his headquarters, "Mrs. Kollontay[28] has spread rumors at Stockholm that the original Russian peace conditions would be modified. Passikivi's trip to Moscow has revealed that those rumors were misleading."

The price the Finnish Government paid for the betterment of its internal situation was a loss of confidence on the part of the German brother-in-arms. Up until this time only the diplomatic relations between Germany and Finland had grown cool to a certain extent, while military assistance continued as usual. Now, however, a reaction set in in the military field. On 19 April, the Commander in Chief of the Twentieth Mountain Army and the German General at Finnish Headquarters received secret information from the OKW that Adolf Hitler had ordered the discontinuance of the delivery of arms to Finland. In future only such equipment was to be supplied by Germany which was absolutely necessary for maintain the fighting ability of the Finnish Army. This heavy blow destroyed all hopes of Finnish Headquarters for modernization and uniformity of the Finnish artillery, equipment of the Finnish Army with modern antitank arms, equipment of the Finnish armored division with modern tanks and many other things. The reason underlying the prohibition of the delivery of arms was the offense incurred by Hitler from the unfriendly attitude on the part of the Finnish press. This hostility stemmed from the measures taken by the Germans for the evacuation of the collections and installations of Tartu University in order to save them from the Russians.

A strange clause in the directive of the OKW stipulated that the Finns were not to be informed of the arms embargo. The German foreign agencies, particularly the German General at Finnish Headquarters, were

---

[28] The Russian Ambassadress at Stockholm.

placed in an awkward position by this obligation to secrecy. If the announced deliveries did not arrive and the Finns then made the natural inquiries, such inquiries were to be passed on to the OKW which would answer them from case to case. This rather doubtful arrangement could only prove an unpleasant surprise to the Finns and undermine the reputation and credibility of the German agencies in their eyes. Independently of one another the German Commander in Chief at Rovaniemi and the German General at Finnish Headquarters immediately protested against this embargo and drew attention to the inevitably evil consequences. They further pointed out that the matter of the Estonian university had gone unnoticed by large elements of the Finnish population and that the Finns would fail to understand why a tactless article in a Finnish newspaper should have such serious consequences. The request to change the Führer directive was declined by the OKW, since Hitler himself had drawn it up. All this seriously disturbed the excellent relations that had up to that time existed between German and Finnish soldiers. Complete confidence had reigned on both sides for almost three years. The strength of the Finnish-German brotherhood-in-arms was based on frankness and honestly which so far had been the supreme law in official intercourse between Germans and Finns.

General Erfurth's position at Finnish Headquarters was a respected one due to the confidence which the Marshal of Finland placed in him. It was well known that, although he always considered his first duty that of looking after German interests, the German General was an honest friend of the Finnish people. That offered him the opportunity to speak his mind freely in difficult situations when the interests of the brothers-in-arms were in disagreement, without running the risk of giving offense. It was, therefore, regrettable that the OKW directive brought about a change in the previously smooth functioning of official intercourse between Finnish and German agencies, causing the German representatives to be suspected of insincerity. It was easy to discern the reasons for the change of mind at the Führer's Headquarters. The Tartu University affair was naturally nothing but a pretext. In reality Hitler was understandably annoyed that the Finnish Government went its own way by taking up contact with Moscow. His distrustful and sensitive nature had been deeply offended by the Finnish peace feelers and the long period over which they had continued. He had, however, suppressed his anger until a decision had been made at Helsinki and the answer containing the refusal had been delivered at Stockholm. One day later he saw the moment he had been waiting for arrive. The peculiar way he chose to let the Finns and the Marshal feel his displeasure, however, can only be explained by the murky, sly character of the dictator. Obviously he could not imagine that his method would not be understood and remain a mystery to the Marshal and the leading Finns.

Nevertheless, the OKW endeavored to re-strengthen the weakened German-Finnish relations by inviting General Heinrichs, the Finnish Chief of Staff, to the Führer's Headquarters. The invitation was readily accepted. On 27 April Heinrichs left Helsinki by plane for Salzburg, accompanied by General Erfurth. They were billeted at a hotel in Berchtesgaden. Since Generaloberst Zeitzler, the Chief of the General Staff, was also living at the Berchtesgadener Hof, General Heinrichs paid him a courtesy call early on 26 April, accompanied by General Erfurth. Zeitzler oriented the Finnish Chief of Staff on the situation at the eastern front and declared that Army Group North, particularly Army Group Narva, were now firmly holding their positions.

He continued that the situation in the sector of Army Group South had been difficult as a result of traffic congestion on the Rumanian railroads. The attempt had been made to switch traffic over to water transportation on the Danube, but the British and Americans had found it out and mined the Danube from the air. Zeitzler expected further Russian attacks in the summer of 1944 south of the Pripyat River, since the Russians seemed bent on getting the Rumanian oilfields into their hands and penetrating to Bulgaria. The Chief of the German General Staff assumed that Army Groups Center and North would experience a quiet summer. That very soon proved to be a great error.

At noon, a conference with Keitel and Jodl took place in Keitel's special personal train. Prior to this conference, Keitel received Erfurth alone, so he took this opportunity to describe in broad outline the situation in Finland, and to point out the danger of the arms embargo. Furthermore, General Erfurth emphasized that the unfavorable criticism in some Finnish papers of the German measures at Tartu had been taken much too seriously by the OKW. Public opinion in Finland had not noticed this affair at all. Besides, freedom of the press existed in Finland even in wartime according to the rules of democracy. The Finnish Government or Finnish Headquarters could not be held responsible for occasional blunders of a newspaper, and nobody in Finland would understand why the necessary arms should be denied the Finnish brother-in-arms on account of some newspaper report. He, therefore, asked that the decision be re-examined.

In spite of the preliminary orientation by Erfurth, the conversation between Keitel and Heinrichs was rather unsatisfactory. The Chief of the OKW condemned the peace parleys held between Finland and the Soviet Union in the past few weeks. He called attention to the great danger which from the German point of view could result from the Finnish Government acceding to the wishes of a political minority. Heinrichs, who was apparently surprised and offended by Keitel's reproachful tone, defended his government's attitude which had to be in accord with the opinion of the Finnish Congress. The ensuing controversy was an example of the fundamental difference existing between the representatives of a totalitarian and a democratic state in the treatment of a political opposition. When Keitel submitted a complaint against the attitude taken by the Finnish press in the Tartu University affair, Heinrichs was completely surprised. The first intimation of this affair was given him through the statements of the Chief of the OKW.

The discussion then turned to the situation at the different fronts on which Jodl made a report. Finally, Heinrichs had an opportunity of advancing a few requests of the Marshal. Jodl, who spoke to Heinrichs in a more pleasant tone of voice, finally asked the Chief of the Finnish General Staff two personal favors:

> 1. In order to continue German assistance to the Finnish Armed Forces by the delivery of arms, Heinrichs should procure an authoritative statement that arms supplies by Germany to Finland would never fall into Russian hands.
> 2. Heinrichs should use his influence to put a stop to any attacks by the Finnish press against measures taken by the Germans and particularly by slandering of the Wehrmacht.

No mention was made of the arms embargo by anyone during the Finnish visit. After the conference, Jodl promised General Erfurth privately that he would use his influence to have the Führer directive cancelled. For this, however, he needed an authoritative declaration of either the President or the Marshal on the points mentioned to Heinrichs.

General Heinrichs was not satisfied with the discussion he had with Keitel. Immediately upon his return to the hotel he told Erfurth that he felt Keitel's tone to have been overbearing. Besides, he found Keitel to be lacking in an understanding of Finnish conditions. After his previous visits to Germany, Heinrichs had expected to be treated as an honored guest. Instead of that he had been reproached and thinly veiled threats had been made, which, from the Finnish standpoint, was scarcely justified. The bad impression made on Heinrichs could not be blotted out by the lavish social entertainment in his honor. Heinrichs, who did not feel too well owing to a severe cold remained quiet and lost in thoughts and occupied himself with listening.

In compliance with his wish, Heinrich's return trip was made by way of Vienna where on 29 April he toured the sights of the old imperial capital. On 30 April Heinrichs and Erfurth returned from Vienna to Helsinki by plane. The impression of a rupture in the Finnish-German brotherhood-in-arms, which Heinrichs must have gained at

Berchtesgaden, was increased by a report of the Finnish Air Attaché at Berlin, which General Heinrichs found on his return to Helsinki. The Finnish Air Attaché reported that he had been officially received on 28 April by the Chief of Staff of the Luftwaffe. On that occasion he had heard, evidently owing to a blunder by the Chief of Staff, that there existed a German arms embargo to Finland. What the Finns so far had until now been only able to guess became a fact. The indispensable assistance from Germany failed to arrive. This embargo which had suddenly been placed on Finland now also began to affect the needs of the civilian population.

After the beginning of May no more grain ships came to Finland from Germany. On 2 May, Marshal Mannerheim received General Erfurth in order to hear the latter's report on his and General Heinrich's trip to Berchtesgaden. Mannerheim emphasized that the trip had been very useful. He understood the German displeasure about various Finnish press reports, but there was no way of preventing such articles. The publication of the Russian peace conditions had achieved a new unity within the Finnish population. The people had become calmer and the Armed Forces had not been affected. A report had been sent to the Prime Minister on the damage done by the Finnish press.

A long discussion at Mikkeli in the beginning of May between the Chief of the Finnish General Staff and the German General made it clear that the Finns had become more aware of the seriousness of the situation. They tried to find a way out of this uncomfortable position and hoped to appease Hitler by agreeing to Jodl's suggestions. After the situation had been thoroughly examined as was the Finnish way, two letters on the matter were dispatched to the Führer's Headquarters on 12 May. One letter from Mannerheim was addressed to Hitler and the other letter from General Heinrichs to Jodl. Mannerheim's letter, however, did not change the situation, since Hitler considered it too noncommittal and composed of generalities as General Erfurth soon learned through confidential sources. The German embargo remained unchanged.

On 25 April the 20.Geb.Armee submitted an estimate of the situation to the OKW. It stated that the thaw had set in in Lapland so that a major Russian attack was not to be expected for the time being. The Commander-in-Chief believed that the Russian measures might well be an assembly of forces in case of emergency. Eight Russian divisions were assumed to be at the front opposite the Twentieth Mountain Army in the beginning of May with two divisions and a few individual brigades in reserve.

On 5 May, General Erfurth made a report as requested by Hitler on conditions at the Karelian Isthmus front, stating that there were two lines of fortifications. The Finnish High Command believed it would be able to ward off even a concentrated attack after strong artillery preparation in the first defense line. Three divisions and one brigade were employed there, while one division, one armored division and one reinforced infantry regiment were held in reserve. Troops as well as commanders were good and intended to put up a fight. Experience in large-scale engagements was, however, lacking.

German requests arriving at Finnish Headquarters in the course of the month of May in regard to the joint conduct of operations were treated by the Marshal with particular consideration. The Finns agreed in principle to the request made on 10 May by the German Naval Operations Branch to station a German naval squadron consisting of the cruiser PRINZ EUGEN and a number of destroyers in Finnish waters near the Åland Islands, from where timely intervention in case of a Russian attempt to break out of the Gulf of Finland seemed possible. The Finns only suggested one change with regard to location, which, however, was immaterial and satisfied the Naval Operations Branch.

The situation in the German theaters of war had by then developed from bad to worse. Russian and Allied offensives in South Russian and Italy continued without interruption. Bitter fighting raged for weeks in the Crimea. Sevastopol was given up by the German and Rumanian troops on 10 May. Rear guards at Sevastopol covered the retreat of the German-Rumanian forces from the Crimea with bravery but heavy losses.

Heavy fighting took place on the lower Dniester and in the foothills of the Carpathian Mountains, as well as in the Nettuno beachhead in Italy, where fighting was shifted under pressure of the Allied offensive from the coastal plain to the mountains behind it. A large-scale battle of material raged by the middle of May on a wide front in the South Italian mountains, forcing the German defenders to retreat behind the Tiber River toward Monti Albani. American armored units entered Rome on 4 June.

Allied bombing attacks on Italian and German towns and the Rumanian oil fields assumed larger and larger proportions. German bombardment squadrons made night attacks on railroad junctions and traffic centers behind the Russian front trying to disturb the Soviet Russian supply service.

On 16 May, General Hölter, the new Chief of Staff of the Twentieth Mountain Army, came to Mikkeli to present himself to the Marshal as successor of General Jodl.[29] He was the bearer of several requests from Dietl on account of the unclear situation before the front of the Twentieth Mountain Army. On the whole, those requests were granted by

---

[29] Generalleutnant Ferdinand Jodl, not to be confused with the Chief of the Wehrmacht Operations Staff. (Translator)

Mannerheim. The Marshal, for instance, agreed that the Finnish 3rd Brigade, which had been transferred on 25 March to the Kemijärvi-Joutsijärvi area remain behind the front of the XXXVI Corps. The Finnish Commander in Chief also agreed that units of the Finnish 3rd Brigade be employed at the left wing of the XXXVI Mountain Corps, but the brigade was to remain assigned to the Marshal. The Finnish 11th Regiment was withdrawn from the Kiestinki sector in order to join its division but was to be replaced by Finnish construction battalions which were to finish the construction of the Sohjana Position. Two of the four frontier guard battalions in the Kiestinki sector were to remain there. Whereas on former occasions Mannerheim had bitterly struggled with Dietl for each individual Finnish battalion, he yielded this time quickly and magnanimously to the German wishes. General Hölter could return to Rovaniemi in the evening of 16 May satisfied with what he had achieved.

As Russian air raids against German shipping traffic to Kirkenes and Liinahamari increased, General Dietl asked for better air protection to avoid endangering the supply of the German army in Lapland. A German Stuka group was thereupon reorganized. On 25 May, seventy of eighty Russian planes attacking a German convoy were shot down. On a similar occasion on 26 May, thirty-seven of one hundred and twenty Russian planes were downed.

Russian mine clearing in the Gulf of Finland became very active in the end of May. New mines were sown in the gaps cleared by the Russians. The German and Finnish navies laid out a double net in front of the barriers at Narva, and a destroyer flotilla, two S-Boot flotillas and other units were kept ready outside to prevent a Russian landing. Engagements in the Gulf of Finland were frequent at that time, but for the time being there was no fear of a Russian submarine breakthrough to the Baltic.

On the Karelian Isthmus, thrusts were made by Russian units up to company strength, but the Finnish General Staff declared that there was no indication of a concentration of Russian forces and the beginning of major engagements.

At the end of May, under the cover of fog and after artillery preparation, the Russians attacked at the Litsa front, but only in company strength. In the sector of the 20.Geb.Armee, major combat actions were not possible for another ten days in the southern part and three weeks in the northern part because the snow was melting.

The Finns now proceeded with unusual severity against those Finnish papers which had provoked justified German criticism. The *Svenska Pressen*, which had irritated all German soldiers in Finland during the war by its anti-German attitude, was suppressed on 8 June for a period of three months. On the same day the Marshal decided that Rauanheimo, a Finnish reserve officer who had given offense by two newspaper articles dealing with the German air operations against England in 1940/41, would have to appear before a court martial.

Meanwhile a letter from Hitler arriving at Mikkeli on 1 June in answer to Mannerheim's letter of 12 May added new fuel to the tension created by Passikivi's trips. Couched in polite and friendly terms as far as the Finnish Marshal was concerned, who was always treated by Hitler with the greatest respect anyway, the letter contained harsh reproaches against the independent way of Finnish politics and serious warnings of its consequences. The Marshal was correct, Hitler wrote, in calling the demands made on the German armaments production enormous. Hitler then explained the vastness of the German efforts and continued that he must frankly state that "we feel all the more offended by the way in which one ally (Italy) has broken faith to a large extent, while other allies consider it a matter of course to go their own ways." It was by no means a purely Finnish affair to enter into peace negotiations or not, and it might have a contagious effect. To beat back Russia and hold out in the west was what mattered. The Marshal should understand, Hitler concluded, that it was not possible to withhold a single weapon from one front unless there was absolute security that it would be utilized at another.

A heavy blow to the Finnish Commander in Chief was Hitler's point-blank declaration that he could no longer take the responsibility toward the German people for withholding urgently needed weapons from the hard-fighting Wehrmacht and for sending them to another front without a guarantee as to their future employment. This signified a formal refusal of the Reich to give further armament assistance to the Finnish brother-in-arms.

It goes without saying that Hitler's letter caused Finnish Headquarters great concern. Mannerheim consulted his Chief of Staff and asked the German General what he could do to appease the Führer. He could well understand Hitler's annoyance, but for internal political reasons it had been necessary to demonstrate to the Finnish people that peace with Moscow was impossible. The Finnish Commander in Chief rightfully pointed out that he was not responsible for Finnish politics. Hitler's complaints were not directed against the military but against the political leadership and could be only settled through diplomatic channels.

Mannerheim's birthday came on 4 June. President Ryti, Prime Minister Linkomies and Defense Minister Walden came from Helsinki to Mikkeli to offer their congratulations. After breakfast, Ryti, Mannerheim, and Walden proceeded to the front for an inspection of the armored division in the Enso area with its new assault gun equipment supplied by Germany. This day brought repeated opportunities for Mannerheim to discuss with Ryti and Walden the situation created by Hitler's letter. It seems, however, that no decision was reached. Ryti returned to Helsinki the night of 4 June. Mannerheim, who returned to Mikkeli the same night, was accompanied there by his friend Walden. General Talvela who had come from Germany to celebrate the Marshal's birthday also used the Marshal's special train to Mikkeli, and the Marshal had a lengthy discussion with him during the night. Probably Talvela gave the Marshal a detailed report on his impressions of Germany, and the two men examined the possibilities of cementing the rifts in the Finnish-German brotherhood-in-arms. Without German armament assistance, the Finnish Armed Forces were bound to come to a desperate situation within a short time. The Finnish Air Forces were entirely dependent on German supplies.

It was not easy to find a way out, since Hitler's demand of a binding declaration by a person with authority (the President or Prime Minister) could not be fulfilled. The Finnish Congress would never have consented to such an obligation which would have made Finnish foreign politics dependent on the Reich. In search of a practicable solution it probably occurred to Mannerheim to discuss matter with Foreign Minister Ramsay. The Marshal brought his friend, Minister of Defense Walden, to Lahti by motor car on 7 June where a meeting with the Foreign Minister took place. The discussion lasted several hours whereupon Mannerheim returned to Mikkeli, while the other two men proceeded to Helsinki. The result of the discussion remained unknown. Mannerheim obviously intended extricate himself from the German-Finnish controversy leaving the matter to the diplomats. When thanking Hitler for his birthday congratulations he took the opportunity to add a few words of thanks for Hitler's letter of 1 June. That brought the affair to a close as far as Mannerheim was concerned. Whatever may have been decided upon at Lahti, nothing was put into effect, and a few days later a large-scale Russian offensive broke loose at the Finnish front, creating an entirely different situation whose seriousness brushed all other questions to the background.

Before proceeding to a narration of the events, some incidents deserve mentioning which happened in the first half of 1944 in Finland independently of events at the front and at headquarters.

The training courses for winter warfare had been continued in the winter of 1943/44 as in the preceding winters. The fifth and sixth training course began at Tuusola on 9 January under Finnish instructors.

Finnish Headquarters had expressed a wish to learn through an experienced German line officer of the attack principles applied by the Russians in their last large-scale offensives at the eastern front. The OKW sent Colonel Nobis to Finland to comply with this request, an officer who was particularly suitable for this mission. Nobis gave a very impressive lecture at Mikkeli on 9 January before the senior officers of Headquarters. The Marshal was also present and was very interested in the information supplied by the German colonel. At Finnish request, Nobis repeated his lecture a few days later before larger circles of Finnish officers at Tuusolaand Petrozavodsk.

The narrow-gage field railway Kuusamo-Hyrinsalmi, constructed by the Germans, was at last finished on 13 January. Many difficulties had to be surmounted by the German engineers, which had been underestimated at first. Construction had lasted much longer than calculated by the railroad contractors, but the time to begin service eventually arrived. The supply service in the Kiestinki sector was thereby much improved.

General Grandell, Chief of the Finnish Economic Office, went to Berlin in February to negotiate about Finnish requests and returned to Finland satisfied with the results. These negotiations had not been influenced at all by the political development in Finland. Military relations had at that time not yet been prejudiced. All German agencies endeavored to fulfill Finnish requests. Grandell's request to increase the Finnish fuel contingent had also been granted.

By order of the Marshal of 12 January, the removal of Headquarters to rural districts in the neighborhood of Mikkeli had been initiated. General Erfurth had also been requested by the Marshal to find billets in the country. Since all billets in the neighborhood of Mikkeli were fully occupied by Finns, the Erfurth decided immediately to build a temporary camp for his staff. A suitable place was found on the shore of Lake Pitkä not far from the outskirts of the town where the forest bordering on the lake offered good air protection. Construction of the camp was pushed with great speed. A German construction squad supplied by the Twentieth Mountain Army performed the technical work. All members of the German General's staff set to work in order to expedite the construction work. The season was very unfavorable for constructing foundations, since during the first week there was deep snow and the ground was frozen hard. When the snow began to melt, at times everything was submerged by the water flowing into the lake, so that time-consuming drainage measures became necessary. During the mud period, the supply route from Mikkeli to the camp could not be used by trucks. The construction of the German camp on Lake Pitkä (Long Lake) gave a lot of trouble, but finally all difficulties were surmounted and a forest camp was erected which nobody needed to be ashamed of. When the Finnish Government on 18 March declined the Soviet Russian peace conditions, Finnish Headquarters feared that Mikkeli would become the target of enemy air raids. Anxious about the fate of the German Staff, Mannerheim asked General Erfurth to move away from Mikkeli as fast as possible. For that reason removal to the forest camp on Lake Pitkä began on 21 March, although construction of the camp had not yet been finished. Its lovely surroundings offered many comforts during the favorable seasons of the year. On 13 June 1944, the third anniversary of General Erfuth's arrival in Finland, Colonel Brunerona, the solicitous commander of Finnish Headquarters, placed a few boats at the disposal of the German Staff which were enjoyed by all German personnel. The "Idyll on Lake Pitkä" will live in the memory of all Germans who got to know it. The splendid comradeship and excellent morale of the small German staff made living together in narrow quarters agreeable. Until the end, morale was high in the camp.

CHAPTER V: The Development of the Political Situation in Finland and Diplomatic Negotiations

Political events played a large role in Finland during the war. The Finns, like the other Scandinavian nations are firm supporters of the democratic system. The democracy of the northern nations is parliamentarianism on the western model.

The supreme political organs in Finland according to the constitution of 1919 are President and Congress. Together with the representatives of the people, the President exercises both legislative and supreme executive power. The Cabinet is responsible for the government of the country. The parliamentarian governmental system in Finland requires the Cabinet to have the confidence of Congress. Congress is elected by all citizens, including women, above a certain age limit in a general and free election.

Congress consists of only one house with 200 members. The following parties were represented in Congress during the war, with the strongest first:

> Social Democratic Party
> Democratic Farmers Party
> National Coalition Party
> Swedish People's Party
> Patriotic People's Movement
> National Progressive Party
> Small Farmers Party

Finland's political approach to Germany beginning before the Winter War and increasing in the short interval between the Winter War and the Third War of Liberation was based on a sober and realistic judgment of the over-all world situation and was not due to any sympathy with National Socialism. This ideology with a few exceptions had taken no root in Finland either prior to or during the war. The Finns were not interested in National Socialist doctrines, in fact often strongly opposed to them. The Finnish press openly expressed this feeling. The development of conditions in Germany under the Third Reich remained unknown to the Finnish public. The picture gained by means of foreign press reports and radio broadcasts was distorted and often incorrect. Those few Finns who travelled to Germany during the war had official missions and were well cared for by the German authorities. What they saw of life in Germany was, therefore, of a limited nature and impressed them very much. The rigid organization characteristics of an authoritarian state and the courageous, self-sacrificing attitude of all classes of the German population during the war had made a strong impression, however. The bulk of the Finnish nation believed that Germany was a strong partner not only for the Finnish Armed Forces, but also for the requirements of the Finnish economy and for assistance in maintaining the nutritional requirements of the population. Hitler was known to be a friend of the Finnish people who had a ready ear for the wishes of the Finns. The fact that he had protected Finland in the winter of 1940 when negotiating with Molotov was not forgotten. Considering the cool nature of the Finns, Hitler could not have been called popular in their country but rather a man in whom they had confidence.

It was good form in Finland not to discuss ideological differences between Germans and Finns. The Germans never attempted to influence the Finns by National Socialist propaganda or to condemn the democratic system of their government. The German Ambassador, a diplomat of the old school and an aristocrat, who discharged the duties of his office with great tact, prevented exponents of the Nazi Party from coming to Finland and creating unrest and served as an excellent model for the German colony in Finland. The small staff of the German General at Mikkeli and the German military agencies at Helsinki also exercised a great reserve in political matters. Though in the course of the years close comradeship, even sincere friendship, developed between Finns and Germans, nonetheless, even in private circles at early hours, disputes about questions concerning current issues never arose. All members of the Finnish Headquarters tried to equal the Marshal who, a master of good form himself, made great demands upon the tact and irreproachable behavior of his officers. A sense of reality and self-control inherent in the soldiers of all countries exercised a beneficial effect on contacts between Finnish and German soldiers at Mikkeli even during the last phase of the war when the brotherhood-in-arms relationship showed serious cracks. In the last war, which was so void of chivalry, few headquarters existed where so much politeness, attentiveness and readiness to help representatives of friendly armed forces lasted until the very end of hostilities. That is the reason why mutual esteem could survive the unhappy end of the war when the roads of the brothers-in-arms parted.

The atmosphere at Rovaniemi was different from that at Mikkeli and Helsinki. There, the vast majority were German soldiers by themselves. Owing to the sparseness of the population in Lapland, the German soldiers had little opportunity to come into contact with the civilian population. Most of the duration of the war (from January 1942 until June 1944), General Dietl commanded the German army in the Arctic region. He was an idealist and a convinced National Socialist who outspokenly advocated his standpoint. Dietl was one of the few generals in high favor with Hitler and the Party. Whenever he came to Germany he was received by Hitler and treated by him with great distinction. The Party leaders often visited Dietl at Rovaniemi. The natural result was that National

Socialism, preached without reserve by the Commander in Chief, formed the key-note of the mental attitude at Army Headquarters and radiated from Rovaniemi to all German sectors at the front. The mountain infantrymen at the front coming from Bavaria and Austria and the men of the Waffen-SS accepted the Party ideology readily. The German propaganda company at Rovaniemi lavishly distributed propaganda material among the troops, which arrived from Germany and naturally also propagated the National Socialist ideas. It would probably be correct to assume that the Twentieth Mountain Army showed the same attitude towards current problems as the other armies at the German eastern front. But all this did not cause any friction in Lapland during the war. At the end of the brotherhood-in-arms relationship on 2 September 1944, Mannerheim acknowledged that the German soldiers had behaved without reproach. The Finnish population liked and respected them, which is the most honorable testimony for an army that had been stationed for years on the territory of a foreign power.

As mentioned before, the entry of Finland into the war with Russia was preceded by a German-Finnish agreement on 22 September 1940 concerning the passage of German troops to North Finland and by several conferences between Germans and Finns during the first half year of 1941. That was the only basis on which Finnish-German brotherhood-in-arms was built.

All decisions of the Finnish President were made according to the constitution in agreement with the Cabinet and with Congress. All questions concerning foreign policy were discussed by the committees for foreign affairs in the Cabinet and of Congress before they were submitted to the President for decision. Questions of particular importance were then voted on by the entire Cabinet. If questions of vital interest to the Finnish people were at stake (for instance, acceptance or refusal of the Russian peace conditions in spring and in summer 1944), Congress was convoked and informed by the Minister of State (Finnish term for Prime Minister) on the intended policy of the government. Congress then gave a vote of confidence if it was in agreement. This procedure prescribed by the Finnish constitution made it necessary that even affairs which demanded strict secrecy had to be brought before large Finnish circles. The disadvantage arising therefrom was outbalanced by the advantage that there was no authoritarian rule in Finland and that he Government's policy was supported by the confidence of the representatives of the people. Between government and people there was full agreement on all vital questions. There can, therefore, be no doubt that the policy of Ryti and the cabinet of Rangell in power in June 1941 had the confidence of Congress. The close cooperation with Germany and anti-Russian Finnish policy were absolutely popular.

The suffering of the Finnish people during the Winter War and the hard terms of the Treaty of Moscow had prepared the ground for Finland's entry into the war against Russia. The whole population was greatly concerned whether Finland would be able to maintain its independence in view of the Soviet Union's urge for expansion. The Finns looked with great hopes on Germany, and they confidently believed, in view of the course World War II had so far taken, that she would be able to smash Russia with quick and heavy blows. No Finn, however, wanted to be drawn into the war between the Great Powers. June 1941 seemed to offer Finland the opportunity to be relieved of the threat from the sprawling eastern empire and to regain what had been lost in the Treaty of Moscow. Any opposition to the Government's policy at that time was very weak. The bulk of the people followed the call to arms readily and full of hope. The admirable calm and order of the Finnish mobilization proved that the Finnish people was of one mind. Moreover, there can be no doubt that the men who bore the supreme responsibility in June 1941 and during the war acted to the best of their knowledge and conscience as good patriots. Who could foresee the end of World War II as it actually developed? To err is human and Finnish history is rich in tragedy. It often leads through night and darkness past dangerous abysses. What, in such situation, is guilt and what is destiny? To find out the historic truth one should first investigate the causes that led to the war and second the responsibility of the men involved.

Finland entered the war against Russia on 26 June 1941 after a radio broadcast by President Ryti to the Finnish people announcing that, since Finnish towns had repeatedly been attacked by Russian airplanes (Helsinki had been bombed several times on 25 June), that Finland considered itself in a state of war with the Soviet Union.

Hitler's proclamation of 22 June 1941 to the soldiers at the eastern front contained the following words with regard to Finland:

> "Our comrades under the command of the Victor of Narvik stand in league with Finnish divisions on the coast of the Arctic Sea. Both the German soldiers under the command of the conqueror of Norway, and the freedom-lovers of Finland under their Marshal are protecting Finland."

These statements were very embarrassing to the Finnish authorities and particularly to Finnish Headquarters. They created the impression that an alliance existed between Finland and the Reich and that Finland had also entered the war against Soviet Russia on 22 June 1941. Since according to international law a state of war did not exist between Finland and the Soviet Union until 26 June, Hitler's statement anticipated the events and compromised Finnish strategy.

Mannerheim's order of the day to the Finnish Armed Forces of 28 June called on the Finnish soldiers to follow him once more, for the last time, in order to secure Finland's future. Field Marshal Mannerheim enjoyed the confidence of all, and the population supported him unanimously, but there was not as much unity shown with regard to the Finnish war aims. Public opinion was divided into three groups. The most modest aimed at a defense against the Russian threat and wanted operations restricted to mere defensive warfare. Another group wanted to regain the territory lost in the Moscow peace, and to restore their native land to the Karelians, who had emigrated after the Winter War and now lived in emergency quarters in the interior of the country. A third group had considerably more far-reaching ambitions. It wanted to free Far-Karelia of Russian rule and to unite the whole area inhabited by East-Karelians with Finland as a new territory won for western culture, which during and after the First War of Liberation could not be liberated. This third group wanted to create a Greater Finland, whose natural boundaries extended to the Svir, Lake Onega and the White Sea.

The first group, the representatives for a mere defensive war, were an unimportant minority among the political leftists at the beginning of the war. The second group, wishing to regain the boundaries of 1939, formed the political majority. The third group, adherents of Greater Finland, had its followers in the ranks of the Finnish Armed Forces and the students.

The number of supporters of a Greater Finland increased in proportion to the successes achieved by the Finnish Army in the summer of 1941, which had reached the natural boundaries of Greater Finland after the first year of war. When the chances for a favorable issue of the war grew less as the years went by, the Greater Finnish dream faded away, however, and opinions were divided between a Finland with the boundaries of 1939 or 1940. All politicians, however, were united in the desire not to be involved in a war with Great Britain and America, an aim which required a very cautious foreign policy. The Finnish situation was complicated by the treaty of alliance concluded on 7 July 1941 between Great Britain and the Soviet Union. Would the Finnish politicians be able to keep their country out of the war of the Great Powers? That was a serious question. When on 5 December 1941 Great Britain rather surprisingly declared war on Finland, the Finnish government increased its efforts to at least not break off relations with the United States. The fact that these relations though more strained were not broken off until 30 June 1944 was due to clever Finnish policy and probably also to the American desire not to declare war on Finland, since the American people were sympathetic towards the Finns. The U.S. State Department repeatedly tried to extricate Finland from the war against Soviet Russia. These diplomatic steps exercised a great influence on the internal political situation in Finland and created a growing distrust of the German brother-in-arms.

Parallel to the efforts of the United States was the influence exercised by Sweden, which had always had strong ties to Finland. The attitude of the Swedish press was thoroughly anti-Hitler. Daily the Swedish papers warned the Finns of the consequences of its government's policy and exhorted them to reach a compromise with the Soviet Union. Swedish official agencies, too, were ready at any time to negotiate between Finland and the Soviet Union. Finland was connected with Sweden by many and old ties, but its war against the Soviet Union was still not at all popular in Sweden. The number of Swedish volunteers remained small. Swedish opinion penetrated Finland through the Swedish radio and the great number of Swedish papers sent to Finland, and furthermore, was spread around the Swedish speaking population by Finnish papers in the Swedish language. Great attention was paid to them particularly in circles of the Swedish People's Party and the Social Democratic Party. The political opposition against the government's policy originated from this segment of the population and increased in the course of the war. The attitude of the Swedish-language Finnish papers in time grew more and more aggressive towards the course steered by the government, causing the Finnish Government much embarrassment and the German brother-in-arms increasing resentment.

At the very beginning of the war when Mannerheim's order of the day alluded to the uprise in Karelia, the division of public opinion in Finland with regard to war aims became evident. Many Finnish politicians did not like this, and it raised objections from those circles who were in favor of a purely defensive war. When, later on, the victorious advance of the Finnish Army in the summer of 1941 reached the old boundary of 1939, the strategic decisions of the Commander in Chief were strongly influenced by consideration of his country's foreign and internal situation.

In August 1941 the first diplomatic attempt was made by the United States at inducing the Finnish Government to terminate the war with Russia. This action caused the Finnish Cabinet to disagree at the end of August on Finnish war aims. On 31 August, Ryti came to Mikkeli to discuss with Mannerheim whether to continue the offensive beyond the old boundary or not. For a great soldier like Mannerheim there was naturally no question that a victoriously advancing army be halted at a political boundary. The offensive had to go on in order not to give the beaten Russians any respite. The requests of the German brother-in-arms became increasingly urgent that the Finns should take off from the direction of the Karelian Isthmus in the attack of Army Group North on Leningrad , and that the Karelian Army should resume its advance toward the Svir line, after having come to a stop at the old boundary.

Considerable time elapsed (from about the end of July until the beginning of September) until Mannerheim obtained the President's permission to let the Karelian Army resume its attack. Only a modest compromise was reached on the Karelian Isthmus, however, which stipulated that terrain and not the political boundary was to be the decisive factor. Even though situated some ways beyond the old boundary, the Finnish troops were allowed to occupy more tactically favorable positions, which enabled them to save forces.

Finnish participation in the attack on Leningrad, however, was out of the question. If the Finns had not had this political handicap in autumn 1941, Leningrad would have probably been taken in the first year of the war by a joint Finnish-German attack from opposite directions. That would have meant an incalculable advantage for the Finnish-German front north of the Gulf of Finland and a great improvement of the strategic situation. Sufficient Finnish forces would have been released to have enabled strong participation in the German offensive against the Murmansk railroad. The greater the difficulties were which prevented a Finnish-German juncture on the Svir or in the area between Volkhov and Svir, the more the military command of the two brothers-in-arms ought to have tried to bring about a union of the two fronts at Leningrad.

In November 1941, the United States through their ambassador at Helsinki exercised strong political pressure on Finland to separate the latter from Germany and to induce her to come to an agreement with Russia. The moment for the American diplomatic offensive was psychologically well chosen. The war was a heavy burden on the Finnish people; the food situation in the towns was uncertain, fuel was lacking and the hope of an early termination of the war with Russia had been given up. The morale at the front was suffering from the still unsatisfied demand of the older age classes to be dismissed from service. Helsinki was hit by another air attack. At that time, the inquiry of the United States as to how the Finnish Government looked at the situation and whether the good services of the United States were desired to bring about a reconciliation with Russia came as a great temptation to the Finns, to whom the thought of a long war was distressing. Witting, the Finnish Minister of Foreign Affairs, a convinced and true friend of the German-Finnish brotherhood-in-arms, cleverly parried the American move by declaring that Finland did not yet feel secure from the threat of its eastern neighbor and, therefore, did not think the time ripe to come to terms with the Russians. He referred to the statement on the political situation made by Minister of State Rangell a few days previously (on 29 November) in the Finnish Congress. Rangell had expressed his appreciation of the German military assistance and stressed the necessity that the Finnish nation not yet slackened in its war efforts, since Finland's situation was not yet secure. Thus the American attempt at intervention had again been warded off.

A few days later, on 1 December, Mannerheim issued a "proclamation to all men and women of Finland," exhorting the Finnish people in a manner similar to Rangell to make every effort to bring the war to a favorable conclusion.

In December, Great Britain declared war on Finland, and a few days later the war between the Great Powers was further expanded by Japan's entry into the war and Germany's declaration of war against the United States. The expansion of the war was most undesirable to the Finnish Government, which tried to stick to its standpoint not to have anything to do with the war between the Great Powers and to be involved only in an armed conflict with the Soviet Union. This thesis was seriously shaken by Great Britain's declaration of war. Merchant and ship-owner circles interested in world trade, who were not numerous in Finland but very influential, were hard struck and disappointed by this development of the political situation.

At the beginning of March 1942, the United States made another attempt at putting Finland under diplomatic pressure to reach an agreement with the Soviet Union or at least to induce it to refrain from an offensive against the Murmansk railroad. This happened at a time when Mannerheim's plan at an offensive against Soroka was being discussed by the two headquarters. Perhaps some information had leaked out to Sweden and had been passed on to the enemy. During the war many channels existed at Stockholm through which news reached the Western Powers and the Soviet Union. At any rate it was peculiar that the plan of an offensive against Soroka, which had already been dropped by Mannerheim at the beginning of the year on account of the deterioration of the situation at the German eastern front, now seemed unfeasible in early March for reasons of foreign policy. Mannerheim cleverly emphasized the military basis of this change in plans by not immediately declining the repeated German demands to attack the Murmansk railroad but instead making them dependent on a previous capture of Leningrad by the Germans. This connection between Operation LACHSFANG (attack against the Murmansk railroad) and Operation NORDLICHT (attack on Leningrad) has already been dealt with when describing the course of military events. It only remains to be explained that in the diplomatic field, too, certain not unimportant influences were applied to keep the Finns from attacking the Murmansk railroad.

On 4 June 1942, Mannerheim celebrated his seventy-fifth birthday. That was a great event for the Finns. All classes of the population rejoiced with the greatest living Finn and thanked and honored him. For various reasons it had been decided to have the birthday celebration at the front instead of in Mikkeli. This arrangement made it possible to limit the number of congratulants to the guests invited by the President. Ryti acted as host on 4 June. A suitable place in beautiful surroundings was found on the southern shore of Lake Saimaa, where the President's special train with the guests from Helsinki, and Mannerheim's train with the leading officers from Finnish Headquarters could be put on a siding. The nearby Imolanjärvi airdrome provided facilities for the landing of those guests who arrived from distant places by plane. Among them were Generals Dietl and Stumpff. After the ceremony of congratulations had ended and the foreign guests had been received by the Marshal, two Dornier planes landed from Germany. They brought Adolf Hitler, of whose intention to come to Finland the President and the Marshal had been confidentially informed only on the evening of 3 June. Hitler, who greatly admired Mannerheim and the heroic Finnish people, had decided to convey personally his own and the German people's congratulations to the Finnish hero. Though this visit of state was an improvisation which decisively changed the program carefully arranged for the day, nevertheless the Marshal's birthday remained a brilliant event satisfying everyone present. The Finnish gift for equanimity and the great tact of Colonel Brunkrona, the Headquarters Commandant, worked together to enable the day to pass smoothly. The officers escorting Hitler were deeply impressed by the high standard of Finnish hospitality. At ceremonial breakfast in the dining car, Ryti honored Mannerheim by naming him Marshal of Finland. Mannerheim thanked the President in a long speech for the honors bestowed on him and praised the brave Finnish Army, "I am proud of being allowed to command this incomparably brave army. It is and will remain forever my finest memory."

Hitler had not intended making a speech at dinner. He rose, however, and made in this entirely strange circle of persons an astonishingly intuitive speech, which was well accepted by the audience. He praised the Finnish achievements in the Winter War and in the present war and expressed his regret that Germany had not been able to come to the assistance of Finland in the first of the two. After Hitler's departure, the two special trains left for Helsinki and Mikkeli respectively on the evening of 4 June, and all participants in the celebration were satisfied with the day's results. The Finnish press commented favorably on Hitler's visit. The Finnish people understood and appreciated that the Marshal of Finland had been rendered a special honor by the visit of the Head of the Reich. In the United States, on the other hand, the reaction to Hitler's visit was unfavorable. Finnish Ambassador Procopé reported that he had been told by the State Department that Finland could not afford to step out of line again.

Marshal Mannerheim hastened to return Adolf Hitler's visit by going to Germany. His trip was delayed a few days owing to an accident which he had suffered at Petrozavodsk when visiting the front. He left Helsinki on 27 June. In order to show his guest particular attention, Hitler sent his private airplane with General Schmundt, Chief of the Wehrmacht Adjutant's Office, to Helsinki to fetch Mannerheim. The Finnish guest was received in Germany with unusual marks of honor. A great military reception was held on the Rastenburg Air Field. The guests were then driven to the Wolfschanze (Hitler's East Prussian Headquarters) where a reception by Hitler, participation in the daily situation briefing and a state breakfast followed. Around 27 June, the German's second summer offensive began, which had been delayed by a series of storms. At the situation briefing Hitler let Mannerheim see behind the scenes and disclosed to him that the Caucasian oil district would be an objective of the German offensive. Russian resistance in the Crimea was at that time coming to an end. The statements of the German officers reporting on the situation at the eastern front sounded very hopeful and made a favorable impression on Mannerheim and his Finnish cohorts. In the afternoon Mannerheim went to OKH in order to pay a visit to Generaloberst Halder. Hitler appeared there too and again acted as host. The Finnish Marshal spent the evening and night as guest of the Reichsmarschall at the Reichsjägerhof in the heart of the Rominten Heath. In the forenoon of 28 June he drove from there to Insterburg Airport where Hitler's private plane waited to bring him back to Finland.

The Finnish Commander in Chief's trip to Germany had an encouraging and invigorating effect on the Finnish-German brotherhood-in-arms. Mannerheim and his entourage were greatly impressed at the Führer's Headquarters, the Army High Command, and the Luftwaffe Commander in Chief's Headquarters, by the confidence and hopefulness of the German leaders in June 1942, and they made no secret of it in Finland, thereby strengthening the hope of the Finns that the new German offensive in the east would soon lead to a favorable end of the war. At that time (about 1 July 1942) the Finnish-German brotherhood-in-arms was at the peak of its popularity. The Finns put their trust in Germany's strength and there was practically no opposition against the Finnish Government's policy.

Feeling began to change in autumn 1942 when it became apparent that the German offensive toward the Caucasus and Volga, though penetrating deeply into Russia, head not resulted in a decisive victory over the Red Army. On the contrary, the Russian Army, which counterattacked in autumn 1942, showed remarkable fighting strength and drive. The German eastern army, which had naturally been weakened by the summer offensive and had occupied positions which were unfavorable for defense soon got into a difficult situation. Mannerheim, an experienced general, who closely followed the operations of the German eastern Army, grew alarmed early at the state of the protruding German positions in southern Russia. News of the resignation of *Generaloberst* Halder as Chief of the Army's General Staff, which became known in Finland in September 1942, was received with regret and concern at Finnish Headquarters. His successor, General Zeitlzler, was a stranger to the Finns. Personal acquaintance between the leading men of all sides is of great importance in a coalition war.

A clear indication to the Finns of the difficulties felt by the German eastern army in the autumn of 1942 was the repeated postponement of the attack on Leningrad, which finally was put off for an indefinite period of time. They drew the correct conclusion that the German forces were more urgently needed at other places on the front than at Leningrad in which the Finns were particularly interested and for the conquest of which the Germans had made extensive promises. Public opinion in Finland felt deceived in the autumn of 1942 and was very anxious about the situation in Russia. President Ryti, who exerted a great effect on his Finnish people, felt it expedient to broadcast a speech on 26 October 1942 criticizing the slackening morale. He had a presentiment that a change in the opinion of the Finnish people was threatening or had even taken place already.

News of the American landing in North Africa on 8 November 1942 had an alarming effect in Finland, creating nervousness in government and headquarters circles. Nobody could understand how the preparations for such a large-scale operation had remained hidden to the German secret service, and the apparent rapid deterioration of the German-Italian situation in North Africa was a cause for concern.

At the same time the Finnish cabinet was made uneasy by Allied attempts at extricating Finland from the war. Repeated air attacks on Helsinki were made in November, lowering the morale of the population.

On 22 December, the American minister was suddenly recalled. A legation secretary remained to represent the United States at Helsinki.

A new presidential election was due to take place on 15 February 1943. The procedure prescribed by the constitution could not be followed owing to the state of war. Congress had, therefore decided on 1 November 1942 that a new election according to the rules of the constitution should not take place until 1 March 1945. That was to be the limit of the term of office of a president to be elected by a simplified method. Since the election of new delegates was out of the question in wartime, Congress decided that the new President be elected by the 300 old delegates. At first the re-election of Ryti seemed to be a matter of course, since there was no other promising candidate. But when, after the great Soviet Russian successes in the Stalingrad area, the situation on the German front in South Russia and also in North Africa deteriorated more and more by the end of the year, and when opposition against Ryti's policy increased, other candidates were mentioned. Their chances, however, were small. By the middle of January political circles at Helsinki who were opposed to a re-election of Ryti suggested Mannerheim as a candidate. The Marshal remained very reserved and did not assent to his nomination as a candidate. He told his entourage at Mikkeli that he would not engage in a doubtful election but would only make himself available if drafted. Ryti was, therefore, finally re-elected on 15 February 1943, receiving ninety percent of the delegates' votes.

When the curtain fell on the German tragedy at Stalingrad on 31 January, morale in Finland was at a low ebb. A speech by Colonel Paasonen on 9 February before members of the Finnish Congress dealing with the opinion of Finnish Headquarters on the situation on all fronts, sounded rather pessimistic and had a depressing effect on the morale of the Congress. At the same time, the Swedish press advocated more and more openly the conclusion of a separate Finnish peace. The State Department in Washington also believed the moment opportune to tempt Finland again. On 11 February, Procopé, the Finnish Ambassador to Washington, was requested by the American Secretary of State to make a statement on the political situation in Finland from the Finnish point of view. That was the beginning of a lively American program to persuade the Finnish government to conclude a separate peace. Reports of the American Embassy in Helsinki on the critical situation in Finland probably had created the impression in the State Department in Washington that the time would soon be ripe for a political change. This declaration was the first to mention openly the possibility of a separate Finnish peace.

After the re-election of Ryti, the Cabinet as usual offered its resignation. That opened the way for a reorganization of the Finnish Government, which, however, made only slow progress. After the unsuccessful attempt of Hakkila, the former President of Congress, Professor Linkomies, the Assistant Dean of Helsinki University, tried to set up a government.

On 5 March the Linkomies Government was finally formed. Ramsay replaced Witting as Foreign Minister. Germany's friends, Rangell and Witting, were thus no longer in command. The new cabinet was composed of still more colorless personalities than its predecessor. It was not exactly a "peace cabinet" but a cabinet with a free hand.

In consequence of the reorganization of the government Reenpä, the former Chief of the Finnish Intelligence Service, was replaced by Dr. Vilkuna.

On 20 March, the United States began a very effective diplomatic offensive. The American Chargé d'Affaires handed the Finnish Foreign Minister a letter offering the services of the United States in bringing about a separate peace with the Soviet Union. That placed Finnish Foreign Ministers Ramsay in a difficult situation. The tense internal political situation of Finland prevented a blunt refusal and required most careful handling of the American offer. Ramsay had no practical experience in diplomacy. He wished to act as correctly as possible both with regard to the Americans and the German brother-in-arms. He treated the Americans inquiry as a top secret, concealing it from the German Ambassador at Helsinki. He only asked him to arrange for him an early meeting with Ribbentrop, the German Minister for Foreign Affairs. He gave a delaying answer to the American Chargé d'Affaires on 24 March, asking him for further explanations of the American intentions.

On 25 March 1943 Ramsay went by plane to Ribbentrop with whom he had a lengthy discussion, about which several versions exist. Both the Finnish and German reports indicated that the first conference of the two foreign ministers was held under an unlucky star. Ribbentop obviously did not realize Ramsay's good intention to discuss matters frankly and confidentially with his German colleague. The curt manner of the German Foreign Minister, who immediately offered reproaches, hurt Ramsay, the sensitive internationalist. After a short telephone conversation with Hitler, Ribbentrop declared to his Finnish colleague that the Germans would consider any acceptance of the American offer as a Finnish betrayal of its brother-in-arms and of the common struggle for the destiny of Europe with all resultant consequences. Ribbentrop demanded that Ramsay, who was surprised by Ribbentrop's attitude, completely clarify the Finnish intentions, give a written promise of the Finnish Government to conclude no separate peace with the Soviet Union, and immediately decline the American offer. The text of the Finnish reply to the United States should be revealed to the German Foreign Minister prior to its dispatch.

Ramsay could not fail to be annoyed by the treatment he had received, and he flew back to Finland very dissatisfied. Factual difficulties have often in history been aggravated by personal dislikes. Ramsay, too, developed a permanent resentment toward Ribbentrop, which extended to the official contacts between the two ministries for foreign affairs. The Finnish answer, the contents of which had been approved by Ribbentrop, was handed to the American Chargé d'Affaires at Helsinki on 10 April. The second German demand, however, of a written Finnish obligation not to conclude a separate peace with Russian remained unfulfilled. If a very favorable and encouraging answer from the United States to Ramsay's request fo 24 March had come, the Finnish Foreign Minister would have been in a very difficult position toward the Cabinet and

Congress. The Finnish Cabinet would not have been able to conceal from Congress the possibility of an American intervention, and Congress would not have approved a foreign policy destroying such concrete chances. It was probably a great relief to Ramsay to read the answer which the American Chargé d'Affaires handed him also on 10 April. The note was rather noncommittal. The United States had not intended to give any guarantees but only to establish contact between Finland and the Soviet Union. As a consequence of the Finnish refusal, the American Embassy announced its departure from Helsinki on 23 April.

Negotiations on Ribbentrop's second demands – written obligation of the Finns – went on between the German and Finnish governments for another few weeks. For one who knew Finnish conditions, this German demand was impossible, and it would have been better if it had never been made. No Finnish Government would ever have obtained the consent of Congress to such an engagement. It was, therefore, quite useless that the angry Reich Foreign Minister ordered the German Ambassador in Helsinki to return to Germany and did not allow him to return to Helsinki for weeks as a means of exerting pressure. The Finns were not disturbed in the least and pretended not to notice the absence of the Ambassador. If they had some request, they would ask Chargé d'Affaires Zechlin who represented Ambassador von Blücher. Exchanges between the Finnish Foreign Minister and the German Chargé d'Affaires grew, however, more and more infrequent and meaningless. Each one had little to say to the other.

This certainly was an unusual situation for two states that were waging a mutual life or death struggle. The fact must be stressed, however, that this estrangement did not apply to military relationships. The German General at Finnish Headquarters continued to enjoy the unreserved confidence of Mannerheim and the greatest respect of the Finnish officers. The Wehrmacht High Command, too, displayed great readiness to comply with requests which Mannerheim occasionally made. The harmony of the brothers-in-arms in military matters was, therefore, still entirely undisturbed.

On Finnish Memorial Day in May 1943, Prime Minister Linkomies made a speech exhorting the Finnish people to hold out until final victory. Public opinion in Finland was divided between war and peace, and so was opinion in the Finnish Cabinet. The great change in the internal political situation since the summer of 1941, however, became evident in the treatment of the question of the Finnish Waffen-SS Volunteer battalion. The battalion which had been organized prior to the Russian war and had fought in the first two years of the war with the German eastern army in South Russia, had on 1 June 1943 returned on leave to Finland. This battalion was cared for by a Finnish committee (Rector Nevanlinna, Bank

Manager Normahn and others). The organization and employment of the battalion had been arranged by the two foreign ministries. The Finns had probably been influenced by memories of the 27th Royal Prussian Light Infantry Battalion formed by Finns in the First War of Liberation, which had an honorable place in Finnish History. The Finnish General Staff had had nothing to do with the founding of the Volunteer Battalion and left control of the Battalion's affairs to the Foreign Ministry and the committee. Mannerheim's standpoint was that he had nothing to do with Finns fighting abroad in foreign armed forces. That was a matter for the Minister of Foreign Affairs.

Obviously a lack of clarity about the future existed when the battalion landed in Hangö on 1 June 1943 and the men dispersed on leave. According to the Waffen-SS, an opinion shared by the committee, the battalion was to return to the German eastern front after expiration of the leave. If individual members of the battalion wished to remain in Finland, the Finns were to send replacements, so that the strength of the battalion would remain unchanged. It was most regrettable that the future of the battalion was not clarified until the volunteers had assembled at Hangö after their leave. The bulk of the battalion had decided to return to Germany. The situation now entered a decisive stage, for at this moment Congress and the Cabinet intervened. Congress passed a law which forbade Finns to perform active military service in foreign countries during wartime. In this way replacements for the volunteer battalion were prevented. Even if no obstacle was placed in the way of a renewed departure, the existence of the battalion was undermined by this veto. Moreover, the Cabinet did not allow the battalion to leave for an unlimited time; the new engagement was restricted to six months.

The question of replacements probably was in agreement with the desires of Mannerheim. The small amount of Finnish replacements formed sources of continual concern to the Commander in Chief, so that he undoubtedly fully agreed to the stopping of the battalion's replacements. Moreover, he did not think it justified that a battalion be diverted to Germany at a time when Finland was at war. The Finnish Army needed its young soldiers itself. But Mannerheim recognized that the manner in which the Cabinet and Congress handled the incident was going to annoy the German Government. He did not wish that an unfriendly act be committed against Germany and therefore used all his influence with the Prime Minister and the Foreign Minister to grant the battalion an extension of its stay abroad from six months to one year. His proposal was, however, declined by the Government. The consequence was that the supreme German authorities were very much annoyed. The OKW informed the Marshal that Germany was willing to abandon the idea of a return of the battalion entirely in order not to cause the Finnish volunteers conflict with their conscience. The battalion was, thereupon, released from the Wehrmacht on 11 July at Hangö and transferred to the Finnish Armed Forces. So this episode in the Finnish-German brotherhood-in-arms came to an end.

At the same time, the German brother-in-arms was further annoyed when it became known that a Finnish-American Society had been established at Helsinki. Mr. Ersko, the owner of Helsinki's largest newspaper, (Helsingin Sanomat) was appointed president.

The deterioration of the Finnish-American relations was shown by the demand for the recall of the Finnish Military Attaché in Washington. On 22 July he was requested to leave the United States. It was obvious that the over-all situation was getting worse both for Germany and Finland. The secession of Italy in June 1943 and the downfall of Mussolini was a bad omen for all small powers who still sided with Germany. Uneasiness increased among politicians in Helsinki. On 23 August, the "Peace Resolution of the Thirty-three" was published in an open letter to the President. The political opposition began their campaign against the Linkomies Government. The opposition consisted of members of the Social Democrats, some members of the Farmer's Party and of the Swedish People's Party. These thirty-three politicians of the opposition did not yet constitute a danger for the government, considering that Finnish Congress had a total of 200 seats. But the resolution demonstrated to the Finnish people and foreign countries that a good section of Congress had lost faith in a final victory of Germany. The large percentage of Social Democrats in the group of thirty-three, furthermore, showed that the strongest Finnish party could no longer be held together by Tanner, its leader. Tanner, perhaps the most able of the leading Finnish politicians, who had done a good deal for the Social Democratic party, was a Cabinet Minister both under Rangell and Linkomies. He was considered an irreconcilable enemy of Soviet Russia and a strong obstacle to a Finnish peace policy. Now members of the Social Democratic Party, included in the group of thirty-three, rose against him and combated his policy, which they called wrong. Among these men opposing Tanner was the trade union leader Vuori, who on the occasion of a meeting of trade unionists at Stockholm on 24 August discussed with representatives of British trade unions the possibilities of a separate Finnish peace. This conversation was published in the Swedish press and caused a sensation in Finland. The foreign press in the Allied countries took up the discussion which and been discussed by the Finnish politicians. The Daily Sketch printed on 29 August a summary of the conditions under which Finland was allegedly ready to conclude a separate peace.

The proclamation of martial law in Denmark on 31 August 1943 by the German occupation forces induced the Finnish press to express its sympathy openly with the Danes and to condemn the German methods. Feeling at Helsinki had come to such a nervous pitch that Prime Minister Linkomies made a reassuring speech in Congress on 3 September. He declared that Finland should continue the war until its independence was secured. The text of Linkomies speech was handed the German Foreign Ministry by Kivimäki, the Finnish Ambassador to Berlin, in order to satisfy Ribbentrop's demand of 26 March of a binding declaration by the Finnish Government not to conclude an separate peace. The German Government took due note of the Finnish Prime Minister's speech and did not return to the subject. It had realized in the meantime that a morer far-reaching engagement of the Finnish Government as desired by the Reich Foreign Minister, was impossible considering Finnish conditions.

A press reception by Linkomies on 12 September to American, Danish and Swedish journalists at Helsinki was to serve the same purpose as the speech in Congress. The Prime Minister made a statement on Finland's relations with the United States which obviously aimed at improving sentiment in the United States, but which created new resentment on the part of the German Ministry for Foreign Affairs.

It was indicative of the political tension in Finland that discussion of a separate peace and of Moscow's conditions went on without interruption. On 12 September Radio Moscow addressed a broadcast to Finland. A Bulle (probably John Bulls Weekly) from London dated 23 September made Soviet Russia's peace conditions for Finland public. They were felt to be extremely severe (unconditional surrender, change of government, and so on) and were emphatically declined by Finnish public opinion.

New fuel was added to the feeling of nervousness and insecurity of the internal political situation by rumors appearing in the world press in the summer of 1943 about German endeavors to conclude peace with the Soviet Union. By the middle of June there was some confidential talk at Mikkeli that the Finnish Military Attaché in Stockholm, who had visited Finnish Headquarters a few days ago, had submitted to the Marshal proof of German-Russian negotiations, which had begun at Stockholm in great secrecy but were later disrupted by a letter from Roosevelt to Stalin brought by Davies, the American Ambassador to Russia.

Since these rumors increased in the next weeks and began to create a stir in Helsinki, the German Government directed the German Ambassador in Helsinki on 24 September to categorically deny the reports of German-Russian peace feelers. In the beginning of January 1944, *Pravda* reported that Ribbentrop had negotiated in Spain with the British. These rumors appeared credible to some Finnish politicians because more and more Finnish circles doubted that Germany would be able to be victorious, if the coalition between the Soviet Union, the United States and England continued till the end. The Finns believed that Germany's only way out of the ugly situation was to eliminate either Russia or Great Britain from the war.

The Finnish press had a large share in disturbing the relationship between the brother-in-arms, which at first had been so cordial and agreeable. Whereas the German press under the direction of the Propaganda Ministry remained reserved in criticism and published only favorable reports on Finland, the Finnish press indulged in increasingly harmful and damaging criticism of German conditions. Prior to his departure on 16 September 1943 to make a report to the Marshal of Finland, the Finnish General at German Headquarters was told by authoritative persons in the OKH that the tone of some Finnish papers was giving offense in Germany. By that time, new fuel was added to the fire by an article in *Svenska Pressen* of 18 September 1943 on alleged looting by German soldiers in Italy, which strongly hurt German sensitivities since it attacked the honor of the German brother-in-arms. Upon the immediate complaint of the German Ambassador in Helsinki and the German General at Mikkeli, *General* Walden, the gallant Minister of Defense, apologized in due form and promised that mistakes like the article in *Svenska Pressen* would not happen again.

At that time, Tanner made a speech before the Social Democratic Party in Helsinki. He rejected the peace-feelers made by various Finnish agencies and stressed the cohesiveness fo the Social Democratic Party. He added that the Finnish Government had a free hand to withdraw from the war. This speech by the party leader indicated that Tanner, too, could no longer shut his eyes to the opinion of the opposition and admitted the possibility of a separate Finnish peace.

The visit of General Jodl had already been mentioned previously. By order of Hitler, he came to Mikkeli on 14 October 1943 in order to discuss the military situation with Mannerheim. Jodl carried a personal letter from Hitler to Ryti which was handed to the President by the German Ambassador. Hitler warned the Finnish Government in this letter not to yield too much to the growing Finnish opposition which would create the impression of weakness and war-weariness abroad. Hitler complained about the unfriendly tone of the Finnish press toward Germany and reproached the President for not recognizing the liberated Mussolini as Chief of State.

Ryti's answer was delivered on 26 October by the Finnish Ambassador in Berlin. It explained that the attitude of the Finnish Government toward the minority in Congress was in conformity with democratic rules and the parliamentary system which the Finns believed in and with which they had so far had good experience. With regard to the recognition of Mussolini, a small nation like Finland could not voice its opinion before the Italian people themselves had spoken. Ryti admitted that the Finnish press had repeatedly touched a wrong note. He promised that measures would be taken to prevent this in future. Hitler, as was expected, was little satisfied by the answer.

The internal political situation in Finland eased considerably during the last weeks of 1943. The situation at the German front in Russia became somewhat more quiet, and there was a lull at the Finnish-German front between the Gulf of Finland and the Arctic Sea. The most calming effect on the internal political situation in Finland, however, was the news arriving in Finland concerning the results of the Allied conference at Moscow (early November 1943) and Teheran (December 1943). Up to that time, many Finns in important positions had deluded themselves with the hope that, after putting down its arms, Finland would be treated by the Allies like the prodigal son in the Bible. Now all Finns realized the seriousness of the situation. It was obvious that the victors planned a hard fate for the small powers who had taken sides with Germany. If they have the intention of destroying us, the Finnish politicians argued, we may as well defend ourselves as long as possible. The result was that a separate peace was no longer mentioned. The newspapers quieted down. The politicians backing the Government's policy wished to draw attention before the end of the year to the unbroken will of resistance of the Finnish people. As if in answer to the open letter of the thirty-three, they handed the President on 21 December 1943 an address with 5000 signatures, expressing thanks for the German assistance, determination to continue the war and the intention of retaining Karelia.

At that time (end of 1943) Moscow began an atrocity propaganda campaign against the Finns. They were accused of maltreating the population in occupied Karelia. The Soviet Russian war of nerves irritated the Finns, since they feared unfavorable reactions in their relations with the United States. In order to refute the charges of Radio Moscow, they invited a group of Swedish journalists to Finland who were brought to the front in Karelia and received at Finnish Headquarters at Mikkeli on 13 January 1944. The Finns expected these Swedish reports from the front to have favorable influence on public opinion in the Anglo-Saxon countries.

The political calm in Finland came to an end with the outbreak of a violent battle south of Leningrad on 17 January 1944. News of a Russian breakthrough through the German positions at Oranienbaum and Uritsk utterly alarmed Helsinki and Mikkeli. On 1 February, Ryti made a speech in the Finnish Congress, declaring that Finland would retain its freedom of action notwithstanding the development of the war situation. At the same time Foreign Minister Ramsay was said to have stated that a new situation would be created for Finland if Narva were not held by the Germans.

By the beginning of February 1944, sufficient signs were apparent to indicated to the enemy a decline of the Finnish will to resist. If one wanted to strike while the iron was hot, now was the time to do it. The Allied diplomatic actions were initiated by a strong air attack on Helsinki on 6 February.

On 9 February, American Secretary of State Hull broadcast an address to Finland asking her to quit the war. A similar memorandum from the United States was officially handed to Foreign Minister Ramsay by the American Chargé d'Affaires.

On 14 February the Finnish press announced that Minister Paasikivi had left by plane for Stockholm in order to learn the Russian peace conditions. Paasikivi did not hold a public office at that time, but as former Finnish Ambassador to Moscow he had good personal relations with Soviet politicians. There were experienced and influential men in Finland who believed it possible that the Soviet Union would grant Finland favorable peace conditions. The Finns hoped, and the Germans feared, that the Russians would offer the Finns the world. The German Foreign Office, therefore, rightfully believed that the situation had become critical and that there was again a danger of Finland concluding a separate peace. The German Ambassador in Helsinki handed the Finnish Foreign Minister a note on 21 February couched in sharp terms saying that Germany would consider a separate Finnish peace an act of treason toward the German brother-in-arms and Finland would have to pay the consequences. Ramsay explained to the Ambassador that Paasikivi's trip was not a peace-feeler but only served to procure information.

Paasikivi returned from Stockholm on 24 February. The Finnish Government which had so far denied any part in Paasikivi's trip (he was supposed to have travelled as a private person without any official mission) admitted on 25 February that Paasikivi had been at Stockholm in order to learn the Russian conditions. Paasikivi, who at first had been disavowed by the Finnish Government, was now acknowledged by Ramsay. The conditions which the Finnish intermediary received were published on 25 February in *Dagens Nyheter* in comparatively correct form (confirmation of the Treaty of Moscow, political frontier of 1940, internment of the German troops stationed in Finland). In order to influence the Finnish population, Helsinki was again effectively bombed on 27 February by Russian planes.

Moscow Radio also broadcast the peace conditions on 29 February. In addition to the Russian demands, which had already become known, Russia demanded crushing reparations from the Finnish people. Hopes of a lenient peace were now finally buried. Without illusions Government and Congress faced the hard facts.

Prime Minister Linkomies explained the situation to the Finnish Congress on 29 February. He declared Moscow's conditions unacceptable but said that Finland would continue its endeavors toward peace. Congress then passed a vote of confidence in the Linkomies Government.

The answer of the Finnish Government was delivered at Stockholm on 4 March. When Paasikivi was in Stockholm, contact had been arranged between him and Mrs. Kollontay, the Soviet Russian Ambassadress, through the good offices of the Swedish Foreign Ministry. The Finnish answer called Moscow's conditions impossible to fulfill, but added that Finland was ready for further negotiations.

The Russian answer to the Finnish note arrived in Helsinki on 14 March and was communicated to the Finnish Congress on the same day. The Kremlin declined any negotiations on the peace conditions announced by Moscow. The Finnish Congress was once more called together and on 16 March sanctioned the stand planned by the Finnish Government. The Finnish Government, thereupon, declined once more the Soviet Russian conditions but stressed its readiness for further negotiations.

When the Soviet Russian News Agency Tass published a summary of the Finnish-Russian negotiations on 22 March, outsiders believed the whole affair closed. But it soon turned out that the negative resolutions of Finnish Congress of 16 March were by no means accepted as a final "No" by Mrs. Kollontay and the Swedish Government. Peace feelers were continued by them. Rumors circulating in Helsinki were supported by news published in the Swedish Press to the effect that the Russian peace conditions were not irrevocable but might be modified by negotiations. The source of these rumors remained unclear. Political circles at Helsinki were stirred by the rumor passed on by word of mouth that Moscow was ready to lessen its demands, but that the Government withheld this fact from the people. Great uncertainty and nervousness, therefore, reigned in the Finnish capital. Into this atmosphere the news burst on 28 March that a Finnish delegation (said to consist of Paasikivi and Enckell, the former Foreign Minister) had left for Moscow. Every precaution had been taken not to let the public know of their departure. Their plane, had, therefore, started from Turku instead of from Malmi, the Helsinki airfield. The delegation flew first to Stockholm and then to Moscow. Nevertheless the secret had leaked out. But the fact that the dispatch of a delegation to Moscow was to be kept secret made the German agencies in Finland all the more suspicious. A confidential orientation of the German Ambassador at Helsinki by the Finnish Minister for Foreign Affairs had not taken place.

The delegation was detained at Moscow for a long time, making the situation of the German agencies even more uncomfortable. Tension between Finns and Germans was growing. Finally Paasikivi sent the following radio message: "Same conditions. Petsamo in addition." The true situation suddenly was clear. The Finnish delegation returned to Helsinki on 1 April. By 3 April the demands made by Moscow in case of a Finnish capitulation were in the open. There was no question of more lenient conditions. The German agencies (German Ambassador at Helsinki and German General at Mikkeli) were now also oriented by the Finns.

The conditions brought from Moscow were as follows:

1. Rupture of relations with Germany. Internment of German troops and ships or their elimination in the course of the month of April, with Russian support if necessary.
2. Reinstatement of the Finnish-Russian Treaty of Peace of 1940. Finnish withdrawal during April behind the boundary of 1940.
3. Immediate release of the Soviet Russian prisoners of war.
4. Reduction of the budget of the Finnish Army by one half, by July to its peacetime size.
5. Reparations amounting to $600,000,000 in kind over the course of five years.
6. Restitution of Petsamo and surroundings.

If those six conditions were fulfilled, the Soviet Union was willing to return Hangö without any compensation.

No deadline was set for acceptance of the conditions but an early decision was demanded. The Soviet Russian conditions were said to have previously been agreed upon with the governments of Great Britain and the United States. The British press called the attention of the Finns to Molotov's declaration that the Soviet Union did not intend to conquer any territory on the other side of the old boundary.

The Finnish Government took its time. Tanner, who had to overcome considerable opposition to the Government's policy among Helsinki Social Democrats wanted to make use of the Easter holidays during the first week in April to influence his party friends in the rural areas and to clarify the matter to the small party units. The Finnish Congress, therefore, only had a short session on 4 April and did not enter into any discussion. The members, however, were handed a memorandum as a basis for the session of 12 April. Over Easter, public opinion in Finland grew more inclined to reject the Russian demands. The Finns resented particularly the so-called points of honor, the demand to intern the German army in Lapland and to disarm the Finnish Army, which seemed unfair to the sense of decency of the Finnish people. The excessive reparation sum also appeared to many Finns impossible to fulfill.

When Congress convened again on 12 April, it was a foregone conclusion that the representatives would support the negative attitude of the Government. The voting method chosen (party voting, without counting the individual votes) concealed the fact that an opposition did exist. Congress approved of the Government's declaration that it was technically impossible to fulfill Moscow's armistice conditions. The Finnish answer was handed Mrs. Kollontay at Stockholm through the good offices of the Swedes. The reply concluded with a declaration that the Finnish Government continued to be ready for discussions. A veiled new offer could thus be deduced, which created the impression that the Finnish Government's "No" rested on a weak foundation.

The Führer's Headquarters followed the situation at Helsinki with great concern. Finnish General Österman, who wanted to fly to Mikkeli for a personal report, was received on 5 April by Keitel and Jodl. Keitel drew the attention of Mannerheim's representative to the fact that in the long run the negotiations with Moscow were not only intolerable for the Finnish people and the Finnish Army but also for the German Army in Lapland. The description of events in Hungary in the version of the Finnish press had been considered insulting to the Wehrmacht. The Hungarian Army was very satisfied with the overthrow of the Kállay Government and was glad to cooperate with the Wehrmacht. Keitel went on to say that the situation in the sectors of Army Groups North and Center had stabilized and that the front in Army Group South's sector would also soon stabilize itself some distance before the Carpathian Mountains. Keitel requested General Österman to return with a clear statement from Mannerheim on what was going to happen. General Österman was given to understand by Keitel that on the occasion of Paasikivi's second contact with Moscow the question had been discussed whether the German arms deliveries to Finland should be stopped. The threat implied in this statement no doubt would not escape Mannerheim.

After the hopes for a separate Finnish peace had been abandoned, official Finnish circles attempted to justify their position, which seemed ambiguous to German eyes, by claiming that in view of the political opposition it had been necessary to prove to the Finnish people the impossibility of coming to an agreement with Moscow. It had, therefore, been absolutely necessary to learn the truth about the Russian conditions, and that had been possible only by Paasikivi's trips to Stockholm and Moscow. Although those in the know had expected the negotiations to be wrecked by the exaggerated demands of Moscow, it had been necessary to take these steps in order to convince the opposition and to re-establish the unity of the people. This subsequent interpretation of Finnish policy did not seem very credible to German ears. With a certain right the German Government took exception to the fact that the Finnish Foreign Minister had neglected to draw the German Ambassador in Helsinki into his confidence with regard to the plans of the Finnish Government prior to the Finnish-Russian negotiations. Not until the Russian conditions had been published in the press did the German Ambassador learn of these through the Foreign Minister. That had annoyed the German Government. It was now obvious that the Finnish-German brotherhood-in-arms, which had lasted for three years, was beginning to crumble. The German Government followed up this experience by placing an embargo on the shipment of German arms and war equipment to Finland. Growing distrust had led the German Government to doubt whether the German arms, which the Wehrmacht itself badly needed, were really employed in Finland to strengthen the fighting power of the Finnish Army and would always remain in the hands of the Finnish soldiers. From the wish expressed by Jodl on 28 April to General Heinrichs and Hitler's letter to Mannerheim of 1 June the scruples of the high level German command could be gleaned.

The Finnish Government discovered that it had been compromised in the eyes of the German agencies and many Finns by the peace parleys with Moscow. It tried to regain face with its critics on the occasion of the Memorial Day celebration at Lappeenranta on 21 May. Minister Salevaara, an honest man who enjoyed great popularity in the country, made a speech with contained the following statement: "Finland will never desert Karelia." That appealed to most Finns and created the hope that the time of anxious wavering of the Finnish Government belonged to the past.

After the decision of Congress, the Finnish press on the whole advocated continuation of the war against the Soviet Union. Only the Social Democratic papers still expressed a desire of obtaining a peace under better conditions.

Since rumors of new negotiations continued, the President informed the German Ambassador on 9 May that he did not believe in any change in the Russian conditions, the acceptance of which had not been recommended by any of the politicians he had consulted.

Marshal Mannerheim appeared satisfied with the result of the peace parleys and was in good spirits. It seemed as if a general relaxation was taking place after the critical weeks. In the beginning of June, however, a complete changed entered into the war picture. Both Germany's and Finland's situation was threatened again, so that the leading statesmen were faced by a new dilemma.

In the night of 5 June, the Allies began the long prepared attack on Western Europe which had been expected by the Germans. Bitter fighting went on along the coastal strip in northern France where the enemy landed. The German defense was not able to prevent the Allies from reinforcing the troops and enlarging their beachhead. The battle in Normandy increased daily in violence.

On 7 June, the Allies began a large-scale attack in the Rome area, making deep penetrations into the German positions and forcing the defenders to withdraw into the Sabine Hills. In the days to follow the pursuing Allies gained ground toward the north. Southern England and the London municipal area were under the fire of a new kind of German long-range gun after 16 June.

CHAPTER VI: The Red Army Offensive against the Finns
in the Summer of 1944

In the course of spring 1944 several indications of Russian preparations for an offensive on the Karelian Isthmus had appeared. Finnish Headquarters had to reckon that the proximity of Leningrad and the fact that an extremely dense net of communication lines spreading from that city in all directions made a fast concentration of large forces possible without the Finnish reconnaissance being able to know of it long beforehand. The Finns began to increase their defense preparations, particularly by accelerating their fortification construction, of which three lines were in the process of preparation, namely a front defense line, one in the nearby rear area (Vammelsuu-Taipale) and another one in a line from Viipuri to Vuoksi. The Valkessaari sector was considered the most threatened of the Finnish front and was particularly strengthened by additional fortifications and reinforcements.

On 9 June 1944 the Russians made a surprise attack on the Finnish positions on the Karelian Isthmus, where so far an almost complete lull had reigned. No sign of an impending Russian attack had been discovered by the Finns. Strong Soviet air forces crossed the Karelian Isthmus on 9 June, carrying out saturation bombing over the Finnish positions between the Gulf of Finland and Lake Lembaloskoye. More than 1000 enemy planes were counted on that day bombarding the Finnish positions, the nearby rear area and important objectives further back. Simultaneously the Russians employed a huge mass of artillery laying a heavy barrage on the Finnish positions. After this strong preparation, the Russian infantry began its attack supported by tanks at several places. Bitter fighting proceeded the whole day on the entire Finnish front on the Karelian Isthmus particularly on its western part. When evening came, all penetrations made by the Russians with heavy losses had been beaten off or at least sealed off. Violent Russian artillery barrages went on throughout the whole night.

On 10 June, at 0500 hours, the Russian fire increased again to a tremendous roar supported by a strong ground attack airplane squadrons. After this particularly violent preparation, the Russian infantry again attacked, this time supported by numerous heavy tank forces.

The Finnish front between the Gulf of Finland and Lake Ladoga was at this time organized as follows:

The right sector was formed by the IV Corps (General Laatikainen) consisting of the 10th Division (General Sihvo) and the 2nd Division (General Martole); the left sector by the III Corps (General Siilasvuo) consisting of the 16th Division (General Paalu) and the 15th Division (General Hersalo). The main Russian attack was directed against the regiment of the 10th Division stationed at Valkaasaari and led by Colonel Viljanen. The noise of the battle was so strong that the window panes in the small town of Mikkeli far behind the front rattled. The cannonade far off to the south reminded one of the drum fire during World War I at Verdun and the Somme River. As usual in large-scale battles, several hours elapsed before Headquarters had clear knowledge of what was happening at the front. All lines of communication to the attacked sector had been destroyed. The roads leading to the front in the battle area were continually attacked by low flying planes so that all traffic to and from the front had ceased. Only after a considerable time did Headquarters get a clear picture of the situation. The regiment of the 10th Division that was attacked had actually been wiped out by the advance that swept over its sector. A stream of enemy tanks and artillery batteries rushed through the breach that had been created in the Finnish front. In spite of Finnish attempts to seal it off, the Russians were able to drive their wedge to a depth of 12 kilometers by noon. The Finnish cavalry brigade attempted to intercept the quickly advancing Russians on the coast but was pressed back too and had to withdraw to the second line of defense. The 10th Division, strongly shaken, had to retreat, forcing the adjacent 2nd Division on its left also to bend back its front and to build up a switch position between the first and second position. The Russians simultaneously deepened their penetration in the course of the afternoon and extended it on both sides. Only in the eastern part of the isthmus where the Russians had not exercised any considerable pressure could the original front be held.

Finnish Headquarters quickly understood that a counterattack to win back the lost positions promised little success. All one could do was to seal off the penetration. The armored division stationed north of the Karelian Isthmus (the light infantry brigade in front), the Estonian 200th Regiment (formed by Estonians who had fled to Finland), the 3rd Division and a few battalions and batteries of the 2nd and 18th Divisions, adjacent to the 10th Division, were employed for this purpose. The 3rd Brigade from the area of the Twentieth Mountain Army and the 4th Division from the Maaselkä front were to be transferred by rail to the Karelian Isthmus.

Furthermore, Finnish Headquarters recalled all men on leave.

In the course of 11 June those parts of the Finnish IV Corps which had so far held out were pressed back to the second position. The III Corps bent back its right wing in order to maintain contact with the IV Corps. All units of the 18th Division were brought forward to the IV Corps. From right to left, the following units were now fighting in the sector of IV Corps:

Cavalry Brigade

10th Division which had seriously lost in fighting power
2nd Division
18th Division
At their rear were the 3rd Division and the armored division

On 11 June, the Marshal sent an inquiry to the German General at Finnish Headquarters asking whether the German embargo on ammunition for Finland could not be lifted. Already on the second day it became evident that the Russian offensive was a large-scale one, whose purpose it was to make the Finns ready for negotiations by military setbacks.

In the morning of 12 June, the Russians attacked the second position at Vammelsuu and were also attacking the Finns in the Kivennapa area. East of Kivennapa, on the other hand, where the Russians also attacked with strong forces, the Finns held out about five kilometers in front of the second position in spite of continuous, heavy enemy attacks. The Russians continued their violent attacks throughout the whole day but were everywhere beaten off with heavy losses. The Finns made good progress in combating Russian tanks; in the course of 12 June twenty-nine Russian tanks were destroyed in this comparatively narrow area.

In the evening of 12 June, the Finnish troops in the attacked sector were all withdrawn to the second line of defense. The Russians continued their attacks everywhere between Vammelsuu and Siiranmäki. In spite of the tremendous odds against them, the Finns were able to repulse all enemy attacks. Particularly at Vammelsuu, Kivennapa and Siiranmäki they took on the proportions of heavy battles of materiel.

The 3rd Brigade and the 4th Division were now approaching the Karelian Isthmus. The Marshal further ordered that the 17th Division and 20th Brigade be transferred by rail from the Svir front. Whether the Finns would be able to hold their own by means of these reinforcements appeared, however, doubtful in view of the eighteen divisions so far employed by the Russians.

Mannerheim on this day sent the following requests to General Erfurth:

> 1. Support from the Luftwaffe by taking over the air area in front of a line Terijoki-Termola- Rolkanjärvi as far as the railroad line Kiviniemi-Leningrad for preventing and harassing the enemy supply service in the attack area.
> 2. Early delivery of the airplanes, assault guns and antiaircraft guns promised to the Finns but retained in Germany. The OKW soon sent word to Mikkeli that the ammunition and grain deliveries from Germany which had been halted would be set in motion again.

On 13 June, the Commander in Chief of the Twentieth Mountain Army and General Erfurth met at Ambassador von Blücher's in Helsinki. They held a short conference at the embassy on the situation at the front. Dietl and Erfurth were in complete agreement on the Finnish chances. In the evening, Dietl brought Erfurth back to Mikkeli in his airplane. Since the plane slid off the runway and could not clear the ground, Dietl postponed his departure for Rovaniemi until the next morning and stayed overnight at Hotel Kaleva at Mikkeli, where he happened to meet Walden, the Minister of Defense. Late in the evening he saw General Heinrichs at Headquarters, and on the next morning he paid a visit to the Marshal at Sairila, his country place. In this way, an exchange of opinions took place on 13 and early 14 June between the top level Finnish and German command agencies. In the forenoon, Dietl returned by plane from Mikkeli to Rovaniemi. He reported on his trip to Helsinki and Mikkeli on 14 June to the OKW, saying that President Ryti, whom Dietl had seen on 13 June at Helsinki, had maintained a quiet and confident attitude. The Marshal, on the other hand, had been very much concerned about the development on the Karelian Isthmus. Holding an opinion which differed from that of Ryti, the Marshal believed the Russian attack an attempt to bring about a decision. General Heinrichs had hinted at the possibility of giving up the Svir and Maaselkä front.

The course of events on 13 June seemed to satisfy the confidence of President Ryti. The result of this day's battles might well have created the impression that the Finnish situation had improved in the new line of defense. Now at the front were the cavalry brigade and the 3rd and 18th Divisions. In the switch position between the first and second position was the 2nd Division and in the first position the 15th Division and the 19th Brigade. That is five to six units on an eighty kilometer front. As a precaution, the coastal front was reinforced too.

On 14 June, however, the situation at the Finnish front grew again more unfavorable. The Russians continued their large-scale attack on this day with undiminished force. The attacks could again be repulsed at Vammelsuu, Kivennapa and Siiranmäki, but at Sahakylä the Russians succeeded in penetrating into the Finnish positions, and a little later they were also able to break through at Kuuterselkä. Sahakulä was recaptured by immediate Finnish countermeasures. A violent tank battle raged throughout the night at Kuuterselkä and north of the village in order to recapture it. The enemy masses pouring in through the breach were, however, able to extend the Russian breakthrough to a depth of eight kilometers and a width of one and a half kilometers by morning. They accomplished this by utilizing hundreds of planes and a heavy artillery barrage to attack the combat elements at the front and Finnish reinforcements coming in support.

Although the furious enemy attacks carried out on 14 June against Siiranmäki by four divisions were frustrated by the fire of the numerically weak but rough Finnish defenders, the Finnish troops were nonetheless also withdrawn from the eastern sector of the isthmus to the second position, while simultaneously all means were employed to narrow down the enemy breakthrough in the western part of the isthmus which the Russians endeavored to extend.

Since more and more new divisions and brigades were coming to the Karelian Isthmus from other fronts, the tactical command of the battle from Mikkeli grew difficult. The Marshal, therefore, decided to recall General Ösch from the area east of Lake Ladoga and to entrust to him the command of the battle on the Karelian Isthmus. Ösch assumed the supreme command over all troops on the Karelian Isthmus on 14 June.

Since the Finns had so far not succeeded in halting the enemy tanks, the Finnish High Command asked General Erfurth to supply German antitank close combat weapons as fast as possible. The first assistance was received from the Twentieth Mountain Army which sent the desired weapons by plane. A larger amount arrived from Germany in a torpedo boat.

On the same day, the Twentieth Mountain Army received a Führer directive regarding the construction of rear positions in Lapland. The Finns, who anxiously watched the Karelian Isthmus, paid little attention to this directive and obviously failed to recognize its full importance.

The enemy continued his attacks on 15 June. Since it would take some time until the Finnish reserves on the way would arrive, and since the Finnish forces on the Karelian Isthmus could not be permitted to lose their fighting power and no longer be equal to all further tasks, the Marshal ordered on 15 June that, although the Russian breakthrough had taken place only in the western sector of the second defense line, the army should pass over to delaying resistance, abandon the second position voluntarily, where it was still held and fall back to a line Viipuri-Vuoksi in order to preserve its fighting strength. The reserves were to assemble in this short line formed by nature and already partly fortified. With a heavy heart the Marshal decided to order the evacuation of Viipuri.

The position of the Finns in those days was as follows:

The cavalry brigade at Inonkylä
10th Division between Lake Ries and Lake Vamuel
Units of the 4th Division, which had meanwhile arrived, at the
    northern point of Lake Suula, Lake Vuot, and Lake Kauk.
The approaching 20th Brigade was to assemble southeast of
    Viipuri.

General Ösch gave the following orders:

> IV Corps (Lastikainen) will carry out a mobile defense from the northwest of Kivennapa toward the west and hold its position toward the east.
> III Corps (Siilasvuo) will withdraw to the second position.

General Talvela assumed the command at the Svir front by order of the Marshal, and General Mäkinen at the Maaselkä front. Both were ordered to fall back on the second position in order to save forces.

Enemy attacks and Finnish retreats continued also on 16 and 17 June. Russian pressure was particularly strong east of the Leningrad-Viipuri railroad. The Finns retired in a delaying action in the western part of the Isthmus to a line connecting Lakes Kipinolan, Xueleman, Hatjalahden, Kauk, Perk, Suula, Vuot, and Ahi. But they continued to hold Siiranmäli and the second position to the east.

In the early hours of 17 June the eastern part of the second position was also evacuated by order of the Finnish High Command, while simultaneously heavy fighting went on in the course of the delaying action in the areas of Lakes Kauk and Perk. The Russians, who employed particularly strong armored forces, had already conquered the village of Perkjärvi and its railroad station but the Finns succeeded in recapturing it in a courageous attack. A Russian tank breakthrough west of Kaukjärvi suffered the same fate. The situation could be saved by the Finns and thirty-four heavy Russian tanks were destroyed in this encounter.

The bulk of the 3rd Brigade and 4th Division arrived on 16 June. In order to comply with the Marshal's request, a bombardment group and a fighter group (Gruppe Kuhlmey) belonging to Luftflotte 1 came to South Finland to aid the Finns, and were stationed at Imola airfield.

Headquarters issued the following new orders through General Ösch:

> 1. General Lagus (under the command of General Lastikainen) will assume the command in the coastal sector of the Karelian Isthmus over the following units: Cavalry Brigade, 10th Division, 3rd Brigade, Armored Division
> 2. Generals Talvela and Mäkinen will slowly withdraw to a line Uuksunjoki-Suojärvi-Porosero-Ssegosero.
> 3. General Svenson will surrender his command over II Corps at the Svir front and go to Viipuri, where he will assume command over the Finnish reinforcements assembling in the Viipuri area.

The Russians had not yet attacked the Svir front, where nothing more than Russian preparations had been discovered by the Finns. The Marshal decided to evacuate the positions in East Karelia voluntarily, releasing in this way two to three divisions for the Karelian Isthmus.

On 17 June, the retreat of the Finns continued on the Karelian Isthmus in heavy fighting. Enemy pressure was exercised in particular on the cavalry brigade fighting in the coastal sector. General Melander, its commander, was replaced by Colonel Tähtinen. The first transports of the 20th Brigade now arrived at Viipuri. Evacuation of the 17th Division from the Svir front began on this day.

The Finnish Government had so far regularly paid its amortization rate on the loan made by the United States after World War I. Now it again paid the interest due, setting a rare example of fulfillment of international obligations. The United States Government accepted the Finnish payment but handed Procopé, the Finnish Ambassador in Washington, his passport.

Finnish Headquarters intended to continue its retreat to a line Viipuri-Vuoksi and to put up all possible resistance there. The position offered good facilities for a defense to the extent that it was situated behind the Vuoksi River. Its particular strength was protection from enemy tanks. The western part of the position between Viipuri and Vuoksi, however, was not so favorable for defense. There were no prepared fortifications. The city of Viipuri was particularly threatened, since the only waterways offering protection were north of the city. There were no barriers either to its south or in the area east of the city. If Finnish resistance in this region gave way, southern Finland would lay open before the Russians. It is true that after the Winter War the construction of fortifications along the new frontier had begun, but these frontier fortifications had not yet made great progress and were of little value for defense. The danger existed that Russian tanks making a rapid advance on the Karelian Isthmus would reach Viipuri before the Finns and block the isthmus leading to the city to the Finns. In such a case there would be no route of retreat left to the north with the exception of a bridge across the Vuoksi near Kiviniemi. Half of all Finnish units would under such circumstances not be able to bring back their heavy arms and war equipment which would deal Finnish resistance a death blow.

A Finnish attempt to receive arms from Sweden was on 18 June unanimously declined by the Swedish Cabinet. The German arms deliveries did not take full effect at the front for the time being. Available Finnish reserves were small. The Marshal, therefore, had every reason for being concerned about the future.

On that day, Ambassador von Blücher and General Erfurth discussed the problem at Finnish Headquarters of making shipping space available at Hangö for the evacuation of the German colony in case the situation worsened and made such a step necessary.

On 18 June fighting proceeded on the following general line: Rokkalanjoki, Summa, Lake Muolan, Lake Yks, Lake Kirkko, Lake

Punnus, Lake Paakkolan, Lake Murmi, Taipale. Numerous Russian attacks were repulsed along this line. The most bitter fighting took place in the Summa-Leipäsuo sector where the Finns offered tough resistance in the ruins of the Winter War positions although they had not since been repaired. The Koivisto Islands were still held by Finnish troops in order to gain time for the defense of the Bay of Viipuri.

Strong enemy pressure in the direction of Viipuri continued on 19 June. A line Kokkalanjoki-Summa-Lake Muolan-Lake Äyräpän-Vuoksi was held in heavy fighting until noon of 19 June, when the army began disengaging itself from the enemy in order to pass over to a delaying action in front of a line Viipuri-Vuoksi which was to be defended under all circumstances. Bitter fighting took place in the outpost area, especially at Nähkkijärvi, Kämärä, and Salmenkaita, but by the morning of 21 June the bulk of the retreating Finnish troops had passed through the defense positions occupied by other forces. The Russians were in hot pursuit so that the Finnish retreat had to be carried out step by step.

Also at the Svir front, the Russians began to attack on 19 June. The Finns had already started to disengage themselves from the enemy. When the Russians began their attack, the bulk of V Corps had already withdrawn its advanced positions south of the Svir so that the enemy pushed into empty space.

On 19 June, German torpedo boats brought 9000 Panzerfausts from Germany to Finland which were particularly needed owing to the enemy superiority in tanks. Upon Mannerheim's request, the German General sent an inquiry to the Führer's Headquarters asking for a larger number of Panzerschrecks and ground attack airplanes for Finland. The Viipuri-Vuoksi position could only be held if these weapons were utilized.

The German Mountain Army in Lapland had meanwhile done all it could to cope with this situation. General Dietl's request that his 14,000 men on leave should return from Germany had been declined by Hitler. The latter had different plans than Dietl and ordered that the men on furlough not be allowed to return to the Twentieth Mountain Army. In order to create a reserve for the German Army in Lapland, a machine gun ski regiment was organized. Besides, the Bicycle Reconnaissance Regiment Norway was to remain in the northern area.

As might be expected, a political crisis followed the military crisis in Finland. The Finnish Cabinet had a long session on 18 June. The German Ambassador did not get a clear picture on what occurred from the Finnish Foreign Minister. The latter had never before been as downhearted and maintained that an appeal to the Finnish people to make a supreme effort was less promising for a solution of the technical problems than tanks and airplanes. The German General at Mikkeli, too, reported on 19 June to the Führer's Headquarters that the military and consequently the political outlook were uncertain.

In the evaluation of 19 June, the Chief of the Finnish General Staff sent an inquiry to General Erfurth asking if Germany was ready to make strong forces (about six divisions) available as a covering force in the southern sector of the boundary position[30] between the Gulf of Finland and Lake Saimaa for the Finnish Army fighting in the Viipuri-Vuoksi line.

On 20 June, General Heinrichs added that he had acted on the Marshal's orders when seeking German assistance. Obviously, the Marshal had in the meantime asked for and received the consent of his government to his call for German help.

The battle south of Viipuri continued to take an unfavorable course. Units of the Red Army entered Viipuri where street fighting took place.

A reply to Mannerheim's inquiry whether he could count on German help came very quickly. The OKW gave assurance by order of Hitler that Germany would render assistance in the fight for the Viipuri-Vuoksi line. But the OKW refused to make covering forces available for the boundary position. Resistance ought to be offered on the Viipuri-Vuoksi line. Finland would have to be aware of the fact that the consequences of its quitting the war would be more severe for Finland than for Germany. The first assistance announced by the German brother-in-arms consisted of one assault gun brigade and one bombardment squadron (from Luftflotte 5). Further assistance was being examined, but it was pointed out that under no circumstances could six German divisions be made available. The OKW doubted the wisdom of abandoning prepared Finnish positions along the Svir and Maaselkä front without fighting.

For the Finns 21 June was a day of sorrow. The Russians closely followed the Finns who withdrew along the shore road, and immediately proceeded to attack Viipuri where they were able to penetrate into the positions on the eastern outskirts of the city almost on the heels of the Finns. After a short combat, the city had to be abandoned leaving the Russians the moral success of entering and capturing the capital of Karelia. Thus, Viipuri, particularly dear to the hearts of all Finns, was lost. Finnish resistance did not stabilize until the waterways north of the town had been reached.

Finnish Headquarters were now confronted with the serious question whether the Finnish troops exhausted by the heavy fighting would still have the stamina to ward off further Russian attacks along the Viipuri-Vuoksi line. It was true that the Finns had been reinforced by fresh troops. The Russians, however, had many ways of rebuilding their

---

[30] The position was known as the "Moscow Position" by the Finns since its construction had been started after the Peace of Moscow.

strength by bringing forward new troops from Leningrad or from other sectors of the Russian front by using the dense net of communication lines.

In order to give thanks for the quick German assistance, Mannerheim sent a telegram to Hitler on 21 June and promised that the Finns, though success was not certain, would make every effort to offer resistance in the Viipuri-Vuoksi line.[31] It was quite obvious that the German promise had pleased and relieved Finnish Headquarters. According to Headquarters' opinion no change of ministers impended at Helsinki. General Erfurth even had, on the other hand, some evidence of a possible Finnish decision to bind themselves closer to the Reich.

The 22nd of June brought heavy fighting at Tali (east of Viipuri). The enemy made a new attempt to break through in this terrain which was particularly suitable for tank attacks. For the immediate future, the Tali area remained the crucial point of the Finnish front, and the Russians attacked again and again. All heavy weapons and antitank close combat weapons supplied by Germany were committed by the Finns at Tali to strengthen their defense.

The Russians crossed the river on both sides of Lodeynoye Pole and closely pursued the retreating Finns on the Svir and Maaselkä front so that in the course of the following day the Finns were obliged to continue their retreat in order to prevent a disruption of their forces.

The advance guard of the 303rd Assault Gun Brigade arrived at Helsinki and marched from the harbor through the town to the railroad station. It proceeded by rail to Lappeenrahta.

In the evening of that day, Reich Foreign Minister von Ribbentrop arrived unexpectedly at Helsinki by plane. He came to Finland by order of Hitler to bring about a clear and uncompromising clarification of Finnish-German relations. Germany was ready, he declared, to assist the hard-pressed Finnish brother-in-arms as much as possible, but it demanded a clear-cut reaffirmation of Finland's stand with Germany. If that was not done, arms assistance would cease.

Ryti received Ribbentrop in the evening of 22 June in Ramsay's presence. The discussion soon ended in a deadlock without any result. Ryti declared that he was no military expert and would have to consult Mannerheim with regard to the necessity and value of German military help.

On 23 June, General Erfurth was called to Helsinki by order of Ribbentrop via the German Ambassador. A discussion between Ribbentrop, Blücher and Erfurth took place in the afternoon at the

---

[31] The fortified Viipuri-Vuoksi line does not refer to the city of Viipuri, but to the terrain to the north, which is particularly suitable for defensive purposes.

German Embassy. The German Foreign Minister left no doubt that Finland must come to a clear decision. If he were to return with his mission uncompleted, German arms deliveries to Finland would stop. Ribbentrop requested Erfurth to obtain Mannerheim's opinion on the value of German help. Erfurth should further learn Mannerheim's standpoint with regard to a proposal that Mannerheim should assume the command over the entire Finnish-German front between the Gulf of Finland and the Arctic Sea with a German Chief of Staff.

In the evening Ribbentrop received a confidential message from the Führer's Headquarters delivered at the German Embassy in Helsinki that General Dietl had met with a fatal airplane accident near Salzburg on 23 June. Ribbentrop desired this news be kept secret in Finland for the time being in order not to complicate the Finnish-German negotiations.

East of Viipuri, the Russians obtained local success on 23 June. According to information gathered by Finnish Headquarters, the Russians now had the following forces opposite the Finnish front whose presence had been established with certainty:

29 light infantry divisions
2 artillery divisions
4 armored brigades
13 armored regiments
8 assault artillery regiments

The Finns had the following reserves available at that time to oppose the Russian onslaught:

10th Division (with considerably reduced fighting power)
20th Brigade
Armored Division
The 11th and 8th Divisions were on their way to the front

Though valuable ground had been abandoned to the enemy, nevertheless the Finnish Commander in Chief had succeeded in withdrawing the army while conserving its fighting power to the defense line which he had chosen for a decisive battle, since the terrain offered good facilities to prevent the Russians from reaching their operational objectives, that is to say, to penetrate into southern Finland by way of the Karelian Isthmus.

On 24 June, a long discussion took place at Mikkeli between Marshal Mannerheim, General Heinrichs, and General Erfurth, while Ribbentrop stayed all day at the German Embassy in Helsinki waiting for a clarification of the situation. Mannerheim declared to General Erfurth that he did not mean to leave the President in any doubt about the importance of the German military assistance. Ryti arrived at Mikkeli in the afternoon. He was accompanied in his plane by Foreign Minister Ramsay and Minister of Defense Walden. After a long conference with the Marshal in the school building of Mikkeli, the two Finnish statesmen left again for Helsinki in the evening. General Erfurth had the impression that a way was being sought to avoid involving Congress, who by right would have to cooperate in international treaties.

Both 25 and 26 June passed by in fruitless discussions at Helsinki. Ribbentrop became impatient and declared he would return to Germany on the next day. The critical moment had arrived when the negotiations threatened to be broken off without result.

A way out was finally found in the evening of 26 June. The main difficulty was the certainty that Finnish Congress would never assent to a clear and public avowal of siding with Germany. According to the Finnish constitution, however, it seemed impossible to omit Congress in the pact negotiations with Ribbentrop. In this seemingly hopeless situation, the Finnish crown jurists found a solution which avoided participation of Congress. Ryti was to make the declaration demanded by Germany in a personal letter to Hitler. The public avowal that Finland would not terminate the war without first reaching an understanding with Germany was to be broadcast to the Finnish people by Prime Minister Linkomies. The Cabinet agreed to this solution and asked the President to write the letter. Thus interference by Congress was avoided.

Late in the evening of 26 June Ryti received Ribbentrop and gave him the letter to Hitler, bringing the German-Finnish negotiations to a close. Ribbentrop flew to Germany the next day.

The Allied press commented unfavorably on the agreement reached between German and Finland. The United States broke off diplomatic relations with Finland on 30 June. The American Chargé d'Affaires, who during the last months had been in charge of the small remnant of the diplomatic representation in Helsinki left Finland. The last tie between the two countries had been cut. Yet a declaration of war by the United States did not ensue. The cautious Finnish statesmen had succeeded in keeping their country at peace with the United States until the end of the war. This success was due to a really masterful political strategy. On 2 July, Swedish Prime Minister Hanson made a speech expressing his disapproval of the German-Finnish union.

On the same day on which the German Foreign Minister flew back from Helsinki, the new commander in chief of the Twentieth Mountain Army landed there. Generaloberst Rendulic came from the Balkans, where he had been commander in chief of the Second Panzer Army in Croatia. He was unfamiliar with the north of Europe. His appointment was communicated to the German Army in Lapland and to Finnish Headquarters on 27 June. Simultaneously *General* Breusing, commander of the German 122nd Division arrived in Helsinki. His division was being transported from Tallinn to Helsinki and to be moved on by rail to the Karelian Isthmus. The 27 June was an unfavorable day for the Finns at the front. The Russians made a deep penetration at Repola which was only sealed off by committing the last reserves.

Rendulic reported to Mannerheim at Mikkeli on 28 June. It was only through the new German Commander in Chief that the Finnish High Command learnt of the tragic death of Dietl who was held in high esteem in Finland. The Marshal was deeply affected by the news of Dietl's sudden death. He sent a sincere telegram of condolence to Hitler and to Dietl's widow and bestowed the highest Finnish war decoration, the Grand Cross of the Finnish Cross of Freedom, on the dead German general in acknowledgement of his services for Finland.

After a short stay at Mikkeli, Rendulic flew back to Helsinki in the afternoon of 28 June and went on from there to Rovaniemi where he assumed command of the Twentieth Mountain Army. The audience with Ryti, which Rendulic had asked for, could not take place since the President had taken sick immediately after the departure of Ribbentrop.

On 29 June, Mannerheim replied to the German offer that he assume the high command over the entire Finnish-German front. As might have been expected he declined the position of Generalissimo in the northern area, giving his old age as a reason. He said that he felt already too old for his present task as Commander in Chief of the Finnish Army and did not intend to take upon himself any additional burden. The problem of a German Chief of Staff as proposed by Ribbentrop and the OKW had not been submitted to the Marshal by General Erfurth, since Mannerheim would never have agreed to accept a German general as chief advisor and assistant. This combination, which occasionally had been used to advantage in World War I, would not have fitted with Finnish conditions and Mannerheim's personality. The Marshal liked to work with approved men to whom he had become accustomed and did not like many changes.

At Repola on the Karelian Isthmus, the situation worsened. The wedge, which the Russians had driven into the new defensive front in this area and which they extended without interruption, became menacing. Counterattacks failed to eliminate it. On 30 June, the front was therefore straightened out. Simultaneously the town of Petrozavodsk was abandoned, and on 2 July the town of Salmi. Russian attack activity now also shifted beyond the Maaselkä sector to the Kiestinki sector occupied by German forces. By the middle of July, therefore, counterattacks had to be made in this sector.

The large losses suffered by the Finnish Army in the battle raging since 9 July and the difficulty in filling the gaps it created with new reinforcements caused Finnish Headquarters considerable anxiety.

Headquarters calculated the losses since the beginning of the Soviet offensive to be 18,000 men. By the middle of June 12,000 men had been brought forward as replacements. The Finnish situation with regard to replacements was very unsatisfactory. It had been decided to redraft the older age class reserves for service at the front, but their number was small. The number of infantrymen of the 1907 and 1908 age classes was estimated to be 9,000 and that of the 1905 and 1906 age classes another 9,000. The untrained reserves, which so far had not been taken into account, numbered at most 10,000 to 12,000. Then as a last resource there remained the infantrymen of the 1902-1904 age classes, altogether not more than 15,000 strong.

It was no wonder the Finns asked for German help. Mannerheim asked General Erfurth on 30 June to request another German division and one more assault gun brigade from the OKW. Though Finnish Headquarters harbored no doubts about the increasing difficulties of the German eastern front, where the Red Army had begun a large-scale attack on 22 June, while a tremendous battle of materiel was developing in Normandy, the Ribbentrop pact, which had just been concluded at Helsinki, gave the Finns the right to demand German help.

The help apparently nearest at hand, namely forces of the Twentieth Mountain Army, was out of the question, since those forces were just sufficient to guard the extensive front where attacks might be expected at any time. Luftflotte 5 would permit a temporary weakening. Only the zone of the interior and the eastern front came into question. The Luftwaffe shifted one fighter and one bombardment squadron from the Twentieth Mountain Army to the Finns in the south.

Owing to her own precarious situation, Germany was obliged to restrict assistance for Finland to the supply of arms and war equipment. Hitler issued orders to expedite the deliveries and increase their size. He demanded that warships be employed to make faster deliveries. Immediately on 20 June, further supplies were ordered to be sent beyond the war equipment deliveries ordered on 13 and 15 June, among other things 500 bazookas and 150,000 stick grenades. 5,000 Panzerschrecks were sent by air on 22 June. 700,000 rounds of artillery ammunition, antitank and assault guns were either on the way or ready for shipment to Finland in German ports. New demands were fulfilled as far as possible in the beginning of July. Transportation of the 303rd Assault Gun Brigade had been carried out on 23 June and it was immediately brought forward to the front east of Viipuri. One third of the combat echelon of the 122nd Division was on the same day ready for shipment at Tallinn so that its arrival in Finland was to be expected around 28 June.

German naval forces opposed Russian attempts to land on the Finnish southern front. Cruisers were sent to the Gulf of Finland. The

Luftwaffe made 940 sorties on 21 June, a total of almost half the amount of the Russian sorties. So all three branches of the Wehrmacht endeavored to render the hard pressed Finnish brother-in-arms as much assistance as was possible in view of the overall situation. The plan to send another assault gun brigade to the Finns did not materialize, however, since the brigade in question had to be immediately assigned to Army Group Center where a grave crisis had arisen on 22 June right after the beginning of the Russian offensive.

The 303rd Sturmgeschutz Brigade was committed at the Finnish front on 27 June. The 122nd Division began to move by railroad through southern Finland from Helsinki to the Karelian Isthmus. The OKW agreed to Finnish Headquarters' request to commit the German division on the right wing of the Finnish front north of Viipuri behind the arm of the Bay of Viipuri.

On the same day, Minister Linkomies made the radio broadcast to the Finnish people as agreed upon by Ribbentrop. He stressed the determination of the Finnish government to continue the war by the side of Germany and not to lay down arms without a previous understanding with Germany. The Finnish Social Democratic Party simultaneously published a declaration disavowing the Government's policy.

On 3 July a crisis threatened at the battle front. The Russians began a new attack at Ihantala on the Karelian Isthmus and also exercised strong pressure on the Finnish rear guards at Salmi and Kolatselkä east of Lake Ladoga. Mannerheim, therefore, urgently requested the assistance of further German forces and early delivery of rifles and submachine guns from Germany, emphasizing that only the prospect of certain German assistance had determined his attitude when conferring with the President on 24 June. He had, thereby, taken on a great responsibility. If the German units did not arrive, not only would the military situation worsen, he concluded, but his personal political reputation would be shaken. A great deal of infantry ammunition had been lost through the abandonment of the Finnish permanent positions north of Leningrad and the retreat to the Viipuri-Vuoksi line. Supplies of the necessary amount from Germany were difficult to get. The question arose, therefore, whether it would be expedient to arm part of the Finnish forces with German rifles. The problem was submitted to the OKW for a decision together with a proposal of the Finnish High Command to rearm the Finnish artillery with German guns for the sake of uniformity.

On 4 July, strong Russian forces attempted to cross the Bay of Viipuri opposite Uuras. The attack struck the 122nd Division, which a short time ago had relieved the Finnish cavalry brigade and had taken over responsibility at the front. The attack was a complete failure and the attempt was not repeated. The Russians succeeded on 4 July, however, in gaining a foothold in the river delta at Viipuri. Owing to the shallow water, torpedo boats could not be employed there and the only existing speed-boat flotilla had been transferred further to the west.

The Finns finally found an opportunity to strengthen their front and to rehabilitate their forces when the Russians started regrouping in the beginning of July. New Russian units were discovered, partly from the Murmansk front and the central reserve opposite Army Group North.

The Stockholm correspondent of the British newspaper *Observer* published excerpts of Ryti's letter to Hitler, which had been handed to Ribbentrop on 26 June, revealing the background of the events at Helsinki on the evening of 22 June. According to this version, the Finnish Government had been in an extremely weak state at the moment of Ribbentrop's sudden arrival and had planned to approach Moscow with the object of terminating the war. Members of the Finnish delegation that was to fly to Moscow had already been on the way to Ryti to receive their last instructions, when Ribbentrop's arrival was announced. The visit of the German Foreign Minister had in the last minute prevented this development in the Finnish policy from taking place.

Mannerheim's request that another German division be sent to the Finnish front was declined on 5 July by the OKW. In view of the difficult situation on the entire German eastern front, where the defense of the central sector had collapsed with surprising suddenness under the blows of the Russian large-scale attack, it was impossible at the time being to comply with the demand of the Finnish Commander in Chief. But the OKW promised strong assistance with heavy arms which the Finnish Army particularly lacked.

The operations and movements of the Finnish troops slowly retreating from the Svir had partly taken a course not in accordance with the intentions of the High Command. Further difficulties had been created by Russian landings across Lake Ladoga at Juulos in the Finnish rear. The consequence was that the Marshal on 8 July exchanged Generals Martola (formerly 2nd Division) and Blick (formerly VI Corps). Mannerheim's commands during the great battle of defense along the Finnish southern front were given with great firmness and energy. Unflaggingly and with close attention he followed the march of events and interfered resolutely if things did not run as he desired. In spite of his age he filled his position of Commander in Chief without the slightest sign of fatigue and allowed those who worked with him no more influence than necessary. His zeal for work and unlimited devotion to the duties of his office were admirable. Moreover, he never lost his own natural dignity. Correct form in dealing with him was essential, all the more so since he himself maintained a meticulous attitude in the face of ever increasing bad news. Cynical in his views on the human race, but wise and mellowed by many years of a life with frequent ups and downs, he looked at the world with sober realism and perhaps often with pessimism as a result of much bad experience. He probably discovered early that he was fighting for a lost cause, the knowledge of which gave his character a tragic aspect in history. Though success was denied him, he will live in Finnish history as the greatest son of the Finnish race, as a shining model of conscientiousness for future generations, as a general and statesman in particularly hard times. It is an honor to say of the Finnish people that they recognized the greatness of this unique man and did not darken his reputation after the unlucky end of the war because success was denied him.

The situation at the Finnish front had by no means become easier during the first ten days of July. The Red Army gained further successes both on the Karelian Isthmus and in the area east of Lake Ladoga. On 11 July, the Russians succeeded in penetrating across the Vuoksi at Äyräpä and in forming a major bridgehead on the northern bank of the river. Within a short time the Russians widened the bridgehead to such an extent as to be able to employ in it a division with ten to fifteen tanks. The weak Finnish lines retreating from the Svir were pierced on that day in the direction of Laimola. Forces were lacking to put a stop to the advance of the enemy in this area. Finnish losses increased to an alarming extent and amounted to 32,000 men between the beginning of the Russian offensive and 11 July. The large officer casualties were particularly alarming. The battle of defense raging for one month had cost the Finnish Army 2,000 officers. In order to fill the gaps thus created, a course of instruction for reserve officers was ordered to take place at Kankaanpä which was to be attended by 1000 officer candidates.

Heavy fighting in the bridgehead of Äyräpä continued during the following days. East of Lake Ladoga, the Finns continued their retreat to the Finnish-Russian boundary area. The Finnish High Command ordered a general line Pitkäranta-Suojärvi to be held. The situation in the Äyräpä bridgehead was, however, particularly difficult for the Finns since the dominating heights were occupied by the Russians. The greater elevation of the southern bank near Äyräpä had in the Winter War facilitated the crossing of the Russians, and now the unfavorable terrain made it difficult for the Finns to narrow down or eliminate the enemy bridgehead. Owing to the hasty construction of the Finnish fortifications, the daily Finnish losses in the battle for the bridgehead were considerable and difficult to replace.

By the middle of the month, Finnish Headquarters estimated the Russian forces on the Karelian Isthmus to consist of twenty-six infantry divisions and twelve to fourteen armored brigades or break-through regiments and at the Aunos front of another ten divisions. Headquarters followed the unfavorable course of operations along the German eastern front south of the Gulf of Finland with great concern. The Red Army offensive in the central sector of the eastern front made rapid progress and spread both north and south. The German eastern front tottered in July 1944 in many places. The initiative had passed entirely into the hands of the Russians. Areas which had formerly been occupied by German troops were increasingly abandoned and left to the Russians. The German divisions retreated westward under heavy fighting in the entire central sector of the eastern front. By the middle of July the line of main resistance was indicated by the following focal points: Area of Kovel, Slonim, Lida, Vilna, Grodno, south of Dvinsk, north of Polotsk. The cities of Vilna and Pinsk had to be abandoned as a result of strong enemy pressure. It was impossible to strengthen the crumbling German front since the Germans were also in a very precarious situation in other theaters of war (Italy and France).

In Normandy, the Anglo-Americans threatened to tear down the German defense front and to penetrate deep into France.

In Italy, the Allies continued their attacks with particular vigor on the Ligurian coast northwest of Siena and on the Adriatic coast pressing the German defenders back toward the north. The Germans were everywhere in a sorry plight.

The dispatch of the 202nd Sturmgeschutz Brigade from Germany was again cancelled on 17 July. The brigade had to be redirected to particularly critical point of the German front. As a consolation the prospect was held out to the Finns of sending the first assault gun brigade ready for employment to Finland. The brigade which was then considered for Finland had to be assigned to the eastern front as well on 18 July.

Finnish Headquarters noticed on 18 July for the first time that the Russians began withdrawing forces from the Karelian Isthmus and transferring them to the Narva front. The question now was whether the Russians had changed their plan of attack against Finland. The next days would perhaps clear matters up further. The total Finnish casualties up to 18 July were 44,000 men including 6,500 dead. Headquarters had only been able to replace these losses to a certain extent. Reserves totaling 31,700 men were brought forward. Infantrymen in active duty of the age classes 1902-1904 were ordered again to report for active duty. Recruits of the 1926 age class forming the last reserve were, on the other hand, not yet sent to the front from their training camps.

The Finnish front east of Lake Ladoga had stabilized by the middle of July. Four Russian regiments could even be eliminated by counterattacks. On 18 July, the Marshal ordered the former group Aunus dissolved. General Talvela whom the Marshal considered for another assignment was placed at the disposal of the Commander in Chief. The two Finnish corps east of Lake Ladoga – VI Corps (General Martola), II Corps (General Mäkinen) – were placed under the direct command of Headquarters.

Information about the enemy received by Finnish Headquarters on 20 July confirmed the withdrawal of Russian forces and their partial replacement by fortress units. But the Russians continued to be superior in number so that another offensive though on a smaller scale might be expected. The Russian forces were now assumed to consist of the following units: More than twenty-nine light infantry divisions (three of which were newly arrived), two light infantry brigades, ten armored brigades, a number of special regiments in fortified positions. They were opposed by eight infantry divisions (one of which was German), one armored division and a few brigades.

Whereas Russian attacks on the Karelian Isthmus had diminished by the middle of July, enemy pressure in the Ägläjärvi and Tolväjärvi area opposite the Finnish II Corps increased as of 19 July. The Finns offered stubborn resistance in the thick forest terrain. Strong Russian pressure continued opposite the left Finnish wing throughout the following days, and the Finns were pressed back on 21 July west of Kuelismaa behind the old boundary.

Late in the evening of 20 July Finnish Headquarters learned that an attempt on Hitler's life had been made that day at the Führer's Headquarters. There was no great reaction to this news in Finland, since the Finns were preoccupied by their own troubles. Besides, the kind of information given by the Germans made it difficult to understand the ins and outs of the affair and the reasons underlying the attempt. In accordance with international form, the Marshal sent a proper telegram to Hitler congratulating him for his escape from disaster. The Finnish press avoided commenting on the internal political affairs in Germany which had been brought to the daylight by the attempt. A considerably stronger impression was made on Finnish public opinion a few days later by the methods employed at the trial of the conspirators. The Finnish people, especially the Finnish soldiers, failed to understand that a field marshal and other top level generals who had deserved well of their country during the war had to suffer an infamous fate by being hanged.

Finnish attention was, however, soon directed by the dramatic crisis on all fronts. The situation in the sector of Army Group North became more critical. The bomber formation Kuhlmey, which had supported the Finnish brother-in-arms in the operations on the Karelian Isthmus, was recalled by the German High Command on 21 July and returned to Luftflotte 1. The Finns regretted the departure of the German fliers.

It became increasingly obvious to Finnish Headquarters that the lack of forces for the defense of the German eastern front was growing more and more acute. On 22 July Mikkeli received the news that the 1122nd Assault Gun Battalion would not come to Finland either (its arrival as a second assault gun battalion of the 122nd Division had been promised by Ribbentrop in the Helsinki negotiations). On the same day, the Wehrmacht High Command announced that it intended to straighten out the front salient at Narva and Pskov in order to economize forces.

The General Erfurth was instructed to ascertain the attitude of the Finnish Commander in Chief with regard to these measures. Mannerheim, who was well aware of the dilemma of the German eastern front, said that he felt no anxiety with regard to the measures of the German command as long as it was simply a matter of local character. He stressed however the importance of not abandoning the area between Lake Peipus and the Gulf of Finland.

Finnish Headquarters announced on 22 July the replacement of General Österman by General Talvela as Finnish General at German Headquarters. Germany reported that General Guderian had been appointed acting Chief of the Army General Staff. The town of Pskov was evacuated by Army Group North on 23 July. On 24 July, General Warlimont telephoned General Erfurth to inquire about the situation and morale at the Finnish front. Warlimont said that Hitler had only reluctantly detained the German troops earmarked for Finnish assistance. He asserted that immediate help would be given the Finns in case the situation at the Finnish front would again grow tense. At the present time there were no signs of this. On the contrary, it appeared that the Russians had discontinued their offensive against the Finnish front.

The Russians continued their attacks only in the direction of Ilomantsi opposite the sector of the II Corps. In order to support the Finnish Corps, the Cavalry Brigade was brought forward to the left wing of the Finnish front by rail from the area north of Viipuri.

On 27 July, the front between Lake Peipus and the Gulf of Finland war straightened out by the Germans by evacuating Narva. Telephone communication between Finland and the Reich was interrupted on that day owing to the quick advance of the Russians towards Svinsk and Shavli. Telephone conversations between Mikkeli and German Headquarters had from now on to be conducted by way of Rovaniemi-Oslo with a resulting lack of clarity.

The continuous lull at the Viipuri-Vuoksi front allowed Finnish Headquarters to transfer further forces from that area to the threatened left wing. For that reason, the 20th Brigade was brought forward to the II Corps on 28 July to support the positions at Tolvajärvi and to its north. An estimate of the situation by Finnish Headquarters on 29 July considered the situation of the Finnish 1st Division on the left wing of the Finnish front critical, but it was hoped that he arrival of the 20th Brigade would ease the situation. In spite of the withdrawal of Russian forces the Finns expected the large-scale attack to be continued at the former focal points on the Karelian Isthmus. A further transfer of forces was, therefore, not yet taken into consideration.

The situation at the Finnish battlefront had undergone a thorough change by the end of July. While in the beginning of the Soviet Russian offensive the operational point of main effort had undoubtedly been in the area between the Gulf of Finland and Lake Ladoga, both sides had now arrayed their forces differently. The Finns spread out their forces on the Karelian Isthmus. The Russians continued to withdraw forces from the former main attack area transferring them to their front opposite Army Group North. It was but a logical consequence of the change in the overall situation that the OKW, always intent on throwing fresh forces into the battle to support the crumbling eastern front began to examine the question whether the reinforcements sent to the Finns at a time of emergency were still indispensable to them. This question had to receive a negative answer after an unprejudiced examination. On 28 July, General Erfurth received an inquiry from the OKW as to how the Finns would be likely to react to a withdrawal of the 122nd Division. Attention of the Finnish High Command was simultaneously to be drawn to the fact that support of the German front at Narva would also serve Finnish interests. It was, however, obvious that this was not only a question of military but to a large extent of political importance, since the 122nd Division represented the most essential help rendered the Finnish front in accordance with the agreement reached in the summer. This agreement concluded by Ryti under pressure of Ribbentrop was anything but popular in Finland. The more the situation eased at the Finnish front and worsened at the German eastern front, the louder the political opposition protested against the treaty tying Finland to its German brother-in-arms. Mannerheim's attitude with regard to the withdrawal of the German division was absolutely impartial. He expressed doubts on military grounds, mainly inasmuch as the Russians had better transportation facilities. They would be able to bring forward new forces to the Finnish front much faster by rail by way of Leningrad than German reinforcements could arrive in Finland by water. Nevertheless, the Marshal was capable of appreciating the necessity of the measures planned by the OKW. He took, however, the opportunity to make a number of other demands.

Hitler decided that Mannerheim's requests should be complied with as far as possible. The still undelivered assault guns and Panzer IV tanks were to be sent within a short time. Assurance was given to the Finns that in case of a new crisis at the Finnish front, they could always count upon German assistance.

The political situation in Finland had become obscure by the end of July. According to Allied reports, a number of deputies were said to have approached the Marshal in consequence of the critical situation at the German eastern front requesting him to renew his endeavors for an armistice with Russia. The report continued that Mannerheim had been chosen by the deputies since only the hands of President Ryti, Prime Minister Linkomies and Foreign Minister Ramsay were tied by the treaty. A secret meeting took place in the evening of 28 July at Mannerheim's country resident Sairila which was attended by Ryti, Linkomies, Walden and Tanner, who had come by plane from Helsinki. The Finnish statesmen examined the overall situation and took counsel together how to act in view of the growing opposition against Ryti's policy and the continually waning prospects of a bearable end to the war. Ryti, who was physically and mentally exhausted, was said to have decided during this meeting to hand in his resignation in order to win back the Finnish Government's freedom of action lost through the Ribbentrop treaty. The result of the meeting at Sairila was for the time being kept secret but was to be announced to the Finnish public shortly. The Finnish statesmen returned to Helsinki by plane on 29 July. Their meeting with Mannerheim and the matter that had been under discussion was kept absolutely secret.

On the same day, the Finnish Commander in Chief was informed by the German General that the 122nd Division had received an evacuation order from the OKW. The Marshal was requested to accelerate its relief as much as possible. Relief by the Finnish 10th Division began on 30 July. Mannerheim asked the German General to choose Hangö and not Helsinki as the port of embarkation of the German division. He probably feared the unfavorable impression which the withdrawal of the German division was liable to create on the inhabitants of the Finnish capital. Every day brought new unfavorable news from the German eastern front. The huge defensive battle between the upper Dniester and the Gulf of Finland increased further in violence by the end of July. The Red offensive in Galicia penetrated deep into the country and reached Lwow. Soviet pressure continued between the Bug and the Vistula. Resistance of the German garrison at Lublin ended on 27 July. The enemy had formed several bridgeheads northwest of Brest Litovsk on the western bank of the Bug. On 28 July the last German defenders evacuated the towns of Lwow, Brest Litovsk, Bialystock and Dvinsk. In the Warsaw area, a breakthrough of strong Russian forces towards the town was prevented on 31 July after bitter fighting. The German troops tried in vain at Bialystock and northeast of Augustow to halt the Russian advance between the middle Bug and Olita. Between the Augustow forest and the Niemen River heavy fighting went on which developed unfavorably for the Gemans. On 30 July the enemy began a large-scale offensive in the

Kaunas area. Kaunas was lost on 31 July. A Russian spearhead advance rapidly by way of Shavli in the direction of Jelgava, reached Jelgava on 29 July and threatened to cut off the entire Army Group North from the Reich. Since the Riga airport was threatened, the German Lufthansa suspended traffic between the Reich and Finland, interrupting any quick, direct communication between the two countries.

The internal political crisis in Finland was more and more openly reflected by the Finnish press. In the views of the Finnish trade unions the war was lost. The daily increasing political opposition endeavored to obtain a peace settlement even under hard conditions, irrespective of the interests of the German brother-in-arms.

CHAPTER VII: <u>The End of the Brotherhood-in-Arms</u>

The political crisis in Finland reached a climax on 1 August. Congress was convened and informed that Ryti had resigned his position as president. Simultaneously the Government submitted to Congress the draft of a bill nominating Mannerheim President of the Finnish Republic. This way had been chosen in order to terminate the presidential crisis as quickly as possible.

The last act of the Finnish tragedy, which was a direct result of the meeting at Sairila, began with the change of presidents and ended with the termination of the Finnish-German brotherhood-in-arms. The reason given to the outside world for Ryti's resignation was his poor health. Official circles believed that the darkest hour of Finnish history demanded that the supreme political and military power be united in one hand. It was but natural that the Finnish people wished in this time of need to have a man at the helm of the state in whom all Finns had the greatest confidence and who was believed capable of steering his country through all dangers into the safe harbor of peace. At the same time, all Finns expected that Mannerheim, the father of his country, would not shun the call of his people if unanimously elected by Congress. Even the former opposition was unlikely to assent without exception to the law appointing the new president. Amid the general unrest and anxiety the seventy-seven year old Marshal stood like an unbroken rock unmoved by the buffets of fate and ready to procure his people the desired peace.

It goes without saying that the development in Finland was followed with the greatest concern by the German Government, which, however, hoped that the Finnish sense of honor would also induce the new President and his Government to stick to the agreement concluded in the summer between Ryti and Ribbentrop. Moreover, in view of Mannerheim's past it was considered impossible that he would conclude a separate peace with the Soviet Union considering his aversion toward Bolshevism. Nevertheless, Ryti's sudden resignation came like a thunder stroke causing greatest uneasiness as to the future development of conditions in Finland. There were many symptoms of a change in Finnish policy in consequence of the change in government. Perhaps owing to nervousness or due to the urgent necessity of obtaining clarity, Hitler's Headquarters decided on the spur of the moment to send General Schörner, who had shortly been appointed Commander in Chief of Army Group North. This sudden decision had apparently been brought about by a conversation between General Talvela, who had been reappointed Finnish General at German Headquarters and Military Attaché, and the German Attaché Branch on 2 August. In order to answer Talvela's questions regarding the situation in the sector of Army Group North, General Schörner was ordered on the night on 2 August to fly immediately to the Marshal, to give him a report on the situation in his sector and to support the maintenance of Finland's former policy. He was instructed further to announce an early visit of the Chief of the OKW and to declare that his orders were to defend the Baltic provinces and that he had sufficient forces to do so. Finally he was to give information on the other sectors of the German eastern front.

Mannerheim happened to be at Helsinki fully occupied with forming his own government. He was most probably exceedingly surprised to learn on 3 August early in the morning that Schörner would land on Malmi airfield near Helsinki at noon asking to be received by the Marshal. Nevertheless, the Marshal received the German envoy with amiable politeness. Reception and conference took place in the Marshal's special train which stood on its usual place at a suburban station of the capital. The conference was attended by Finnish Generals Walden and Heinrichs and General Erfurth. Schörner made his report, as ordered, on the situation in the sector of his army group and gave the assurance that the Baltic provinces would be held under all circumstances. Since the overland supply route had been interrupted by the Russians, supplies would be sent by water or by air. Armored forces advancing from East Prussia would restore the situation of Army Group North, re-establishing communication with the eastern front. Schörner's report was followed by a short discussion of combat experiences which the German Commander in Chief had made in the heavy fighting of the last weeks in the southern and northern sectors of the eastern front.

After that, the meeting was finished. Political questions were not touched upon, as was to be expected. The sending of Schörner was not a measure suited to clear the political atmosphere. Besides, it was probably much too early to obtain information about Mannerheim's intentions, since so far no efforts had been made to form a new cabinet. Hitler's obvious attempt to impress a man of the Marshal's character by a spirited and carefully colored report on the situation seemed rather naïve. One of the strongest virtues of tiny Finland is her ability to navigate on the choppy waters of international politics. The ruling class in Finland was formed and politically educated over a long period of foreign rule. The Finns lived in a world of ideas and tradition inherited from astute ancestors and they deliberately forgo adventures based on illusions and wishful thinking. For that reason they have acquired a sense of reality and the ability to act with sober realism. To the Finnish mind it was clear that there were but a few grains of sand left in the hour-glass of German-Finnish brotherhood-in-arms. The wheel of destiny cannot be stayed or turned back. This wisdom enabled the Finnish people to endure the heaviest buffets fo fate with dignity and composure.

General Schörner made a favorable report on his visit to Mannerheim. According to information received by the OKW from outer sources, however, the situation was not so good. There were rumors of another Paasikivi visit to Moscow, and the names of new Finnish ministers mentioned did not all inspire confidence to German Headquarters. On 3 August, General Rendulic in a report to Hitler said that the cause of the quick development of the political crisis was a message from Roosevelt to Ryti, furthermore, parleys with British representatives at Lisbon promising peace, and finally the withdrawal of the 122nd Division. The Commander in Chief of the Twentieth Mountain Army, expecting the Marshal to make peace overtures, advocated that the 122nd Division be left in Finland and that the Chief of the OKW pay an early visit to Mannerheim.

General Erfurth reported on 4 August that internal political entanglements were the cause of the crisis (unpopularity of the German-Finnish agreement, unrest in the ranks of the Swedish People's Party and Social Democrats, influence of the Swedish and Allied propaganda, growing opposition, rumors of insufficient military help, withdrawal of forces, rumors of peace proposals). The change of Presidents had been a clever move to appease the opposition. Ryti had always liked quick decisions. Since the Marshal would not have participated in an election campaign, the change of presidents was only possible by extraordinary methods, Erfurth's report continued. The reasons officially stated (concentration of power in one hand, Ryti's poor health) had in part probably been correct. The main point, however, had been that the Finnish people got rid of the undesirable Ribbentrop agreement. The Marshal would probably make a few concessions to the opposition when forming a government, but no reactions were to be expected for the time being on the military situation at the front. Judging from his personal knowledge of Mannerheim and his past, Erfurth did not believe the new President to be ready to come to an understanding with Russia. Other observers of events in Finland, however, were of the opinion that Finland's connection with Germany would probably be given up on the ground that the promise of military help had not been fulfilled.

Finnish Congress unanimously voted into law on 4 August the motion nominating Mannerheim President of the Republic. In a solemn meeting of Congress the Marshal swore his oath of allegiance to the constitution. He spent most of the following days in Helsinki holding conferences regarding the formation of a new government. Procopé, the former Finnish Ambassador to Washington, had returned from the United States to Finland. He categorically denied rumors spread at Helsinki of American peace proposals brought by him and declared that no American help for Finland was to be expected.

In reply to a telegram from Hitler congratulating Mannerheim on his election as President, the Marshal wired his thanks wishing the Wehrmacht good luck in its heroic fight against the common enemy.

Mannerheim's cabinet, which was not formed until 8 August after several days' negotiations, showed considerable changes as compared with the old government. Linkomies, Ramsay, Tanner, Salovaara and Reinikka had resigned. Their places had been taken by Hackwell (conservative, Prime Minister), Enckell (independent, Foreign Minister), Hillilä, von Born, and Aaltonen. Walden was also a member of the new cabinet in his capacity of Minister for Defense. Five of the fifteen cabinet members belonged to the Social Democratic Party and four to the Agrarian Party. The other parties had one representative each. Three ministers were independent. The Transocean News Agency defined the cabinet as Mannerheim's confidential cabinet, since its tendency was more conservative than radical leftist. Paasikivi, who had made a declaration in the press on 7 August stating that Finland would have to sue for peace, was not a member of the new government.

Finnish public opinion interpreted the change of presidents and government as meaning an opening of the way for a new Finnish policy. All political circles were united in the belief that Finland could not continue the war for any length of time and that the wish of an early peace shared by most Finns would have to be seen realized. Everyone felt that the Finnish-German brotherhood-in-arms was nearing its end. But there was a wide divergence of opinions as to which conditions could be considered tolerable. Those circles who objected to an imposed peace were still strong. There was no doubt that the Marshal would not risk losing his reputation by accepting a dishonorable peace. It went without saying that the Marshal would find it hard to separate from his brother-in-arms and to surrender to the Soviet Russian rulers. It could, however, be foreseen that the political development in Finland would increasingly aim at a termination of the war and also influence Mannerheim's policy. The number of Congress members advocating a continuation of the war side by side with Germany decreased from day to day. The former majority which had supported Ryti's policy became a minority now. Fate moved irresistibly onward. The German agencies in Finland as well as Hitler's Headquarters were fully aware of the eventual outcome but hoped to be able to postpone a Finnish separate peace for a little while.

The request of Finnish Headquarters to rearm the Finnish Army with German weapons was declined by the Chief of the OKW on 2 August. He decided that the Finns would have to look out for themselves with regard to armament and ammunition. German assistance would remain the same as before. The plight of the German Army did not permit any major support.

On 9 August, a conference took place at Mikkeli between General Erfurth and the German Naval Attaché at Helsinki about a possible evacuation of German agencies from southern Finland in case the situation took a turn for the worse. The Kriegsmarine unobtrusively made the necessary preparations.

General fear of the uncertain future also took hold of the Estonians who were organized in the 2nd Infantry Regiment and fought along the Vuoksi River in the Karelian Isthmus. They were troubled by the unfavorable state of affairs in Estonia and wanted to return to their families. The Chief of the Finnish General Staff asked General Erfurth on 6 August for his good offices in inducing the OKW to permit those Estonians who had fled to Finland to return to Estonia and to grant them an amnesty for any infringements of German law. The OKW agreed to the Finnish request on 8 August to the great relief of the Finns.

The last successful day for the Finns in this war was 10 August, when the excellent qualities of the Finnish soldiers were once again spotlighted. Russian pressure had continued on the left wing of the Finnish front (II Corps) throughout the first week of August, while at all other sectors east and west of Lake Ladoga there was a lull. Together with reinforcements coming from the Karelian Isthmus (Cavalry Brigade and 20th Brigade) II Corps proceeded on 10 August to attack, pocketing the Russians in the difficult forest terrain between Ilomantsi and Kuolismaa-Ontronvaara and eliminating two Soviet divisions. After this Finnish victory this part of the Karelian theater of war also quieted down, a state of affairs which continued in all sectors of the Finnish front until acceptance by the Finnish Government of the Soviet Russian ultimatum. The last major battle in the war was, therefore, a definite Finnish victory. Finnish Headquarters estimated the Russian forces by the middle of August still to number more than twenty-one divisions, after the withdrawal on 17 July of ten light infantry divisions and a number of minor units. By the construction of rear positions, particularly the Moscow position behind the frontier of 1940, an attempt was made at giving the Finnish front greater stability and depth. Since the enemy did not make any moves in August after the Finnish victory on the left wing of the Finnish front and even withdrew further forces, the attitude of the Finnish Government did not undergo any change for the time being. Nevertheless, the calm, which had set in in the internal political situation of Finland after Mannerheim had taken over the government and formed a new cabinet, lasted but a few days. By the middle of August, the capital was again a hotbed of alarming rumors. Those politicians who were in a hurry to see the war terminated found the time too long before the new government entered into negotiations with Soviet Russia. News that a Finnish delegations was on its way to Stockholm or that Paasikivi made a trip to

Moscow was spread at Helsinki. It was asserted that negotiations proceeded between Finland and Sweden with regard to the defense of the Åland Islands. No sooner had these rumors been refuted that new assertions were made complicating the situation. Rumors spread with a rapidity befitting Vergil's words: "*Vires acquirit eundo* (It gains strength by its movements).

A leading member of Finnish Headquarters assured General Erfurth on 14 August that no negotiations were under way with foreign countries at the present time. Minister for Defense Walden confirmed this statement on 16 August to the German Military Attaché and the Commander in Chief of the Twentieth Mountain Army who had come to Helsinki.

On 17 August, Field Marshal Keitel arrived in Finland from Hitler's Headquarters in order to bestow the Oak leaf cluster of the Iron Cross to Marshal Mannerheim and the Knight's Cross to the Iron Cross to the Chief of the Finnish General Staff. The plan to honor General Heinrichs and his Chief of Staff by bestowing upon them the highest German war decorations had already been arrived at by the end of July when the impression became rooted that the Red Army's offensive against the Finnish front on either side of Lake Ladoga had been discontinued. The defensive victory gained under very difficult conditions by the Finnish Army was also appreciated by the OKW. In order to express this feeling to the Finnish brother-in-arms in a dignified manner and in order to emphasize their unaltered mutual relationship, the Chief of the OKW was to deliver the war decorations personally by order of Hitler.

This plan had been delayed by the great political changes which took place in Finland in the beginning of August. Keitel's announced visit had to be postponed until the Marshal had formed his new government. The Chief of the OKW, therefore, arrived at a time when thoughts of Finland's new political orientation assumed the foreground. Keitel's visit did not, however, pursue any political aims and was strictly a military affair. Mannerheim received the Chief of the OKW in the Mikkeli school building and after the welcome and bestowing of the decorations he made a lengthy statement explaining the situation in all theaters of war as seen by the Führer's Headquarters to the Marshal and a great number of Finnish generals who had been invited. Keitel's words were very optimistic. He described the situation as perhaps Hitler and his entourage would view it, but certainly not Mannerheim and his generals. He passed lightly over the greatest difficulties, the fast, complete breakdown of the German defense in Brittany and Normandy, the Allied landing in southern France, the retreat of the German troops in Italy at Florence and in the Adriatic coast area, the advance of the Russians northeast of Warsaw, in Lithuania and Latvia, and the continual air attacks on German towns. His statements, therefore, failed to impress his audience. Keitel's report on the situation was followed by a luncheon for a small group of people at Sairila, where Mannerheim's splendid gift for conversation was once again demonstrated. The Finns announced that all losses suffered at the front since 9 June amounting to 60,000 men had meanwhile been replaced but stressed that Finland would not be able to survive another such blood-letting.

After luncheon Mannerheim took the opportunity to discuss with his guest the changing situation in Finland. He withdrew for this purpose with Keitel to his study at Headquarters and explained to him in the presence of his chief of staff the Finnish standpoint with regard to the political situation. When Ryti entered the agreement with Ribbentrop by the middle of summer he had acted under constraint and had taken over obligations which the bulk of the Finnish refuses to accept. According to Finnish opinion, the agreement with Germany was not valid any more after Ryti's resignation. The new Finnish government had regained its freedom of action. Keitel immediately opposed this opinion and declared himself not authorized to accept political statements concerning German-Finnish relations. If Hitler had wished to discuss these relations he would have sent another man to Finland. Mannerheim replied that he did not want his guest to leave without having learned of the changed situation in Finland. The OKW Chief left Mikkeli in the afternoon very upset by this conclusion to his visit.

Two days later, on 19 August, General Heinrichs returned again to the subject of the conversation between Mannerheim and Keitel and told General Erfurth that nothing was decided as yet and everything would depend on the development of the situation on the principle German fronts, particularly in the Baltic provinces. If the German forces were successful, those who wished to sue for peace would decrease in number in Finland and vice versa. Whether peace with Russia was possible at all remained an open question, for Finland would not be willing to relinquish its freedom and independence. Heinrichs on this occasion confirmed the fact that as far as he knew no Finnish delegation had gone to Moscow.

The war situation in France and Russia deteriorated, however, in the next few days to a threatening extent. It had become quite obvious that the German front in France had completely broken down and that it was impossible to turn the tide by a major German counterattack. The Allied forces spread quickly across France and advanced rapidly eastward. In southern France, too, the Allied landing had been a complete success and the enemy was in hot pursuit of the retreating German forces between the coast and the Durance River. In Italy the enemy continued his breakthrough attempts successfully in the Adriatic coast area. In the east, the Red Army extended its large-scale attacks to the southern sector after

21 August. German troops southwest of Tiraspol and between the Pruth and Sereth Rivers were engaged in heavy fighting.

Southwest of Lake Pskov the Russians had made a deep penetration which they continued to extend. At the narrows between Lakes Pskov and Peipus, the Germans were engaged in bloody battles with the Russians who had crossed to the western shore.

On 24 August it was learned that an armistice had been concluded between the Soviet Union and Rumania, so that another German ally had withdrawn from the war. Rumania's secession was carried out under dramatic circumstances bringing the German troops on the Pruth and Sereth Rivers and in the Rumanian hinterland into great distress.

The Finns watched with great anxiety the capitulation of Rumania and the costly collapse of the German-Rumanian front. We Finns, Finnish generals said in these days, will be the last to fight side by side with Germany. In the last week of August there could be no doubt that the last days of German-Finnish brotherhood-in-arms had arrived. Everything pointed to a decision. The air attacks, which the Russians carried out against Finnish towns on 23 August, were part of a war of nerves against Finland. They were to show the Finns that they still had to take the Russian danger into account.

Kivimäki, the Finnish Ambassador in Berlin, was instructed by Mannerheim on 26 August to inform the German Government officially that Mannerheim as President of the Finnish Republic did not feel bound by Ryti's prior engagements. Almost a month had elapsed since Mannerheim had taken over the government. He could not put off a decision any longer since in view of the fast development of the situation his government would otherwise not be able to cope with the opposition that had become too powerful.

The press in the Finnish capital took up a more and more unfriendly attitude towards Germany and advocated termination of the war. A great part of the Finnish people was convinced that the war was lost. The quicker it could be terminated, the better it would be.

After a stay of several days at Helsinki, the Marshal returned to Mikkeli on 27 August, and when met General Heinrichs, he declared that the situation was very bad. There was no doubt whatever about that. Heinrichs, full of apprehension, had drawn the attention of General Erfurth to the loss of Tartu and had added that something had to be done soon. That led indeed to the conclusion that at present no negotiations had taken place yet. On 30 August, Moscow Radio requested Finland follow the example of Rumania and Bulgaria and to give in too. The Finnish people, deprived of all hope, were no longer able to resist this new temptation.

The German Ambassador in Helsinki was informed by the Finnish Foreign Minister on 31 August that the Finns had contacted the Soviet Union a few days previously. General Erfurth prepared the evacuation of German wounded lying in south Finnish hospitals.

On 1 September, the two generals Rendulic and Erfurth met in Helsinki at the residence of Ambassador von Blücher. The three men responsible for the German interests in Finland discussed the situation and measures to be eventually taken. Rendulic and Erfurth were received by Mannerheim at noon on 2 September at the summer palace of the President at Tamminiemi in the presence of General Walden, Minister for Defense, and General Heinrichs, Chief of the General Staff. The Finnish generals were in low spirits. Mannerheim, who was otherwise a splendid conversationalist, remained taciturn and occupied with his thoughts. Political questions were not discussed. Rendulic's occasional attempts at touching the all-important questions of the day failed owing to Mannerheim's dignified inaccessibility and the reserve of his generals. One had the feeling of being in a house of mourning from which the corpse had not yet been removed.

In the afternoon of 2 September it was announced that the Finnish Congress would be convened in the evening of the same day in order to discuss the Soviet Russian peace conditions which had arrived on the previous day.

Prior to the Congress' meeting, Lieutenant Colonel Crönvall, Mannerheim's Chief Adjutant, handed the German General at Finnish Headquarters a letter from Mannerheim to Adolf Hitler, in which he asked him to exercise a proper understanding of Finnish decisions. He was convinced, the Marshal explained, that the salvation of his people made it his duty to find a way out of this war as soon as possible. Owing to the unfavorable overall war situation, Germany would find it increasingly difficult to assist the Finns in proper time and to the extent necessary in case of need. Finland, on the other hand, unlike Germany was not able to carry on a war indefinitely. Finland could not afford to suffer another blood-letting as in June, and, in case of defeat unlike Germany it could be exterminated. A growing majority in the Finnish Congress shared his unfavorable view of the war situation. Even if he were of a different opinion, it would not be possible for him in view of the Finnish constitution to neglect for a long time the clearly expressed will of the majority of the people. It appeared certain to him that the Finns would physically not be able to stand a prolonged war. The large-scale Russian attack in June on the Karelian Isthmus had already exhausted the Finnish replacements. "We cannot afford another such blood-letting," Mannerheim wrote, "without endangering the very existence of our tiny Finnish nation." He hardly dared hope, Mannerheim continued, that his explanations and statements would be appreciated or approved by Hitler. Nevertheless he wished to send him these lines prior to his decision.

Mannerheim's sense of chivalry was given particularly stirring expression in the last sentences of his letter to Hitler where he gave high praise to the German brother-in-arms at the moment when the paths of the two nations diverges:

> "Our German brothers-in-arms will forever remain in our hearts. The Germans in Finland were certainly not the representatives of foreign despotism but helpers and brothers-in-arms. But even in such a case foreigners are in difficult positions requiring such tact. I can assure you that during the past years nothing whatsoever happened that could have induced us to consider the German troops intruders or oppressors. I believe that the attitude of the German Army in northern Finland toward the local population and authorities will enter our history as a unique example of correct and cordial relationship."

At the end of his letter, Mannerheim addressed the Head of the Reich in great earnest and full of honest apprehension in the following imploring words:

> "I deem it my duty to lead my people out of the war. I cannot and I will not turn the arms which you have so liberally supplied us against Germans. I harbor the hope that you, even if you disapprove of my attitude, will wish and endeavor like myself and all other Finns to terminate our former relations without increasing the gravity of the situation."

This letter of the Finnish President thoroughly clarified the situation. There may be a difference of opinion about the Finnish Government's right to demand freedom of action, but one will have to admit that the instinctive tact of the Marshal found the best form to explain the step which he felt forced to take. That his action would be appreciated by the Germans he himself probably did not expect. German and Finnish opinions were diametrically opposed to each other. According to international law it might be considered questionable whether the German or Finnish conception was more correct. The German standpoint based on the principles of an authoritarian state insisted that the new Finnish government was also bound by the agreement made between Ryti and

Ribbentrop. The Finnish standpoint based on democratic principles argued that the pact between Ryti and Ribbentrop had no binding power since it had been concluded without the cooperation of the Finnish Congress and the majority of the Finnish people rejected it.

Events now moved rapidly. In the evening of 2 September the Finnish Congress sanctioned the declaration of Foreign Minister Enckell regarding the Government's intended policy of accepting the Soviet Russian conditions for terminating the war. The vote was 113 in favor, 46 against. Immediately after the session of Congress, at 2200, the Finnish Foreign Minister requested the presence of the German Ambassador von Blücher and informed him of the result of the session in a voice full of emotion. Finland was forced now, he said, to break off relations with Germany and to intern the German troops still on Finnish territory on 15 September. At 2300 the Prime Minister gave the reasons for the Finnish Government's step in a radio speech, explaining the deterioration of the Reich's and of Finland's situations. After the loss of the southern coast of the Gulf of Finland, the Finnish front had become less important to Germany. Finland was therefore obliged to face the fact that in the future Germany would not be able to render assistance. Relations had been based solely on common military interests. In the summer, Germany had rendered assistance only under the conditions that no separate negotiations be made. Finland had to agree on account of the situation at the front. The assistance then rendered had been valuable but not as great as expected. When Germany again withdrew forces, the opinion prevailed that cooperation was nearing its end. After the change of government, the hands of the new president were no longer tied. The German Government had been officially informed accordingly. Since the situation had grown more threatening, Finland had begun new negotiations, which had now led to the decision of Congress. The Prime Minister emphasized that an early evacuation also served German interests, for Germany would, thereby, continue to live in the memory of the thankful Finnish people as brothers-in-arms who had the welfare of Finland at heart.

Official death notices had thus been given to the Finnish-German brotherhood-in-arms and the paths of the two nations separated irrevocably.

Concerning the negotiations between Finland and Russia which led to Finland's secession from the war, the following transpired: According to an official declaration by Radio Moscow on 4 September, Gripenberg, the Finnish Ambassador to Stockholm, handed Mrs. Kollontay on 25 August a note from the Finnish Foreign Minister Enckell giving Gripenberg authorization to request the dispatch of a Finnish governmental delegation. Attached to this declaration was a verbal note stating that Marshal Mannerheim, the Finnish President, had informed Field Marshal

Keitel on 17 August that he did not consider himself bound any longer by the agreement concluded between Ryti and the Reich. Mrs. Kollontay answered on 29 August that the Finnish delegation could be received only after accepting the following conditions:

1. Immediate breaking off of diplomatic relations with Germany.
2. Request that Germany withdraw her forces by 15 September. Otherwise disarmament of the German forces and their delivery to the Allies as prisoners or war.

It was added that the answer was given in agreement with the British Government and that the United States Government had made no comment.

It was learned on good authority that the Soviet Union had informed Finland on 30 August of her readiness to enter into armistice negotiations at Moscow up until 15 September provided that Finland broke off relations with Germany and caused the German troops to evacuate Finland by that date, an action which with the best intentions of everyone concerned could not be carried out in so short a time.

The Foreign Affairs Committee of the Finnish Congress had a session on 1 September to discuss the Russian answer. After the announcement of Radio Moscow, Ambassador Gripenberg handed Mrs. Kollontay a declaration of the Finnish President on 2 September, who proposed that Finland, before answering the preliminary conditions of Russia, herself carry out the voluntary withdrawal or internment of the German forces in Finland, furthermore that military action cease and the boundary of 1940 be occupied. A declaration that relations had been broken off should follow after receipt of the Russian reply. Finland was also ready to take part in the disarmament of the German forces in North Finland, but it wished previously to open negotiations in Moscow regarding coordination and help. The Soviet Union declined these counterproposals on 3 September and declared that it would be ready after 15 September to cooperate in the disarmament. The Soviet Union agreed, however, to cease fire on the Finnish southern front.

So 2 September became the fateful day in the history of Finnish-German relations.

On 3 September, negotiations began at Finnish Headquarters at Mikkeli between General Heinrichs and General Erfurth about the evacuation of the German troops in southern Finland and about questions of cooperation between Germans and Finns with regard to developments on the boundary between the German and Finnish fronts. According to the Soviet demands the Germans had to clear out of Finland by 15 September. Those who had not left Finnish territory up to that deadline were to be interned. The Finns desired that up to 15

September as many German troops as possible were to have left the country. The small German agencies in southern Finland were quite able to evacuate in due time, but it was obvious that the German army in Lapland could not possibly terminate its evacuation by 15 September. This fact caused the Finns great concern, and they were at a loss to know what attitude the German Army in Lapland was going to take. General Erfurth, who had received no directives orientation from the OKW, could not give any explanation either. General Heinrichs promised that Finnish Headquarters would support the German evacuation transports in every respect. In case the right wing of the Twentieth Army would be bent back, Finnish Headquarters wished to distribute a security line of Finnish forces along the Finnish frontier. In preparation of these measures, Finnish Headquarters intended bringing the 6th Division to Kajaani and the 15th Division to the Oulu area. The Twentieth Mountain Army was informed accordingly on 4 September and considered it a threat to its southern flank. In order to protect itself, the Army High Command formed two task forces which should be at hand for intercepting a Finnish assault if it became necessary. In this way an atmosphere of distrust between Rovaniemi and Mikkeli was created on the very first day after the Finnish capitulation.

Hitler's and Ribbentrop's reaction to Finland's withdrawal was curt and without understanding for Finland's position. Both the German Ambassador and General Erfurth received a directive from Ribbentrop on 3 September to break off immediately all personal or official relations with the Finns. In view of the situation of the German agencies, whose endeavors to leave Finland were entirely dependent on Finnish support, this directive was difficult to understand. If it had not been for the fact that Germans and Finns had so far been on excellent terms, Ribbentrop's ban on contact would have caused serious frictions. Owing to the honest wish of all Finnish agencies to help the former brother-in-arms and to facilitate his exit, all possible assistance was offered the Germans without waiting for them to ask for it. The Finns endeavored in the spirit of Mannerheim to wind up the former relations without causing the situation to become even more grave.

The office of the German General at Finnish Headquarters was dissolved on 3 September with undue haste by a decree from the OKW. General Erfurth with his staff was appointed "Evacuation Staff South" and received orders to conduct the evacuation of German troops and agencies from southern Finland and to carry it out by 15 September.

The armistice became effective at the Finnish-Russian front on 4 September. In the evening of that day, Marshal Mannerheim, who had remained in the capital, urgently requested the presence of General Erfurth on 5 September in Helsinki for a discussion. Since such a step was not permissible because of Ribbentrop's ban on contact, Erfurth asked for OKW permission to attend the meeting with Mannerheim, which was granted by Field Marshal Keitel. During the night of 4 September Erfurth went to Helsinki by train. On his arrival in the capital he made a long distance call to Rovaniemi. General Rendulic authorized Erfurth on this occasion to inform the Finns that the Twentieth Mountain Army had begun its withdrawal from Lapland. Naturally it would not be possible to carry out the entire evacuation by 15 September. Erfurth drew the conclusion from Rendulic's words that the Twentieth Mountain Army would do everything in its power to begin the evacuation of the German army immediately.

The Marshal received Erfurth in his summer palace of Tamminiemi in the presence of General Heinrichs. At the request of Erfurth, who wanted to say good-bye to the staff, Mannerheim bade Lieutenant Colonel Grönvall and Dr. Kalaja also to come in.

Mannerheim gave the assurance in this last conversation that he wished to assist the German evacuation in every possible way, and that he would give the necessary orders to the Finnish Chief of Transportation. He desired to be informed by Erfurth on Rendulic's intentions. Erfurth informed the Marshal that his mission in Finland as German General at Finnish Headquarters had come to an end. Regarding the attitude of the Twentieth Mountain Army he told the Marshal what had heard by telephone from Rendulic in the morning. Mannerheim and Heinrichs were apparently relieved by the news that the German army had begun its withdrawal. The Marshal admitted that 15 September was too early a deadline for terminating the evacuation, but the Finns could do nothing against this stipulation of Moscow. The conversation between Mannerheim and Erfurth was held in the same cordial spirit which Mannerheim had shown the German General during the past three years. Each side sincerely regretted the separation brought about by inevitable fate. Mannerheim took leave of Erfurth with warm words of thanks.

The situation made it inevitable that much friction would occur in the following days, since German and Finnish interests were now at variance, but through mutual good will a suitable way was always found. All requests made by General Erfurth were readily met by the Finns. The German agencies at Mikkeli and Helsinki endeavored to understand the difficult Finnish situation. It was but natural that the Finns wished to avoid appearing incorrect toward the Soviet Union. In the position in which the Finns found themselves there was little room for freedom of action. In contrast to the frank exchange, based on confidence, between the Finnish High Command and the German agencies in southern Finland, the old congenial relations between the Finns and Rovaniemi had ceased to exist. Neither Finnish Headquarters nor General Erfurth had received any information on the intentions of the Twentieth Mountain Army and the OKW.

As the first objective of the intended withdrawal movement, the Twentieth Mountain Army had provided an intermediary position running behind the former right wing in a north-southerly direction and then bending to the west. The XVIII Corps was to withdraw into this position after 16 September and the XXXVI Corps after 11 September with their mobile forces. Meanwhile, the bulk of the two corps was to march off in a northwesterly direction.

On 4 September, General Rendulic requested an early decision from the OKW as to whether the movement of his army should continue as far as northern Norway. He did not think it advisable to inform the Finns of his plans but left it open to notify them of the actual position of the movement, as proposed by General Erfurth. The OKW sent him directives on the same day to carry out the withdrawal as far as the Karesuando position and gave him command authority as a Wehrmacht commander.[32] The withdrawal of the German army was not to reveal the intention to hold the Ivalo-Petsamo position in the north with the XIX Corps and was to be carried out in agreement with the Finns.

Hitler and many German agencies had formed quite erroneous ideas about the probably attitude of the Finnish soldiers. On 5 September, Hitler had, for instance, approved a proposal of Army Group North to reactivate the Finnish 27th Light Infantry Battalion based on the traditions of World War I days in order to organize Finnish soldiers opposed to the capitulation into a unit under German command. Simultaneously the Twentieth Mountain Army High Command endeavored to incorporate Finnish stragglers into the German Army in Lapland. Finally, Himmler attempted to recruit Finnish soldiers on the strength of old Finnish relations to the Waffen-SS. But as more rational experts in Finnish affairs could have predicted it soon turned out that Finns wishing to join the Wehrmacht were the exception and that the majority did not think of opposing the political decisions of the Finnish Government and of disobeying the Marshal.

Hitler answered Rendulic on 5 September that a withdrawal to northern Norway was not planned and that the Finns should be informed only as far as compatible with the interests of the Twentieth Mountain Army. Furthermore, Hitler gave directives about the extent of destruction to be carried out during the withdrawal which proved very important for Finnish-German relations. The Kolosjoki nickel plant, from Finnish

---

[32] The powers of a commander with Wehrmacht command authority extended to other than army units.

workers had been withdrawn, was to continue work with German labor by order of Hitler.

No difficulties were expected in supplying the German army during this withdrawal which had been prepared for a long time. Since time was short for transportation across the Baltic it was decided to evacuate the superfluous personnel on this route, some 23,000 strong, as well as 23,000 tons of valuable Wehrmacht material and 5,000 tons of fuel. The total stock of Wehrmacht material was estimated to be 150,000 tons. There remained no alternative but to destroy the material which could not be removed.

These transports again drew attention to the question of shipping space in the northern region. Gauleiter[33] Kaufmann, National Commissioner for Maritime Commerce, therefore, went to Norway on 6 September to discuss matters with Reich Commissioner Terboven and General von Falkenhorst, the Military Administrative Commander, and to determine the construction projects to be abandoned and the laborers to be withdrawn. The result of the discussion was that the construction program would have to be cancelled in case the Mountain Army had to be transported back, since both could not be done simultaneously. In order to bring the interests of the Kriegsmarine and the merchant marine into harmony, negotiations went on about the repair capacity of the dockyards.

A strong Russian air attack was made on 6 September on the Alakurtti-Salla railroad, an important supply route of the XXXVI Corps, causing temporary suspension of traffic.

On the same day, the staff of General Erfurth left Mikkeli for Helsinki in a special train provided by the Finns. There, provisional billets were kept ready for the next few days until the departure of the boat and where the last German affairs were dealt with.

The Finnish delegation (Hackzel, Enckell, Walden, Heinrichs) flew on 6 September from Helsinki to Moscow in order to sign the capitulation.

The former Finnish General at German Headquarters, Talvela, reported that he departed from German Headquarters with great courtesy displayed on both sides.

On 6 September at 2100, the first phase of the withdrawal of the German Lapland Army, the so-called BIRKE movement, began with the retirement of the right wing of the army to the Sohjana position .

The Kriegsmarine evacuated the base at Kotka and its positions on Suursaari Island. The Military Administrative Commander in Norway was ordered on 7 September to transfer immediately the Bicycle Brigade

---

[33] Official in charge of a Nazi Party administrative area

Norway to Skoganvarre as GHQ reserve to be employed in the sector of the Twentieth Mountain Army.

Evacuation of the German units and agencies in South Finland by boat from Helsinki also began on 7 September. The first transport included the 303rd Assault Gun Brigade, the difficult loading of which was carried out under Finnish assistance. The bulk of the German agencies boarded on 8 September and weighed anchor on 9 September. On 9 September the Finnish Government ordered the evacuation of Lapland and permitted no one to enter the region.

Task Force East had been established on 8 September at the new southern front of the Mountain Army. The formation of Task Force West on the other hand, was delayed for some time. The bicycle brigade was brought forward from Norway to be employed as reserve. Operation TANNE OST (occupation of Suursaari) was postponed on 9 September for the time being, for lack of forces (to be dealt with in Chapter Eight). The Russians followed the withdrawal of the Twentieth Army's right wing to the Sohjana sector quite slowly. They attacked, on the other hand, in the Kandalaksha sector, probably assuming that the German troops were already retiring and suffered heavy losses. Later on they continued their attacks with more success, as will be dealt with later.

The Finnish Chief of Transportation announced on 9 September that the Finnish railroads would not be available to the Twentieth Mountain Army after 14 September. General Erfurth immediately lodged a protest and demanded that traffic on the Salla-Kemi line be upheld for German use. Rendulic believed the Finnish Transport Chief's mode of dealing with the matter an unfriendly act and categorically demanded in threatening terms that the railroads in the army's area be handed over after 15 September to be run by German personnel. Relations between the Twentieth Mountain Army and Finnish Headquarters became considerably more strained by the railroad dispute. General Erfurth warned that this matter should not be carried to a breaking point. The OKW, which had been advised of the threatening conflict, did not think too rigorous an attitude wise either. It was only too obvious that the Soviet Union was able to exert a stronger pressure on the Finns than the Germans.

The Finns, too, apparently wished to adhere to the German requests as far as possible and not to let an explosion come about over the use of the railroad. Lieutenant Colonel Haahti, Chief of the Army Operations Branch, flew to Rovaniemi as liaison officer of Finnish Headquarters in order to harmonize Finnish and German views. There could have been no better person for this delicate mission than Haahti. As a result of the negotiations, Finnish Headquarters agreed to have the Salla-Kemi railroad operated by the Germans for the time being.

On 10 September, Ambassador von Blücher and his staff left the capital by train for Turku. Many Finns who had remained true friends of Germany gathered at the Helsinki railroad station to bid farewell. The departure of the German Embassy was carried out in a very dignified manner. The Finnish population showed much tact in these grave days and no German soldier was molested in the streets of Helsinki. On many occasions, the Finnish population gave the German soldiers spontaneous proofs of unchanged sympathy and friendship, which were noteworthy considering the cool nature of the Finnish people. It would have been alien to the Finnish character if this most hospitable people in the world had treated the German brother-in-arms in an unfriendly way. The evacuation of the German civilian population from Finland took place on 9 and 10 September.

In the evening of 12 September, General Erfurth with his staff and the balance of the German agencies left Finland on the steamer LAPLAND. By order of the Marshal, General Valva, Commander of the Finnish Navy, came on board in order to bid farewell on Mannerheim's behalf. Erfurth's activity at Finnish Headquarters had lasted for exactly three years and three months. Mannerheim's last act of courtesy showed his affection had remained unchanged by the separation caused by the trend of politics.

The LAPLAND left the harbor of Helsinki as the last evacuation vessel. The evacuation of German agencies in southern Finland had thus come to a close before the set term had expired.

Independent of the fluctuations of the political situation in Finland, the OKW had as a matter of course made military preparations in case Finland should sign the separate peace expected at any moment. The following two operations had been prepared for a long time: Operation BIRKE, withdrawal of the Twentieth Mountain Army to North Finland and North Norway, and Operation TANNE, occupation of the Åland Islands.

At the time of Paasikivi's trip to Moscow in late March 1944, the only available route of withdrawal in northern Norway in case of a separate Finnish peace (Operation BIRKE) was the road along the Norwegian coast (State Highway 50) since the road from Muonio to Skibotten was not good enough to be able to be used so soon after winter. Evacuation from Bothnian ports applied only to supply troops, since combat troops were needed to carry out Directive 50 of 28 September 1943 which was authoritative for Operation BIRKE. The threat to the southern flank was considered less important by the Twentieth Mountain Army after the Uhtua sector had been taken over. Preparation of the supply base in northern Norway had commenced, as well as the transfer of supply goods from southern and central Finland to the north, where Ivalo had been chosen as supply base. By the end of March 1944, the Kriegsmarine had completed its preparations for Operation TANNE (occupation of the Åland Islands) which was to be carried out simultaneously. The group of islands was expected to be occupied by about 3,000 men, another newly arrived Finnish light infantry battalion, and eleven batteries. The 416th Division stationed in Denmark was earmarked for this operation and, in addition, Army coast artillery and naval batteries from Norway, the 6th Parachute Light Infantry Regiment, and forces of the Kriegsmarine and Luftwaffe.

The Military Administrive Commander of Norway was informed on 4 April of the manner the Twentieth Mountain Army intented to carry out Directive 50. As a precaution, he was requested to reconnoiter a switch position in a general line of the Swedish frontier and Lyngen Fjord with was to include Bardufoss Airfield and the fortress of Tromsö. The Military Administrative Commander of Norway and the Twentieth Mountain Army were instructed to proceed with preparations for Operation BIRKE (preparation of supply bases at Ivalo and in northern Lapland, transfer of supplies from central to northern Finland, construction of the road from Muonio to Skibotten, evacuation of unnecessary units of the Mountain Army and Luftflotte 5 by way of the Bothnian ports). The Todt Organization provided the necessary forces for the construction of the supply bases, but major forces could not be employed before May because of the frost.

On 8 April the following code names were definitely chosen: For the operation against the Åland Islands, TANNE WEST, against Suursaari Island, TANNE OST, and for the withdrawal movement to the north, BIRKE. The overall commander of TANNE WEST was to be the Commander in Chief of the Kriegsmarine; the air landing was to be under the command of the Commander in Chief of the Luftwaffe. Operation TANNE OST was to be carried out by the Army General Staff (Army Group North).

It was now planned to carry out Operation TANNE OST prior to or simultaneously with TANNE WEST.

The Military Administrative Commander of Denmark was informed on 13 April that he was to make the 416th Division available for Operation TANNE. It was to be equipped with 200 trucks. Assignment of the batteries was arranged on 15 April. The Twentieth Mountain Army was made more mobile by the assignment of 400 tons of truck space.

In order to protect the Petsamo nickel plants[34] which were indispensable to the Wehrmacht, the Twentieth Mountain Army was instructed on 23 April to improve the fortifications planned for Operation BIRKE, as soon as the weather became better, in such a way that it would be possible to hold them.

The Kriegsmarine High Command was ordered on 24 April to discuss with the Finnish agencies the transfer of German naval forces to the Åland Islands to ward off a possible assault by the Russian navy from Kronstadt against Bothnia and other coastal areas which was to be expected if the situation worsened. The inquiry of the German Naval Staff, Operations Division, was forwarded to Finnish Headquarters on 10 May.

The Twentieth Mountain Army was informed on 4 May that there was at present no intention of withdrawing the Louhi front, that is to say, the right wing of the army. It might, however, become necessary in order to form reserves. The switch position in the Sohjana Isthmus on the right wing of the army should, therefore, be constructed as strong as possible.

The Twentieth Mountain Army questioned on 26 May further construction of the BIRKE position (the position which included Ivalo and Petsamo), since the construction would reveal the German intention of offering resistance on Finnish territory. The Twentieth Mountain Army, therefore, proposed to reconnoiter the position only. The

---

[34] 10,000 tons of pure nickel were annually obtained from Petsamo. Moreover, Germany purchased 18% of Finland's entire production of molybdenum and 38% of its wood fiber production.

20.Geb.AOK added that the construction of the Sohjana position had meanwhile started and proposed to abandon the Louhi front in the coming autumn in order to withdraw to the Sohjana position which was better and permitted the formation of reserves. The OKW sanctions on 9 June the withdrawal of the German front to the Sohjana position after its completion. Hitler reserved, however, the decision to himself when to withdraw the German right wing. Simultaneously, AOK NORWEGEN was ordered to dispatch construction troops to Finland. General Erfurth was instructed to inform Finnish Headquarters of the intended construction of fortifications in Lapland. He was simultaneously to give the assurances that these positions would never voluntarily be occupied. The German General transmitted this information on 14 June. Obviously the Finns did not attach particular importance to the German plans.

All participants knew that a withdrawal of the Mountain Army to the Arctic region would be an unusually difficult operation even if no major fighting occurred, and all the more so if its last phase reached into Arctic winter. It was a question of withdrawing about 200,000 men (the number of men drawing rations was 2,4,064 by the middle of August 1944, of which 132,554 were members of the Army) and of evacuating considerable stocks which had accumulated in Central Finland for four months and in North Finland (Murmansk sector) for nine.

20.Geb.AOK had reported on 1 and 19 June on the additional forces required for carrying out the march. On 24 August it requested the assignment of the 303rd Sturmgeschütz Brigade, which was still employed at the Finnish front, in order to be in a better position to counter a possible Finnish secession. The StuG brigade was, however, urgently needed at the German eastern front and was evacuated by water as of 7 September.

Obviously acting upon erroneous conceptions gained from General Dietl's last report at Berchtesgaden on 23 June, Hitler instructed General Dietl to win over in case of a Finnish collapse as many Finnish units as possible in order to use them to build up a defense front at his southern wing. A German corps headquarters was to be prepared for the German units at the Finnish front. The V Corps headquarters had been earmarked for this purpose, but since Finnish Headquarters did not want it and the corps headquarters was needed at the German front, it was again assigned to the General Staff of the Army on 9 July.

Simultaneously, preparations for Operation TANNE proceeded. When the Finnish front in the Karelian Isthmus tottered seriously on 20 June, Hitler gave instructions, in view of a possible Finnish collapse, that orders be issued to reinforce this front at the first sign of a crisis. Two parachute battalions were, thereupon, made available at Danzig and Gdynia. As replacement for the 416th Division (Denmark) which was to occupy the

Åland islands, the 50th Division, recently transferred from the Crimea to Perleberg, had been selected, but this division also had to be transferred to the eastern front on 1 July.

The OKW considered whether Hangö or another base on the Finnish southern coast should be occupied to blockade the Gulf of Finland. On 24 June Hitler ordered the reorganization of a task force formed of men belonging to the 20.Geb.Armee who had returned from leave but had been held back at Danzig. This unit was placed at the OKW's disposal in order to obtain forces for Operation TANNE. This force, however, had to be transferred shortly to the sorely beset eastern front.

Although the situation at the Finnish front had improved during the first half of July, the long-range political attitude of the Finns was still considered doubtful by the OKW. German preparations in Lapland, therefore, continued. Construction of the Ivalo position by 3,300 laborers began on 1 July and that of the Karesuando position, which was situated in the tip of Finland protruding into Norway, on 1 August by 1,800 workmen under the direction of the Todt Organization.

Investigations by the OKW had led to the conclusion that Suursaari Island was the most suitable place for blockading the Gulf of Finland. Hitler ordered on 4 July that Operation TANNE OST (occupation of Suursaari Island) was to be carried out entirely by the Kriegsmarine. The 500th SS Parachute Battalion was to be transferred from Gdynia to the area of Army Group North as a precautionary measure. The alert was, however, lifted on 9 July on account of the stabilization of the Finnish front. In connection with Operation TANNE the fact had to be taken into consideration that Sweden as a co-guarantor of the statute of Åland would increase its unfriendly attitude should German occupy the islands; this had to be avoided in view of the necessity of getting supplies of ores and roller-bearings from Sweden. No decision was, therefore, taken yet with regard to Operation TANNE WEST (Åland Islands).

After the Marshal had become President, the OKW re-examined the question of the attitude to be taken by the Germans in Finland. On 21 August Hitler again broached Operation BIRKE at a discussion of the situation. Answering his question about the necessary cover for the southern flank of the Twentieth Mountain Army, the Chief of the Wehrmacht Operations Staff told Hitler that General Rendulic had forces available for this purpose. Movements in connection with Operation BIRKE would be made more difficult but not impossible through the winter weather. It was arranged, thereupon, on 24 August to occupy the Sohjana position. Preparations were to be made to carry out the occupation within a few days.

The difficulties the OKW expected during the withdrawal movement were the following: At sea there was a monthly shortage of 13,100 tons and 500 cubic meters of shipping space for fuel. Supplies, with the exception of hay, could probably be handled. Attacks at sea were to be expected along the coast between Cap Nordkyn and Petsamo, and in the skerry district between the Forsang Fjord and the Skagerrak; mines were to be expected between Norway and Denmark. The German security forces were already fully occupied and it was impossible to increase them. Reverses were expected on the western coast. Traffic could be interrupted by mines or raids. The Luftwaffe in the northern area was considered temporarily adequate and needed reinforcements.

On 31 August arrangements were made to orient the naval attaché in Helsinki.

The discontinuance of relations between Finland and the Reich on 2 September had an immediate effect on shipping traffic between the two countries. On 3 September at 1705 German ships in Finnish waters were ordered to leave as a precaution. But the Finns prevented their departure as was also the case in Germany with the Finnish ships. The warning order for Oeration TANNE was issued in the night of 4 September. Since it was expected to have far-reaching political consequences, Hitler reserved the final decision for himself. In addition to the serious political qualms there were also military objections in the operation against the Åland Islands. The 416th Division selected for the operation was urgently needed in Denmark since further Allied operations against the northern region seemed possible after the landing in France. Transportation space was needed elsewhere, and the forces withdrawn from the Twentieth Mountain Army were not for replacements, since they lacked combat value. Operation TANNE OST, on the other hand, was looked upon with misgivings by the Naval Operations Staff which needed its forces for the blockade of the Gulf of Finland.

On 3 September Hitler decided at the discussion of the situation that further measures concerning Finland should be dealt with in a spirit of compromise. The detention of Finnish ships in German ports was therefore also discontinued. Hitler further ordered that operation TANNE WEST be dropped. The reason behind this decision was probably lack of forces. This was undoubtedly a lucky stroke of fate, for an occupation of the Åland Islands would certainly have given rise to no end of complications.

The planning and directives of the OKW in the northern area during the last months of the Finnish-German brotherhood-in-arms and after the secession of Finland gave an impression of inconstancy and uncertainty, which is perhaps explained by the coercion under which the OKW was acting owing to the course the great offensives in France and Russia had been taking since June. With battles which would decide the outcome of the war being fought in the west and east, little time remained at Hitler's

Headquarters for questions of the northern area. From the German point of view, Finland had become an unimportant theater of war, which had to take a second place behind the main German fronts with their more pressing demands. But a sober viewing of the situation would have led to the conclusion that nothing could be gained in Finland by halfway measures. The dream of having the Petsamo nickel available as long as possible had to be abandoned in favor of withdrawing the Twentieth Mountain Army to northern Germany with the least possible losses. The sooner the withdrawal began, the better could the time until 15 September be utilized. The deadline imposed by the Russians on the Finns (and Germany) was so short that any delay would increase the dangers connected with the German withdrawal. The German measures, however, paid no heed to this line of reasoning. Hitler's strategy had always included a refusal to abandon untenable positions voluntarily, and he acted accordingly in Lapland and also in Estonia.

Army Group North had not retired on account of the Finns. After the great successes of the Russian offensive against Army Group Center its situation had become very precarious and it was needless for the Germans to remain any longer in Estonia after Finland's secession. It would seem natural, therefore, to withdraw Army Group North to East Prussia without any delay. Nevertheless, this decision was not taken, and Army Group North was even ordered to hold the Narva line, as this controlled the Baltic Sea. Thus, wishful thinking in this case prevented the taking of necessary measures in time.

The withdrawal of the Twentieth Mountain Army to the north was carried out in so far as northern Norway was designated as the goal. It was, however, intended to halt while still on Finnish territory. This plan of General Rendulic was sanctioned by Hitler on 4 September but withheld from the Finns.

Economically, the secession of Finland meant a loss of copper, cellulose, molybdenum and so forth. The most burning question, however, was whether Petsamo should be held or not on account of the nickel.

The fact that use of the Swedish port of Lules with a railroad line to the ore mines of Narvik would probably be made more difficult or be interrupted entirely had no practical influence for the time being, since traffic to that port would come to a standstill during winter anyhow. It was, however, to be expected that relations with Sweden would become more difficult heretofore.

General Erfurth reported on 4 September that the Finns did not intend to impede the Finnish withdrawal. Finnish pilots were to be made available to the Kriegsmarine.

28,000 tons of Wehrmacht supplies left the Bothnian ports (mainly Oulu, Kemi, Tornio) by 15 September, that is to say 5,000 tons more than expected. On 15 September, the Kriegsmarine evacuated the port of Uno, and Oulu on the following day. German submarines were stationed in the Gulf of Bothnia and near the Åland Islands. On 18 September the Twentieth Mountain Army decided to shift the focal center of the evacuation from the Bothnian ports in the direction of Skibotten. The last German transport left the port of Kemi on 21 September. The evacuation from Finnish ports included a final total as follows:

> 4,049 soldiers
> 3,336 wounded
>   332 political refugees
>   746 vehicles
> 42,144 tons of Wehrmacht supplies (13,064 tons were lost by
>   Finnish ships withdrawing to Finnish and neutral waters).

The situation of the German troops in Finland became complicated again when Hitler decided on 13 September to carry out Operation TANNE OST in spite of his former decision. The operation was to take place on 15 September. It was a complete failure. The first German wave succeeded in landing on Suursaari Island according to plan. The Finns offered but little resistance at first, for form's sake, but after the German initial successes, however, Finnish resistance stiffened in the course of 16 September and the Russian Air Force intervened so that the second German wave was unable to land. This strange operation had, therefore, to be broken off. Finnish public reaction was very strong, as might have been expected, and the encounter encouraged anti-German activities in Finland.

The first result of the unsuccessful German surprise attack against Suursaari was a deterioration of the Finnish-German relations at sea, which so far had been correct. At the blockade line in the Bothnian Gulf, Finnish batteries on the Åland Islands began to fire on German boats. Hitler, thereupon, sanctioned an order of the Commander in Chief of the Kriegsmarine issued in the evening of 16 September to support the German interests by force of arms and if necessary to enforce a breakthrough through the Finnish blockade line. Moreover, an order was again given to retain Finnish ships. Besides this, Hitler decided on 25 September that in case of a Finnish attempt at clearing German mines they should be prevented from doing so, notwithstanding the danger that the Finns, who previously had received plans of the German mine fields, might consider it a reason for declaring war as stipulated in their treaty with the Soviet Union. It was considered imperative to protect German shipping in the Baltic against submarines.

The Swedes had already declared that they had closed their waters to any kind of traffic. The Finns now demanded the evacuation of a tip of their territory southeast of the Twentieth Mountain Army as well as of the Bothnian coast from Oulu to the Swedish frontier. Since the vital points of those areas had already been evacuated, the Twentieth Mountain Army answered that it would comply with the Finnish request. But the Mountain Army made no haste to fulfill this promise so that serious complications arose.

On land, things developed differently. Although during the first two weeks of September the little official intercourse as was absolutely necessary between the former brothers-in-arms had been transacted in due form and the Finns had loyally endeavored to facilitate the German withdrawal, frictions and even serious clashes occurred soon after the departure of the German diplomatic and military representatives from Helsinki and Mikkeli. The question of guilt for these events has not yet been quite cleared up. Most probably, both sides committed blunders and acted rashly, as understandable though not excusable in such troubled times. It goes without saying that the Finnish secession came as a shock to the German soldiers in Finland. Confidence in the brother-in-arms, which had been unlimited, changed suddenly to the contrary. To many, an incident which formerly had been passed over with forbearance, great importance was now attached. Though most liaison officers assigned to the German staffs behaved correctly and tactfully unit the end of their assignments, yet individual officers gave occasion for distrust. Relations with the Finnish liaison officers at the Twentieth Mountain Army Headquarters (Colonel Villamo, Lieutenant Colonel Voss) remained sincere and trustful. But the same harmony did not prevail in the subordinate staffs. In some cases it happened that Finnish liaison officers were disarmed by the Germans. The German liaison officers assigned to Finnish units on the boundary of the Finnish and German fronts were withdrawn on 15 September. The detention and confiscation of the heavy baggage, which had been forwarded by the German Corps to the Bothnian ports early enough for shipment, caused the German soldiers much chagrin. The baggage of the XXXVI Corps, for instance, had been dispatched to Oulu already in August and put aboard a Finnish boat for shipment to Germany. But the departure of the ship was delayed by continuous difficulties. When the boat finally left, it was ordered back by the Finnish authorities. Actually, the heavy baggage of the German troops was not dispatched but lost in consequence of Finnish interference.

By the middle of September the OKW again gave orders to carry out Operation BIRKE according to the original general plan. It remained, however, an open question whether the operation should be terminated before winter or only in the coming spring. Hitler reserved the final decision for himself. On 19 September, the German command agencies concerned were informed that a decision would be made only after clarification of the economic questions. In case of need the operation would have to be carried out even in winter.

The German evacuation program was as follows: The XIX Corps was to remain for the time being in its former sector at the Murmansk front, while the XXVI Corps was to retire to the Ivalo switch position and the XVIII Corps to withdraw to the Norwegian frontier. Since the Germans could not use the Bothnian ports any longer, only three routes of retreat were available to the Twentieth Mountain Army for its personnel and supplies. These were the following:

> The "Russian Road" from the Murmansk front by way of Parkkina to Kirkenes, which links up at the latter place with the road along the Norwegian coast (State Highway #50).
> The road between Alakurtti and Ivalo, which continued by way of Inari to Krasjok and joined the road along the Norwegian coast at Lakselv.
> The road from Rovaniemi by way of Muonio to Skibotten.

The first two roads had been built during the war by Organization Todt. But despite the existence of these three roads, the situation of the Twentieth Mountain Army was very difficult since it was not very mobile, the unfavorable season was coming, and both Russians and Finns were obstructing the evacuation.

According to the Army Headquarters' intentions the march was to start on the right wing since the troops in the Uhtua and Kiestinki sectors had to cover the longest distances. As the Russian plans were unknown and the attitude of the Finns acting under Russian pressure did not promise much, the Twentieth Mountain Army had taken measures in due time to cover its southern flank. The army reserve (a motorized regiment under the command of General Stäts), reinforced by units hastily withdrawn from the Louhi and Kandalaksha sectors, advanced toward the south to the chain of lakes extending from Lake Oule by way of Kajaani to the east. This flanking position was aimed at preventing a threatening advance of Finnish forces towards the north against Rovaniemi, and the troops were then to retire gradually to the north corresponding to the movement of XVIII Corps. The mission of these security forces was to protect the lines of communication of the XVIII Corps (General Hochbaum) and later to destroy them as far as required for military reasons.

The evacuation of the XVIII Corps (7th Mountain Division, 6th SS Mountain Division Nord, and Division Group Kräutler) began by the middle of September.

In the Uhtua and Kiestinki sectors, the Russians followed as far as the Finnish frontier, which led to major combat actions for the first time on 16 and 17 September west of Kiestinki.

Finnish forces meanwhile assembled from the south opposite the German flanking position. The Germans assumed that the Finnish armored division and a Finnish brigade (3rd?) were involved. The German security forces had been reinforced by units withdrawn from the 6th SS Mountain Division Nord and the 7th Mountain Division. During the second half of September repeated clashes and local skirmishes occurred between Germans and Finns for the possession of important bridges. These engagements were by no means sham fights in order to make the Russians believe that the Finns had fulfilled their obligations, but the fighting was real according to German and Finnish standards. The Germans maintained that Soviet Russian commissars had been assigned to the Finnish units who supervised the orders of the Finnish officers. On 16 September, General Rendulic informed the OKW of his negotiations with the Finns about the requests they had made. He declared it his aim to avoid friction and to settle differences of opinion in a friendly spirit. He believed the Finns had the same intention. On 20 September Rendulic reported on a further agreement stipulating a temporary boundary line. Other measures, too, made a loyal attitude of the Finns toward the former brother-in-arms seem likely. Soviet Russian pressure, which was soon to change the situation, could however, be felt already.

Reports of destruction and terrorist acts by German troops during the retreat, spread by foreign broadcasting stations, have probably been exaggerated by enemy propaganda. Finnish eye witnesses were lacking since the civil population of Lapland had been evacuated by order of the Finnish Government, so that the foreign radio reports could not be investigated and contradicted. It has, however, been proved that numerous bridges and other road constructions were destroyed and that also villages in Lapland and later in North Norway were burned in retaliatory moves by the Germans. The Germans believed that the Russians would penetrate Finnish territory and occupy Finland. They feared that Russian motorized forces would advance deeply into Finland and roll up the Twentieth Mountain Army from the south. They believed themselves justified according to the rules of war to secure their withdrawal by blowing up important railroad and other bridges and to deprive the enemy of billets (for instance the great camp at Hyrynsalmi constructed by German troops) which were of utmost importance for arctic warfare. The Finns naturally looked at these measures dictated by military necessity from another point of view than the Germans. They were deeply embittered by the fact that their former brother-in-arms carried out destruction in their country, which had been jointly protected by Germans and Finns during long years of bitter warfare. The scorched earth policy in the Arctic had aroused exceedingly angry feelings in the three Scandinavian countries and in Finland. Anti-German feeling increased in consequence of the Russian assurance given from the first not to advance beyond a line Kirkenes (Norway) - Lake Inari (Finland) to the west. As Hitler did not trust the Russians the destruction had to be carried out nonetheless upon his order. Germany was thus put in the wrong. The destruction in Finland was attributed to its desire of revenge for the secession of the former brother-in-arms.

An incident occurred on 28 September at the German southern wing which led to a short fire fight, to another one on the following day and to a third on 30 September. Moreover, the Germans were of the opinion that the Finns were not observing agreements any longer.

On 1 October, General Rendulic addressed a note to Finnish Headquarters announcing that he would be forced to take countermeasures if the Finnish Army did not adhere to previously made agreements. The Finnish Commander in Chief felt very much offended by this reproach, since loyalty is an essential Finnish virtue, and Mannerheim believed he had done more for the Germans by discreet assistance than he could justify to the Russians.

On 3 October, the German Commander in Chief reported to the OKW that relations with the Finns had further deteriorated. On 4 October he transmitted the wording of the Finnish answer to his note. The answer which indignantly refuted the German reproaches was entirely unsatisfactory from the German point of view.

Thus, tension between the former brothers-in-arms had very much increased by the beginning of October, so that any new incident might have unforeseen consequences. Such a fateful event occurred in the beginning of October when the Finns landed at Tornio. Before going into the details, a description will be given of the events at the front of the Twentieth Mountain Army during the second half of September.

While at the southern flank of the army the above-mentioned clashes between the German security forces and the Finnish troops advancing from the south increased in size, the evacuation of the XVIII Corps proceeded smoothly after the pursuing Russians had been repelled on 16 and 17 November west of Kiestinki, since the Russians gave up their pursuit at the Finnish frontier. The vacuum created by the evacuation of the XVIII Corps in the southern sector was filled by the Finnish 6th Division instead of by the Russians as the Germans had expected. The XVIII Corps reached the Kuusamo position according to plan and withdrew further to the Rovaniemi position. The spearhead of the 6th SS Mountain Division Nord reached Rovaniemi on 22 September.

Conditions in the Kandalaksha sector turned out more difficult. The XXXVI Corps (General Vogel) began the withdrawal movement in the evening of 11 September. A Russian attack probably intended to arrest the withdrawing Germans penetrated into the retiring German 163rd and 169th Divisions but was repulsed. The Russians also showed activity south of the route of retreat from Alakurtti to Salla but without any serious consequences. Soon afterwards, however, a serious crisis occurred at the northern flank of the German corps. As explained in Chapter IV, the Russians had long ago made extensive attack preparations in this sector and General Dietl had to come to Mikkeli on 6 April 1944 in order to discuss the situation in the Kandalaksha sector with Marshal Mannerheim. No decision had been reached at that time to remove the clearly visible Russian threat. Now the Russians believed their day had come. The German withdrawal movement was mainly dependent on the Alakurtti-Kairala-Salla road. Parallel to it to the south, the Germans had constructed a new road, which, however, had no great capacity. The 169th Division started first, while the 163rd Division remained for the time being in its old position and was to follow as a rear guard.

The Russians had not contented themselves with using their system of approach roads and trenches but had made a flanking movement through the virgin forest around the German positions taking the XXXVI Corps completely unawares in the rear. That a Russian armored brigade and a reindeer brigade cut their way through the trackless wilderness was an amazing performance which enabled them to launch a surprise attack against the German security forces to the west toward the Kairala-Salla road. The XXXVI Corps was split into two parts by the Russian assault. The 169th Division, with which the commanding general had remained, formed a hedgehog position around Salla. It could not, however, prevent the Russians from penetrating between Kairala and Salla and cutting off the withdrawal route of the 163rd Division. The latter division had to attack toward the west in order to reopen its withdrawal route and to carry out its junction with the 169th Division. This goal was accomplished on the third day after heavy fighting. Since the Russian task force attacking Salla showed no more desire to attack the crisis was removed. Most probably the supply services of ammunition and so forth had broken down in the trackless wilderness.

The XXXVI Corps was now able to withdraw unhindered towards the west behind the strong Kemijärvi-Kemijoki sector where the corps remained until 3 October. The withdrawal was then continued after demolishing the huge railroad bridge across Lake Kemi, a masterpiece of German construction which had been erected in a very short time in the beginning of the war.

On 28 September, the Twentieth Mountain Army Headquarters submitted its plan to the OKW for the conduct of battle in the Rovaniemi defensive position and the further withdrawal to the next two positions.

At the end of September, the OKW took the following view of the strategic situation at sea and its effect on Norway: The Arctic Sea and Norway had been secondary theaters of operations during the first half of 1944. The Anglo-American invasion in France had, however, brought about a complete change. The bulk of the British Navy was now available for an attack on Norway, the only German strategic naval position, which had become of decisive importance for submarine warfare after the loss of the western bases. This position was dependent on the command of the coastal waters. The supply service across the sea, the life-blood of Norway, had so far been secured by a thin veil of light security craft. The TIRPITZ squadron together with submarines had so far formed the backbone in the north, which by its very existence held heavy British naval forces tied at Scapa Flow. The Twentieth Mountain Army, after the secession of Finland and the latest attitude of Sweden, was entirely dependent on sea transportation for supplies. The enemy was aware of this fact and would try, as the OKW believed, to cut off the Mountain Army. Haste might well be induced on the enemy's part by fear of a revival of submarine warfare and of a Soviet Russian advance to northern Norway. The Allies could control the Norwegian coastal area even without a major landing, and the first thing to do was to eliminate the battleship TIRPITZ. The Anglo-Americans were now in a position to employ air forces which had formerly been tied down by the submarine bases in the west. In the long run it would not be possible to guarantee the supply by water of all Norway all the more so as increasing losses had to be taken into account. The bulk of the German force was of necessity concentrated in the Baltic Sea. In Norway they would lack the necessary air support. The German submarines could be employed on the defensive, but probably with little success owing to the increasing enemy superiority in the air. The following was, therefore, deemed necessary:

1. A relief of the excessively strained situation with regard to German shipping space.

2. A transfer of army units to the area east of Narvik as a cover against Sweden.

All these prerequisites were fulfilled by evacuating the area from Petsamo to Lyngen Fjord. Since Reich Minister Speer had recently declared that the Reich was not dependent on nickel from Petsamo, the OKW believed that there was no further reason to hold the BIRKE position in the Murmansk sector. After the expected enemy attacks at sea and from the air, evacuation of the Twentieth Mountain Army would only be possible under heavy losses. Since the attacks would be directly mainly against southwestern Norway, an increase in the capacity of the Mo-Oslo railroad was considered imperative. The Wehrmacht Operations Staff concluded its estimate of the situation by stating that every day of hesitation would render the evacuation of the area east of the Lyngen position more difficult.

On 30 September, the Wehrmacht Operations Staff made a report to Hitler on the advantages and disadvantages resulting from a withdrawal to Lyngen Fjord. After the Finns had landed at Tornio, Hitler agreed in principle to the withdrawal of the Twentieth Mountain Army to Lyngen Fjord. A warning order was given on 4 October, but the final order to commence the evacuation of the Murmansk sector was again postpones. As soon as the order had been issued, the movement was to be carried out in the following way: One mountain division was to reach the Narvik area as rapidly as possible in order to defend the Swedish frontier crossing points on either side of Bjornstjel; strong units were to withdraw on the road to Skibotten in order to secure State Highway #50; the bulk of the XIX Corps was to reach the Lakselv River by the middle of November and cover the arctic ports with its mobile rear guards. Attention of the Twentieth Mountain Army was drawn to the great difficulty of the planned movement which could only succeed under a strict and uniform command. The Twentieth Army headquarters was authorized by Hitler to take all necessary measures. The Luftwaffe, the Kriegsmarine and the Assistant Chief of Staff in Scandinavia were assigned their respective missions. Besides the units of the LXXI Corps stationed in Norway, the following units of the Twentieth Mountain Army were earmarked for the defense of the Lyngen Fjord-Narvik area:

> XIX Corps Headquarters
> 6th and 7th Mountain Divisions
> 210th Division (stationary)
> Machine Gun Ski Brigade Finland
> Bicycle Reconnaissance Brigade Norway
> The necessary GHQ troops

Twenty-nine coastal batteries were to be emplaced immediately, and the construction of the Lyngen position was to be expedited.

On 6 October the withdrawal movement received the cover name NORDLICHT. The Twentieth Mountain Army was told it would have to get along on its stock of fuel until April 1945.

The way the weather would develop was an unknown factor for the German plans, as well as the question whether it would be possible to cover the difficult routes in the Arctic prior to the winter storms.

In the discussion between the Wehrmacht Operations Staff, the Military Administrative Commander of Norway and the Reich Commissioner for Norway about the evacuation of northern Norway, the Wehrmacht Operations Staff took the standpoint that the population should be evacuated and the enemy be prevented by demolitions from gaining a foothold in the evacuated area. It was expected in this connection that Norwegian forces would in all probability be landed from England, which was considered dangerous in view of Sweden's uncertain attitude and the resistance movement in Norway. This opinion was strengthened by a radio announcement by the King of Norway on 26 October that Norwegian forces would soon intervene in cooperation with the Russians.

We come now to the description of the Finnish landing in Tornio which gave the Germans occasion for strong complaint about the former brother-in-arms. The details and motives of this regrettable incident, which largely influenced German-Finnish relations, have not yet so shaped up as to form a clear picture for historians. There is a possibility that the local Finnish commanders took another attitude than that intended by Finnish Headquarters. It is a fact that on 1 October Finnish troops, which had crossed the gulf from the direction of Oulu, landed in the German rear at Tornio, the port near the frontier east of Haparanda, and on the island in front of the port of Kemi situation further to the east. The Germans believed these forces to have consisted of the 15th Brigade under the command of Colonel Halsti. The Finns entered the German hospital at Tornio by surprise, where acts of violence are said to have been committed. The Finns then attacked the large German fuel dump north of Tornio and overpowered the guards stationed there. Fighting increased during the following days and became more fierce. German forces were sent from the right wing of the army in order to recapture Tornio, whereas the Finns landed reinforcements. The Luftwaffe joined in and German submarines were employed. Both the Finns and the Germans suffered heavy losses in this combat which lasted for several days, but the Germans failed to dislodge the Finns from Tornio and the fuel dump and in pushing them into the sea, since the Finns received timely reinforcements (the 3rd Division under General Pajari). The reasons for the Finnish attitude can only be guessed at. The regrettable incidents at Tornio were probably caused by Finnish concern that the railroad bridge across the Tornen-Elv, which was of vital importance for traffic between Finland and Sweden, would be blown up by the Germans. German preparations for such a demolition are said to have taken place, and this probably made the Finns suspicious. There may have been good reason to expect such action from the Germans, since the Finns had learned of the destruction of other structures and traffic installations by

German soldiers during their retreat from the Russians. What everyone familiar with Finnish conditions had believed impossible happened as a result of the tragic conflict of Tornio: The former brothers-in-arms pointed their guns at one another and in sudden enmity began a bloody fight. Finally, the Germans gave up hope of retaking Tornio and withdrew. The Finns tried to place themselves in the way of the German retreat to the north on the road along the Swedish border. The German troops broke through the Finnish switch position on 7 October and cleared their withdrawal route of enemy forces. The last German forces left the Tornio area on 10 October.

The reaction of both Finns and Germans to the fighting at Tornio was considerable. The news broadcast by foreign stations, that the retreating Germans took Finnish hostages along with them, enraged Finnish public opinion. The leftist press stirred up the sudden hatred against the German brother-in-arms who only now was showing his true character. On 7 October, the German Commander in Chief in Lapland announced the instructions which he had given to his troops: In consideration of the Finnish civil population and the honest Finnish soldiers who were not responsible for their government's treason, German countermeasures would even now be carried out with moderation and without severity. The OKW gave strict orders on 9 October not to retain any hostages.

As Finnish ships carrying Wehrmacht supplies, which had taken shelter in Swedish harbors, made preparations to return, the OKW gave the permission to capture or if necessary to sink such vessels.

In the speech by a Finnish Minister, it was declared on 8 October that Finland had correctly fulfilled its obligation, but that Germany had not withdrawn from northern Finland and a breach of international relations resulted.

Not only the Finns but also the Russians now became active. On 7 October, a large-scale Soviet Russian attack began at the Murmansk front against XIX Corps, the divisions of which (6th and 2nd Mountain Divisions) were still in their old positions on the Litsa and south of it. The Russian attack had by no means come as a surprise. All attack preparations and the reinforcement of the Soviet Russian troops had been observed for time in the open country of the Tundra. The construction of numerous roads and approach trenches, which had lasted for weeks, could not remain unnoticed by the German reconnaissance. The division commanders and General Jodl, the Commanding General, had pointed to the threatening danger and stressed that it was necessary to hurry the withdrawal movement before the great Russian attack could break loose. 20.Geb.Armee had not shut its eyes either to the admonitions of its subordinate commanders. It appears that it tried repeatedly to win over the OKW to the policy of the commanders on the Lapland front. If the Commander in Chief of the Mountain Army urged that the retreat from the northern sector be started as soon as possible he took into consideration the fact that the sections of State Highway #50 were usable only to a certain extent and that snow storms were to be expected in November. The OKW, however, paid no heed to the warnings from the German Arctic Army. The Wehrmacht Operations Staff believed that the withdrawal of the XIX Corps could still be carried out in November, an opinion which afterwards proved true owing to the unusually favorable weather conditions which lasted right into December 1944.

There were, it was true, several reasons for a prolonged halt of the XIX Corps. In the first place, the withdrawal of the two southern corps had to make sufficient progress. Furthermore the far-extending coastal front of the XIX Corps along the Arctic Sea had to be evacuated, the Luftwaffe had to remove the numerous ground personnel, and the Kriegsmarine had to withdraw its bases on the Arctic Sea. For all this, naturally, a certain amount of time was needed. The main reason for retaining the XIX Corps on the Litsa, however, was quite different. Hitler was obstinately of the opinion that the Kolosjoki nickel plant in the Petsamo area had decisive important in the war, although Reich Minister Speer held a contrary view. The dictator had reserved the decision on the deadline of the XIX Corps' withdrawal to himself and demanded that the corps should hold out in northern Lapland in order to protect the nickel plant. A redoubt was to be defended, formed by the position ot the XIX Corps on the Litsa, the so-called Ivalo position, which extended east and south of Lake Inari, and the Karesuando position in the Finnish tip northeast of Muonio stretching far into Norway.

When the Soviet Russian attack against the XIX Corps broke loose on 7 October, the Russians endeavored to envelop the Germans and lunged so far southward that the security of the 2nd Mountain Division, which was very weak in that area, was quickly pierced. A Russian reindeer unit quickly penetrated through the gap and blocked the Arctic Highway west of Loustari. The Russians then advanced along the Arctic Highway toward the south as far as the vicinity of Salmijärvi. The 2nd Mountain Division was disrupted. The 6th Mountain Division was threatened with envelopment in its positions on the Litsa. The situation quickly took an unfavorable turn for the Germans. Coherence of the army was soon destroyed. If the Russians had continued their advance along the Arctic Highway as far as Ivalo, the XXXVI Corps would have been able to use the withdrawal route by way of Karasjoki. That had to be prevented under any circumstances. Units of the XXXVI Corps which had already withdrawn beyond the Kemi River, were wheeled off for this purpose from the Arctic Highway toward the north under the Command of

General Rübel and sent in the direction of the Russians in order to prevent them from approaching Ivalo. The army reserve under General Steets, which in the meantime had fought at Tornio, was also dispatched for Corps Group Rübel and advanced northward together with the latter. It was joined by dispersed units of the 2nd Mountain Division, which had been force toward the south. Corps Group Rübel had the mission of slowing down the Russian advance by a delaying action between Ivalo and Salmijärvi or of preventing it altogether.

The situation of the 6th Mountain Division had become more dangerous. In order to avoid its envelopment it was withdrawn behind the Litsa by night from the salient protruding far to the east. But on 9 October the situation of the XIX Corps became more acute owing to Russian landings from Rybachi Peninsula at the northern flank. From there, the Russians enveloped the new position of the 6th Mountain Division, which though frontally strong was threatened on each flank. The situation became worse on 11 October. The Russians lunged far westward and interrupted traffic on the Arctic Highway. A German counterattack was unsuccessful. The 6th Mountain Division, therefore, soon withdrew from the intermediate position to the Petsamo position.

On 12 October the crisis took on larger proportions since the Russians had now occupied the Arctic Highway for a distance of eight kilometers and had landed troops from speedboats in the Bay of Petsamo. German attempts to clear the Arctic Highway of enemy forces also failed on 13 October. Only the Petsamo-Kirkenes road, which had also been cut off, could be reopened. The bulk of the 2nd Mountain Division had also made an evading movement across Norwegian territory and marched past to the south of the Russians who had blocked the Arctic Highway at Salmijärvi. It was covered by Corps Group Rübel coming from the south. Contrary to expectations, the Russian forces which had halted at Samijärvi remained inactive so that the area between Ivalo and Kilosjoki remained in German hands until the German forces from northern Lapland had also been evacuated.

How did the OKW now look at the situation in northern Finland? The laboriously constructed Murmansk position had collapsed after one week's combat, which meant that the evacuation had to be carried out much faster than intended. Hitler, however, still hesitated to draw the necessary connections from the events which speedily followed one another. It was a great surprise for the OKW that six Russian divisions and various brigades had advanced into a tundra-like area which had been thought only to allow the employment of small units with special equipment. The situation at Petsamo had developed by the middle of October in such a way that the necessary destruction had been prepared, but not as much material had been removed as might have been possible without enemy pressure. For in the meantime more ships had been made available for the northern area, part of which had already arrived. Not only were Russian speedboats and planes very active along the coast of the Arctic Sea, but also British naval forces which worked hand in hand with the Soviets.

In spite of the very unfavorable course of events the OKW stuck to its decision to temporarily halt the XIX Corps after the abandonment of the Litsa front in a line Kolosjoki-Arctic Highway-Parkkina in order to recover the unusually high amount of supplies that had accumulated there and to continue to run the nickel plants at Kolosjoki.

The fact that XIX Corps had lost much of its fighting power in consequence of the heavy combat, however, was not taken into account (the Russians were estimated to be attacking with a superiority of forces of 8:1). The territory was unsuitable for defense, and arctic winter though unusually late could appear very suddenly. Soon, State Highway #50 would not be able to be kept open any longer. Also, the front had approached Kolosjoki too closely to allow exploitation of the nickel mines.

Maintaining the German mission would probably lead to a catastrophe for the XIX Corps and even for other units of the Twentieth Mountain Army. No assistance was to be expected from the zone of the interior. On the contrary, the other theaters of war requested that the arctic front be given up and these forces be assigned to them. At this point, General Hengl, who was particularly familiar with conditions at the Murmansk front and who had been assigned in the autumn of 1944 to the Army High Command as special-services officer, intervened.

Hengl had been stationed in the arctic region from spring 1940 until summer 1944 as regimental commander, commander of the 2nd Mountain Division and commanding general of the XIX Corps. The development of the situation in the arctic region and the hesitancy of the OKW naturally caused him concern for his former corps. He took advantage of his position in the OKH and his good personal relations with important personages in the OKW to discuss the situation in northern Finland with General Jodl, and he succeeded in convincing the Chief of the Wehrmacht Operation Staff of the necessity of an immediate evacuation. After a lively discussion, Hitler also assented to order the immediate withdrawal of the Twentieth Mountain Army to Norway. Parallel to Hengl's efforts, 20.Geb.AOK had also initiated similar negotiations with the OKW. So finally the OKW listened to reason. General von Hengl was ordered to fly to General Rendulic and he was given authority to give the necessary instructions in accordance with the local situation to the Commander in Chief of the Twentieth Mountain Army with regard to the withdrawal. Whereas the principle had so far been first to save the materiel and then the men, the maxim was now to be that men were more important than materiel.

Hengl left Berlin on 14 October and arrived in North Finland at the XIX Corps Headquarters on 15 October. An immediate discussion took place with General Rendulic in the presence of the Commanding General of the XIX Corps and his divisional commanders. It is probable that no one in this war-council proposed a longer stay in Lapland. Once Hengl had convinced himself that the XIX was no longer in a position to resist the Russians who were superior in tanks and planes although it continued to put up a stubborn fight along the Arctic Highway under heavy losses and even made minor counterattacks to get breathing space, he exercised his authority. The Russians were obviously assembling for a new attack. Speedy action was therefore imperative. The last act of the German drama in Finland began.

The movement began with the withdrawal of the right wing of the army from the Rovaniemi position. The march was arranged in such a way that the motorized units of the 6th SS Mountain Division Nord were sent ahead to Narvik while the infantry followed so that the division as a whole would be ready for shipment in three weeks. When the last German troops (units of the 6th SS Mountain Division Nord) passed through Rovaniemi, destruction took place in the capital of Lapland, according to Finnish and German reports, far above that permitted by the exigencies of war. It appears quite a lot of damage ensued from the explosion of several ammunition trains, which got stranded at Rovaniemi station. Many wooden houses burned down. Also the beautiful Hotel Pohjanhovi was destroyed where the German High Command had lived for more than three years. Rovaniemi's hard fate must be deeply deplored by the Germans too.

The withdrawal of the German troops from Lapland was carried out after 16 October in the following manner:

a. XIX Corps Headquarters.
   Division von der Hoop \ which had been stationed along
   210th Division   / the Arctic coast.
   6th Mountain Division
   by way of Kirkenes

b. XXXVI Corps Headquarters
   2nd Mountain Division
   169th Division
   163rd Division
   Detachment Steets
   by way of Karasjoki

c. XVIII Corps Headquarters
    7th Mountain Division
    6th SS Mountain Division NORD
    Division Group Kräuter
    Horse-drawn artillery units of the XXXVI Corps
by way of Muonio to Skibotten

The Army Headquarters had ordered the corps to disengage itself from the Russians. In caes of strong Russian attacks, resistance was to be offered. Otherwise, the withdrawal was to be carried out slowly in order to facilitate the removal of materiel.

The Russians pursued the Germans only in the beginning. Later on they left them unmolested. They never crossed the old Finnish and the Norwegian frontier in the direction of Finnmarken. At the Arctic Highway they did not advance to the south beyond Nautsi. In spite of the hesitating attitude of the Russians, the German evacuation from Lapland was only carried out with considerable losses of arms, equipment and all kinds of supplies. The German fortifications, which had been held for years, contained much unmovable equipment and huge amounts of supplies had been stored there by order of Hitler.

Operation NORDLICHT, that is to say, the removal of all materiel from the northern sector of the Lapland front, had first been ordered by the OKW on 6 October. Since, after the Soviet Russian attack on 7 October, one could foresee that it would not be possible to remove all the material, the program of evacuation was based on a priority system. The first stage comprised vital goods, the second stage valuable good, the third stage such goods the salvage of which was desirable but which probably would have to be abandoned. It was a foregone conclusion that only the goods of stage one could be expected to be brought to safety. And that is what actually happened. Very little of the nine months' supplies of the XIX Corps could be evacuated.

As a precaution, food supplies had been placed along the routes as follows:

XIX Corps on State Highway #50 as far as Lakselv (exclusively) and on the Arctic Highway as far as Ivalo

XXXVI Corps on the road Ivalo-Lakselv

XVIII Corps on the Finland Highway (what the Germans called the Rovaniemi-Muonio-Karesuando road) as far as west of the Karesuando position

It was early established that an evacuation of goods from the Petsamo area was no longer possible. The Twentieth Mountain Army, therefore, endeavored to save at least the valuable fuel. By increasing the transportation capacity at Kirkenes an attempt was made to rescue what could be saved from the "burning house." By 22 October, when the evacuation came to an end, 30,000 tons had been removed from Kirkenes, which was, however, much less than expected. From the area Ivalo-Inari, not quite 10,000 tons were transferred to Porsanger Fjord. The evacuation of the goods which had been temporarily stored by the XVIII Corps at Muonio was much delayed by the muddy state of the road.

Evacuation of the large area Porsanger Fjord-Lyngen Fjord was carried out under less enemy pressure and followed more or less according to plan.

What the German troops left in the Petsamo area fell into Russian hands. On 17 October, 20.Geb.AOK ordered the Kolosjoki and Kirkenes areas held for the time being.

The Ivalo defensive position was occupied in the night of 18 October. At the same time the evacuation from the north began in such a way that two brigades of the 6th Mountain Division retired along the northern road, while all other units of the division were led back southwestward to Ivalo, which, therefore, had to be held until all forces from the Murmansk front had been channeled through. The Arctic Highway between Petsamo and Ivalo was thoroughly destroyed by the Luftwaffe behind the retiring German troops.

By this time a march had to be carried out to Narvik, covering a distance of 1,100 kilometers from Ivalo and 1,000 kilometers from Kirkenes. The German Anabasis[35] of 1944 was burdensome and difficult to execute.

The movement was a success although the Russians pursued the northern and at first also the Ivalo group and were able to interrupt the road to Kirkenes temporarily.

The right wing had no difficulties since contact with the Russians was soon lost and the Finns only followed slowly.

On 21 October, the nickel plant and the Kolosjoki settlement were evacuated by the Germans after thorough destruction. In the night of 23 October the Kirkenes position was occupied after the last convoy had left the harbor the same day. Heavy losses had been suffered there during the embarkation owing to Russian air attacks lasting for twenty hours. It was ascertained afterwards that one third of the supplies had been evacuated from Kirkenes while two thirds had been destroyed. The town and port of Kirkenes were evacuated on 25 October. Though the evacuation could not be carried out according to plan, a considerable amount of materiel and supplies had been successfully removed from the northern area in

---

[35] Anabasis – Xenophon's history of the Greek retreat form the Euphrates to the Black Sea in 400 B.C.

spite of the great haste in which it had been done. The main achievement was that no units had been cut off so that the Mountain Army remained fully intact with the exception of losses in action[36].

Evacuation of Varanger Peninsula began on 26 October. On the same day the withdrawal started from Nautsi at the southern corner of the Norwegian territory which extended into Finland. Nautsi was evacuated on 28 October and simultaneously Vatsö on Varanger Peninsula.

Muonio at the Swedish frontier was reached on 29 October where the great ammunition dump had already been removed. Then German motorized forces crossed the Norwegian frontier. On 30 October the withdrawal began from the Luto sector and on 31 October from the Ivalo defensive position. On the same day the last units left Vardö by water.

The 2nd Mountain Division which marched back on the Arctic Highway reached Norwegian territory on 2 November, where Finns and Russians now exercised joint pressure. Ivalo was evacuated on 3 November. In the north, Tanajoki and Tana Fjord were secured. The German forces then also withdrew from here without enemy pressure and marched on to Lyngen Fjord, Only four mobile rifle battalions on skis were left behind. Moreover, the area around Hammerfest and the area west of the Alta fjord were held until the next year. By the middle of November, only the northwestern corner of Finnish territory was occupied by the Germans.

An important factor for the success of these movements was the fact that the Russians did no pursue. In the beginning it appeared that they would disregard the Norwegian frontier which was crossed by Russian advance elements. But in December it became apparent that the Russians were not going to advance beyond Tana Fjord. They occupied only the extreme corner of northern Norway and then withdrew forces to other fronts. Since the Finns also did not advance against Porsanger Fjord and made no preparations to attack the Karesuando position, the OKW was able to form its decisions independent of Russians and Finns.

The fact that the Russians did not continue the pursuit cannot have been due only to the road destruction carried out by the Germans but it is difficult to determine how political reasons played a role. The rear guards of the Twentieth Mountain Army withdrew on 17 December to Bille Fjord after destroying all artificial structures along State Highway #50. The Kautokeino position was evacuated on 18 and 19 December.

---

[36] The amount of German losses in the battles with Russians and Finns in September and October 1944 is unknown. Some units, for instance the 2nd Mountain Division, must have suffered considerably.

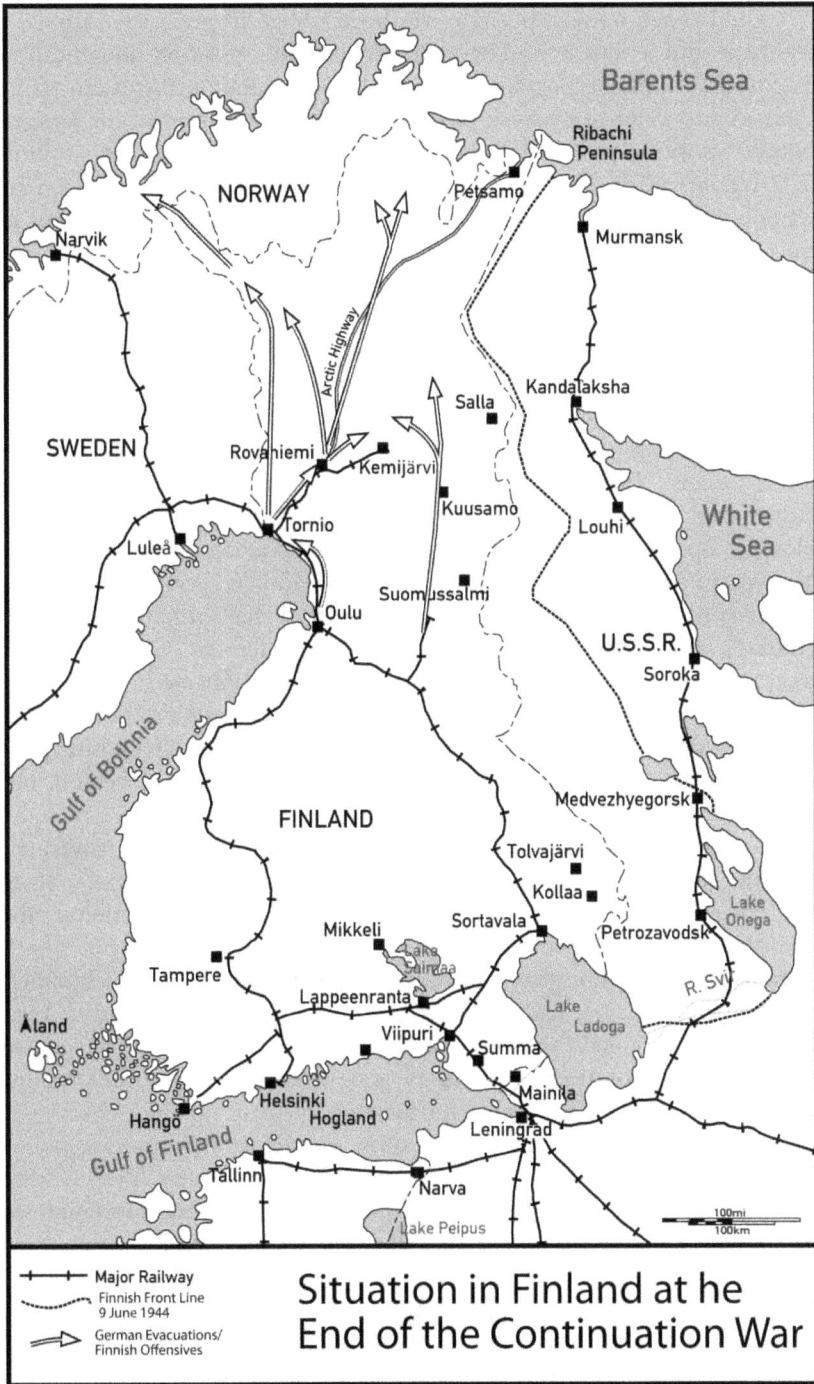

Barents Sea

Ribachi
Peninsula

NORWAY   Petsamo

Narvik   Murmansk

Arctic Highway

Salla   Kandalaksha

SWEDEN   Rovaniemi
                              Kemijärvi
                                        Kuusamo   Louhi
Luleå   Tornio   White
                                                              Sea
                    Oulu   Suomussalmi
                                              U.S.S.R.
                                              Soroka

Gulf of Bothnia

FINLAND   Medvezhyegorsk

                    Tolvajärvi

                    Kollaa
                                              Lake
Mikkeli   Sortavala   Petrozavodsk Onega

Tampere   R. Svi
          Lappeenranta
Åland   Lake
          Viipuri   Summa   Ladoga

          Helsinki   Mainila
Hango   Hogland   Leningrad

Gulf of Finland
          Tallinn   Narva   100mi
                                          100km
                    Lake Peipus

Major Railway
Finnish Front Line
9 June 1944
German Evacuations/
Finnish Offensives

Situation in Finland at he End of the Continuation War

Map 2

The Lyngen outpost position was occupied at the end of January by a regiment and a battalion. The area between this position and the also occupied Semmering position at the boundary of the northwestern tip of Finland was watched by weak German forces. Still in front of the Lyngen outpost position was the garrison of Hammerfest and an evacuation detachment on the Alta Fjord, both of which were to be evacuated by water after a short time. There were also weak German security forces in the outpost area.

State Highway #50 had been destroyed to such an extent beyond the German area that major movements on it were not possible at present. The northern Norwegian area was, therefore, sufficiently secured on land.

That brought to an end a movement which caused great concern for it took place in the middle of a hard winter with temperatures of thirty centigrade below zero. The weather had been comparatively favorable to the Germans. It was wild and not much snow had fallen in Norway in November. Norwegian and British partisans harassed the retreat by blowing up artificial structures at more places along the railroad. The Norwegian population east of Lyngen Fjord had been evacuated by order of Hitler on 28 October. The march back from the northern area to the railroad, the entraining to Oslo, the transfer to Denmark and transportation to other German fronts was connected with many difficulties which required close cooperation of the three Wehrmacht branches and of transportation facilities on land and sea. The difficulties were great enough already owing to the inclemency's of the season, but they were increased by enemy attacks from the air and on sea. Yet the losses suffered by bombs and mines during this transportation movement until the spring of 1945 kept within bounds.

The situation in the northern area permitted in addition the employment of transport vessels for the withdrawal movement, which were used for the transportation of wounded and of Wehrmacht supplies. The troops, however, had to march to the Lyngen position and its rear, form where they had to proceed on foot to Mo in so far as they were to be transferred to other theaters of war. Some units marched on to Trondheim in order to relieve traffic on the Mo-Oslo line which only allowed the passage of eight trains daily. Ferries at the crossing points were increased in order to accelerate the march movement. Vessels were also employed south of the Narvik position for the transportation of equipment. On 12 November, the Allies employed for the first time heavy naval forces (1 cruiser escorted by an aircraft carrier and destroyers) against German ships sailing around southwest Norway. Two German ships totaling 3,000 tons were sunk, two others could be salvaged, the balance escaped. Five of the six escort vessels which tried to intercept the enemy were sunk however.

On the same day, the Allies succeeded in causing the battleship TIRPITZ, which had already been attacked several times, to capsize in the Alta Fjord after several hits from aerial bombs.

From 1 to 30 November about 50,000 soldiers and 6,030 trucks crossed Lyngen Fjord on 2,130 trips, that is to say a daily average of 1700 men and 600 vehicles.

Parallel to the deterioration of relations with Finland in the course of October, a deterioration of relations between the Reich and Sweden developed. The Swedish Foreign Minister made a speech in the Swedish Congress on 30 October declaring the continuation of neutrality as long as circumstances permitted and speaking in unveiled support of the neighboring Scandinavian countries.

In the beginning of November, the German Government declared the Baltic Sea a theater of war. The Swedish Naval Security Office, thereupon, ordered all Swedish vessels to enter Swedish waters by 10 November 2400 owing to the increased danger of war. On 11 November, the Swedish Government contested in a note the validity of the German warning and held the Reich Government responsible for possible consequences. Little border incidents were dramatized by the Swedish press. The Swedish Government launched a sharp protest against the German scorched earth policy in North Finland and North Norway during the evacuation of these territories in autumn 1944. Sweden's entry into the war threatened at the eleventh hour.

In December the Swedish Government declared that it would probably not be in a position to extend the expiring German-Swedish commercial treaty.

Dark clouds gathered over Finland in autumn 1944. It is true that the Russians did not occupy the country and even transferred their troops to other fronts, but the Soviet Russian armistice commission, which arrived in Helsinki, consisted of about 800 members. It protected the "Finland-Soviet Union" society and the Communist Party, whose newspaper advanced radical demands and requested that more "war criminals" be arrested.

By the middle of November, the Finnish Government had been reorganized. Paasikivi became chairman, Enckell remained Foreign Minister. The leftist tendency of this coalition government was increased by the inclusion of the Communist editor, Leines, and Dr. Holo, the President of the Finnish-Soviet Society.

Demobilization of the Finnish Armed Forces was terminated at the end of 1944. One age class about 32,000 strong remained under arms. The Finnish security forces, which were a thorn in the eye of the Communists, had to be dissolved. The highly praiseworthy Finnish women's organization "Lotta Svärd" was dissolved as well. The final chapter to German-Finnish relationship was not attained as long as Mannerheim was still President. Not until March 1945, after Mannerheim had resigned and a new government had been formed under his successor Paasikivi, did Finland declare a state of war existing between Finland and German as of 15 September 1944.

From a retrospective point of view the historian will ask why the OKW did not confidentially discuss with Mannerheim and prepare the withdrawal of the German Army from Lapland in due time, cooperating with the Finnish Chief of the Armed Forces, as long as good relations still existed between the OKW and Finnish headquarters. In the last year of the brotherhood-in-arms, the Finnish Marshal occasionally dropped the comment, "I do not understand why the Germans attach such great importance to a strong German army in Lapland. They could employ these troops much better somewhere else. By preventing the Russians from reaching the industrial area of Petsamo they act in the interest of the British."

The time of broaching the question of a German withdrawal had obviously come in April 1944, when a Finnish delegation had the first parleys with the Russians and Paasikivi returned from Moscow with the Soviet Russian conditions. From this date it became an established fact that in case of a Finnish capitulation the Russians would demand the interment of the German troops in Finland. From that time on there could be no doubt that the situation of the Twentieth Mountain Army would become very serious if the Finns made peace with the Russians. Also General Dietl became early aware of the dangers threatening his army and urged the OKW to order the evacuation. The German withdrawal from Lapland had been prepared in theory by the Twentieth Mountain Army Headquarters since the end of 1943 on the basis of a withdrawal southward to the Bothnian ports as well as northwestward in the direction of State Highway #50.

A confidential inquiry regarding a timely German withdrawal in agreement with the Finns would probably have been fully understood by the Marshal and would have saved the German troops much trouble and sacrifices. But it was not Hitler's character to give up untenable positions in good time. The bitter cup had to be drained to the dregs.

The question of German reaction to the Finnish capitulation still remains to be answered. Up until then the German press had painted all events in Finland in the rosiest hues and entirely concealed the political changes in that country from its readers. But after the impending break had taken place, everything Finnish was described in the slackest of tones. The German newspaper reader learned now to his great surprise that the Finnish brother-in-arms, who had hitherto been admired and respected, was a faithless traitor. The totalitarian press did not even try to understand that a small nation in utmost danger was endeavoring after the hopeless shipwreck of the Reich to reach the safe shores before it was too late. The German newspapers reviled the men who were now in control of Finland and branded Mannerheim's treason.

Thus the German-Finnish brotherhood-in-arms was buried under such tragic circumstances.

History will judge Finland's attitude and the Proteus[37] nature of Mannerheim more justly. It will come to the conclusion that the Finnish nation had no other choice unless it preferred to commit suicide. The Marshal of Finland was the only man with the necessary actual and moral authority to lead his people along the way to safety in the darkest hour of Finnish history. The human greatness of Mannerheim was demonstrated by the fact that he did not try to escape this unthankful task which must certainly have been bitterly hard on a true patriot. The statesmanlike qualities with which he brought the almost insoluble mission to a successful conclusion in spite of many unforeseen difficulties were displayed by his political and diplomatic skill. When has a small nation faced a similarly difficult situation as the Finnish people in 1944! Self-preservation demanded a complete rupture with the former brother-in-arms while a considerable amount of German troops occupied a Finnish territory in the north. Without the Marshal, the Finns would hardly have found a way out of this immense danger. The Finnish people owe much, if not everything, to this unusual man.

The picture of Mannerheim obtained in the years of war by those around him recalls the description which Saint Simon has left to posterity of Louis XIV when he said: "This man knew how to preserve his kingly attitude under much heavier blows of fate." During the defeat and the misery of his last years, Saint Simon declared that the king stood at the head as long as he could with indefatigable care, hoping against hope, with the demeanor of a true king. With like dignity and composure, Mannerheim, too, accepted the heavy burdens allotted him by fate and brought them to their conclusion.

When, on the evening of 2 September 1944, Finland's Congress sanctioned the decision of the Finnish Government to terminate the war against the Soviet Union, the iron ties which had held Finns and Germans together during the war were broken. Each of the former two brothers-in-arms went his own way toward a dark future. But hope lived on in the hearts of the German soldiers who had gotten to know and love Finland that one day Germany and Finland would again join hands, united by the

---

[37] Proteus, the one who easily changes his appearance or principles (translator)

bonds of old friendship, in order to work together to fulfill the missions of peace in a new Europe.

BOOK TWO: The German Liaison Officer With the Finnish Armed Forces

CHAPTER I: Liaison Staff North

During the war German Generals were sent as liaison officers to the high commands of the allied or friendly armies. Their tasks and their activities will be shown in the following by means of the example of the "German General with the High Command of the Finnish Armed Forces":

In the discussions between representatives of the Finnish and German high commands in Salzburg on 25 May 1941, and in Zossen on 26 May 1941, it had been agreed that a German general was to be sent to the Finnish headquarters as liaison officer of the Army High Command (OKH) and the Wehrmacht High Command (OKW). On 12 June, the then Oberquartiermeister V (Fifth Senior General Staff Officer) (Military History) General Erfurth, was instructed at Zossen by the Chief of Staff, General Halder, to fly to Helsinki on the following day to represent the German Army at the headquarters of the Finnish Commander in Chief, Marshal Mannerheim, as "Commander of Liaison Staff Nord" (this title was changed in the fall of 1942 to "German General with the Finnish Armed Forces. The position thereupon was made a Wehrmacht function, the reason being that the General had become increasingly involved in political questions. In addition, Finland now became a theater of war of the OKW). When this instruction was given, it was still an open question whether there would be war with the Soviet Union. Though the political situation between the two countries had become very tense on 12 June, the end of the crisis could not be foreseen. At Finnish headquarters, where General Erfurth reported on 14 June, complete uncertainty likewise prevailed concerning the further development of the political situation.

I. Mission

The tasks of the Commander of Liaison Staff North had not been written down in detail. They gradually took shape and became more and more comprehensive in the course of time, covering the following spheres:

(1) Establishing and maintaining contact between the German and Finnish High Commands
(2) Coordination of planning and measures
(3) Representation of mutual wishes regarding warfare in common
(4) Briefing of both sides on situation of the war at any given moment

(5) Liaison between the German sectors and the Finnish sectors adjacent to them

(6) Exercising the powers of a commander of a military area (Wehrkreis) in regard to the German agencies and troops in the Finnish zone of operations.

Consequently the following agencies were involved in the message and signal communication traffic of Liaison Staff North:

OKW (Wehrmacht High Command)

OKH (Army High Command)

AOK (Army Headquarters); (the headquarters at Rovaniemi was renamed Army Headquarters Lapland in the beginning of 1942, and the Twentieth Mountain Army Headquarters in the summer of 1942)

Army Group North

Eleventh Army Headquarters (only in the summer and fall of 1942)

The German General at Mikkeli daily received detailed information about the situation on all fronts from the OKH and OKW; in addition he received the reports of AOK NORWEGEN and of the Eighteenth Army (left flank of Army Group North). Finally he received the so-called "policy lines" issued by the Attaché Branch of the OKH, as well as the information given to the Finnish Liaison General in the OKW and OKH. In spite of all this, Mannerheim's desire for the fullest information about the situation could not always be satisfied, since all information, especially that provided by the Attaché Branch, tended to put a favorable light on the deterioration of any given situation, and the obvious understatement of failures aroused the mistrust of the Finnish Commander in Chief. He was a man with sound common sense and sometimes he regarded the German optimisms as not quite objective.

The German Luftwaffe had sent a liaison officer of its own to Finnish Air Forces Headquarters. The same applied to the Kriegsmarine. This caused a great deal of friction. The Finnish High Command was pronouncedly an armed forces command. Matters concerning the three branches of the Finnish Forces were centralized at the headquarters at Mikkeli. Marshal Mannerheim made a point of maintaining his authority equally in all branches. There was no attempt in the Finnish Army to bypass or eliminate the authority of the Commander in Chief. He was considered and respected as such not only by all agencies of the Finnish Army, but also by the Government and the politicians. Even the Finnish Prime Minister, Ryti, was extremely correct in his attitude toward Mannerheim, although under the constitution, the Prime Minister was the head of the Finnish Armed Forces. He refrained from any encroachment upon the domain of the considerably older Commander in Chief. The relationship between the Head of the Government and the Commander in Chief was cool, as is the Finnish way, but objective and free from jealousy. Mannerheim kept the President posted about the situation at the front and his intentions, and carefully avoided impairing the powers given to the President in the constitution or neglecting the latter's instructions.

The Commanders in Chief of the German Luftwaffe and Kriegsmarine repeatedly tried to find and establish separate channels to Marshal Mannerheim. But these attempts invariably failed, since Mannerheim, who had soon recognized the weaknesses inherent in the dispersion of the German top-level organization, held that, in all questions concerning the German Armed Forces, he had to deal only with the German General attached to his headquarters. Mannerheim's generals behaved in the same way. If any matter interesting the Germans did occasionally reach the Finnish headquarters without the knowledge of the German General, the Finns passed it on to the German headquarters in Mikkeli.

Similar friction resulted from the fact that the representatives of the various branches were not under the German General at Finnish Headquarters. When, on 25 June 1941, Finnish Headquarters were transferred from Helsinki to Mikkeli, these representatives stayed in Helsinki, leading and independent life, as it were, of which the German General had a little knowledge. Since a number of difficulties arose from this situation, the military attaché in Helsinki was finally place under the German General in the summer of 1944 (shortly before the capitulation of Finland).

The Finns had handled this quite differently from the very beginning. When a Finnish general was sent to Berlin as Mannerheim's representative, they detached the Finnish Military Attaché in Berlin to Budapest, and made the other military attachés subordinates of the Finnish General at the German High Command. The general had made a request that this be done on being sent to Berlin and Mannerheim had agreed, since he was of the same opinion. According to my own experience the Finnish system is to be given preference.

II. Composition

When the German staff arrived in Finland its composition was as follows:

> Commander,
> Chief of Staff0
> 3 General staff officers
> 1 Adjutant
> 2 Aides
> 1 Liaison Officer to GHQ, Press section

1 Administrative Officer
1 Paymaster in charge of finances
1 Medical Officer
1 Communications Officer
1 Economics Officer

The lower echelon consisted of:
Clerks and draftsmen
Teletype operators
Drivers
Interpreters

During the Finnish-German offensive in the summer of 1941 it became clear that the staff was too large. For that reason, in the fall of 1943, the following persons were placed at the disposal of the High Command in Germany as dispensable:
Chief of Staff
1 general staff officer
1 aide
1 medical officer

The Chief of Staff lacked sufficient work, since discussions with Marshal Mannerheim and his generals were in the main conducted by the commander himself.

In view of the scarcity of general staff officers and officers suited for service in the higher staffs at home, and since the offensive had gradually shifted to a war of position, one of the junior general staff officers (Ib, the Supply Officer) and the aide could be dispensed with. Finally the medical officer could be sent back, since the small German staff could consult and be treated by the Finnish medical officer at Mikkeli if necessary.

The tasks of the commander of the headquarters had been performed by the adjutant (IIa, Personnel Officer) during the summer in addition to his own work. But this arrangement proved inadequate in the long run. The tasks of the IIa steadily increased (Finnish personnel data, proposals for award of decorations, duties of presentation). There was little time left for the adjutant to deal with the welfare and supervision of the lower echelon. This was the reason why, at the beginning of 1942, a regular headquarters commander was requested and sent to Finland.

III. Echelons

So as not to be too great a burden on the Finnish Headquarters, which moved from Helsinki to Mikkeli on 25 June 1941 (the small town of Mikkeli was already greatly overcrowded), the following parts of the staff of the German General remained in Helsinki as Echelon II:
1 administrative officer

1 communications officer
1 economics officer
1 paymaster

Since the concerns of the first two had chiefly to be discussed with the Finnish War Ministry, which had stayed behind in Helsinki, and since the finance administration had to be available to German soldiers passing through from Germany to Rovaniemi, the fact that these three agencies were left in Helsinki was justified. The three officers occasionally went to Mikkeli to make a report to the German General, if the latter had been unable to discuss matters with them on his frequent journeys to Helsinki.

The local German administrative headquarters of Helsinki was also under the German General; it was in charge of billeting, welfare and forwarding of German soldiers passing through Helsinki.

Loosely affiliated with the German General were the following agencies: K.O.F. (field office of the Foreign Group/Counterintelligence of the OKW) and also the Chief Transportation Officer (under the Wehrmacht Chief of Transportation).

IV. Helsinki Echelon

The personnel and tasks of Echelon II soon grew and were transformed into Wehrmacht offices. Thus the administrative officer became Wehrmacht Administrative Officer in Finland; the communications officer, the Wehrmacht Communications Officer in Finland; the economics officer, the War Economics Officer at Helsinki.

a. Wehrmacht Administrative Officer. His mission included the procurement of foreign currency and its distribution to the German headquarters and troops in Finland; measures for the protection of the Finnish currency and the Finnish market; restriction of purchases by German soldiers in Finnish shops; establishing quotas for Finnish personnel working for the German agencies; preparation of agreements between the German Wehrmacht and the Finnish Defense Ministry regarding joint use of Finnish utilities; representation of German interests in law suits (such as rents, indemnities, liabilities, etc.).

b. Wehrmacht Communications Officer. This officer, together with the Finnish Communication Inspector, governed the German use of Finnish signal or communications installations and the installation of new communication lines and circuits in the Finnish network. As a rule, new materiel had to be provided by the Germans. The Finns furnished the necessary labor. In the course of time a large Wehrmacht message center was organized in Helsinki (Station "Zentrum") for teletype and telephone communications. This center handled communications to the General at Mikkeli, the German headquarters at Rovaniemi, Army Group North, the Army High Command, the OKW, Hitler's headquarters, and Berlin.

The Wehrmacht Communications Officer was in charge of the big German trunk lines in Finland, and he supervised the technical transmission of the communications of the German General at Mikkeli. All teletype and telephone calls by Finnish headquarters to German agencies in Finland, on the Eastern front, and in the Reich, went through the communications system of the German General in Mikkeli and Station "Zentrum."

c. War Economics Officer. This officer's agency was affiliated with the Economic and Armaments Branch of the OKW in Berlin. Finnish economy and industry were in no way equal to the requirements of a war waged for Finland's existence and extending over several years. Even in the Winter War, which had lasted about 100 days, serious difficulties had cropped up in the supply of the nation and the armed forces. In the last Finnish-Russian Finnish imports had been considerable (wheat, coal, fuels, rubber, etc.).

After the declaration of war by Britain on 5 December 1941, Finnish imports were restricted to those from Germany. But in practice free importation by Finland across the seas had stopped earlier, at the end of July 1941, when a strong British naval unit appeared near Murmansk, and air raids were launched from aircraft carriers on Petsamo and Kirkenes. At that time the Finnish Government had caused its representative in London to inform the British Government that Finland considered its diplomatic relations with Great Britain "suspended." Germany, though she had to be very sparing of her supplies, helped her Finnish brother-in-arms generously. This has often been given grateful recognition by authoritative agencies in Finland. From Finland, Germany bought lumber, paper, nickel and copper. Finland's trade balance remained "passive" all through the war. In the latter part of the war German firms increasingly passed their orders on to Finnish firms (through the shifting of contracts, as was done in the case of occupied countries). The official channel for these transactions was the German War Economics Officer in Helsinki.

The negotiations concerning the German-Finnish trade agreement took place at short intervals in part in Helsinki and in part in Berlin. At the head of the German delegation was the German Ambassador Schnurre; the Finnish chairman changed several times. The negotiations on the German side were prepared in the Embassy at Helsinki and the officer of the War Economics Officer in Helsinki. The latter was the only German participant in the negotiations concerning the Finnish armaments requirements; for this purpose he kept in close contact with the Finnish Defense Minister and the Chief of the Finnish Economics and Armaments Board, General Grandele. The latter, accompanied by the German War Economics Officer, participated in all negotiations on the trade agreement and often personally represented the Finnish demands at the German Economics and Armaments Branch of the OKH in Berlin. Grandele was an especially able negotiator and was held in high esteem by Mannerheim. When the war with Soviet Russia began the Finnish Armed Forces were rather old-fashioned as to armament and equipment. Moreover it had not been possible to replace the losses of the Winter War. The Finnish infantry lacked heavy weapons for attack and defense; the artillery was not at all uniform and its guns were obsolete. Reserves of ammunition were used up after the first weeks of the summer offensive of 1941. Finnish manufacture of ammunition was so small that the striking power of the troops could not be maintained. There was a great scarcity of motor vehicles and signal equipment. This was also true of uniforms, coats, underwear and boots. The Air Force entirely depended on Germany for aircraft and spare parts. Finland did not produce a drop of gasoline. All the fuel for motor vehicles and aircraft had to be supplied by Germany. To carry on naval warfare in the Finnish Gulf, the small Finnish fleet received its entire requirements in mines and obstacle equipment from the Kriegsmarine. The Finnish Chief of Transportation, during the crisis of the winter of 1941-42, needed substantial assistance from the Germans to be able to cope with the situation (in view of the scarcity of locomotives and railway cars). Since the Finnish and Russian railroads have the same gauge, Germany could only help by making Russian booty available. This was shipped from Reval to Helsinki. Considerable, too, was German aid in the food supply of the Finnish soldiers. A few days after General Erfurth had arrived in Finland the Chief Administrative Officer of the Finnish Armed Forces paid him a visit and submitted a list of the goods that were scarce in the Finnish Army. These were canned meats, cereals, sugar, jam, fats and potatoes, all items that were also scarce in Germany. Requests by the Finnish Army like this were frequently repeated in the course of time, and they were in most cases granted. But the greatest concessions were made with regard to the rations of the Finnish III Corps. In the General Staff discussions of 25-26 May 1941, the Germans had agreed to give German Army rations to all Finnish troops under the command of the German Army in Lapland. The Finnish III Corps was also included in this agreement. This corps was employed on the right flank of the German army in the Kiestinki and Uhtua sectors. When, at the beginning 1942 at Mannerheim's request, the OKW agreed to relieve this Finnish corps with German troops, its food supply was continued by the Germans. But since this corps did not remain as one unit, but was divided and employed at various places in southern Finland, its food supply by the army headquarters all the way from Rovaniemi was no longer possible. General Erfurth was entrusted with this task. The details were worked out the by War Economics Officer and the Wehrmacht Administrative Officer in

Finland. This concession to the Finns was maintained until the capitulation of Finland.

V. Mikkeli Echelon

Mannerheim had set up his headquarters in the small town of Mikkeli in southern Finland, on the same spot where he had exercised the supreme command of the Finnish Army in the final phase of the Finnish 1918-1920 War of Liberation. The life of the Finnish officers there was almost peace-like in form and custom. The German staff had been housed in a Finnish barracks near the school house where Mannerheim and the most important agencies of the High Command had their offices. Whereas the officers of the German staff were in constant contact with the chiefs of the Finnish departments, contact with the Commander in Chief and the Chief of Staff was exclusively through General Erfurth. There were almost daily talks between General Erfurth and General Heinrichs and frequently also with the Marshal, to whom General Erfurth submitted important questions in person. And in the same way, Mannerheim, if some urgent and important matter was on his mind, asked the German General to come up to his headquarters.

VI. Characterizaion of Mannerheim

The old principle of *minima non curat praetor*[38] was definitely not Mannerheim's. General Heinrichs once said to General Erfurth that the Finnish Commander in Chief was not only interested in kilometers, but also in millimeters! And indeed, there has hardly ever been a more diligent Commander in Chief and one who was more interested in all spheres of warfare, than Mannerheim. Very little independence was left to his General Staff; he demanded to be informed about everything, and could be quite unpleasant if the information came late. This extraordinary man united the greatest contrasts in himself; he had the habits of a *grand seigneur*; he loved to live in comfort, was passionately fond of hunting and traveling, and introduced an almost regal ceremonial for visitors from abroad; at receptions and on special occasions he supervised all details personally. He was a charming and most considerate host, making the nicest distinctions in the treatment of his guests according to their rank and personality. His gift for languages was phenomenal, so that he could converse in the language that was most convenient to any of his guests. He was also greatly interested in all political and economic problems and events in the wide world, kept up a correspondence with numerous personalities from abroad, and, as a true *pater patriae*, was deeply interested

---

[38] The King does not care about trivial things.

in all the public matters of his nation. He also gave encouragement and support to ministers and politicians, who, worried by the deteriorating situation, often came from Helsinki to Mikkeli to seek his advice. Mannerheim had frequent talks over the telephone with the Finnish President, and through his friend, Defense Minister Walden, he kept in close touch with the Cabinet at all times. Although without doubt Mannerheim was the center of public life in Finland, and all affairs of his country were dealt with at his desk, he found the time to concern himself thoroughly with questions affecting the war and the conduct of operations. He was a hard worker and kept his headquarters busy. This fanaticism for work may have been a natural disposition, but the ability to spur his co-workers and assistants to the highest achievement had probably been developed and enhanced during his long term of service in the Imperial Russian Army. There he must have learned that a generalissimo must know how to be omnipresent and to hold the reins firmly. He applied this method, which he recognized as the right one in St. Petersburg and Warsaw, to the Finnish Army, which was his creation. Like all great commanders Mannerheim had a sympathetic understanding for his soldiers. He took special care of them and personally and most actively pleaded for help from Germany for them in the way of clothing, linen and food.

General Erfurth's attitude toward Mannerheim and the Finnish generals was determined by the fact that Finland was neither an ally of Germany nor bound by the instructions of the German High Command, but waged war as an independent and sovereign state against a common enemy. Thus German requests had to be presented by General Erfurth in such a manner that the rights and feelings of the Finns were respected. Though it is the main task of a liaison officer to protect the interests of his own armed forces, there was no way of preventing the Finns from trying to interest him in their own affairs and making him the spokesman of their own requests. The Finns greatly overestimated the power of the Germans to help them. Their trust and confidence in the capabilities of the Reich was unlimited and almost naïve. After the rapid rise of Hitler, the dazzling successes of his policy, the victories of the German Army in Poland, Norway, France and the Balkans, in 1941 the Finns regarded the power of German as very great. If the Finnish statesmen had not had an unshakeable belief in a German victory, they would not have decided, in the spring of 1941, to wage war against Russia on the side of Germany. Once this decision had been taken the almost complete dependence of the Finns on the supply of food and war materials from Germany left them no other choice but to continue the fighting on the side of Germany as long as possible. There were two official channels through which the Finns could make their requests and desires heard in Germany: One was via the German Embassy, the other via the German War Economics Officer in Helsinki. In both cases the Finnish requests reached the competent branches of the German ministries via the Foreign Office in Berlin or the Economics and Armaments Branch of the OKW. This channel contained too much red tape for the Finns; in their impatience they pressed for quick help. They had soon recognized that under a totalitarian regime quick decisions are made only by the highest commander, and that General Erfurth alone had the possibility of reaching Hitler directly with his reports. Since General Erfurth sent daily reports to the OKW and these, if Hitler was in Berlin, were forwarded to him as quickly as possible, this channel alone seemed to hold prospects of a quick decision. Once they had recognized this the Finns exploited the channel. This conduct was favored by Hitler's great personal interest in Mannerheim and his high esteem of the soldierly qualities of the Finns. After the Finnish offensive in the summer of 1941 Hitler repeatedly declared that the Finns were the most valuable allies of Germany and that the other allies lagged far behind them. Hitler considered Finland as a political matter and demanded the friendliest reception of the Finnish requests. It was inevitable that the Finns would eventually discover Hitler's favorable attitude towards them. Many a statement by the dictator and his environment, which was influenced by him, reached Finland and was heard there with satisfaction. The Finns, being a true nation of farmers profited by this. Thus it happened that economic questions and later, when there was some disagreement between the Foreign Ministers of the two nations, also political questions were shifted from the competent civil departments to the military. The Field Marshal encouraged this development and often used General Erfurth to ensure quick fulfillment of Finnish wishes. There was never any friction in this cooperation between German and Finns. Mannerheim had confidence in Erfurth, listened to his suggestions, and treated him with distinction and courtesy. The good relations between the German Staff at Finnish Headquarters and the Finns remained untroubled until the end. The Finns took the greatest care of the Germans until the last evacuation steamer with the German Staff on board left Helsinki on 13 September 1944. The farewell visit of Erfurth to Mannerheim, who in the meantime had become President, took place in the most honorable forms. The grave friction that occurred when the German troops left Lapland occurred only after General Erfurth's departure. The question of guilt for these incidents cannot be clarified at present.

CHAPTER II: Participation of German General in Military and Political Questions

In the three years and three months that General Erfurth was a member of the Finnish Headquarters he often helped to solve military and political problems. A few examples will suffice to show the way in which this happened.

I. The Finnish Army and the Fighting for Leningrad

This was a military and political question at the same time. For a long time, it was in the foreground of the German and Finnish discussions. In the Finnish war, especially, politics and strategy were closely interlinked. Important military decisions by the Finnish Commander in Chief cannot be understood without knowledge of the political background. Consideration for the Finnish foreign policy and the inner-political situation often influenced military decisions. In the German-Finnish General Staff discussions in Germany on 25-26 May 1941, it had been agreed that the Finnish Army, in case of war with the Soviet Union, was to assemble to the northwest of Lake Ladoga in such a way that its bulk could take the offensive either west or east of the lake. The decision as to the assembly and attack of the Finnish Army was to depend on the advance of the German Army in the East (Army Group North). Since the latter pushed through the Baltic counties with great rapidity during the first ten days of the German offensive, the Finnish Army, at the request of the Germans, entered its area of concentration in such a way that its bulk could attack east of Lake Ladoga (Karelian Army). The goal of the Finnish Army was to be the Svir River, and, by advancing in the direction of Ladeynoye Pole, it was to contact Germen Army Group North, advancing south of Lake Ladoga.

There was as yet no talk of a Finnish offensive across the Karelian Isthmus in the direction of Leningrad. In an instruction to the German High Command of 2 August 1941, given to the German troops in Finland, emphasis was laid on the fact that the point of main effort of the joint attack was to lie east of Lake Ladoga. The offensive of the Karelian Army had begun on 10 July. The Finnish attack broke the Russian resistance, and the Finns thrust through the gap deep into Soviet-occupied territory.

In the first week of August Finnish troops also attacked west of Lake Ladoga with the intention of engaging elements of the Red Army that were facing their front. But it was only a restricted sector of the Finnish front, between Imstra and Unkunjemi, that launched this attack and its objective was limited.

However, since the advance of Army Group North had come to a standstill south of Leningrad, the German Army High Command suggested that the Finns advance along the Karelian Isthmus in greater force (10 August). The Finns complied with the wishes of the Germans from 21 August onward. This offensive soon led to the seizure of Käkisalmi and, on 30 August, of Viipuri.

In the course of August the Karelian Army rapidly advance east of Lake Ladoga, into Karelia. In a continuously victorious drive, the Finns advanced to the former 1939 border. Here, however, they halted for the time being and limited themselves to mopping up the important district of Suojärvi on the left flank of the Karelian Army. Presumably, Mannerheim, before deciding to resume the advance of the Karelian Army toward the Svir, intended to wait until German Army Group North had advanced farther south of Lake Ladoga.

Since the German-Finnish offensive against the Murmansk railroad had come to a dead stop in the first weeks, it seemed important to the German High Command to keep the operations of the Finnish Amy in Karelia and on the Isthmus moving. On 20 August 1941, a discussion on this point took place between Mannerheim and Erfurth and the following wishes of the OKW were dealt with:

(1) Finnish forces, as strong as possible, were to participate in the encirclement of Leningrad by pushing down from the north. In this way the junction of the German and Finnish attackers was to be established between Lake Ladoga and Leningrad.

(2) Along the front between Lakes Ladoga and Onega the Finnish Karelian Army was to reach the Svir sector, advance beyond it, i.e. establish a bridgehead roughly near Lodeypoje and Swirstroj. From this bridgehead a mobile group was to be sent out to join up with the German forces south of Lake Ladoga. Mannerheim at once raised objection to this.

According to prior agreement the Finns were to advance down the Karelian Isthmus only as far as the old frontier line of 1939, and east of Lake Ladoga only as far as the Svir. But now the Finnish Army was asked to push considerably farther. The Marshal could not decide this question and would first have to ask his Government. The tasks demanded of the Finnish forces were too big for their strength. Even the German troops would not be able to implement this plan. The Marshal did not seem to like the idea that his troops should advance or that he should move them up close to Leningrad. The Finns, he declared, would not have anything to do with Leningrad. They would prefer the Germans to take and keep Leningrad. Then they would have peace. How was he to get through the fortified system north of Leningrad? All necessary prerequisites for this mission were missing.

Further discussions on the same subject took place between Mannerheim and Erfurth during the following days. The German General told Mannerheim that it would be incomprehensible from the military viewpoint if the Finns stopped dead in their advance at the old Finnish frontier north of Leningrad while the Germans attacked the city simultaneously from opposite directions. Though Mannerheim held out the prospect of a new offensive of the Karelian Army east of Lake Ladoga in the near future, he firmly stuck to his decision that the Finns halt their offensive along the old frontier on the Isthmus and refrain from participating in the German attack on Leningrad.

On 21 August a meeting took place in Mannerheim's headquarters with Ryti, the State President, who had come over to Mikkeli accompanied by Walden, the Defense Minister. After Ryti's departure Mannerheim and Walden visited General Erfurth to inform him of the result of this conference. Little had been changed with regard to the Finnish viewpoint: The Marshal declared that the Finns would neither cross the old frontier on the Karelian Isthmus nor cross the Svir east of Lake Ladoga. The Karelian Army would stay where it was until the Germans, from the direction of the Volkhov, had neared the Svir, so that a Finnish crossing of this river would be quite unnecessary. Mannerheim gave an evasive reply to an explicit question put by the German General as to when the Karelian Army would be ready to attack; the Defense Minister countered by asking whether there was any news from the German front south of Leningrad.

The Marshal asked General Erfurth to see him in his headquarters on the following day and somewhat mitigated or qualified the Finnish viewpoint of the previous day. He said that he had had another discussion with the Finnish President over the telephone and now made the concession that the Finnish troops on the Isthmus would cross the old frontier on both sides of the road from Viipuri to Leningrad to reach a line designated by the General on the previous day, and, from this favorable position, would then begin a wide encirclement of Leningrad on the northwest front. In return Mannerheim, at the request of the President, asked for 25,000 tons of rye from Germany, of which the Finns were in urgent need to bridge the time until the new harvest.

On the same day the German Ambassador in Helsinki sent a confidential message to General Erfurth to the affect that the defensive viewpoint had gained the upper hand in the Finnish Government. This was in accordance with information from Swedish sources (8 August), which stated that there was a growing tendency in the Finnish Government (the Social Democrat Minister Tanner was mentioned) to bring about a decision of limited warfare (i.e. up to the old frontier of 1939 with some corrections).

The Swedish informant held that these views were strongly supported by the U.S.A. The Finnish Cabinet reflected the conflicting ideas of the Finnish nation as to war aims. The majority was of the opinion that the territory which had been lost in the Winter War, i.e. the old Finnish frontier of 1939, should be taken back. A minority, supported by very influential groups (officers and university people) thought that the time had come when the East Karelians, who had lived outside the Finnish frontier under Russian rule and under the influence of the Orthodox Church, should be liberated from the Russian yoke and returned to the Finnish nation. The Finnish victories of the summer of 1941 were a great stimulus to the champions of "Greater Finland." Finally there was a small minority, but increasing considerably in number in the course of the war, which supported the idea of a purely defensive war, and even rejected the idea of regaining the territories lost in the Winter War. The strongest party in the country, headed by Tanner, the Social-Democrat Minister, in the summer of 1941 belonged to the first group (frontiers of 1939), but when the situation along the German fronts deteriorated it went over to the third group (purely defensive warfare). This was the background of the decisions taken in the Finnish Headquarters in August 1941.

The Finns stuck to their decision. They would neither cross the old frontier (with the slight concession made by Mannerheim on 1 August) nor go beyond the Svir, east of Lake Ladoga. But since it seemed more favorable from a tactical viewpoint, the positions at some points of the river front were moved onto the southern bank of the river. This was a military necessity. However, the bridgehead on the Svir was under no circumstances to serve as a jump off point for a Finnish offensive into the area east of Leningrad; the Finnish front on the Karelian Isthmus also remained unchanged until, in June 1944, the storm of the Russian offensive broke over the Finns. Repeated attempts on the German side to make the Finns launch an attack on the northern front of Leningrad (especially in the summer and fall of 1942) met with unshakable resistance on the part of the Finns. The defensive tendency of the political front in the country grew so strong that Government and Headquarters were chained down.

II. Mannerheim's Plan for an Operation Aiming at Soroka

The German-Finnish offensive against the Murmansk railroad in the summer of 1941 had not led to full success at any point of the front. After initial advances the front had come to a standstill in all sectors and the war had become a war of position. The reasons for this failure were manifold; the great difficulties in the road less wilderness of Karelia, which was entirely unknown even to the Finns, and along the coast of the Arctic Ocean, had quite obviously been underrated by both Finns and Germans.

Probably the forces they had sent into action had been insufficient, and they had set their hopes too high.

The Murmansk railroad was so favorably situated for the Red Army that it gave the Russians most valuable superiority in transportation. The summer, in the opinion of the Finns, which was based on ample experience in the northern area, was less well suited for military action and operations than the winter when lakes, rivers, and moors freeze over and the terrain can be traversed easily. Since it was considered very important for the Murmansk railroad be cut at some point, so that Russia would be deprived of Anglo-American supplies arriving by way of the White Sea, the idea occurred again and again to Germans and Finns alike to repeat in winter the operation which had been such a failure in the summer. Towards the end of 1941 Mannerheim had had the intention to participate more vigorously in this winter offensive than he had done in the summer, but he was greatly hampered in his decisions and actions by consideration for the foreign policy of Finland.

The Finnish nation had become war-weary in November 1941. The summer campaign against Russia, despite the great Finnish successes in Karelia, had been a great disappointment in the end. The illusion of a blitz war against the Soviets had been given up. The Finns, with their characteristic matter-of-factness and coolness, had soon enough recognized that nobody could see the end of the war, which had been started with so much optimism. This mood was exploited by the U.S. State Department, which sent a note to the Finnish Government in November 1941, inquiring whether there were any chances of a settlement between Finland and Russia. Perhaps this note was also intended to warn against a new offensive. A reply was most difficult for the Finnish Government, for they had to consider both their German brothers-in-arms and the Finnish nation, which wanted peace. There was fierce controversy in the Finnish Cabinet over the formulation of the reply to the United States, in which the Finnish Government finally declared its willingness to cease fighting Soviet Russia as soon as the danger had been warded off and guarantees been given. The Finnish-American negotiations, which had resulted from the demarche of the American Ambassador in Helsinki, were the subject of a discussion between Mannerheim and Erfurth in the Finnish Headquarters on 10 November 1941. The Marshal said with a smile that the big U.S.A. and small Finland were at the moment fighting a diplomatic duel. He continued with a sigh, "If only there were not Soroka! I am convinced that, if the Finns gave an assurance that they would not go on to Soroka, the storm would abate. The Anglo-Saxon powers would probably have no objection against an expansion of the Finns' positions in the south (Karelian Isthmus and east of Lake Ladoga). But Soroka is the point of conflict! It is tragic what importance the Murmansk railroad had gained. They all want to have it safe in their hands. It is a pity that this line was ever built!

After the Finnish reply had been sent off to the United States, Mannerheim quite frankly voiced his opinion to Erfurth on 20 November 1941, with regard to a continuation of the war on the Finnish front. He said that in his opinion Murmansk, Kandalaksha and Soroka should be taken in the winter of that year, the sooner the better. He recommended that the winter offensive be started in an eastward direction in January 1942, i.e. simultaneously against these three objectives on the railroad. Though, naturally, there should be a point of main effort in the fighting, the three pieces should be attacked at the same time, so as to deprive the Russians of the possibility of shifting their forces and concentrating them at the points of attack by using the railroad line, as had been the case in the summer and fall of 1941 during the repeated attacks by General Falkenhorst.

The Marshal found the present situation at the front of Army Group North very distressing. "We cannot remain in this position. Too many Finnish forces which cannot be used effectively are engaged and tied down outside Leningrad and on the Svir." With regard to the mood of the Finnish nation it seemed most desirable to him that a final and decisive step be taken on the Finnish southern front. As long as two-thirds of the Finnish Army were tied down in the south, the campaign in the north could not be continued with sufficient vigor.

At the time of these considerations by the Finnish Commander in Chief, General von Falkenhorst at Rovaniemi was planning to resume his offensive in the Kandalaksha sector. He had also interested the OKW in this plan. On 24 November 1941, the Chief of the OKW wrote the Finnish Marshal about a German winter attack to be launched against Kandalaksha. Keitel asked Mannerheim to make two Finnish ski brigades available for this purpose, if possible. Mannerheim, in his reply of 5 December, quite clearly pointed out that he Finns could participate in this campaign against the Murmansk railroad in greater strength only if the Finnish and German forces on the Svir were united, since then the Finns would be to a certain extent relieved on the southern front. In this case Mannerheim would be willing to launch an attack against Bjelomorsk-Soroka, simultaneously with the German attack against Kandalaksha, and to reinforce the southern group of the German attackers aiming at Kandalaksha by two Finnish brigades.

The OKW was not very pleased with this reply from the Finnish Commander in Chief, for Mannerheim demanded more for his participation in the attack than could be given by the Germans. The rendezvous on the Svir which Mannerheim demanded was now quite impossible, due to the unfavorable situation of Army Group North. The counter-offensive of the Red Army in the direction of the Volkov was launched with such vigor against this overstrained army group, which had dwindled greatly, that withdrawal of the wedge which had pressed forward in the direction of Tichwin seemed inevitable.

On this same day the OKW informed General Erfurth that relief of the Finnish southern front as well as simultaneous attacks on the Murmansk line in the north were unrealizable demands. The OKW had begun to doubt whether the German attack on Kandalaksha could be launched at all.

On 14 December a meeting took place at Rovaniemi between Falkenhorst and Mannerheim, who was accompanied by Erfurth. The discussion led to no results. No agreement could be reached concerning the relief of Finnish troops by German troops in the sector of Kiestinki and Salla, as demanded by Mannerheim. Mannerheim wished to attack Soroka, Falkenhorst stuck to his intention of attacking Kandalaksha. The negotiations were broken off without an agreement having been reached. On the return journey to Mikkeli in the Marshal's special train, Mannerheim discussed with Erfurth what was to be done. According to Mannerheim's plan for the 1941-42 winter offensive, the point of main effort was to be Soroka (called Bjelomorsk on some maps), since he considered it to be the most important of all the localities along the Murmansk railroad, on account of the branch line that started from there to Oboserakaja (on the line from Wologda to Archangelsk). He was willing to launch this attack mainly with Finnish forces, and then to roll up the Soviet-Russian positions to the west of the Murmansk line from south to north, provided that the situation on the German Eastern front did not take a turn for the worse. Mannerheim's plan (attack on Soroka) was taken to the German teletype operator when the train passed through Helsinki, and sent to the OKW by General Erfurth as Mannerheim's proposal. On their arrival in Mikkeli they learned that a complete change had taken place in the situation on the German Eastern front. The German forces in the east were passing through their first grave crisis. Tichwin and Wolchowstroj had had to be evacuated by the German troops. The prospect of uniting the German and Finnish fronts to the south of Lake Ladoga and on the Svir had thus dwindled to the vanishing point.

Marshal Mannerheim was much shaken by the withdrawal of the German Eastern front. He had now lost all confidence in the success of an attack against Soroka, since he considered his Svir front greatly endangered.

Repeated attempts on the German side, in the beginning of 1942, to cause the Finnish Command in Chief to carry through his own proposal of an attack against Soroka naturally met with rejection by Mannerheim. The Marshal did not wish to take any new decisions for the time being, but intended to wait and see in which way the situation on the Russian front developed.

Toward the end of the winter a well-informed officer from Finnish Headquarters maintained that the Marshal would have liked to launch the winter attack against Soroka, but that the Finnish Government had thwarted his plans for political reasons. The Finnish Government had held that it would be better to wait and see which course the German summer offensive would take in 1942. Presumably it was less inner-political reasons than the menacing attitude of the U.S.A. that caused the Finnish Government to stop Mannerheim from launching an attack in the late winter 1941-42. At that time the Finnish Government was under American pressure. The purpose of this pressure was to force the Finns into a settlement with Russia or at least stop them from launching an attack against the Murmansk railroad. The Finnish Government had heard that the Americans, like the Finns, were trying to keep up normal relations, and that a declaration of war by America was not likely, on condition however, that the Finns did not start a new offensive. On the other hand, a successful Finnish offensive against the Murmansk line and the conclusion of a treaty of alliance with Germany was more than could be tolerated, and would most certainly result in a declaration of war by the U.S.A. The Finnish Government, in full agreement with the Finnish Parliament, did not wish to break off diplomatic relations with the United States under any conditions.

In the summer of 1942 the problem of an attack on the Murmansk line was again brought up, but this time by the Germans.

III. The German Plan for an Offensive Against Soroka (Operation LACHSFANG[39])

On 9 July 1942, General Erfurth visited the Commander in Chief for Lapland, General Dietl, in Rovaniemi.

At that time the German offensive of the second war-time summer was in full swing in the south of Russia. The German successes exceeded all expectations. The news sent by the OKW to Finland was very optimistic. Dietl and Erfurth agreed that it would be unjustifiable to leave the entire German-Finnish front inactive while the German forces in the south were fighting for a decision. The attack on the Ribachi Peninsula, which, according to the OKW's plan was to be launched by the German army in Lapland in the late summer of 1942, did not seem to promise

---

[39] Operation Salmon Catch

much success. Only if the Murmansk line could be reached and held at several points could supplies from the U.S. be interrupted. This would be a victory of great import. Dietl decided to launch an attack on Kandalaksha and probably a secondary attack from Kiestinki on Louhi. He intended to start operations in December, on condition that Mannerheim simultaneously attacked Soroka-Kem. Erfurth at once pointed out that there would not be sufficient Finnish forces for an attack on Soroka. The Finns could only be won over for this plan if Army Group North would first take Leningrad or the Finnish encirclement troops north of Leningrad were relieved by this army group.

OKW consent was quickly obtained for this plan of a joint German-Finnish attack against the Murmansk railroad. General Jodl, who had come to Rovaniemi on 14 July, promised that Leningrad would be attacked in September. The heavy artillery was already being transported there from Sevastopol.

Dietl thought he would be able to launch his attack on Kandalaksha on 15 October, so that the entire operation against the Murmansk railroad could be completed by Christmas.

Everything depended on Mannerheim's willingness to cooperate. Erfurth was instructed by the OKW on 22 July to inquire in what way the Finnish High Command intended to participate in Dietl's offensive against the Murmansk line. The Finnish Chief of Staff, with whom operation LACHSFANG was first discussed, said that it seemed important to him that the Murmansk line should be first reached and cut by the Germans, so that the Finnish Parliament could not blame Finnish Headquarters for the declaration of war by America that was to be expected.

Marshal Mannerheim had doubts because of the season. It would not freeze hard enough in October. But he realized that delay would give the Soviets the advantage of more supplies from the U.S. via the Murmansk railroad. Mannerheim's written reply was handed to Erfurth on 2 August 1942. The Marshal declared that in the main he was willing to participate in the campaign. But his consent depended on several conditions. The most important was that Leningrad be taken by the Germans in September, and that the Finnish divisions on the Karelian Isthmus be relieved for the Finnish offensive against Soroka. In addition, Mannerheim pointed out that an advance east of the left flank of Army Group North and south of Lake Ladoga into the area of Wytegra (south of Lake Onega) or as far as the middle of the bend in the Svir would have the best chance of relieving some of the Finnish divisions which were so urgently needed.

Mannerheim's conditions were accepted by the OKW, except the one in which he demanded that the Germans advance south of Lake Ladoga.

The reply was brought to Mikkeli on 15 August by the Finnish liaison officer to the OKH, General Talvela. "If the Marshal" ran the reply, "insisted on an advance by Army Group North south of Lake Ladoga in an eastward direction, the German-Finnish offensive against the Murmansk would likely have to be cancelled." The Germans could not, in addition, advance across the Volhov. By reason of these objections Mannerheim, though not very willingly, gave up his demand for an offensive by Army Group North.

Thus everything seemed to be in order, as far as the Finnish and German plans went. The Finnish President Ryti, who had been kept informed by the Marshal about his negotiations, gave his consent to Operation LACHSFANG. But at that very moment the heavy Soviet attacks against the eastern front of the forces ringing Leningrad (the battle south of Lake Ladoga) upset the German-Finnish agreements. The initiative had passed to the Russian side. The German divisions being moved up north from the Crimea for the attack on the southern front of Leningrad now had to be employed for defensive purposes on the endangered front southeast of Schlüsselburg. The consequence was a postponement of the joint offensive against the Murmansk line from the fall of 1942 to the winter. Under these circumstances the OKW suggested participate by strong Finnish forces in the German attack on Leningrad (Operation NORDLICHT[40]).

IV. Operation NORDLICHT

As in the summer of 1941, the German request to actively support the attack on Leningrad was extremely undesirable to the Finns for political reasons. "The situation was quite different," said General Heinrichs to General Erfurth on 2 September 1942, "when participation by the Finns in the attack against the Murmansk railroad was decided upon." At that time the offensive in the direction of Soroka had corresponded to the desire of the nation to liberate the Finns in Eastern Karelia. But the Finns did not want anything to do with Leningrad. It was extremely unpleasant to them, he declared, to give a foundation to the propaganda of the Soviets in this way, who had always maintained that Leningrad was endangered by the Finnish border close to it. As was to be expected, the Marshal's official consent on 4 September was non-committal. He would attack with weak forces at the appointed time, but only with a restricted objective. If Operation NORDLICHT had actually been implemented, the Finnish share would probably been extremely modest.

---

[40] Operation Northern Lights

But Fate willed differently. On 11 September a message from the Finnish General Talvela in Germany arrived at Mikkeli, saying that the attack on Leningrad would be delayed, because the plan was to widen the narrow passage on Lake Ladoga, southeast of Schlüsselburg, by means of a prior offensive.

At the beginning of October, General Talvela was informed by the Chief of the German Armed Forces Operations Staff that the attack of Leningrad would have to be postponed indefinitely. The forces of the Eleventh Army, which had been employed on the left flank of Army Group North south of the Gulf of Finland had been weakened by losses and strain and needed rest. In addition, the enemy had assumed a menacing strength in the big breach on the right flank of Army Group North and on the left flank of Army Group Center, roughly on both sides of the railroad to Veliki Luki, in the area of Toropetz. The German line around this breach was said to be very thin. This tense situation seemed to make it advisable to refrain from an attack on Leningrad.

What, in the beginning, had been meant only as a postponement became conclusive in the course of the ensuing weeks: on 30 October 1942, the German General at Mikkeli received instructions from the OKW (Armed Forces Operations Staff) to inform the Finnish Commander in Chief that the necessary conditions for an attack on the Murmansk line, i.e. for the execution of Operation LACHSFANG, in which Finns and Germans were to have participated, were no longer present and could not be reestablished until the late winter of 1942-43. Twentieth Mountain Army headquarters in Lapland had shifted to defense tasks. The Finns could take it that there would be no important tasks for them during the winter. The LACHSFANG and NORDLICHT operations were never referred to again by either Finns or Germans. The effects of the Russian offensive against the German Eastern front in the winter of 1942-43 became so decisive, that the idea of an attack in the northern area was irrevocably given up by both Germans and Finns. Once again the words of Thucydides had come true – "Time and tide wait for no man." The time and tide, or fair chance, to seize Leningrad had undoubtedly existed in the summer of 1941. The fact that, due to the reduced striking power of the Germans and the political inhibitions of the Finns, this opportunity was not seized, decisively influenced the course of the war on the Finnish front.

V. Deterioration of the German-Finnish Relations (Spring 1943)

During the entire war the U.S.A. repeatedly tried to draw Finland from the German side and make her agree to a settlement with Russia. Each time the Finns were on the verge of war with the U.S. A all Finnish politicians and official statements endeavored to avoid this. The Finnish

Government demanded that Finnish Headquarters give no cause for American to declare war on Finland. This is the reason why tactical questions like the Finnish offensive against the Murmansk line in the winter of 1941-42 were handled with the greatest care by Finnish Headquarters. If, at any time and in any place strategy was linked to foreign policy, it was in Finland. With great forbearance the German Government watched the tortuous ways of the Finnish politics, considering the frequent exchange of notes between the U.S. and Finland as a harmless and platonic flirtation. But in March 1943 this attitude changed radically. By reason of a deterioration of the general situation of the Axis Powers (Stalingrad and the wavering of the German Eastern front) a crisis had occurred in the interior policy of Finland, which found its expression in a reorganization of the Finnish Government. The staunchest friends of Germany (Prime Minister Rangell, Foreign Minister Witting and some other ministers) left the Cabinet, and Professor Linkomies became Prime Minister, and Eric Ramsay, Foreign Minister. Some days after the latter had taken office, on 20 March 1943, he was given a note by the American Chargé d'Affaires from the State Department in which the U.S.A. offered their services to the Finns for mediation of their differences with Soviet Russia.

Minister Ramsay kept the German Ambassador in Helsinki in ignorance of this note, which was discussed in the Foreign Committee of the Cabinet (Ramsay, Linkomies, Tanner, Walden).

On 22 March, Ramsay asked the German Ambassador to arrange a secret flight to the German Foreign Minister for him.

On 24 March, Ramsay gave a personal reply to the American Chargé d'Affaires, in which he expressed his gratitude for the generosity shown in the American note. He said that the American proposal was of the utmost importance for Finland, and asked for a more detailed statement of American intentions.

On 25 March, Ramsay flew to Berlin, where on 26 March he had a long discussion with Ribbentrop. This meeting of the two Foreign Ministers was ill-fated. Ribbentrop reproached his Finnish colleague bitterly with having entered into close relations with the Americans. After a consultation with Hitler over the telephone, Ribbentrop demanded a clear statement of Finnish intentions and a precise declaration by the Finnish Government, to the effect that it would not conclude a truce or peace treaty with the Soviet Union without the concurrence of Germany.

Ribbentrop insisted on an immediate and definitive refusal of the American offer without waiting for a reply to Ramsay's last note. The German Government, said Ribbentrop, would be happy if the Finnish Government would contact it as to the wording of the note. The continued flirtation of the Finns with the U.S.A. would have to be stopped once and for all.

Ramsay departed disappointed and full of resentment. He felt deeply offended by Ribbentrop's unfriendly attitude. The relations between the two Foreign Ministers remained strained and never improved again. This disharmony spread to the ministries. The German Ambassador in Helsinki was offended because Ramsay had not taken him into his confidence form the beginning and had not asked for his mediation. The result was that diplomatic relations between Finland and German considerably cooled. Consequently the Finns tried to transfer all matters to the military channel. A great deal of debating ensued as to an objective settlement of the questions raised by the American note.

In respect to the reply to the U.S., the Finnish Government complied with the wishes of the Germans. The text of the Finnish refusal was submitted to the German Government before it was sent off. It satisfied the latter. But with regard to the second request of the Reich Government (a formal promise by the Finnish Government) great difficulties arose, since such a thing was unconstitutional. For this reason this question could not be settled between the Finnish and German Governments; it was passed from one government to the other through diplomatic channels, until greater events occurred which made it seem insignificant. The diplomatic channel between Berlin and Helsinki remained blocked for several months. Ribbentrop, so as to exert pressure on Finland, called the German Ambassador to Berlin and kept him there for several months. The German Chargé d'Affaires in Helsinki complained that he did not receive any information from the Finnish Foreign Minister and that his conferences with the Finns were fewer and fewer.

In the meantime other incidents caused new disharmony between the two countries fighting together. Thus, at the beginning of July 1943, when Berlin was about to close and forget the German-Finnish difference of opinion, a Finnish-American Society was formed in Helsinki. The German reaction was that all official visits from German to Helsinki were cancelled. There was complete uncertainty about the return of the German Ambassador to Finland.

The latter's return to Helsinki on 17 August was a great surprise. The German Foreign Minister, who had finally given up the diplomatic struggle with the tough Finns, believed that in this way the stagnant German policy could be revived; but the success was not great. The relations between the German Ambassador and Ramsay, the Finnish Foreign Minister, remained frosty. In addition, the Finns, during the five months the diplomatic struggle lasted, had got accustomed to taking all matters to the Marshal at Mikkeli, who increasingly made use of General Erfurth in the representation of Finnish wishes.

From the spring of 1943 it became a custom for the statesmen and politicians who came to report to the Marshal at Mikkeli, to also pay a visit to General Erfurth. The railroad schedule was such that travellers from Helsinki to Mikkeli used the night train for the journey there and back, and spent the day at Mikkeli. Since it was Mannerheim's custom to invite his visitors for lunch, it became a habit for the German General to invite them for dinner. They stayed in the small German mess until it was time to drive to the station. At these informal meetings at Erfurth's table all matters of importance for Finnish economy and policy were discussed. As the Finns knew that the General had their Marshal's confidence, they talked without restraint. This did not lead to any unpleasant incidents, since the harmony between the Finns and the small German staff was never disturbed by indiscretions.

Moreover, the relations between the German Ambassador and General Erfurth were not disturbed by the latter's growing importance. They kept up a close and frequent exchange of ideas; they were not touch in such matters and became permanent friends.

VI. Efforts by Paasikivi to Obtain Separate a Peace (Spring 1944)

At the beginning of 1944 Finnish-German relations passed through a serious crisis, due to a diplomatic move by the U.S.A.

On 9 February the Secretary of State, Mr. Hull, made a last appeal on the air to the Finns to withdraw from the war; otherwise they could not count on clemency when the peace treaty was signed.

The same ultimatum was handed in the form of a memorandum to the Finnish Foreign Minister in Helsinki by the U.S. chargé d'Affaires.

Simultaneously the Moscow radio began to broadcast threats against Finland. The American ultimatum cause great nervousness among the Finnish politicians. The opposition considered the war lost for Germany and urged the Government to inquire after the conditions of the Soviet Union. Other political circles deemed it necessary to show Finland's good will toward the U.S.A. Although the Finnish Government did not seem willing to reply to the memorandum at first, it was to be expected that there would be great tension in Parliament and in the press.

The political situation in Finland had undoubtedly become most difficult. A growing desire for peace was noticeable in the entire Finnish nation: few people believed in a German victory. But to men of understanding the possibilities of a peace seemed slight. What had become known through press and radio of the Russian demands and conditions was considered unacceptable by all authoritative Finns. Now the Social-Democrat Party appealed to the Government to enquire about the Soviet peace conditions. The Government was at the time wrestling with the problem as to whether to comply with the wishes of the Social-

Democrat Party and answer Hull's memorandum. Everywhere there was a desire not to impair relations with the U.S.A. The general nervousness was enhance by the news of 14 February that the Finnish statesman Paasikivi, who was known to be a Russophile (former Finnish Ambassador to Moscow and co-signatory of the Moscow peace treaty of 1940) had flown to Stockholm as a private person in order to obtain information about the Soviet intentions.

On 24 February, Paasikivi returned from Stockholm with the Soviet conditions. It was only then that the Finnish Government admitted to the German Ambassador that Paasikivi had been to Stockholm for this purpose. The conditions were published in the Swedish newspaper *Dagems Nyheter* of 25 February in a form that was generally correct (provision of Moscow Peace Treaty, frontier of 1940, internment of German troops). The Parliament passed a vote of confidence in the government of Linkomies and adjourned so as to give the members a chance of consulting their constituents in the lonely forest farms. It was reported that Mannerheim had given the Government a serious picture of the situation on the front in the East. The Finns were especially interested in the situation of Army Group North, which had deteriorated greatly during the previous weeks.

The Foreign Minister, on 16 February, had said that a withdrawal by the Germans to the Dvina would create an entirely new situation for Finland. Prominent Finns, on every occasion, pointed out how important it was that Narva be kept by the Germans on any account. Mannerheim had mentioned this to the German General on 2 March.

The situation in Finland in the beginning of March 1944 was such that while large and influential circles were striving to end the war, the majority of Parliament was not yet inclined to accept the peace conditions Paasikivi had brought from Stockholm.

On 14 and 15 March 1944, these conditions were debated in the Finnish Parliament and rejected. But the 'nays' were hesitant and cautious; it was noticeable that the Parliament would have preferred to answer in the affirmative. The Finnish reply contained a request for an interpretation of the Soviet conditions. It also emphasized the Finns willingness to make peace.

The German political influence on this decision was very slight. It was the severity of the Soviet conditions what was of decisive importance.

This "peace-feeler" which the Finns had sent out through Paasikivi was by no means nullified by Parliament's decision of 15 March. Through the diplomatic mediation of Sweden, at the suggestion of the Soviet Ambassadress in Stockholm, Mrs. Kollontay, the Finnish Government was offered the interpretation it had asked for in its reply. This diplomatic battle of wits, which was directed from Stockholm, led to another reconnaissance journey by Paasikivi. On this second journey, which he started in secret on 28 March, and which led him to Moscow, Paasikivi was no longer a private person. He was accompanied by the bank director Enckell, who later became Foreign Minister when Mannerheim became State President and formed his new Government. The German Government had not been informed about this Finnish step.

When details about this second journey gradually began to come out, Finnish Headquarters explained the motivation to General Erfurth in roughly the following way: "There is no reason why we should not receive the interpretation of the Soviet conditions offered to us. Only if these throw some new light on the matter, which may influence our opinion on the situation, will they be brought before Parliament. The attitude of the Finnish Government is the same as before, namely that the original conditions are unacceptable.

The personal reasons which Foreign Minister Ramsay offered were that the Finnish nation was divided as to the peace question and that it would have been a fatal omission on the part of the Finnish Government not to try to obtain the information offered.

The Finnish delegation to Moscow had three meetings with Molotov. It was a great disappointment to the Finnish negotiators to find out that the Soviet Union did not think of mitigating in any way the peace conditions they had been given in Stockholm. On the contrary! Moscow, in addition, demanded cession of the Petsamo region. Paasikivi returned to Helsinki in the first days of April. The Finnish Parliament passed a vote of confidence in the Government concerning the reply they intended to send to Moscow. The Finnish reply, in which the Russian conditions were called or designated as technically impossible to fulfill, was passed to the Soviet Government through Stockholm.

During the entire period of the Finnish peace campaign General Erfurth had been in close and almost daily contact with the Finnish Commander in Chief and his Chief of Staff and was thus able to supplement the reports of the German Ambassador to the OKW about the development of the political situation in Finland.

In the statements he made to General Erfurth, Mannerheim approved of the policy of his Government and considered it right that they had asked for an interpretation of the conditions. "Mrs. Kollontay," said the Marshal, "had spread rumors in Stockholm to the effect that the original conditions would be considerably or essentially mitigated. The fact that these rumors were false was not learned until Paasikivi had returned from Moscow."

The Finnish policy caused great resentment on the part of the German Government. The Chief of the Wehrmacht Operations Staff had asked General Erfurth on 16 February what the attitude of the Finnish

Headquarters was, and he had demanded full information as to when the development of the Finnish policy would require security measures to be taken for the German troops in Finland.

On 21 February, the German Ambassador in Helsinki had given the Finnish Foreign Minister a sharp note.

Although the reports from General Erfurth were in a calm tone and the fact was emphasized again and again that there did not seem to be imminent danger, for the time being, of secession by Finland, Hitler and the Wehrmacht Operations Staff became much excited about the situation in Helsinki. On 8 February Erfurth was again instructed to keep the OKW posted and, if necessary, point out whether the German Commander in Chief in Lapland was to be given new instructions.

When on 4 April, the Finnish General in the OKW took leave from Keitel to fly home for Easter, the Chief of the OKW pointed out to him the great strain which would be placed not only on Finland and its Army but also on the German army in Lapland because of the negotiations in Moscow.

General Östermann, successor to General Talvela, was asked to bring a clear answer from the Marshal on his return from Finland as to what was to happen. He was told by Keitel that even when Paasikivi started on his second journey the question had been under discussion in the OKW as to whether the German supply of arms to Finland should be stopped. This was a veiled threat by Hitler to a brother-in-arms who seemed about to pursued a separate course.

Hitler's sympathy for the Finnish nation, which had been great during the first two years of the war against the Soviet Union, had decreased in the course of time. Some not very tactful articles in Finnish newspapers and the statement, repeated not only by the press but also by official agencies, that Finland was waging a separate war with the Soviet Union, and did not participate in the war of the great powers, had made him resentful. But the climax came when the Finnish Government entered upon negotiations concerning a truce without previously informing the German Government. Distrustful and resentful as he was, Hitler had probably only been waiting for the moment when he could show the Finns their mistake. This moment seemed to him to have come when, on 18 April, the Finnish refusal had been handed to the Russians in Stockholm.

VII. The German Embargo on Arms to Finland

On 19 April General Erfurth received information from the Führer's Headquarters to the effect that the German supply of arms to Finland was to be stopped at once. Exceptions could be made for single items which served the immediate maintenance of Finnish fighting strength. This was a heavy blow to the Finns, who could not continue the war even for a few weeks without German supplies.

The reason given for this grave measure was the unsympathetic way in which some Finnish papers had written of the evacuation of the University of Tartu in Estonia. This poor pretext did not convince the Finns, since the Tartu incident had remained practically unnoticed by the Finnish public. More dangerous was the order given to the German agencies in Finland to keep this embargo secret from the Finnish agencies, with which the Germans had up to that time cooperated closely; they would be suspected of unreliability and insincerity, for the Finns would very soon notice that supplies from Germany were not arriving as announced. Thus the independent notion of the Finns and Hitler's resentment had deeply disturbed the brotherly relations between Finns and German. During the ensuing weeks all persons who cared for these good relations worked hard to calm Hitler's anger and to restore the old brotherhood-in-arms. But all that was undertaken in this respect (a visit by General Erfurth, accompanied by General Heinrichs, to Hitler's Headquarters on 26 April, where discussions with Keitel and Jodl took place; and correspondence between Mannerheim and Hitler) could not remove the obstacle. Neither war materiel nor grain ships arrived. The 40,000 tons of grain that had been promised the Finns to tide them over until the new harvest never arrived. There did not seem to be any way to restore Hitler's confidence.

On 4 June, Mannerheim and his German General discussed at great length a letter of Hitler's written on 1 June to the Marshal, in which he complained about the policy of the Finnish Government. In it Hitler declared curtly that at a time when the Germans were fighting perhaps the most decisive war in the world's history he did not feel he could take the responsibility of depriving them of a single weapon without knowing for certain that it would be put to good use elsewhere.

Mannerheim had been much impressed by this letter. Although he himself had made use of military channels during the past years to present Finnish wishes quickly and directly, he found it inconvenient when as a result Hitler pushed the responsibility for the Finnish policy onto his shoulders and placed all German grievances on his desk, since he did not consider himself competent.

This was the result of the drying up of the diplomatic channel between Germany and Finland due to the disharmony between Ribbentrop and Ramsay, and the fact that the Finns had not tried to pour new life into it. "What am I to do?" asked the Marshal on 4 June 1944 to his German General, "How can we pacify the Führer?"

General Erfurth pointed out that the Führer's words, as far as they concerned the Marshal personally, showed warmth and cordiality, and that he had talked of the Finnish Armed Forced with undiminished respect.

In Hitler's opinion the Finnish policy of the last months had impaired the over-all conduct of operations. He felt resentful because he had not been informed about the Finnish intentions to sound the Russians out as to peace conditions, with the intention of bringing about a consolidation of the political situation in the interior (so the anger was directed against the politicians alone). Through this omission Hitler's confidence in the Finnish Government had been seriously shaken. Mannerheim replied that he understood the Führer's feelings completely; but the nation had to be shown that a tolerable peace with Moscow was not to be obtained. Then the Marshal suggested that the fact that the Reich Government had been informed so late might perhaps be traced back to the tension between Ribbentrop and Ramsay. The latter, who had just taken office without any experience in the conduct of foreign policy, had met with a bad reception when he had flown to Berlin to discuss with Ribbentrop the U.S. note to Finland. At that time he had been stiffly told that a "reply by Finland would be a betrayal of the common cause."

"Since that time," Mannerheim continued, "Herr von Ribbentrop bears a grudge against us. But what is to happen now? If we do not get any arms from Germany, we shall be defeated. If we had known that Germany would one day refuse to give us arms, we should never have decided to enter the war. Our belief in Germany's victory, but also in her help, made us choose this course. The political conditions in Finland are such that government and public opinion as represented in the Parliament must concur."

On that same day Erfurth had a talk with Heinrichs about Hitler's letter. General Heinrichs said that he had not understood why in Berchtesgaden, on 28 April, all this resentment had been expressed toward him, and why Keitel and Jodl had pushed all the responsibility for the Finnish policy onto his shoulders. In the same way he could not understand why Hitler had voiced his grievances in a letter to the Marshal, since the latter was not competent in the matter.

General Erfurth pointed out that he also was in an extraordinary situation, since the German Ambassador was the one to handle political complaints by the Reich. But the ambassador would probably not know anything about Hitler's letter. The diplomatic channel was unfortunately as yet unavailable. However, the fact that Hitler had written to Mannerheim showed that the confidence between them still existed.

The same day again General Heinrichs said, "Evidently we shall be asked to make binding promises and undertake definite responsibilities. It will be most difficult to give the assurance which Germany demands."

On the following day the Finnish General in the OKW – again General Talvela – came to see General Erfurth. He knew about the tension in German-Finnish relations. From his activities in the Reich, he said, he knew that Germany had repeatedly tried to conclude a written pact with Finland. But the latter had always avoided it, since the Finnish Government knew that Parliament would never give its consent.

Nor were the Germans clear as to how the disharmony between Finns and Germans would be removed. On 6 June General Jodl sent a wire to General Erfurth saying that Hitler seemed to expect a political declaration or an attempt to establish contact on the part of the Finnish Government. In his opinion this crisis of confidence could only be solved through political channels.

The situation was entangled still more by the fact that the German Ambassador in Helsinki had received no instructions as to how he was to continue to implement German policies. He had not even been informed by the Foreign Officer about Hitler's letter to Mannerheim. Nor had he any information as to the status of the embargo on arms and grain decreed by Hitler. Urged by Foreign Minister Ramsay to inquire about the missing 40,000 tons of rye he had contacted the Foreign Officer in Berlin and Ambassador Schnurre, but had not learned anything.

It seemed as if the Gordian knot in the German-Finnish relations could not be untied by an diplomatic or political means. At that moment fate intervened and cut the knot with one stroke.

On 9 June, the Soviet offensive on the Karelian Isthmus began. In view of the imminent collapse of the Finnish defense system, an entirely new situation had been created politically and militarily.

VIII. The Soviet Offensive Against the Finnish Front

With the elemental force of a tremendous storm, the Red Army's attack broke loose over the Karelian Isthmus on 9-10 June 1944, crushing any kind of resistance in the Finnish sector under attack. To the Finns this attack came as a complete surprise. Like water through a breach in a dam the Russian tanks and batteries, supported by an enormous number of aircraft, thrust through the gap in the Finnish front, penetrating deeply into the hinterland. An attempt to seal off this penetration proved hopeless.

As early as 11 June General Heinrichs asked General Erfurth to petition the OKW to get the arms and ammunition supply from Germany to Finland going again as quickly as possible. On the following day the situation on the front had deteriorated. Mannerheim addressed two requests to General Erfurth. Since the weak Finnish Air Force was unequal to the pressure of the tremendous Soviet superiority, the Finnish Commander in Chief asked for the support of the Luftwaffe in the area under attack. Furthermore, the Marshal asked for speedy delivery of the aircraft, assault and antitank guns that had been stopped in Germany. Despite the previous dissension Germany quickly helped the Finns. As early as 12 June, Finnish Headquarters was informed that the supply of ammunition and grain had been continued. In addition, a large number of 88mm antiaircraft artillery was released by the OKW for Finland.

The lack of modern antitank close-combat weapons in the Finnish Army was especially critical. The Finnish soldiers, who fought with the utmost bravery, could not cope with the Russian tanks. At the request of the Finns, on 12 June the German General asked the Wehrmacht Operations Staff for speedy delivery of close-combat antitank weapons.

The situation on the Finnish front worsened rapidly. On 15 June Mannerheim asked Erfurth through his Chief of Staff to do his utmost to speed up the German supply of war materiel.

So as to relieve the vulnerable lack in antitank close-combat weapons, General Erfurth furnished quick assistance from Lapland through the Twentieth Mountain Army.

On 16 June one fighter and one close-support squadron (cross check this in the other book) from the area of Army Group North arrived and were placed at the disposal of the Finnish Commander in Chief for employment on the Karelian Isthmus. A torpedo boat and aircraft brought antitank close-combat weapons from Germany. The artillery that had been promised by Germany in March, but had been stopped, was released by the OKW. On the same day Mannerheim asked for additional assault guns and tanks from Germany.

As the situation on the Karelian front continued to deteriorate, on 17 June Mannerheim decided to withdraw to a line running from Viipuri to Vuoksi and to link up his troops with the forces that had been moved up from the area east of Lake Ladoga. It also became necessary slowly to withdraw the troops on the Svir front in a northerly direction.

The situation was rightly considered very grave by the Finnish Government. The Cabinet had long conferences, but its decisions were not made public.

The strongest enemy pressure was directed against Viipuri. On 19 June a Russian attack was launched against the Finnish positions on the Svir, which had been partly evacuated. The Finns withdrew but engaged in a delaying action.

General Heinrichs, on this day, submitted two questions to General Erfurth:

(1) Is the continuation of the war by the Finns of such importance to Germany that she is willing to furnish other aid than that hitherto granted?

(2) Is Germany able and willing to make stronger forces (about six divisions) available For action in the southern sector of the Moscow Position (the Finnish name for the uncompleted defense line along the new frontier of 1940) between the Gulf of finland and as far as Lake Saimaa so as to guarantee protection for the Finnish Forces fighting along the Viipuri-Vuoksi Line?

On the following day, 20 June, General Heinrichs resumed his talks and admitted that on the previous day he had spoken with the consent and at the request of the Marshal.

Several discussions over the telephone with the OKW took place. To his first inquiry Erfurth got the answer that Hitler was willing to help Finland. The OKW was especially interested as to whether Mannerheim's request for German aid was also supported by the political agencies in Finland. Hitler obviously reckoned with the fact that the Finns, forced by circumstances, would now make concessions they had up to then withheld.

Somewhat later in the day the OKW telephoned that Hitler was willing to help Finland, but on condition that the Viipuri-Vuoksi line was held. Erfurth was instructed to place great stress on this. Employment of German forces in the frontier position in the rear was out of the question. The Finns would have to fight to hold the above line. As a first installment of German aid the Finns would obtain one assault gun brigade and one close support squadron (from the area of Army Group North).

Further German units were to follow. The June and July quotas of war materiel were to be sent with the greatest speed.

It was pointed out to Erfurth how important it was for him to watch the military-political situation.

Viipuri was lost on 21 June. This was especially painful for the Finns. There were no signs of a change in the political situation. Mannerheim held a meeting in his headquarters with the highest Finnish personalities: The Finnish President, the Foreign Minister, and the Defense Minister came to Mikkeli.

It was learned that the Marshal had reported on the situation and his intentions and that although he had left no doubt as to the seriousness of the situation, the Finns would have to hold out.

The first echelon of the German assault gun brigade arrived and was unshipped in the port of Helsinki. The German OKW announced by wire that the German 122nd Division would begin to arrive in Finland on 27 June.

The German dive bombers were sent into motion on that day and proved most satisfactory in defense against the Russian attacks east of Viipuri. Joyfully Mannerheim told his German General that the Finnish soldiers had cheered wildly when the German bombers had dropped their bombs over the Russian position. The atmosphere at Finnish Headquarters had somewhat improved.

On 22 June, the Red Army crossed the Svir on both sides of Ladeynoye Pole. The Russians came in contact only with Finnish rear guards who withdrew northward. On 23 June there was a great surprise. In the early morning General Erfurth was informed by telephone by Ambassador Schurre that the Foreign Minister had arrived on the previous evening and was staying at the Embassy. Ribbentrop had to talk to the General that same afternoon, come what may.

Thereupon General Erfurth flew to Helsinki and in the afternoon had a long conference with Ribbentrop; the latter gave the following information:

Hitler had sent him to Finland to bring about an unambiguous clarification of German-Finnish relations. The Führer demanded a clear and public declaration that Finland was on the side of Germany. If this declaration was not given there was danger that the aid, part of which had already arrived, would be stopped. This would cover not only the units that had arrived and those that were on their way to Finland, but also the arms supply and even the situation of the German army in Lapland. Hitler felt that he could no longer assume responsibility before the German nation for continuing to give German weapons for a cause which had become uncertain. The theory put forward by Finnish politicians and statesmen of a separate Finnish war was no longer tenable, since the request for increased aid in arms had not only been expressed by the military but also by the political leaders of Finland. Hitler had assigned the following aid to Finland: two assault-gun brigades and one infantry division with an assault gun battalion.

Hitler would also be willing to grant additional help if the situation required and it was possible to do so.

Ribbentrop said that he had had a long conference with the Finnish President the previous evening, but that it had ended in a deadlock. Ryti had indicated doubts as to whether the promised German aid would be sufficient. He had admitted that he was not a military expert, but that Mannerheim had given him a pessimistic picture of the situation on the front and also of the military possibilities of Finland.

Ribbentrop explained that General Erfurth had been placed at his disposal by Hitler as a military expert. It would be General Erfurth's task to make Mannerheim send an opinion to the President with approximately the following wording: "If this German aid arrives the Finns will probably be in a position to master the situation at the front."

It would also be very important if Mannerheim could be induced to give his opinion on how essential and decisive the German aid was. The Marshal, Ribbentrop declared, would probably be convinced that the

Finns could not hold out without German aid. Erfurth should indicate in his meeting with Mannerheim that this decisive hour had come for Finland.

The German Foreign Minister's journey to Helsinki was a great stake to risk but also a last attempt made by Hitler. Such a step could not be repeated. If Ribbentrop had to fly back without having attained his end, Finns and Germans from that day onward would pursue different paths. Ribbentrop would stay in Helsinki for another day and be ready to continue discussions with the Finnish Government, but he would have to return on 25 June.

IX. The Midsummer Pact Between Germany and Finland

It was evident that the German Government thought that the time had come to make the alliance pact with Finland to which the Germans had aspired for a long time. But the opposition in Finland against this pact had not become any weaker, in spite of the great distrust of the Finnish people. Conditions were not so simple as Ribbentrop imagined.

General Erfurth flew back to Mikkeli on 24 June and was at once received by the Marshal in the presence of General Heinrichs. After a long discussion Mannerheim declared himself willing to contact the agencies in whose hands the political decision rested. He did not wish to leave any doubts as to the value and importance of the German aid.

Immediately after the General had left Mannerheim, President Ryti, Foreign Minister Ramsay and Defense Minister Walden arrived at Mikkeli and had a long conference with the Marshal. From a confidential source General Erfurth learned that the difficulties lay in the correct formulation of the political and constitutional questions which were to decide the fate of the Finnish nation. The difficulty was not so much the military opinion, but to find the most suitable words for it. In the evening the Finnish statesmen flew back to Helsinki without a decision having been taken.

The next day, too, was full of waiting and tension. Ribbentrop, who had intended to leave on that day, became impatient and in the afternoon began to press for a decision. He refused to discuss further formulations and insisted on a precise declaration by the Finnish Government, without any compromise.

Uneasiness and apprehension prevailed in Finnish Headquarters lest the inner political situation became difficult if foreign affairs came to a head. The Government needed the confidence of the Parliament. A conflict on this matter might again revive the old hostility between White and Red in the Finnish nation, as had been the case in the 1918-1920 Finnish War of Liberation. Disturbances in the country might result in a weakening of the front.

Mannerheim indicated a desire that General Erfurth help by presenting the situation to the Wehrmacht Operations Staff. But Erfurth had to decline this request, since the conduct of German foreign policy was in the hands of the Foreign Minister, who was acting in accordance with the instructions he had received from Hitler. Erfurth pointed out that, on 24 June, he had a limited mission assigned to him by Ribbentrop, which had been completed after his report to the Marshal.

So as to be near the center of tension Erfurth again flew to Helsinki on 26 June, where he found the situation very obscure. A sitting of the Cabinet had taken place on the preceding evening. The majority of the Ministers was said to have been in favor of compliance with the German requests. But all members of the Cabinet had been of the opinion the matter would have to be submitted to Parliament. Ramsay had been very pessimistic.

Ribbentrop had postponed his departure, waiting with impatience for a solution.

In the course of the afternoon the situation suddenly changed. The state lawyers had meanwhile found out that the President could make the declaration desired by the German Government without the participation of the Finnish Parliament. In the evening the news was that President Ryti had stated that he was willing to make the declaration in a letter to Hitler. In addition, after the agreement with Ribbentrop, Prime Minister Linkomies was to go on the air to speak to the Finnish nation, inform it about the situation, and express the determination of the Finnish Government to continue the war against Russia on the side of Germany, and not to put down its arms without previous agreement with the Reich Government (this address was given on 2 July).

When, on 27 June, Ribbentrop returned to Germany from Helsinki he had the letter of State President Ryti to Hitler in his pocket. It looked as if German diplomacy had achieved a great victory in Finland. But it was clear to all persons of judgment that the "Midsummer Pact" between Germany and Finland could endure only if the situation of the Reich and its allies did not deteriorate. Only if the German Eastern front was able to withstand the assaults of the Red Army was there some prospect that the Finns could continue the war against Soviet Russia on the German side.

X Resignation of President Ryti

In the vast expanse of White Russia the German Army in the East received a serious setback in the summer of 1944. The Red Army's offensive against Army Group Center led to a quick and complete collapse of this group. The Soviet breach was soon widened and expanded to take in the front of Army Group North. The OKW had to move every available unit to the German Eastern front in support of its forces. This the prospects for aid to Finland deteriorated.

Of the unites that had been promised by the German Foreign Minister, one assault-gun brigade, and the 122nd Division had arrived in Finland by the end of June.

These units had arrived very quickly, and the Finnish press had been very pleased about the swift German aid. But then the transportation of German troops to Finland stopped.

The Marshal, on 3 July, expressed his uneasiness to his German General about the fact that no more German units were arriving. Even the units that had already been announced had been retained. The Marshal said that as a soldier he had a full understanding of the difficult situation which the German High Command was at the moment. He added that his own responsibility only covered Finland. The Finnish Army was already fighting on old Finnish territory. It was absolutely necessary for the situation on the Finnish front to be stabilized. But this was only possible with German aid. On the Finnish front politics and warfare were closely interwoven. Each setback on the front would agitate the politicians in Helsinki, he said. He had to inform General Erfurth that it was only due to his own intervention that the political pact with Germany would never have been signed. Without his advice Ryti and the Finnish Government would never have given their consent to the conclusion of the Midsummer Pact. He had said to the Finnish President and the Ministers: "Philosophizing is of no use to us. Aid in arms must be accepted where it comes from."

But weapons were not enough. Additional units would have to come from Germany. If these did not arrive, not only would the situation on the front deteriorate, but in addition his authority with the Finnish President and the Government would be shaken. The Marshal asked Erfurth to do his very best to start transportation of further German troops to Finland.

The attitude of the Marshal was understood by the Germans, since the Red Army was not only continuing its attack on the Karelian Isthmus east of Viipuri, but was also exerting great pressure on the weak Finnish forces east of Lake Ladoga.

Unfortunately the German High Command, due to the crisis on the Eastern front, was no longer in a position to fulfill the assurances made by Ribbentrop. The reply to the Marshal's wishes for German aid arrived on 5 July from Hitler's Headquarters. The OKW stated that it would be impossible to send a further German division to Finland but promised aid in heavy weapons. Hitler had personally given his attention to the Finnish request. He knew very well – such was his message to Mannerheim through General Erfurth – that he could not fulfill all of Mannerheim's requests, but he had done what he could. And even that had been very difficult. He much regretted that, at the moment, it was impossible to send another division; but in compensation he would send heavy arms in great quantity to Finland.

It was to be expected that Mannerheim would be disappointed by the German answer. But with the realism that is characteristic of all Finns, he saw that he could not expect more help from an ally engaged in fierce fighting. He had a conference with General Erfurth on 8 July at which General Heinrichs was also present. After Mannerheim, with the courtesy of a *grand seigneur*, had thanked General Erfurth for "the inestimable services he had recently rendered to the Finnish Armed Forces by sponsoring the wishes of the Marshal to the OKW in respect to aid in weapons and troops," he passed on to the core of the matter and stated that he was very worried about the situation on the Finnish front. According to the information about the enemy, he had to conclude that a new large-scale attack was about to be launched. This offensive without interruption, which would probably continue for some length of time, was a great strain on the strength of the Finnish forces. The losses sustained since the Russian offensive were very considerable; the possibility of filling the gaps with new troops was very limited. For this reason he urgently needed the weapons promised by Germany. He asked Erfurth to do his utmost to speed up the transportation of the arms and ammunition, and to see to it that the dates fixed were not postponed.

The following days brought bad news from the front. The Russians succeeded in forming a bridgehead on the Karelian Isthmus by crossing the Vuoksi north of Äyräpää. This bridgehead resisted all attempts by the Finns to eliminate it. East of Lake Ladoga the Russians penetrated deeply into the Finnish front in the direction of Loimola. This led to a further withdrawal by the Finns in this theater of war. In addition, the development of the situation south of the Gulf of Finland caused great anxiety.

Although the Finnish General in the OKH wired that the Germans intended to hold the Baltic countries, serious doubts prevailed in Finnish Headquarters as to whether Germany would have sufficient forces to do this.

The growing uncertainty of the Finns and the pessimism that prevailed in Helsinki caused Prime Minister Linkomies, Foreign Minister Ramsay, and Defense Minister Walden to come to Mikkeli on 13 July for a conference with the Marshal.

It was a favorable circumstance that on arrival of the Finnish ministers a wire came from the Finnish General at the German OKH, with roughly the following mornings: "Large-scale measures to stabilize the situation in central Eastern front have been initiated. Fresh troops being concentrated. Intention is to hold the Baltic States. Report follows."

After the Ministers had listened to a report on the situation on all fronts, they had flown back to Helsinki on the morning of 14 July, satisfied with the news and information they had received.

But the Marshal obviously did not have very great confidence in the information from his representative in Germany, especially as General Erfurth had not learned anything about the "large-scale measures on the German Eastern front." For this reason he summoned General Talvela to his Headquarters, to obtain a clear picture of the German counter-measures against the Russian offensive.

The information which the Finnish General brought to Mikkeli from the Wehrmacht Operations Staff sounded most promising.

Owing to the Russian large-scale offensive the strength of the German front had been decreased by roughly ten divisions. The other divisions, whose strength had been impaired and which had been withdrawn, could be replaced again.

Motorized units and infantry divisions were being moved up to the front (part to be sent into action in July, the bulk probably at the beginning of August). The intention was to defend the Baltic countries and to hold every inch of the soil. Rear positions along the San and Vistula Rivers and the border of East Prussia had been under construction for some time.

The consolidation of the situation thus depended only on whether the Soviets would give the Germans time to carry through the counter-measures they had initiated. From the fact that two assault-gun brigades, which had been announced for delivery in South Finland on 17 and 19 July, were cancelled without the promise of a substitute, the Finns had to draw the conclusion that the German High Command had no other resources to fill the gaps in the Eastern front. The Marshal took this cancellation very seriously.

On 18 July the first signs of a change at the Finnish front were reported at Finnish Headquarters. The Finns began to reckon with the possibility of a withdrawal of Russian forces on the Karelian Isthmus for transportation by way of Leningrad or the Gulf of Kronstadt to the Russian front south of the Gulf of Finland. The situation in the interior of Finland seemed to have been consolidated. On 19 July General Erfurth received the following information from Helsinki: "The responsibility undertaken by the Finnish Government in the midsummer talks with Ribbentrop is an unpopular as ever but it is respected. Discussions about a Finnish separate peace have stopped. The chief attention in Helsinki is focused on the development of the situation on the German East front."

The situation of Army Group North quite obviously became worse and worse from day to day. A German officer who returned to Mikkeli from Germany on 20 July, gave the following confidential report about his impression of the Germans in military agencies: they had been most depressed about the situation on the East front, whose seriousness and importance completely overshadowed the situation of the other fronts (Atlantic coast, Italy). Opinions differed as to whether the Baltic States could be held. But there was doubt that an evacuation was still possible. Hitler had decided, said this officer, that they should be held and defended. Political reasons must have been decisive in this question. People quite clearly saw that after the loss of the Baltic countries Finland could no long be kept in the war, and this would mean losing the war in the northern area, for after Finland had left Norway would have to be given up, on account on the menace from the rear. As the situation of Army Group North became more and more disastrous, further German forces which had originally been destined for Finland were moved up to this group on 21 July. The Wehrmacht Operations Staff made the following communications by telephone to General Erfurth: Hitler had most unwillingly retained the German special troops that had been intended for aid to Finland. But he assured the General that the Finns would be helped if the situation on the Finnish front should become tenser. Moreover, compensation would be given to the Finns in the form of increased war materiel.

The anxiety that the Finns might leave Germany in the lurch grew more and more oppressive with the increasing disintegration of the German East front. On 22 July, Erfurth was given instructions by the OKW to inquire about the Finnish High Command's opinion of the OKH plan for straightening the salient at the front near Narva and Pskov. The answer was that the Finnish High Command would have no misgivings if this was merely a local evacuation of the two salients. However, the Narva sector between Lake Peipus and the Gulf of Finland would have to remain in German hands on any account.

More difficult was the question which came to Mikkeli as 28 July from the Wehrmacht Operations Staff to ask what effect the withdrawal of the 122nd Division from the Finnish front would have on the Finns?

This question, apart from its political aspect, was rather important. In the Finnish Headquarters the opinion had gained ground that the Russians had stopped their offensive against Finland. As they quite obviously withdrew forces from the Karelian Isthmus and transferred them to the other side of the Gulf of Finland, it seemed quite natural for forces to be shifted across the Gulf from the Finnish front. The 122nd German Division, as the sole German division on the Finnish front, seemed to be the only unit that could be considered in this respect. This division was in a quiet position behind the Bay of Viipuri, and could easily be relieved by a Finnish division from behind the front if the latter was first rehabilitated.

But to give up the 122nd Division did not seem as simple as all that to the Finns. The Finnish Chief of Staff , with whom the German General discussed the matter first, seemed shocked and said the Marshal would be most unhappy. Mannerheim, like many a commander in chief, always parted most unwillingly with forces under his command. In addition, the question naturally was of a certain military importance.

General Erfurth pointed out to General Heinrichs the seriousness of the situation on the East front. The Soviet assault armies had assembled in front of the Narva army ready to attack. If this army group could not be reinforced quickly there was the danger that the Soviets would break through and thrust in the direction of Reval. This would also seriously endanger the Finnish front.

Heinrichs had to admit that all this was correct. But his objection against a weakening of the Finnish front was that the Russians had better lines of communication. They would be in a position to reinforce their forces on the Karelian Isthmus very rapidly again.

The Marshal's reply arrived late in the night. It said that he would regret it very much if the 122nd were taken from him. This might mean a risk, perhaps even a danger, for the Finnish front. The position of the Finns would become more difficult. But he would also regret the departure of this division for another reason: he would have to consider it as a symptom of growing difficulties on the German East front.

The conversation which the German General had with the Finnish Chief of Staff concerning this reply showed that the Marshal had some understanding for the difficult German situation and that his doubts were of a military rather than a political nature.

Since on the following day, 29 July, the situation on the East front, especially of Army Group North, became more and more menacing – the Soviets were advancing quickly in the direction of Jelgava – a reply from the Führer's headquarters arrived without delay. Hitler had decided that the 122nd Division would be withdrawn from the Finnish front and moved up to Army Group North.

It has not been proven that the departure of the German forces from southern Finland had any immediate political consequences. But it is certain that public opinion in Finland was unfavorably influenced. The value of the pact that had been made with German only a few weeks before was thus reduced, in the opinion of many Finns.

Mannerheim's request to select Hangö and not Helsinki as the port of embarkation for the 122nd Division suggested that the Finnish Commander in Chief did not wish to focus the attention of the Finnish public on the departure of the German division that had marched through Helsinki to the Finnish front at the beginning of July.

XI. Mannerheim Becomes President

Toward the end of the month the political situation in Finland began to become obscure. According to the opinion of the Finnish trade unions the war was lost. The decision was to be expected very soon. Efforts were made by the trade unions to bring about peace, even if the conditions were hard. In this situation there were only two alternatives in the political sphere; either a government under Ryti that would free itself more and more from constitutional restrictions or a new government whose task would be to lead Finland out of the war.

The solution of this crisis came surprisingly quickly.

On 1 August, General Heinrichs asked General Erfurth to see him and informed him that President Ryti had resigned and that the Government, on the afternoon of the same day, would bring in a bill to Parliament, according to which Mannerheim would be made President. The reason for the change of office was that the military and political powers should be united in the hands of one man.

The Marshal would place himself at the disposal of the nation if Parliament made him President. It was not strange for the Finns to turn to Mannerheim to steer the foundering ship safely into the harbor. The entire nation had the greatest confidence in his wisdom, political vision and diplomatic abilities. There was no better man for this infinitely difficult task.

But it seemed strange that Mannerheim was willing to shoulder this great burden. The highest office in the land was a thankless task. There were many experiences in the past of this unusual man that would make it difficult for him to agree to a settlement with the Soviet Union. Perhaps this decision of his is the one that should be admired most and indeed was the greatest in his long life. Mannerheim will be one of the most interesting figures in the history of modern times. He can be certain of the gratitude of his nation for having steered the ship from the beginning of August 1944 onward, and for having solved his task in such a masterly fashion.

On the evening of 1 August, the Finnish Parliament unanimously passed the law (normally the Finnish President is chosen by electors), according to which Mannerheim became President. He was sworn in on 4 August and took office that same day. But he also remained Commander in Chief of the Finnish Armed Forces.

This change in office had an alarming effect on the Reich Government. Hitler tried to find ways and means to influence Mannerheim and to keep him on the side of Germany. On 3 August in the afternoon, by order of Hitler, the Commander in Chief of Army Group North, General Schörner, landed at the Helsinki airfield, "to inform the Marshal about the situation of Army Group North and to strengthen the attitude of the Marshal and Finland."

Such was the information Erfurth received shortly before Schörner's landing. This was an astonishing event, which completely disregarded the fact that Mannerheim was fully occupied with the task of taking over his new office and with the formation of a new government. In spite of this the Marshal sent word politely that he was expecting his visitor in his special train in one of Helsinki's outlying stations.

Schörner gave the Marshal a short report on the situation of his Army Group. That was to have a soothing effect. The Baltic States would be held. The supplies that had been cut off by the Russian advance on land would be sent by sea and by air. Armored units advancing from East Prussia would re-establish a connection with Army Group North and with the Eastern front. The activation of fresh troops in Germany had considerably increased in the meantime. At the beginning of September at the latest, ten further infantry divisions and eleven armored brigades would be ready to be sent into action. Attacks to regain the San line were being launched. Further defense positions close behind the San-Vistula-East Prussia line were being organized.

Schörner's report was followed by a light lunch in the train, and the reception was over. Political questions had not been touched. Although this hasty visit must have been rather inopportune for the Finns they did not show it. Mannerheim, as always on such occasions, was courteous and dignified, so that Schörner, before his departure, asked Erfurth why he had had to fly to Finland in such great haste. Everything seemed quiet to him in Helsinki. Hitler's idea that it was possible to influence a man like the Marshal by an embellished report on the front situation seemed almost naïve. For it is one of the strong points of the Finnish nation to act wisely in politics. During the long time spent under foreign yoke the ruling classes in Finland had been formed and trained in politics. The experience of his forefathers and tradition influence the modern Finn's actions; he consciously remains aloof from adventure and fantasy; instead he has a clear knowledge of what can what cannot be done, as well as the ability to act within sober realism.

It was clear to the Finns that there were only a "few grains left in the sandglass of the German-Finnish brotherhood-in-arms." Fate cannot be circumvented. In the realization of this great truth the Finns have always suffered the severest blows with dignity and composure.

The formation of the new government took several days. On 9 August the list of ministers had been fixed. General Heinrichs said to General Erfurth: "The situation seems clear, and probably no changes will take place in our foreign policy if the situation on the German fronts does not continue to deteriorate."

The new Prime Minister, Enckell, characterized the new Cabinet to the German Ambassador in the following way: "It is not a pronounced peace cabinet, but it is open to proposals."

The uncertainly of the political situation showed itself in the rumors which kept the public in Helsinki alarmed. It was not easy for the Germans there to find out what was true and false.

One of these rumors was spread on 12 August. It mentioned another journey by Paasikivi (who incidentally was not a member of the new Cabinet) to Moscow.

The assurance was given by the new members of the Government that at the moment there were no negotiations.

But since the rumor continued to spread that, as in the spring of 1943, a connection had been established by Mrs. Kollontay via the Swedish Embassy in Helsinki with the "Peace Circle of the Thirty-Three" (on 22 August 1943, thirty-three members of the Finnish Parliament had brought in a peace resolution, which had been the first parliamentary attack on Ryti's policy), on 16 August Defense Minister Walden categorically declared to the German Military Attaché that all rumors alleging that a Finnish delegation was on its way to Sweden or Moscow were false. An objective observer would have gained the definite impression that many elements in the Finnish nation seriously occupied themselves with the idea of a separate Finnish peace.

In the Finnish Parliament the number of those who were in favor of peace with the Soviet Union had greatly increased. What had been a minority had now become a majority, due to an increase in the size of the Social-Democrat Party, the Swedish People's Party and the Farmer's Party. On 16 August the German Ambassador estimated that of the 200 deputies 120 were for peace. This would have an influence on the duration of the Government, which had to have the confidence of Parliament.

On 17 August the Chief of the OKW paid a visit to Mannerheim in Mikkeli. The visit, which was considered urgent by the OKW, had been intended to take place at the beginning of the month. But Mannerheim had asked Keitel to wait until he had attended to tasks that could not be postponed, and until the Marshal, after the formation of the new government, had returned to his Headquarters. Evidently the Marshal made a point of receiving the Chief of the OKW not amid the turmoil existing in Helsinki, but in the quiet of Mikkeli.

After the amenities had been observed, Keitel presented the Finnish Marshal with the oak leaf cluster to the Knight's Cross. To General Heinrichs he gave the Knight's Cross, to honor in this way the Finnish

Army for the defensive victory they had won on the Karelian Isthmus and east of Lake Ladoga in the preceding weeks. Then Keitel gave a lengthy report, in the presence of the generals of the Finnish Headquarters, on the situation on all German fronts. This report had been expected eagerly, for the Finns hoped to hear from the Chief of the OKW how the Germans were going to master a situation that was becoming more hopeless from day to day on the Eastern front, in France and Italy. They hoped to get some encouragement. Keitel's report was a disappointment, although he spoke with great confidence. To the Finns, who are realists, positive statements and data were missing as to how the Germans could offset the superiority of their enemies on the various fronts.

Thus there was no discussion after Keitel's report. Mannerheim asked no questions, but invited his guest for lunch in his country house. After lunch Mannerheim withdrew with Keitel into the study he had in his headquarters for a long conference.

The only other person present was General Heinrichs. Keitel, who was accompanied by Erfurth on his return flight to Helsinki, gave an account of the conference, his memory still fresh with the experience he had just been through. Mannerheim had said that Ryti, at the end of June, had been pressed by Ribbentrop to undertake an obligation at a moment of great distress, although it was against the wishes of the majority of the Finnish nation. For this reason, Ryti and the other ministers that had participated in the midsummer pact had had to resign. And therewith, according to the opinion of the Finns, their alliance with Germany had come to an end, too. The Finnish Government had regained its freedom of action.

Keitel had answered that he was no empowered to make or receive political declarations.

Keitel's statement was supplemented by the account given of the discussion by Heinrichs to Erfurth on 19 August. According to this Mannerheim had not made a categorical declaration to Keitel involving the cancellation of the Ribbentrop pact; he had merely given him a chronological description of the events that had led to Ryti's resignation. Perhaps there had been no necessity to make these statements, for Keitel had not come as a political negotiator; but the Marshal had not thought it morally correct to let Keitel depart without explaining to him the changes that had taken place in the interior policy of Finland.

Ryti's position, the Chief of Staff continued, had become untenable because of the following factors:

(1) He had signed the Ribbentrop Pact in disregard of the Finnish constitution.

(2) The situation on the German fronts had become most unfavorable since the end of June.

(3) The Finnish nation was willing to wage a war of defense; but it did not want to fight for Germany's sake just because it was obliged to do so.

According to Finnish judgment, owing to the resignation of Ryti and the government of Linkomies-Ramsay, the obligation toward German resulting from the Ribbentrop Pact had become null and void. Finland had thus regained her freedom of action. This was the core fo the difference between Finland and Germany. Finland held that the obligation had been cancelled. Germany contested this. It is a question which can be explained from the differences of the governmental forms. A democratic state does not think the same as a totalitarian state about the question: "Is a new government bound by the obligations undertaken by its predecessor?"

Concerning the talk with General Heinrichs, General Erfurth asked in which way Finland would use her new freedom of action?

General Heinrichs answered that there were a number of possibilities. The situation on the chief German fronts would decisively influence the development of things. He also point out the difficulties that would obstruct the conclusion of a Finnish-Soviet peace. The peace which the Finns desire, he said, was a peace which would leave the Finnish nation its freedom and independence. These precious rights could not be given up. It was thus very doubtful if a peace between Finland and Soviet Russia could materialize at all.

To the disadvantage of the German position in Finland, the situation on the German fronts deteriorated from day to day in August 1944. The old troubles on the Eastern front, in Italy and France, were increased by new troubles in the Balkans and Romania. The Soviet Union and Romania concluded a truce on 24 August. The German troops of Army Group South were in a fatal situation.

Mannerheim, on 26 August, returned to Mikkeli from several days stay at Helsinki. It was to be admitted, he told Heinrichs on arrival, that the situation was very bad. The latter, full of anxiety, told Erfurth that a good piece of news was most urgently needed. "You may be sure," he added, "that the peace party in Finland is rapidly growing." And, as if speaking to himself, he added: "Something will have to happen soon. The Marshal has been President for three weeks." And again turning to General Erfurth, General Heinrichs said, "I am sorry for you. You must feel terribly alone."

XII. Secession of Finland

On this day a meeting took place between the German Ambassador in Helsinki and Finnish Foreign Minister Enckell. The latter told the

Ambassador that the Finnish Ambassador in Berlin, Mr. Kivimäki, had been instructed by the Marshal formally to announce to the German Government that Mannerheim did not feel himself bound by the obligation undertaken by Ryti, which had been brought about without the cooperation of the Finnish Parliament.

The Finnish-German brotherhood-in-arms was irrevocably nearing its end. Alarming telegrams arrived at General Erfurth's office in Mikkeli from the Ambassador on 30 August. The Ambassador reported a rapid deterioration of the atmosphere in the country caused by the bad news from France and Romania. His informants thought it possible that under this pressure public opinion in Finland would tolerate concessions in regard to former points of honor such as the attitude toward the German army in Lapland and the demobilization of the Finnish Army.

The press in Helsinki pleaded with growing frankness for peace with Russia and abandonment of the brother-in-arms. On the evening on 30 August the Ambassador sent word that he had been informed by the Finnish Foreign Minister that contact had already been established for some days with Russia. The consequences remained to be seen. The Finnish Parliament had been summoned for 2 September.

On 1 September, the Commander in Chief of the German Army in Lapland met with the General Erfurth in the Embassy in Helsinki to discuss the situation. General Rendulic had asked for an audience with Mannerheim on 2 September to discuss military matters. He hoped to be able to start a discussion on politics with the Marshal. The Ambassador and Erfurth, who had long been familiar with Finnish customs, tried to dissuade him.

But Rendulic stuck to his intention. As was his custom the Marshal asked General Erfurth to be present at this reception. Rendulic did not succeed in speaking to the Marshal alone. General Heinrichs and Defense Minister Walden were also present. The conversation was kept in general terms.

All attempts on the part of Rendulic to touch topical questions were evaded by the Finns. Mannerheim was a master in leading a conversation in any direction he wanted. This reception did not bring any clarification of the political situation.

Mannerheim quite incidentally put forth the question, "Why are the Germans staying in Petsamo? They are only helping the British and their divisions are so urgently needed at other places." It was clear that Mannerheim aimed at a voluntary withdrawal of the Germans from Lapland.

On the afternoon of this fatal day the German Military Attaché reported that the Russian conditions had arrived on the previous day. In the form of an ultimatum the Reds demanded that Finland break off its relations with Germany. This was the reason for the hasty summoning of the Parliament.

Shortly thereafter, Ambassador Schnurre saw General Erfurth in his hotel room in Helsinki. He corroborated the news of the Military Attaché and expected that Parliament would accept the Russian conditions.

The decision came in the evening. While Parliament convened Mannerheim's chief aide came to the hotel where Erfurth was staying and gave him a letter from the Finnish President for Hitler. In the introductory part Mannerheim wrote that in this hour of decision he felt a desire to inform the Head of the Reich that it would be his duty, in order to save the Finnish people, to find a way out of the war soon.

The unfavorable general situation restricted Germany's possibilities of giving the Finns the help they urgently needed in time and in sufficient measure. He pointed out the experience of the preceding summer and the length of time it had taken to transport adequate German aid to Finland. Mannerheim's unfavorable opinion on the military position was shared by a growing majority of the nation's representatives in Parliament. Even if he were of a different opinion, it would not be possible for him – in view of the Finnish constitution – to disregard the will of the nation's majority for any long time. Merely from the physical viewpoint the Finnish nation would not be able to stand a long war. The Russian large-scale attack in June had already exhausted Finnish replacements. The Finns could not afford similar losses without endangering the existence of the small Finnish nation. Although he hardly dared hope that Hitler would recognize his statements and arguments as correct or agree to them, Mannerheim continued, he wished to send these lines to him before the decision was taken.

After Mannerheim had spoken in appreciative terms of the correct and cordial relations of the German soldiers with the population of Finland, he expressed his hopes that Hitler, like Mannerheim and all Finns, would be anxious to wind up these relations without letting things come to a crisis.

The Finnish Parliament, as was to be expected, accepted the Russian conditions in its evening sitting. In the same night the Finnish Foreign Minister made a corresponding communication to the German Ambassador. General Heinrichs, on 3 September, asked General Erfurth to see him and handed him a written statement like that which had been passed to the German Ambassador by the Finnish Foreign Minister on the evening of 2 September. Thus the relations of Finland with her former brother-in-arms had been broken off in due form.

There was only the question of the departure of the German troops from Finland to be discussed. According to the Soviet Russian conditions of the Finnish capitulation, Finnish territory had to be cleared of German troops by 15 September. The Finns declared themselves willing to help with the evacuation. In view of the small number of troops in South Finland it was clear that the evacuation would be completed in due time. But the case was more difficult for the German Army in Lapland. Heinrichs indicated that the Finns thought that the German Twentieth Mountain Army might not leave Lapland. He wished Erfurth to inform him as to the German plans. The latter unfortunately did not know. The Finns would obviously be very glad if the Twentieth Mountain Army were withdrawn from Finnish territory with the greatest speed possible, so that the country would not become a theater of war.

It was quite clear to the Finns that, even though the Germans were ready to evacuate Finland, it would be technically impossible to carry through the evacuation in time. This problem overshadowed all others and was the main subject of the conferences which took place and filled both the Finnish High Command and the German General with anxiety.

On 4 September the Marshal, though Heinrichs, asked Erfurth to come to Helsinki as soon as possible. He had a desire to exchange ideas concerning the future with the General.

Erfurth arrived on the morning of 5 September and was at once taken to the President's summer palace at Tamminjemi by the Marshal's chief aide. Mannerheim received General Erfurth in the presence of General Heinrichs.

In the ensuing conference the Finnish desire that the evacuation of Lapland by the German troops be carried out smoothly and quickly became quite clear.

Erfurth point out that it would be impossible for the Twentieth Army, numbering roughly 200,000 men and whose bulk was still in East Karelia, to reach Norwegian territory on the coast of the Arctic Sea or the Bothnian ports of Finland within 12 days. The Finns had to admit that the day had been fixed too early by the Russians. But the Marshal declared himself willing to help the Germans with all means to accelerate and facilitate their withdrawal. He ordered the Chief of Staff to give the necessary instructions to the Chief of Transportation.

Then General Erfurth took his leave from the Marshal, who thanked him warmly, and completed his mission to the Finnish Headquarters. Although the sending of the German General to Finland had ended in a failure, the parting was cordial.

On 12 September the evacuation in South Finland had been completed.

In the early morning of 13 September 1944, General Erfurth, together with his staff, left Finland on board the last evacuation steamer from Helsinki.

XIII. Conclusion

    Mannerheim's wish, as expressed in his last letter to Hitler, that the winding up of relations be carried out without conflict unfortunately did not materialize. Friction, sporadic fighting and even regular combat took place between German and Finnish troops after 15 September. It will be regretted by Germans and Finns alike that this brotherhood-in-arms, which had endured so strong for more than three years, ended so unpleasantly. As far as the conditions prevailing after 15 September can be judged, the early date of evacuation was chiefly to be blamed for the difficulties the German troops met with during their withdrawal. In addition, there may have been rash actions, which can be explained by the total change of position and human inadequacies on both sides. The breach with German was a risk in view of the fact that a well-equipped, strong German army was on Finnish soil. A happy solution was possible only if both sides actual firmly and carefully.

    That Finns finally achieved their political goal they owe to Mannerheim, who shouldered all responsibility at the decisive moment, and solved the most difficult problem that can be put to a statesman in a masterly fashion. Indeed, the Finnish nation owes him everything! It is true that the German soldiers felt bitter about being left in the lurch by their brothers-in-arms. But what else could Finland do, without committing suicide and being pulled into the whirlpool that threatened to swallow up Germany?

    Subsequent developments in Finland have shown that the Finnish decision was right. The Marshal must be given credit for having waited until the last moment before making his decision, which was probably very difficult for him. But, then, he acted with a steady firm hand. The Finnish nation was fortunate that in its darkest hour the right man was at its disposal; it proved its political insight by unanimously putting Mannerheim at the helm when conditions steadily deteriorated.

www.ingramcontent.com/pod-product-compliance
Lightning Source LLC
Chambersburg PA
CBHW070025100426
42740CB00013B/2592